Uncertain Honor

Uncertain Honor

Modern Motherhood in an African Crisis

JENNIFER JOHNSON-HANKS

THE UNIVERSITY OF CHICAGO PRESS   CHICAGO AND LONDON

JENNIFER JOHNSON-HANKS is assistant professor in the Department of Demography and an affiliate of the Department of Anthropology and the Center for African Studies at the University of California, Berkeley.

The University of Chicago Press, Chicago 60637
The University of Chicago Press, Ltd., London
© 2006 by The University of Chicago
All rights reserved. Published 2006
Printed in the United States of America
15 14 13 12 11 10 09 08 07 06   5 4 3 2 1

ISBN (cloth): 0-226-40181-2
ISBN (paper): 0-226-40182-0

Library of Congress Cataloging-in-Publication Data

Johnson-Hanks, Jennifer.
    Uncertain honor : modern motherhood in an African crisis / Jennifer Johnson-Hanks.
        p.   cm.
    Includes bibliographical references and index.
    ISBN 0-226-40181-2 (cloth : alk. paper) — ISBN 0-226-40182-0 (pbk. : alk. paper)
        1. Women—Education—Cameroon.   2. Birth control—Cameroon.   3. Family
    Planning—Cameroon.   4. Beti (African people)—Social life and customs.   5. Fertility,
    Human—Social aspects—Cameroon.   6. Women—Cameroon—Social conditions.
    7. Women—Cameroon—Economic conditions.   I. Title.
    HQ1809.5.J64   2006
    306.874'3'096711—dc22   2005016187

Contents

Preface

M beya is hardly thirty miles from Yaoundé, but on a bad day the trip by shared minivan can take two hours. It was that kind of day when I arrived in Mbeya for the second time, in January of 1998. I had come to see the parish priest who, eighteen months earlier, had given me a letter of welcome to conduct research in his church, school, and community. After a noisy week in a dubious hotel in the capital, I was eager to get settled and start working. But my would-have-been benefactor was gone, and the new priest had many supplicants to see that day. Shy, tired, and embarrassed that I did not speak Eton, the most common local dialect, I sat silently with the others.

The anteroom where we waited is part of the original mission, built by Pallotin priests and Beti converts in the first decades of the twentieth century. Even after more than eighty years, the stucco and timber construction, with a second-floor balcony and red tile roof, remained one of the finest buildings in the district. The florescent tube lights hummed from the high ceiling, somehow making the space seem even more cavernous and more quiet. It smelled of hot, dank wood, like the summer church camps I remember. Looking down at the floorboards, made in a pattern I recognized but out of tropical hardwood, I thought how the room felt at once familiar and strange. I thought about luck, and my own luck in particular, by which a series of near catastrophes had turned out all right in the end. I thought about the circumstances that would lead an American agnostic to seek an audience with a Cameroonian priest. Then it was my turn.

Père Charles Amarin, an elegant and intellectual man, was unimpressed with my wrinkled letter from his predecessor. I too felt unimpressive: I was too short to sit on the chair and have my feet reach the floor, my shoes were dusty and my clothes crumpled. I answered the father's questions limply and in disorder, trying to remember my project and French vocabulary and why Mbeya was the perfect place for the study. The discomfort reminded me—viscerally—of years of Bible school when I had failed to memorize the weekly verse. Then, with an abrupt generosity that I would come to recognize as a fundamental part of his character, Père Charles Amarin said yes.

If ever we anthropologists could fancy ourselves as more cosmopolitan or educated than our local interlocutors, that era is forever gone. Whether studying scientists (Hayden 2003; Rabinow 1996, 1999), NGO officials (Riles 2000), or bankers and financiers (Maurer 1997; Miyazaki 2004), contemporary anthropologists have to confront ethnographic subjects who are not only as sophisticated in their own worlds as we are in ours, but who are in fact part of the very same fields of scientific production and institutions as we are. In this spirit, however, the indigenous Catholic clergy, arguably one of the most important groups of cosmopolitan culture brokers in the contemporary developing world, remain understudied. Unfortunately, this book does not redress that failing—the clergy themselves are almost entirely absent here. In the brief time I spent in Mbeya, I often wished that I could write a biography of Père Amarin. With a doctorate from a prestigious European university and equal passions for life and learning, he sometimes seemed to me a personification of the hope of the global church. But that first day, I knew only that he would let me work in his parish, and I was thankful.

The trip had not begun smoothly. The parcel from the embassy containing my passport and visa had gotten mixed up in a corporate mailbag, and was finally found and delivered just five hours before my flight. The finding was thanks to my newfound love (now my husband), whom I now had to leave behind in Chicago. CamAir lost my luggage. And within twenty-four hours of my arrival in Cameroon, I was riotously sick. Admittedly, good news was in short supply, and I was glad for every break I could get.

In many ways, the research project that brought me to Cameroon was ten years in the making. In January of 1988, I had started tenth grade at an international boarding school in Mbabane, Swaziland. I had gone to Swaziland because I wanted to become a "frontier" medical doctor like my dad, who was in the Indian Health Service when I was born, and this school gave me a chance to see Africa firsthand. I imagined myself with a Jeep and a Coleman cooler of cholera vaccinations: the Indiana Jones of African medicine. But in addition to the naïve condescension of this plan, the problems facing Swazi children in that last decade before the AIDS pandemic were not "medical" in the sense that I understood the term. Instead, they suffered from intestinal worms, bilharzia and other parasites, malnutrition, and respiratory infections from smoky indoor fires: "only development problems!" in the words of the exasperated doctor whom I had pestered with questions. So I decided to study development problems.

The development problem that most demanded my attention appeared that same year in a newspaper article, which—as I remember it—outlined the plight of a Swazi girl about my age whose family could not afford to send her to school. A teacher paid her school fees, and they became lovers. When she discovered herself pregnant, however, the teacher disavowed any responsibility, and the girl lost her schooling, her social standing, and her passionate companion. Pregnancy seemed both the outcome and the antithesis of the seduction of knowledge, Eve's fruit, embodied in the teacher. The eroticism of pedagogy is, of course, not unique to schooling in Africa. The Scylla and Charybdis tale resonated in an awful sense that it could have been me, all the more because, in the Alaskan town where I grew up, teen pregnancy and dropping out of high school were (and are still) not uncommon. The boundless horizons or secret gardens of learning glisten before every book-drunk kid; the sensuality of the relationship between teacher and protégé reverberates from classical Greece to Nabokov (see also Hawhee 2004). But when schooling represents the path to development, sex the path to school, and pregnancy the limit to hope, poetics becomes political economy. That is, development problems.

When one begins to think about schooling, sexuality, and childbearing, the relations between them seem to multiply. The three intersect in a multitude of ways: each can cause changes in the others; they are all used metaphorically to talk about the others; and all three are fundamental both to the making of persons and to social reproduction. We are seduced by theory, give birth to dissertations, and are "educated in romance" (Holland and Eisenhart 1990). In policy and development circles, it is the causal links between education and childbearing that receive the most attention. For more than a decade, international NGOs and aid organizations have viewed the schooling of girls in poor countries as a practical means of increasing their status and autonomy vis-à-vis men and of persuading them to bear fewer children and to bear them later. Like marriage in George W. Bush's welfare policy, school is presented as a primrose path out of poverty. For example, in the documents of the United Nations 1994 Cairo conference on population and development, the presumed power of school to transform women from "victims of tradition" to rational, liberal, choice-bearing subjects is nothing short of enchanted:

> Improving the status of women also enhances their decision-making capacity at all levels in all spheres of life, especially in the area of sexuality and reproduction. This, in turn, is essential for the long-term success of population programmes. . . . Education is one of the most important means of empowering women with the knowledge, skills and self-confidence necessary to participate fully in the development process. (United Nations 1994: sec. A.4.1–4.2)

The enchantment with school suggested here and reiterated by policymakers in development throughout Africa resembles the breathless fascination that I remember from my own grade school books. The books were portals to somewhere else, "off the rock" we said, referring to the island that is home to our town. Perhaps even more, the enchanted power of education in development policy parallels the magical allure of modernity held out to schoolchildren by schools throughout sub-Saharan Africa. There is nothing pedestrian, bureaucratic, or even secular about this other, African modernity. As Geschiere has argued, modernity is a most powerful form of magic in Cameroon, both in the sense that modern things have invisible powers, and in the sense that the acquisition of modern things is best achieved through magic. He writes, "To the villagers, it is obvious that the ascension of the new élites . . . is linked, in one way or another, to the occult force of the *djambe*" (Geschiere 1997: 5; see also Comaroff and Comaroff 1993; Ferguson 1999; Moore and Sanders 2001).

The enchantment of the modern and the seduction of knowledge may seem like strange starting places for a work in demographic anthropology, that most "dismal" of anthropological sciences (if Thomas Carlyle's comments on Malthus are to be taken seriously). But ever since Malthus, population studies have addressed politics, as well as both the sexual and moral passions. Malthus argued that it was the necessary and almost immutable "passion between the sexes" (1970: 70) that rendered impossible Godwin and Condorcet's revolutionary vision of the perfectibility of human nature through political change. Malthus, like other eighteenth-century political economists, saw population as "no longer something pliable, to be manipulated by enlightened leaders, but the product of recalcitrant customs and natural laws which stood outside the domain of mere politics" (Porter 1986: 26). And yet certain late-twentieth-century demographers have been seduced by an evolutionary morality play no less radical than Condorcet's.

The politics of girls' education plays the part of just laws and the moral state, but the resolution—a stable population and ever-increasing personal welfare—is the same.

I am interested in how we can think about the causes of statistical patterns in social life, and I argue that mechanical models of causation (of the school-causes-lower-fertility type) have done us more harm than good. Beginning with schoolgirls' impassioned visions of possible futures, this book tries to develop an alternative way of thinking about demographic facts, based more on hopes for the future than on the quantitative associations of outcomes. Whereas statistical associations—such as between more school and fewer births—can be deeply revealing, causal interpretations of them may have the same dangers as the historical "backshadowing" critically analyzed by Bernstein (1994) and Morson (1994).

Schooling and fertility are "development problems" everywhere in Africa, and to some degree this study could have been done just as well in Mali, Gabon, or Botswana. I first went to southern Cameroon as a graduate student because I could: one of my advisors (Caroline Bledsoe) had a colleague there working on related topics, and the other (Jane Guyer) had done extensive research in the same district. Soon, however, the analytic advantages of working with the Beti for this project became clear: the long-standing emphasis on individual training, the specific colonial history, the dramatic shifts in women's roles in recent decades.

The field research on which this book is based began in 1996, with a two-month tour of southern Cameroonian villages and secondary schools. On that trip, I conducted sixty-odd short and informal interviews, mostly with elder men and village chiefs, about schooling, schoolgirl pregnancy, and childbearing in general. For the most part, these elder men considered girls' schooling at once necessary and dangerous: necessary because of its potential to train the girls in domestic and religious virtues, and dangerous because some girls got pregnant and dropped out, while others could be snatched by certain spirits and rendered permanently incapable of conceiving. This was exactly the kind of moral paradox that I had expected. It was not until I returned in 1998 and worked primarily with schoolgirls that I understood how specific these concerns are to older, rural men. For all the difficulty and internal contradiction that school may generate in the perceptions of young, southern Cameroonian women, the risk of spirit-induced sterility is not among them.

I conducted the primary field research from January to August of 1998. The research relies heavily on structured methods of data collection: classroom observations, time-use surveys, a demographic life-history survey, and interviews. Between February and May of that year, I observed more than 140 hours of classes at the Catholic high school la Trinité, taking notes on classroom activities, time use, and curricular content. These data gave me a good sense of what happens during school, but in order to have a clearer sense of student's lives outside, I collected forty-eight week-long time-use surveys. Here, students self-reported their activities in fifteen minute intervals for seven days, and completed a brief questionnaire about household composition. Although these data suffer strong reporting bias, they roughly indicate some empirical trends and are very interesting as modes of self-presentation. They offer interesting images of what the students thought that I would respect or value, such as rising at 4 a.m. to pray and studying in secret, after everyone had gone to bed.

During June and July of 1998, I worked with six research assistants to conduct a demographic life-history survey in Yaoundé and Mbeya, which consisted of 184 women who had attended at least one complete year in a Catholic high school in the south-central province and who were no longer attending high school. The sample is not statistically representative, but it does indicate some clear trends in the experiences of Catholic educated women in this area. To diversify the sample of respondents, we used six different methods to locate eligible women. First, each of the surveyors conducted a series of interviews with women known to her or to her mother. These included the mother herself, aunts or cousins, neighbors and colleagues. Second, we selected two small neighborhoods of Yaoundé and went door-to-door, identifying and interviewing all eligible women in each household. One of the neighborhoods was a four-block-square section of an old, working-class *quartier,* the other a new residential-only, relatively wealthy area on the periphery of the city. Third, the director of the pediatric ward at a major public hospital generously offered me very open access to his ward. We interviewed both nurses and women who had come for postnatal care for their infants. Fourth, we looked for interview candidates in three very different workplaces, where the manager or ranking person gave us permission to present our project to the assembled women. One of these was a regional ministry, another a private company, and the third an open-air fruit and vegetable market. Fifth, we interviewed thirty-five women who reside in two small villages near Mbeya. Finally, I went to the meetings of two women's *tontines* (rotating credit associations), presented the project, and then asked for volunteers to make appointments. Altogether, the survey provides a broad sense of the experience of high-school educated women in the south to the degree possible in the absence of a sampling frame.

The questionnaire focused on the relative timing of various events in the domains of schooling, work, residence, relationships with men, and reproduction. I conducted 14 of the interviews myself and attended 21 interviews conducted by my assistants. The remaining 149 were conducted by an assistant alone. I proofread the results from each interview and sent the interviewers back to the field to complete or correct the account when it seemed necessary. Most interviews were conducted in the respondents' homes; a minority were conducted in women's workplaces, or in nearby cafés or bars when that seemed more private. My assistants were instructed to attempt to avoid having anyone else in the room at the time of the interview, although this was not always possible. About two-thirds were conducted in Eton or Ewondo, with the remainder in French, according to the preference of the respondent.

To complement the formal survey, I also conducted open-ended life-history interviews with thirty-six women. These were tape-recorded and transcribed, and most of the quotes in the book come from these interviews. All of them address the personal life history of the respondent, as well as her aspirations for the future. Many also explore her opinions about Catholic schooling, womanhood, and marriage and motherhood. In addition, I conducted and tape-recorded four "focus-group" discussions, where a group of people discussed topics that I gave them, and recorded another half-dozen informal conversations with friends or neighbors on related topics. Finally, I learned much of what is written here while peeling manioc, eating dinner, or visiting a new mother and baby. It was often in the moments that I was not taking formal field notes, eliciting, or surveying that I was able to actually *see* the relationships between apparently disparate things, understand something that I had been told earlier, or recognize a distinction between two similar phenomena.

I left Cameroon about halfway through my scheduled fieldwork, in August 1998, because I was seriously injured in a car accident. I have never been so glad to see an American Marine as the one who fetched me from the hospital! It turns out that convalescence is a good time to code data and transcribe interviews, because you can't do much else. By the time I was well enough to travel, the momentum of analysis and writing had caught me, and I decided not to return for another lengthy stay. Most of the book relies on those eight months of fieldwork in 1998; the epilogue recounts what became of some of my interlocutors between my departure that August and July 2001, when I was able to return and visit. All names, and a few particularly revealing life-historical details, have been changed to protect people's anonymity. All translations from French and German are my own.

*   *   *

This book could not have been researched or written without generous assistance at every stage. I gratefully acknowledge the financial support of the Program of African Studies at Northwestern University, the Social Science Research Council, the National Science Foundation, the Spencer Foundation, the Wenner-Gren Foundation, the Population Council, and the Hellman Family Fund.

In Cameroon, Ghislaine Ateba Nomo, Melanie Eboa and her family, Parfait Eloundou-Enyegue and his family, Kisito Kisito, Jacqueline Mballa, Nicole Moandjel, Paulette Florence Nga, Barbara Ngah, Marie Ngono Awono, Monsieur Odilon, and Noah Pantaléon all offered me kindness as well as practical help. *Je vous remercie tous.* In addition, the women whose stories are recounted here—you know who you are—were generous beyond description. My heartfelt thanks to all of you.

I gratefully thank Alaka Basu, Guilia Barrera, Sara Berry, Anthony Carter, Jean Comaroff, John Comaroff, Amal Hassan Fadlalla, Michael Herzfeld, Pamela Feldman-Savelsberg, Elise Levin, Elinor Ochs, Clementine Rossier, Helen Schwartzman, Rachel Sullivan, Susan Watkins, and Ken Wachter, who offered significant comments or critiques on the manuscript or the ideas it contains. Much of what is valuable about the book comes from their advice. Elizabeth Kuhn-Wilken edited the manuscript with passion and precision, a rare combination of talents that I am sure will serve her well as she begins her own graduate studies. I am sorry to lose her help, but eagerly anticipate the research that she will produce. Sarah Walchuk and Kate Jordan offered excellent administrative assistance. At the University of Chicago Press, David Brent, Elizabeth Branch Dyson and Carlisle Rex-Waller went above and beyond to bring the project to fruition. I also thank two anonymous reviewers for their exceptionally useful suggestions for revision. Of course, the errors and omissions are my own.

Caroline Bledsoe and Jane Guyer inspired the project throughout. They are role models both as scholars and as people, and their contributions to the ideas herein are extensive and fundamental. So, too, are the contributions of my dear husband William Hanks; our constant conversation so underlies this book that I am honestly unsure which of the best ideas are really his. Finally, the book is dedicated to my grandfather, Professor James E. Johnson, whose generous mentorship in academia I hope to have deserved.

CHAPTER ONE

Introduction

Without adequacy on the level of meaning, our generalizations remain mere statements of statistical probability, either not intelligible at all or only imperfectly intelligible. . . . On the other hand, even the most certain adequacy on the level of meaning signifies an acceptable causal proposition only to the extent . . . that the action in question really takes the course held to be meaningfully adequate with a certain calculable frequency. — Max Weber, *Economy and Society*

One of the most remarkable and resilient findings of social science in the later half of the twentieth century is the inverse correlation between women's schooling and their fertility. Throughout the developing world, educated women bear fewer children, and start bearing them later, than do their less educated counterparts (Adamchak and Ntseane 1992; Bledsoe et al. 1999; Castro Martin 1995; Cleland and Rodriguez 1988; United Nations 1995). This basic relationship appears surprisingly impervious to local context: given the variability across countries in the quality and distribution of schooling, in the social meanings ascribed to education and to childbearing, and in the forms of families and households, it seems frankly implausible that the relationship between education and childbearing should be consistent in direction. And yet it is. Whether the unit of analysis is the nation or the individual, the statistical relationship between education and reproduction emerges. Schooling does not predict fertility perfectly—indeed, we find substantial variation—but that it predicts fertility at all is quite astonishing.

Why, and how, do educated women so limit their childbearing by comparison to their less educated compatriots? Why should this limitation so often include postponing the first child? Although these questions may appear to have obvious answers—such as "modernization" or "a rational curriculum"—empirical tests of these easy answers produce mixed results, at best. Despite a detailed body of data characterizing the shape and density of the education-fertility correlation, remarkably little is known about the causes or mechanisms of that correlation. This uncertainty constitutes part of a larger dilemma in studies of population, culture, and society, where the social and economic causes of fertility levels and trends—the "distal determinants"—remain undertheorized (Caldwell 1997; Hirschman 1994; but see also Mason 1997). Despite significant contributions from anthropology, demography, economics, and sociology, we frankly do not yet understand the social processes that underlie fertility rates or changes in those rates.

This demographic dilemma constitutes half of the impetus for this book. Seeking to understand the social mechanisms through which the statistical correlations arise, I focus on one aspect of the schooling-fertility correlation, in one country, and ask: Why do educated Cameroonian women wait so long to bear their first child? How do they achieve this delay? A second stimulus for this book lies in the mystery of coming of age for girls in southern Cameroon. What does it mean to become a Beti woman, particularly one who is educated? How has womanhood been transformed by the social forces of school, church, and economic underdevelopment? This book demonstrates how the answers to these two questions, apparently so discrete, are deeply intertwined. To become an educated Beti woman means, in part, to practice disciplined reproduction; educated Beti women wait so long to bear a first child in order to attain the identity of an educated, disciplined, and honorable woman.

The book comprises three central arguments. First, I propose that educated Beti women delay their childbearing because they view motherhood as appropriate only in a limited set of social contexts, and these contexts are slow to coalesce. It is entry into the social category of "mother," rather than the biological event of giving birth, that women seek to regulate. Educated Cameroonian women characterize their rigorous management of motherhood as an expression of their modernity, discipline, and honor—characteristics that they attribute to their schooling. Thus, the relationship between schooling and fertility cannot be adequately described either as causal or as classic selectivity; instead, the demographic outcomes are the result of culturally mediated aspirations and attempts to capitalize on perceived opportunities. That is, when confronting vital life-history transitions, individuals and their families draw on assembled understandings of what is plausible or desirable; they put themselves into social positions to facilitate certain anticipated outcomes. In the Beti case, these desired outcomes are framed in a system of honor that valorizes self-dominion as measured in autonomy and discretion.

My second central claim is that educated Beti women discipline their reproductive lives not only before conception, but also during pregnancy and after delivery. In each of these moments, they see and act on opportunities to control the timing and conditions of their entry into socially recognized motherhood. In many cases, this control comes in the form of delay—delaying a pregnancy, especially through the use of periodic abstinence, delaying giving birth by aborting certain pregnancies, and delaying socially recognized motherhood by giving up certain children to essentially permanent fosterage. These practices result in a situation where educated women not only bear their first child later than do the less educated, but are also less likely to experience their first pregnancy, first birth, and entry into socially recognized motherhood all at the same time. We therefore need to broaden our view of reproduction to include not only live births, but also the reproductive processes that surround them: the "mishaps" (Bledsoe, Banja, and Hill 1998) and methods of baby making that constitute a reproductive career.

Finally, I build on this ethnographic case to propose an approach to social organization in diachronic perspective that integrates demographic aggregates with systems of meaning, using a unit of social description that I call the "vital conjuncture." Vital conjunctures are structures of possibility that emerge around specific periods of potential transformation in the lives of one or more participants. Although most social life is indeed conjunctural, in the sense that action is conjoined to a particular, temporary manifestation of social structure, *vital* conjunctures are particularly critical durations when more than usual is in play, when certain potential futures are galvanized and others made improbable. For my purposes, the prototypical vital conjunctures are those surrounding the three moments of childbearing: conception, pregnancy, and birth. However, all life transitions—such as migration, marriage, or career change—can be theorized as vital conjunctures. The analysis of vital conjunctures relies on their horizons and on the possible futures that social actors envision, hope for, or fear, and which thereby motivate the actions that make demographic facts. Thus, an understanding of population-level fertility patterns requires attending to quite nondemographic phenomena. The claim that the demography of fertility is inextricably bound to social form underlies the organization of this book; we will work back and forth between statistical and social patterns, seeking to illuminate each with the pale light of the other.

The Shape of the Correlation

The fact that schooling and fertility are often inversely correlated was observed by Malthus (1970: 90), and has been conclusively demonstrated over the past three decades. It is a relationship that appears at several levels: countries in which a large proportion of women are educated generally have lower fertility rates than do countries in which few women are educated, and within specific countries, women with more education generally bear fewer children than do women who are less educated. The occurrence on multiple levels is significant for the kinds of explanations that might be adequate. It matters also that this is a correlation in the statistical sense, and not a universal pattern. The specific form of the relationship between schooling and fertility varies substantially. It is not always monotonic, or constantly downward sloping: sometimes moderate amounts of school are associated with higher fertility than no school at all, and the predicted inverse relationship only applies after extended schooling. The degree of fertility decline associated with schooling is also quite variable: in some cases, even extended schooling is associated with only a slight reduction in fertility, whereas in other cases, the decline is precipitous. The tightness of fit between education and fertility differs as well: in some cases, the variation in schooling levels can predict most of the variation in fertility, while in other cases, schooling explains relatively little. The relationship between education and fertility is, in fact, a whole set of relationships.

Figure 1.1 shows the cross-national relationship between schooling and fertility. The data points on this scatter plot are countries; the measures of schooling and fertility are thus national aggregates. The proportion of women who are literate serves here as a proxy for women's education, and the total fertility rate (TFR) is used as the measure of fertility. The total fertility rate is the number of children a woman would bear over the course of her life if she bore children at the age-specific rates prevailing in her country at a specific time: it is a useful synoptic illusion. This graph shows two things: first, countries with higher literacy rates (on the right hand side of the graph) have generally lower fertility that those with lower literacy rates. Second, the graph shows that literacy is not the complete explanation of fertility practice—at any given level of literacy, we find countries with wildly differing total fertility rates.

The cross-national correlation indicates that something of significance is going on here, but what? As we move inward, to more detail, the picture gets more complicated. National rates elide important differences.

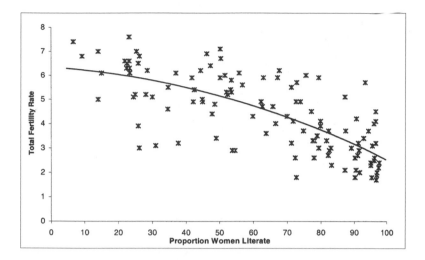

FIGURE 1.1. Total fertility rate as a function of female literacy. Data from World Bank Data Indicators Online (http://devdata.worldbank.org/dataonline).

The next series of graphs moves inside the scatter-plot points to show how the relationship between schooling and fertility works within specific countries. Each line on these graphs represents the fertility rates of women with different degrees of education in a single country—each country chosen solely because the data were available. The countries are grouped by national total fertility rates, read loosely as children per woman. Figure 1.2 pertains to countries where total fertility is under four children per woman, primarily in Asia and Latin America. These countries show substantial variability in the character of the relationship between schooling and fertility. A couple of the countries in this group demonstrate a monotonic downward slope of fertility with increasing schooling. Others show almost no relationship at all—the line is flat. In one country, women with a couple of years of schooling have significantly *higher* fertility than those with none, a pattern called the "inverted-j" by Jejeebhoy (1995).

The middle group of countries, which includes Cameroon, have total fertility rates between four and six (fig. 1.3). Although these countries, some sub-Saharan, some North African, and some Latin American, vary substantially in history, economy, and culture, they share a relatively unambiguous inverse relationship between schooling and fertility. Here, women with no education bear between five and eight children, while the most educated—women with at least ten years of school—bear no more than

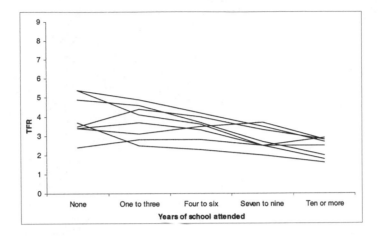

FIGURE 1.2. Total fertility rate by years of schooling in countries with total fertility rates 2.0 to 3.9. Data from United Nations 1995: 65.

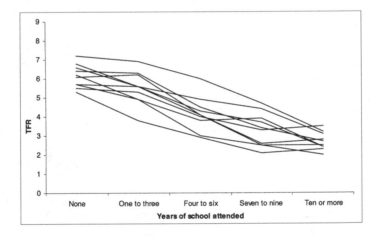

FIGURE 1.3. Total fertility rate by years of schooling in countries with total fertility rates 4.0 to 5.9. Data from United Nations 1995: 65.

four. In all but two of these countries, the relationship is monotonic, such that even low levels of schooling are associated with declines in fertility.

The last group of countries, countries with total fertility rates over six, are all in sub-Saharan Africa or Muslim West Asia (fig. 1.4). In only two of these countries does the monotonic inverse relationship appear; in the other countries, it is only women who have attended seven or even ten

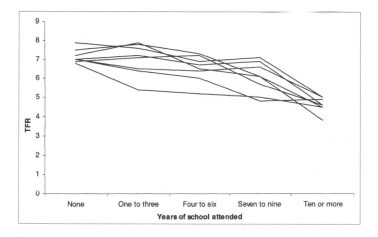

FIGURE 1.4. Total fertility rate by years of schooling in countries with total fertility rates 6.0 and more. Data from United Nations 1995: 65.

years of schooling who bear fewer children than those with no schooling. In many of these high-fertility countries, such women are extremely rare, inviting the interpretation that their elite status, even more than their schooling, induces innovative fertility practices.

Looking comparatively across these figures, the correlation between schooling and fertility is strongest in countries with moderate overall fertility levels. In some cases, these are countries where fertility is falling, and it is simply falling fastest among the more educated. In other countries, these moderate fertility rates, and the differentials by education, appear stable. The variation in the shape of the association between schooling and fertility among these different countries is a reminder that this statistical relationship always works through social processes in specific contexts. Here, Weber's call for an integration of "adequacy on the level of meaning" with "calculable frequencies" from statistical aggregates starts to make intuitive sense (1978: 12). Although educated women do indeed bear fewer children than do less-educated women in most countries, they do so in different ways and to different degrees.

This variation in manner and degree is even clearer when we turn from total fertility rates to age-specific rates. Age-specific rates give a sense of the pattern and pacing of childbearing, details that are invisible in more aggregated data, but that are essential to an understanding of the experience of reproduction, its place in social life, and how fertility differentials are made over the life course. Let us look specifically at Cameroon

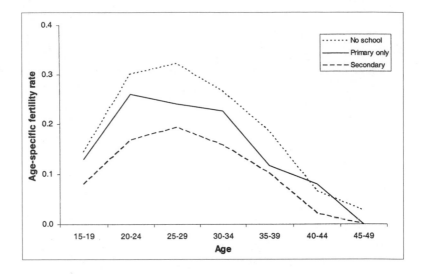

FIGURE 1.5. Age-specific fertility rates by educational level in Cameroon. Data from 1998 Cameroon DHS in Fotso et al. 1999.

(fig. 1.5). Data from the 1998 Cameroon Demographic and Health Survey, a nationally representative survey conducted by Macro International in collaboration with Cameroonian researchers (Fotso et al. 1999), indicates that the fertility differentials persist across all ages, although they are largest at younger ages (below thirty-five).

The fact that educated Cameroonian women bear fewer children at all ages than do the uneducated implies that the explanation of the rates must be based in a broad, social understanding of reproductive practice. Whereas Henry (1961), Coale and Trussell (1974), Knodel (1987), and others have suggested that the fertility decline begins with certain women deciding to stop bearing children after reaching a certain, desired family size, that does not appear to be the pattern in Cameroon. Here, educated women are restraining their childbearing at all ages, and presumably all parities, in relation to women with no schooling.

The Beti of Southern Cameroon

At the center of this book are a group of young, educated women who call themselves Beti. "Beti" is both a status category and an ethnic affiliation, much like "Nuer" (see Evans-Pritchard 1969: 3–6). A century ago, Beti society was organized into segmentary lineages practicing swidden horti-culture. Through taxation, physical violence, and the establishment of a lo-cal political hierarchy, German colonials instituted sedentary, centralized communities in the decades before World War One (Mveng 1963; Ngongo 1987). At the same time, Roman Catholic missions and mission schools brought about one of the most rapid and complete conversions known in Africa (Laburthe-Tolra 1977). Following World War One, southern Cam-eroon was administered by France under a mandate from the League of Nations. Increased production for the cash economy reconfigured patterns of kinship and residence in this period, as rural men took as many wives as possible in order to capitalize on the women's labor on their plantations. So strong was the demand for women's labor that some men took wives who had not yet reached puberty (Guyer 1985). Some of the profits from these enterprises were reinvested in formal education for children, who entered state employment. Thus, the institutions of the state, the church, and the school together came to define a newly emergent elite (see Bayart 1989).

French Cameroon became independent in 1960 and joined with a por-tion of former British Cameroon in 1961. Schooling was a major priority of the newly independent government, and educational institutions at all levels were built in record numbers in the 1960s and 1970s. The expan-sion of public schooling was possible, in part, because of the strength of the national economy at that time. Cameroonian imports of cocoa and coffee were well remunerated, and the state was solvent. But in 1987 the value of these exports collapsed. In 1986, Cameroon earned over CFA 800 billion from exports; in 1987, that value scarcely exceeded CFA 500 billion (Asuagbor 1994: 41). From this grew *la crise,* a disintegration of socioeconomic order that persisted at least to the turn of the millennium. Civil service salaries were cut twice, and the currency was devalued by 50 percent in 1992. But the effects of *la crise* are as much social as economic. Many southern Cameroonians talk of generalized distrust caused by *la crise morale,* which makes every step radically uncertain.

Since the establishment of mission schools in the early twentieth cen-tury, Catholic schooling has been a powerful social force in Cameroon (Berger 1978). Most of the nation's leaders attended Catholic schools, and the schools retain an aura of power and prestige, particularly at the sec-ondary level (Nkoe 1991). Catholic schooling maintains a distinct moral agenda in reference to family formation processes; its students attend cat-echism classes and lessons like "Education in Life and Love," in addition to the classic academic subjects. The schools are thought to impart discipline, a trait considered central to both economic independence and judicious action in sexual relationships, the dual bases of honor for Beti women. Highly valued for both moral and economic reasons, Catholic schools are seen as the path to formal-sector employment and elite status.

Catholic education is arguably not only a path to elite status, however, but also an assertion of such status. For Catholic school is not available to all: attendance requires command over significant resources, financial and otherwise. Women who have attended Catholic schools thus share not only educational experiences, but also some aspects of family background, since the institution effectively selects its students from the relatively privileged. There are notable exceptions—the talented child from a poor family whose school fees are paid by a priest, or the beautiful young lover of a successful man—but these exceptions are few.

This book proposes that Beti women educated in Catholic schools navigate family formation processes in reference to a local system of honor, similar to what Hammel has called a "moral economy" (see, e.g., Hammel 1990). They bear their first children late because the social conjunctures they will accept as conditions for honorable childbearing come together slowly. Concepts of honor are widely shared throughout southern Cameroon; however, actors in different social positions understand these concepts differently as a result of their histories of interaction with them. Thus, educated women construe honorability and the paths to its attainment differently than do the uneducated. This is accentuated by the fact that women who attend Catholic secondary schools are disproportionately selected from families connected to the formal sector, from urban families, and from families with educated parents. Through family and school, educated women acquire schemata of honorability focused on a normative order of life-history events in which marriage and childbearing follow the establishment of a career. Disciplined timing is thus the key to honorable childbearing for women of the educated Beti elite. Educated women often significantly delay family formation while seeking to create its appropriate conjunctures.

Although education in the abstract plays a significant role in the honor system, on-the-ground activity within schools both contributes to and contradicts that general role. School provides a context in which students get to practice certain kinds of action, and this practice may matter as much as much as any lesson plans or curriculum. The simple fact that students spend the entire day with unrelated age-mates of the opposite sex, engaged in the same spheres of activity, stands in stark contrast to the forms of social organization outside of school. School thus serves as a central locus for practicing heterosexual relationships. The insults that boys call out to girls, girls' acquiescence to such taunting, and the coexistence of (sexual) attraction and conflict all serve to habituate young men and women into the forms of heterosexual relations that will later form the context of sex and pregnancy. The formal curriculum gets little classroom time in the school where I observed, especially compared to waiting for the teacher, enduring punishments, and taking verbatim dictation. In part, these are the forms of discipline that make Catholic schools so highly valued in the honor system: they are said to teach patience and respect. Educated women regularly assert that these traits distinguish them from the uneducated. This is not at all to imply that discipline, patience, and respect are limited to the educated, or that they are not needed in other aspects of Beti society. To the contrary, they are precisely the marks of a well-socialized Beti person, educated or not, and are needed in situations from traditional funerals to interactions with state bureaucracy. Indeed, the fact that Catholic schooling is thought to impart them so well demonstrates the equation of schooling and successful socialization. It explains why an educated person is sometimes called *mfan mot*, a "real person."

To understand Beti motherhood, the first birth must be distinguished from entry into socially recognized motherhood; the first is a demographic event, the second a social process. Part of my goal is to delineate the relationship between the first birth and entry into socially recognized motherhood among the Beti. I will show that educated women's aspirations to enter motherhood honorably play a critical role in their delaying first childbearing. First childbearing offers a rich locus for studying fertility, both in its own right and as a pivotal moment in a reproductive career. The social context of the first birth may have significant, although not determinative, consequences for the mother's future opportunities (Alter 1988; Delaunay 1994).

Schooling and childbearing in southern Cameroon relate to one another as parts of a system of social reproduction. At issue in decisions about education, sex, and motherhood is the remaking of socially structured relationships. This fact underlies the correlation between education and fertility; the statistical relationship rests on a social one.

The Ethnography of Reproduction

In the past three decades, fertility has become an increasingly central topic in social anthropology. This is in part due to the increased ethnographic attention to women, and in part related to the move away from structural-functional and toward activity-centered approaches to the life course. The majority of ethnographic research on fertility has focused either on the political economy of kinship and marriage (Collier and Yanagisako 1987; Ginsburg and Rapp 1995; MacCormack 1994; Robertson 1991; Sargent 1989; Strathern 1992a, 1992b) or on the discursive arena of cultural meaning in which sex, birth, food, and gender are represented and symbolically elaborated (Boddy 1989; Devische 1993; Inhorn 1994; Martin 1989). Both perspectives offer important insights into the Beti material.

Political-economic approaches to fertility are eloquently represented by the work of Marilyn Strathern and Faye Ginsburg. Locating fertility in a structure of economic value, Ginsburg has focused largely on the consequences of the new reproductive technologies, such as in vitro fertilization and ultrasound. Fertility and its control are seen as resources that can be strategically employed and are therefore valuable. With Rayna Rapp, Ginsburg has argued that reproduction should be approached as a locus of power inequality (Ginsburg and Rapp 1991, 1995). These scholars argue that access to reproductive choice is intimately related to political legitimacy; that is, there is a direct mapping between the reproductive body and the body politic (1995: 3). As we will see, reproduction is "stratified" in southern Cameroon, both through access to fertility limitation methods and through perceptions of what constitutes legitimate or appropriate reproduction.

Strathern comes to the study of fertility from studies of kinship, gender, knowledge, and the construction of value (1992a, 1992b, 1995). She considers the relationships between the new reproductive technologies, systems of kinship, and national identity. Throughout, she argues against classic distinctions between the cultural and the natural, demonstrating, for example, the ways that in vitro fertilization and models of kinship intersect and are mutually constitutive. Strathern argues that the new reproductive technologies may transform procreation and kinship, taking them ever further outside the domain of reproduction and family, as kinship is "dispersed" (1995: 352). Like Ginsburg's work on how power inequalities shape reproductive choices, Strathern's dissociation of physical from social reproduction resonates in the Beti material, where socially recognized motherhood, rather than biological reproduction, is salient. Both Ginsburg and Strathern have significantly advanced studies of the political economy of fertility; however, their emphasis on power and politics has led them to neglect the question of how sex, gender, and fertility are symbolically mediated and therefore experienced.

A second group of ethnographers have approached fertility through its symbols. Emily Martin's 1989 work *The Woman in the Body* opened new vistas for research focused on the cultural meanings of fertility, sex, and gender. The hegemony of current medical practice, she argues, alienates contemporary American women from their bodies. She analyzes women's talk, primarily from interviews, about their bodies, health, and reproduction. She suggests that American women use one central image in thinking about bodies: "Your self is separate from your body" (1989: 77). Martin's work has been instrumental in drawing attention to the body as the ground of symbolic contestation between the medical establishment and women themselves. Yet the consequences of this symbolic contestation either for social organization or for demographic outcomes is ignored.

Janice Boddy similarly focuses on the cultural meanings of fertility, but also attends to social organization. In *Wombs and Alien Spirits* (1989), Boddy demonstrates how religious practice, including spirit possession, is intertwined with marriage and reproduction. She argues that spirit possession is a central modality of coping with reproductive and marital disorder in Sudan, where reproductive capacities are thought to be largely under the sway of potentially possessing spirits. In this dense ethnography of gender relations and religion, Boddy argues that reproduction and its absence constitute the core cultural concern, without which both possession and marriage are incomprehensible. These symbolic perspectives suggest several productive paths of inquiry into the Beti material, but the symbolic mediation also has quantitative consequences, and understanding these consequences requires a complementary approach.

The interrelationship of the political economy and symbolic representation of fertility is now beginning to be enunciated. The work of Pamela Feldman-Savelsberg provides one model of potential integration. Feldman-Savelsberg has explored the cultural meanings inscribed in fertility in west Cameroon, focusing on the symbolic equation of fertility, cooking, and the power of the chiefdom (1994, 1995, 1999). She convincingly argues that the Bamiliké equate the disempowerment of the chief vis-à-vis the Cameroonian state, particularly in the period of economic crisis, with collective infertility. Although Bamiliké women in fact have fertility levels just above the average for Cameroon, infertility constitutes a central locus of anxiety about social relations, the breakdown of traditional authority, and the declining power of the chief. Feldman-Savelsberg has shown that the symbolic meanings of fertility are constructed through tangible practices in economic, political, and historical time and space. Her work is particularly generative for comparative studies, because Feldman-Savelsberg has developed a way of interweaving social facts of different kinds and at different levels of social organization, pushing the analytic logic of Weber (1978) in a case where the community, the ethnic group, and the state might each be seen as the "social group" over which meanings and statistical patterns are distributed.

At the same time as Feldman-Savelsberg has been developing an integrative approach to fertility out of the close analysis of her field data, a small group of thinkers have been engaged in a parallel, if somewhat more ambitious, project, explicitly defining the emergent field of demographic anthropology. Susan Greenhalgh has been one of the most outspoken and eloquent of these scholars. The introduction to her edited volume *Situating Fertility* (1995) is a plea for fertility studies on the borders of demography and anthropology. Greenhalgh argues that we need a "culture and political economy of reproduction" that will employ political economy approaches, feminism, and social constructionism (1995: 12–13). She is not alone in this project. Anthony Carter, for example, has cogently argued for the integration of a theory of practice into studies of fertility, proposing to view reproductive life through the lens of social action, where the production of meaning and the production of demographic aggregates have the same source (1995: 84). Thus, the ethnography of fertility has made great progress toward understanding the social situations of childbearing. What this literature lacks is a method for addressing the population-level consequences of the meaning structures that have been so elegantly explained. For this, it is necessary to turn more toward demography.

The relationship between demography and ethnography has been rocky, although most demographic anthropologists have tried to smooth over the epistemological differences. Townsend writes that "both anthropology and demography are concerned with the relationship between elements and structures and with the coordinated reproduction of both individuals and the structured relationships in which they exist" (1997: 96). But while this may be true, the anthropological and demographic understandings of "relationship," "structure," and "individual" are often so radically different that the fact of common concern seems to fade to insignificance. Demographic models of reproduction seek to purge the data of precisely the things that inspire anthropologists, such as the variation in social experience and multiple interpretations of social facts. Anthropological approaches, by contrast, neglect the issues central to demographers: comparability, causation, statistical significance, and external validity. This dichotomy is captured in the questions that members of the two disciplines consider compelling. For most anthropologists, fertility relates to socialization, the life cycle, ritual, kinship, and gender, as well as concepts of personhood; schooling and fertility are connected as parts of the process of coordinated social reproduction. For most demographers, by contrast, fertility relates to contraceptive use, modernization, and the national labor market; schooling and fertility are connected in that the distribution of the first drives the patterns of the second.

Education and Fertility in Demography

The correlation between education and fertility has been extensively studied in demography, almost always using national-level survey data. Much of this research has focused on measuring the strength and consistency of the relationship (Ainsworth, Nyamete, and Beegle 1995; Cochrane 1979; Jejeebhoy 1995). Nearly all of this research confirms that the correlation is strong and consistent in direction, as we saw earlier in this introduction. Most researchers have assumed that this correlation arises from a causal link: that education in some way induces women to bear fewer children. This assumption is supported by the fact that educated women differ from their uneducated age-mates to a statistically significant degree in a variety of domains. Differences found in various studies have included not only lower fertility, but also lower infant mortality, decreased tolerance of polygyny, increased participation in wage labor, and increased income (Cleland and Kaufman 1998; Cohen and House 1994; Koenig 1981; Pitt 1995; Schultz 1993; Shapiro and Tambashe 1997). The key problem in the contemporary demography of schooling and fertility, therefore, has been framed in terms of mechanisms: *how* does education induce fertility decline? Whereas anthropologists have explored the contexts and meanings of social and biological reproduction separately; demographers have focused on the mechanisms of the correlation between them.

Explanatory models of the correlation in demography have largely been of two types, which I will roughly categorize as cognitive and instrumental change. The first group of theories have proposed that schooling alters people's values and ways of seeing the world, changing women's perspectives, ideas, and modes of thought (Goody 1968; Goody and Watt 1963; LeVine and White 1986; Ong 1982). In these modes, the schemata that women use to evaluate the world are transformed by the educative process, but the objective world itself is not. For example, van de Walle (1992) has argued that in some "traditional" societies, fertility has not entered Coale's famous "calculus of conscious choice" (1973); in a cognitive model of fertility change, formal education would be seen as serving to bring fertility into that calculus. Theories of instrumental change, by contrast, emphasize the ways in which schooling changes the objective conditions under which decisions are made (e.g., Caldwell 1980; Blanc and Lloyd 1990). Most of these models are microeconomic, including the innovative models of Becker (1991), Easterlin and Crimmins (1985), and the common model of "opportunity costs," which proposes that educated women—making exactly the same type of rational choices as uneducated women—will bear fewer children as children become more costly to rear (see, e.g., Ainsworth 1988).

Both groups of theories emphasize that education encourages women to desire fewer children, although for different reasons: they are "demand-side" theories. Cleland and Kaufman (1998) have countered that schooling affects not the numbers of children that women wish to bear, but rather their ability to achieve their reproductive goals: schooling makes women more able to convince their husbands of the need for contraception, negotiate with difficult clinic workers, and properly use contraception. In this way, Cleland and Kaufman argue that education changes the "supply" of children, rather than parents' demand for them. Although their supply-side model offers an innovative revision to classic understandings of the association of fertility and education, Cleland and Kaufman continue to assume that fertility practices are carried out in reference to a desired number of children. This has been taken for granted by the demographic community for decades; however, Bledsoe, Banja, and Hill (1998) propose that women in Gambia bear children according to a calendar established by their physical well-being, rather than by the number of children born or surviving.[1]

In a series of major works, Bledsoe has laid out a systematic theory of African fertility that serves as a critique of the standard demographic model. First, she criticizes the close association that demographers assume between childbearing and childrearing, noting the complexity of fosterage and adoption arrangements that parents employ throughout West Africa; her data indicate that the processes of childrearing are implicated in diverse social and economic relationships that bind households to one another. The costs and benefits of childrearing do not necessarily accrue to those who bear children (Bledsoe 1990c, 1993). Second, she proposes that women in Gambia, rather than seeking to bear specific numbers of children, structure their reproductive practices in reference to their own degree of "maternal depreciation" (Bledsoe, Banja, and Hill 1998), delaying pregnancies to protect their fragile bodily resources. Women time their births in reference to their own physical health, as well as to their status in the household. In Bledsoe's model, women's childbearing is ordered not by the maximization of some utility curve in which children have costs and benefits, but rather by a series of situated practices, decisions made on the basis of bodily well-being and the socially constructed view of timing of births. In Bledsoe's alternate view of African fertility, "reproduction and aging [are] highly related processes and . . . both of these processes can be managed" (Bledsoe 2002: 164).

Bledsoe's critique hits at the core of demographic theories of fertility. By demonstrating that reproductive practices derive from a social logic with a long temporal horizon, rather than from the maximization of short-term utility, Bledsoe has countered the central tenet of demographic causality. When social actors, as people with histories and hopes, navigate reproductive lives, they are not stand-ins for economic "factors" or demographic "forces." Bledsoe's evidence of reproductive agency thus undermines models of causal links between aggregate variables.

Students Participate in Their Schooling

Contemporary studies in classrooms echo Bledsoe's emphasis on social actors as agents in the making of social facts: neither students nor reproductive women are passive receivers of economic or demographic forces. A number of studies of schools have demonstrated that students participate actively in their education, constructing schools as sites both of social reproduction and of its transformation (e.g., Aronowitz and Giroux 1991; Heath 1983; Johnson 1985; McLaren 1993). These school-based studies are fully consonant with research on socialization in other domains that posits an active learner (Ochs 1993; Pelissier 1991; Schieffelin 1990; Schieffelin and Ochs 1986; Street 1993). Although most of this work has been conducted in schools in the United States and Europe, research in Africa has contributed by documenting the multiple social ends to which students and communities have employed education (Barnes 1986; Comaroff 1985; Serpell 1993; Stambach 2000).

Schools are perhaps the most explicit arena of instruction and enculturation in contemporary society, and a foundational body of work on the culture of education explored this role, drawing heavily on culture-and-personality and socialization studies (Hansen 1979; Kimball 1974; Ogbu 1974; Spindler 1974). Formal education may reproduce or contradict aspects of socialization that occur in the other institutions of family, church, or economy; the processes unfold in ways that are neither discrete nor independent (Spindler 1963; Wolcott 1967). Contextualizing schooling in the larger frame of socialization allows us to view it as instrumental in providing knowledge, skills, and opportunities, as well as in constructing subjectivity. It also implies that all of the significant advances in the study of socialization of the past twenty years apply equally to studies of schooling, whether or not schooling was their locus.

In addition to contributing to the socialization of individuals, schools are a significant site of the reproduction of social inequality, as a number of sociologists and ethnographers have demonstrated (Bourdieu and Passeron 1971; Gintis and Bowles 1976; Willis 1977). They are sites of the formation of postcolonial urban elites (Barnes 1989; Mann 1985; Moran 1990), and places of gender construction (Anyon 1983; McRobbie 1978; Thorne 1993; Weis 1988). Exemplifying this approach to schools, Willis explores the oppositional culture of working-class schoolboys in Britain. He argues that they inadvertently recreate their own economic and social subordination through actions "experienced, paradoxically, as true learning, affirmation, appropriation, and as a form of resistance" (1977: 3). Willis provides an elegant argument of unintended consequences: these boys resist school norms intentionally, and with a partial understanding of the class-based economy, but their actions systematically force them into low-paid factory work with few prospects for advancement. Willis's dissociation of intention and effect makes possible an approach to action based not in outcomes, but in aspirations. Similarly, Thorne describes how North American grade-school children learn gender identities through schoolyard play. She demonstrates that "children act, resist, rework, and create; they influence adults as well as being influenced by them" (1993: 3). Thorne's work has transformed studies of children and children's activities. She has shown, as has Schwartzman (1978), that studies of children must focus on the present as the present, and not only on childhood as preparation for adult life.

Thorne's emphasis on the ways that children create and transmit cultural forms is consonant with studies of learning across the life course. Lave and Wenger (1991) have developed a model of learning they call "legitimate peripheral participation," in which novices learn skills by engaging in activities on the periphery of the social group, incorporating knowledge through practice as they become involved in increasingly central ways in the activity. Lave and Wenger argue that learning is not a process of acquiring and applying abstract knowledge, but is constituted instead in practices through which novices increasingly act like experts. Becoming an expert thus means behaving like one in a context where that expertise is recognized. Learning is not, therefore, an individual activity. Instead, "communities of practice" create and transmit knowledge; learning is socially distributed. This approach implies an "emphasis on comprehensive understanding involving the whole person rather than 'receiving' a body of factual knowledge about the world" (Lave and Wenger 1991:33).

Despite major differences in method and style, a single thread runs through the work of Willis, Thorne, and Lave. All these researchers have demonstrated that students are active participants in their schooling, and that schools do not impose values, norms, or ideas on students in any clear or unidirectional manner. Schooling must therefore be construed as a participation frame in which students, teachers, administrators, parents, and others collaborate in a systematic way to produce social form. A key corollary of this point is that schooling does not—*cannot*—cause demographic change independent of the agency of social actors. Insofar as this work holds, then, the common assumption that education directly transforms individuals' demographic behavior *cannot* be correct. Instead, schooling and childbearing are situated in life histories and in communities; their correlation is an artifact of social process.

Selectivity and Theories of Practice

If the well-established inverse correlation between education and fertility cannot be explained simply as a causal relationship, what models shall we call on? One classic alternative in the statistical social sciences is selection, those processes by which individuals with certain characteristics differentially enter certain demographic or analytic groups (Collier 1995;

Heckman 1976). This presorting results in groups with different compositions, clouding the analysis of variables whose causal direction is often taken for granted. That is to say, when experimentation is impossible, you cannot know that the study group and the control group do not differ in ways other than the variable of interest. In fact, there is often good reason to assume that they do, and these hidden differences may cause the divergent outcomes between groups. For example, throughout Africa children from wealthy families are more likely to attend school than children from poor families; therefore, the school population is composed of more wealthy children than is the general population. Some of the differences in fertility between educated and uneducated women likely arise as a result of this variation, rather than as the result of schooling per se (for similar arguments, see Fuller et al. 1995; Lloyd and Gage-Brandon 1992; Pitt 1995).

Understood in this way, selectivity poses a direct problem for data analysis. In response, researchers in economics, sociology, and demography have argued that the selectivity problem should be avoidable through the addition of variables that account for the differences in groups' compositions—such as the wealth of parents in our example, generally using multivariate regression analysis (e.g., Axinn and Thornton 1992; Belman and Heywood 1989; Bennett et al. 1988; Gronau 1974). However, this solution assumes that the selection occurs as a result of some isolated variable that more refined statistical techniques can capture. This is not always the case. Many processes of selection cannot be reduced to single variables, because they emerge and evolve jointly over the life course (see Corgeau and Lelièvre 1992). In some cases, selectivity effects are not threats to the data quality, but are instead the processes most central to understanding a phenomenon.

An ethnographic approach could bring new life to these configurations of heterogeneous factors that must be analyzed in conjunction, such as those linking education and childbearing, by confronting selectivity squarely as a set of social and cultural processes rather than attempting to delete it from the data. Unfortunately, anthropologists have largely failed to capitalize on this opportunity. In ethnographic writing, a persistent focus on the processes within groups has elided questions of the very composition of those groups. We rarely ask how our ethnographic units have arisen or what are the analytic consequences of those processes.

Bourdieu (1977, 1990) has sought to propose a theoretical language for analyzing the daily processes through which social form is concretized.

Practice theory has been elaborated and applied to institutional reproduction, language use, socialization, and other domains (Carter 1995; Hanks 1996; Lave 1988; Starett 1995). It proposes a constant interplay between structure and subjective disposition, such that social structures are embodied by social actors as generative principles of action, which guide actors' engagements with the world. The actions of agents working from productive schemata born of social structure result, largely, in the reproduction of those embodied structures. Thus, the reproduction of social order is neither inevitable nor mechanical, but occurs through the everyday practices of participants in the social world. Bourdieu explains as follows:

> The conditionings associated with a particular class of conditions of existence produce *habitus*, systems of durable, transposable dispositions, structured structures predisposed to function as structuring structures, that is, as principles which generate and organize practices and representations that can be objectively adapted to their outcomes without presupposing a conscious aiming at ends or an express mastery of the operations necessary in order to attain them. (1990: 53)

What Bourdieu describes suggests a way to radically refigure the analysis of reproduction, schooling, and socialization, insofar as systematicity may inhere neither in intentionality nor in visible coercion, but in "structuring structures," habits of thought and preference so common as to become invisible. Social structure is thus both processual and contingent and therefore deeply challenges rational-choice theories of reproduction, which often assume "that fertility decisions are made once-and-for-all, generally at the beginning of the reproductive lifespan" (Greenhalgh 1995: 22). Indeed, this assumption collapses in the face of the contingency and uncertainty inherent in unfolding reproductive careers. Instead, a practice approach, as formulated by Carter, suggests that reproduction is part of the "reflexive monitoring and rationalization of a continuous flow of conduct" (Carter 1995: 61) that constitutes all social interaction. This view of fertility emphasizes that reproduction, like schooling outcomes, results neither from coolly rational choices nor from passive inculcation with norms, but rather from practices that emanate out of *habitus*. Practice theory thus offers an ethnographic approach to the processes through which selectivity effects emerge.

Statistical selectivity and theories of practice in fact explain many of the same phenomena, but from different perspectives and with different emphases. Bourdieu and Passeron imply as much in their classic work, *Reproduction in Education, Society and Culture* (1971): they use evidence of selectivity effects in schooling achievement as the basis for an argument of the class basis of *habitus*. This exceptional work connects the unequal school outcomes of children from elite and working-class backgrounds to their cultural preparation for school. The authors suggest that habitual relationships to language, expectations for school outcomes, and systematic preferences for and against specific subjects put working-class children not only at a disadvantage in school, but at odds with school values. These students are unequally selected against as they continue through school. Selectivity is therefore an iterative, long-term, and semiconscious process that arises out of structured daily practice. It is this integration of statistical models of selectivity with cultural models of practice that grounds my empirical work. Such an integration makes it possible to uncover how the mutual constitution of agent and social context underlies the most quantitative of demographic phenomena.

The Vital Conjuncture

In this book, I offer a specific empirical argument about the role of the Beti honor system in giving shape to the education-fertility correlation in southern Cameroon. But I also am making a more general, methodological claim about the unit of social description I call the vital conjuncture, proposing a way of integrating statistical selectivity with practice theory as a means of addressing the social basis of statistical facts (Johnson-Hanks 2002a). As mentioned above, vital conjunctures are socially structured zones of possibility that emerge around specific periods of potential transformation in a life or lives. They are temporary configurations of possible change, critical durations of uncertainty and potentiality.[2] A familiar example is the duration around the completion of an academic degree, when career, residence, and professional identity are all at stake. Will I find a job? Where will I live? What will the future hold? This experience of future-orientation, extreme uncertainty, and the potential for radical transformation defines degree completion as a vital conjuncture; young Cameroonian women face the same combination of circumstances in the vital conjunctures of first pregnancy and motherhood.

Although vital conjunctures arise when previously assumed futures are called into question, and although they often entail a transformation in what social actors envision as their trajectories, they are not "choices" or "decisions" in any usual sense. As Schutz argues, in models of choice "the deciding Ego stands at the crossroads O and can decide freely whether to go to X or to Y. . . . [However,] these goals do not exist at all before the choice, nor do the paths to them exist until and unless they are traversed" (1967: 66–67). Unlike the diverging roads in Frost's yellow wood, there are no leaf-strewn paths leading out from a vital conjuncture; vital conjunctures are not junctions on experiential landscapes, but rather periods in which a social actor suddenly—and often painfully—sees the easy, taken-for-granted clarity of the stream of future events as false. On the island where I grew up, the road ends about fifteen miles south of town. A half mile before that stands a sign that reads: "Warning: Road Ends." That is a better metaphor for the experience of the vital conjuncture than a forked road.

Young women facing an unintended pregnancy are not choosing *between* an abortion and a premarital birth, because both of these exist only as imagined potentials at the time of the "choice." Instead, they envision themselves in a succession of possible future states in which the abortion or birth is only one step, until the conjuncture eventually closes as one of these potential futures grows thick and ripe, absorbing all imagination. The conjuncture closes when the major outlines of the future again appear stable, whether those outlines are the same or different as the outlines of futures expected before the conjuncture. In retrospect, the resolution of the conjuncture may be seen as inevitable, or as a major turning point. Either way, however, this perspective is only possible in the retrospective gaze of the actor or the social scientist: prospectively, there is only the momentary configuration of historical events to which the actor must respond.

We can understand vital conjunctures through their horizons, the borders of possibility, desirability, and potential danger as perceived by the participants. These horizons are the socially constructed guideposts, the *points de repères,* the expectations and aspirations that underlie and motivate social action. "Pregnancy can ruin your chances for school" and "you can't wait forever to have a baby" are examples of horizons that will become important here. Participants in a vital conjuncture will experience "the possible" differently, as they will have access to varying amounts and kinds of information, and are authorized to act in diverse ways. Furthermore, they will experience the outcomes of the conjuncture differently. Even if the horizons are the same, their consequences—or even their relevance—may appear different to different participants. Schoolgirls, whose futures are centrally at stake in the conjunctures recounted here, often disagree with their parents about what outcomes would be desirable. They are also often overruled: with relatively limited access to knowledge and relatively little authority to act, the schoolgirl may be a "legitimate peripheral participant" (Lave and Wenger 1991), although it is her own future that is at stake.

Both the words "vital" and "conjuncture" are borrowed from the literature, but from very different domains. "Conjuncture" in this sense comes from Bourdieu, who employs the term to express the relatively short-term conditions that manifest social structure and serve as the matrix for social action:

> Practices can be accounted for only by relating the objective *structure* defining the social conditions of the production of the habitus which engendered them to the conditions in which this habitus is operating, that is, to the *conjuncture* which, short of a radical transformation, represents a particular state of this structure. (Bourdieu 1977: 78)

For Bourdieu, then, the conjuncture is the effective context of action; it is the site in which *habitus* is made and its consequences enacted. This usage is almost identical to that of Sahlins (1985).[3] Like Bourdieu, Sahlins sees conjunctures as intermediate between social structure and individual events. What he calls the "structure of the conjuncture" is "the practical realization of the cultural categories in a specific historical context, as expressed in the interested action of the historical agents" (1985: xiv). The ideas are obviously similar, although Sahlins's usage seems to imply that the conjuncture's outcomes are more heavily determined, the range of possible action narrower. My own usage, particularly through the focus on horizons, emphasizes the intersection of structured expectations with uncertain futures. I use the word "conjuncture" to emphasize the dual character of vital conjunctures: manifestations at once of recurring systematicity and of unique possibility and future-orientation.

"Vital" is taken from the demographic term "vital event," which refers to any occurrence "which [has] to do with an individual's entrance into or departure from life, together with changes in civil status" (IUSSP 1982: 211), such as birth, death, marriage, or change of residence. Indeed, the vital conjunctures model is an alternative way of conceptualizing the life-history elements described by demographers as vital events, for incipient or recent births, deaths, and marriages often evoke precisely these durations of uncertainty and potential creation. When viewed from within a life history, however, the birth of a child or dismissal from school do not constitute discrete events, but rather elements in a subtly structured conjuncture. The differences between events and conjunctures are dramatic. Whereas classic demographic events happen to individuals, conjunctures are distributed over social groups; they involve multiple, differentiated participants. Whereas events are discrete and conceptually instantaneous occurrences, conjunctures have duration, and are variable in character. Whereas events are outcomes in themselves, conjunctures may have multiple outcomes over different time frames. It is significant that the contributing elements of a vital conjuncture are not necessarily in themselves "vital": religious conversion, domestic residence, or the clandestine promises of a lover may not appear vital, but when conjoined, these constitute the generative locus of the so-called vital events.

Concomitant with the departure from an event-based model is the move from actuality to potential, for vital conjunctures are defined in part by their horizons, their structured sphere of possibilities. In an analysis of vital conjunctures, we need to ask what kinds of futures are imagined, hoped for, or feared, and how these orientations might motivate specific courses of action. By thinking about life histories in terms of vital conjunctures, rather than in canonical stages, we can ask whole new sets of questions. When and how do life domains cohere? Which elements of the life course are cumulative, periodic, or waxing and waning? How are transitions in specific life domains navigated, and their implications for other life domains interpreted?

In this book, I seek to make sense of social reproduction both demographically and ethnographically, by focusing on vital conjunctures in the lives of Catholic-educated Beti women as the generative loci of our well-known correlation. It is here, I argue, in the potential turning points of a lived trajectory, that the differential fertility of educated women is made. A careful study of the kinds of vital conjunctures through which educated women navigate, the horizons that they envision from the context of those conjunctures, and their evaluations of those horizons will begin to explain why and how educated women wait so long to bear a first child, as well as why they eventually bear so few. Placing fertility in its experiential context offers the potential for a coherent model of fertility levels and trends that has so long eluded students of population, for educated Beti women are managing lives, not just births, in the vital conjunctures of marriage, sex, and reproduction. The relationship between education and fertility in Catholic Cameroon is mediated by concepts of discipline and honor; elsewhere, the mediating concepts will certainly be different. But what will not differ is the fact that fertility is not an end in itself, not outside the structures of family and household, not apart from cultural values and identities.

Through the lens of vital conjunctures, fertility per se—that is, the number of live births to a woman or couple—is the wrong unit of analysis, at least as a first step. Numbers of births should come at the end of the analysis, as they come at the end of the stream of social practice that itself is oriented to structured social relationships in a context much broader than births. A baby may be the seal of a marriage, a future caretaker for the parents, and the bearer of hopes for the honor of the family; frequently, a baby is all these at once. Reaching for an ever-uncertain honor, educated Beti women postpone motherhood while trying to bring about the contexts in which it will be socially sanctioned. Managing vital conjunctures, they make demographic facts. As we look comparatively, I think we will find that it could hardly be otherwise.

CHAPTER TWO

A Social System in Transformation

"Traditions" did not necessarily stop changing when versions of them were written down, nor were debates over custom and social identity resolved, either during the colonial period or afterward. In general, the colonial period in Africa was less a time of transition—from isolation to global incorporation, from social equilibrium to turbulence, from collective solidarity to fragmented isolation—than an era of intensified contestation over custom, power, and property. — Sara Berry, *No Condition Is Permanent*

The "contestation over custom, power, and property" that Berry argues intensified in the colonial period (1993: 8) continues into the present in Cameroon. And social reproduction, in the form of fertility and formal education, remains central to these contests. The clear, monotonic relationship between schooling and fertility in Cameroon that we examined in chapter 1 emerged only over the course of the 1990s. As recently as 1991, Cameroonian women who had attended some school bore more children than did those who had never been to school. The nature of the statistical correlation has changed, not in isolation, but rather as part of a broad sweep of transformations of Cameroonian, and more specifically Beti, society and culture over the past century. In less than four generations, the Beti have shifted from swidden horticulture to incipient e-commerce, from acephalous segmentary lineages to multiparty elections, from having no writing system to having upward of 70 percent of the population literate in French. The twentieth-century history of the Beti is one of increasingly institutionalized economic inequality, alongside significant ideological change, as opinions have both altered and diversified. In this context of change, it is tempting to suppose that nothing has remained of the proud, independent Beti of the late nineteenth and early twentieth centuries, as they were so richly described in the classic works of Largeau (1901) and

Tessman (1913). But many traditional qualities have endured. Concepts of honor in self-dominion still serve to orient social action; the logic of "wealth in people" and its accompanying emphasis on self-improvement continue to organize social life; premarital sexuality remains—or, more accurately, is again—widely accepted; kinship is still reckoned through the *mvog,* or minor lineage. Beti social organization may have been transformed dramatically in the contestations over power and property since 1900, but it has not been entirely transformed. This chapter explores what has changed and what has endured, providing the ethnographic, demographic, and historical contexts for the contemporary childbearing of educated Beti women.

Precolonial Social Organization

In contemporary local discourse, the term "Beti" implies enduring membership in a circumscribed ethnic group that has resided in southern Cameroon since before human memory. Like many ethnonyms, however, this coherence and immobility themselves are recent rhetorical constructs (Hobsbawm and Ranger 1982). Laburthe-Tolra (1981) argues that the group called Beti is really an amalgam of several different kin-based groups, and that the term originally meant only "honorable ones" or "Lords": it was not an ethnonym at all. Rather than descending from a single overarching category, the segmentary clans and lineages of today's Beti—including, for example, the Eton, Ewondo, and Manguissa—were partially assimilated out of originally unrelated groups. Today, the relationship between the minor lineage, the major lineage, and the entirety of the Beti is one of progressive inclusion, consistent with other segmentary lineage societies (see Evans-Pritchard 1951; Fortes 1969). Thus, a person may belong to the *mvog* Belinga, to the major lineage Bënë, and to the Beti and may emphasize one or another identity depending on the circumstance. However, these nested lineages and sublineages were not all produced through a historical process of iterative splitting.

Laburthe-Tolra further shows that not only is the ethnic designation of the Beti of recent origin, but so also is their residence in the lands around Yaoundé. He argues that the migration of those called Beti into their contemporary homeland occurred only during the eighteenth and nineteenth centuries, as one phase in an ongoing process of migration that began perhaps in the 1500s. The migration was, generally, a slow movement toward the south and the west. Laburthe-Tolra estimates that Nkometou, a village just south of Mbeya, may have been occupied as early as 1730, but that Minlaaba, some hundred kilometers to the south, was not settled by people today classified as Beti until 1850 (1981: 169). The present lands occupied by the people called Beti are arguably just as far as the long migration happened to get before the colonial administration forcibly ended it, and the boundaries of the Bulu-Beti-Fang thus may simply define assorted independent groups that happened to be incorporated before their language, customs, and borders were codified by scholars and colonial bureaucrats such as Savorgnan de Brazza (1887–88), Curt von Morgen (1893), and Georg Zenker (1895).

It appears that the Beti's slow migration occurred through a specific pattern of residence linked to the system of segmentary lineages. Villages consisted primarily of the members of one *mvog*.[1] When a man attained a certain stature, he left his natal village to found a new one. Complete male adulthood consisted of the establishment of a new community, and with it a new lineage. The *mfan mot*, or "true man," had opened a plot of land to plant and founded a household and a family (*bonde nda bot,* literally "to found a house of people"). Opening new land had not only political and economic consequences, but also important personal ones. *Esep,* fields cleared from virgin forest, were symbolically important for marriage, as we will see in chapter 6, and full male adulthood depended on them. In order for the fields to be cut from virgin forest, and to maintain a man's autonomy from his father, new villages associated with the establishment of a minor lineage were some distance from the old. In this way, the migration southward into the forest occurred by generational leaps (see Laburthe-Tolra 1981, part 2, chap. 2). There were no political authorities higher than the village: each *mfan mot* was his own highest authority, his own head.

Today, the generational migration into virgin forest, the clearing of *esep,* and the *mvog* as a residential and political unit are emotionally and mentally distant for many young, educated Beti, who imagine their own futures in terms of urban residence and formal employment. The complex set of gifts and countergifts, particularly of raw foodstuffs and cooked food, that once structured Beti marriage have been simplified or even fallen away. But these old and new forms of social and economic organization that seem so distant from one another are in fact linked by a social system of "wealth in people" in which asymmetric alliances of patronage and clientship serve—at least in part—the interests of each party. "Wealth in people" deserves a detailed discussion, as it continues to shape Beti social life significantly, providing the means through which social and economic inequalities are manifested.

Wealth in People

The term "wealth in people" has been used by anthropologists and historians to describe a system common to many African societies in which affluence and power are mediated through affinity, consanguinity, and dependence.[2] A number of social and economic relationships, including slavery, pawnship, and polygynous marriage, have been interpreted in terms of the wealth-in-people paradigm. In its classic incarnation, wealth-in-people theory proposes that in African societies, a "person's status and influence depend directly on his or her ability to mobilize a following" (Berry 1993: 15). That is, people—usually but not always senior men—gain power and prestige through social relationships in which they acquire rights over the labor, loyalty, or legal status of others. The labor of women, children, and low-status men generates material wealth for elder men, who then employ this material wealth in procuring the support of other dependents. Through the strategic manipulation of systems of mutual obligation, certain adults and corporate groups come to control the products and prospects of juniors and other subordinates.

"Wealth in people" describes a system of social inequality, whereby power and prestige are monopolized by certain senior men. Like any functioning social system, it is maintained both by coercion and something like consent, albeit not an unproblematic consent. Jean and John Comaroff argue that "hegemony is habit forming" (Comaroff and Comaroff 1991: 23), and these habits are one part of the consent with which women and junior men engage in the system of wealth in people. The other part of their consent is explicitly strategic. Women and junior men participate in asymmetric alliances as clients to powerful patrons because of the benefits that patronage can bring them: access to land, money for school fees, help assembling bridewealth, or an advantage in the competition for a salaried job. Finally, they engage because they have no real alternative. When access to resources is organized through patronage, establishing firm ties to the best patron available offers the only real chance for advancement.

Among the precolonial Beti, the absence of any form of institutionalized political domination, such as chieftaincy or kingship, meant that relations of marriage and patronage were the only means to accumulation.

As Lembezat argued, "The most real powers are exercised by the family head, and one could have written that these are the powers of a proprietor, and that the family is a man's only valuable" (1954: 54). The authority of the *nkukuma* of a village, its leader and usually its founder, lay only in the loyalty his kin gave him. This loyalty took three important forms: his wives and children farmed for him; the junior and dependent men provided him with political support and physical defense if necessary; and any of his dependents with unusual skills or accomplishments brought renown to the *nkukuma* who was his patron. Today, patronage may bring these same benefits to a local chief, but it is also—and perhaps better—seen in the former schoolboys who now work in the capital and send money home or in the ability of a village chief to promise blocks of votes in elections.

Models of wealth in people highlight the relationship between fertility and social organization, because biological parenthood constitutes a particularly important social relationship. Childbearing and childrearing enhance the wealth and status of the parents. Parents create children; this act of creation itself is prestigious (Boddy 1989; Feldman-Savelsberg 1995; Oppong et al. 1976). But the act of creation also promises parents unusually strong rights in their children. As Guyer has argued with special reference to the Beti, parenthood is a form of authorship, and so parents have rights in their children not only as elders and patrons, but also as creators. Historically, these rights included not only the authority to command their labor or lend them to kinsmen when they were young, but also rights to the support and assistance of adult children. Today, economically successful children are expected to support their parents and to pay school fees for younger siblings. Children can also be strategically married or fostered out, building further alliances on which their parents can draw (see Bledsoe 1990c, 1993). Because of the ways in which childbearing and childrearing enhance the wealth and prestige of parents, kinship structure and reproductive practice have long been considered part of economic and political organization throughout sub-Saharan Africa (Comaroff 1980; Evans-Pritchard 1969; Radcliffe-Brown and Forde 1967). The old system of the *mvog,* which so completely collapsed political authority and paternal authorship, is merely one example among many.

Given that dependent people were the wealth of *nkukuma,* and that children are dependent in a particularly intense way, men sought children through a variety of means, including demanding the children born to their unmarried daughters. Laburthe-Tolra claims that fathers in past time would pressure their daughters to bear them children before marrying, and suggests that some fathers would even forbid their daughters to marry without fulfilling this expectation (Laburthe-Tolra 1981: 24). Control over the sexual and reproductive status of female kin—especially daughters and sisters—constitutes a significant resource for Beti men. According to one myth, a young orphan boy who is sheltered by a great man is so thankful for the generosity of his patron that he offers to give him his sister in marriage. Instead of taking the girl, the great man arranges to perform the *tso* (a ritual to mitigate the deleterious effects of incest) and marry them to each other (Laburthe-Tolra 1981: 128). The boy is thus transformed from "a miserable boy, very ugly and all dirty," to a young man officiating over his sister's proposed engagement, to adult man and husband. His promotion in status occurs through his increasing control over a woman's sexuality and reproductive power. Not only in history and in myth, but also in present social practice is reproductive management strategically important. Its importance, however, has waned and changed form. Today, children born to an unmarried Beti woman may be claimed by her father, but as children have grown more expensive, their loyalty less complete, and young women's claims over their own children stronger, fathers increasingly view their daughters' nonmarital pregnancies as liabilities rather than benefits. Rights in children remain valuable, but they are increasingly partible. Men invest in the education or upbringing of a variety of children, rather than seeking solitary "authorship."

Guyer (1993, 1996) has argued for a revision of the classic wealth-in-people model to include greater recognition that not all dependents have the same value. Because of their access to certain kinds of esoteric knowledge or social positions, particular people become especially desirable as followers. The value of people, Guyer proposes, is tied to the same kind of creative tension that Appadurai (1986) has discussed for the value of objects: the tension between singularity and comparability. While a skill or kind of knowledge must be comparable with others in order to be recognized, its value—the value of the person who has it—arises from its uniqueness. Valuable people are therefore unique in recognizable ways: as storytellers, leather workers, catechists, or mothers of many children. Among the precolonial Beti, only one man in a region might be a spoon maker, another the maker of fine arrows or stools: skills were highly specialized and highly individual (see Tessman 1913). As soon as we return to thinking about people not as interchangeable units, but as bearers of innovation and individual skill, it becomes clear that the strategies in a wealth-in-people system must focus on the choreography of diverse skills, rather than simply on increasing numbers. That is, at least among the Beti, wealth in people is defined not by sheer demography, but by "the extraordinary people—the named heroes, virtuoso performers and craftsmen, the most deeply concentrated of spiritual adepts" (Guyer 1993: 253). The power that accrues to an *nkukuma,* or for that matter, to a contemporary civil servant, because of his ability to mobilize a following depends not only on the quantity, but also on the qualities—and particularly the diversity of the qualities—of his people.

This emphasis on singular knowledge transforms not only our thinking about politics, but also our understanding of the socialization process. Instead of rearing children in a uniform way to conform to standardized notions of adulthood, Guyer proposes that Beti parents attended—and still attend—to the unique talents of their children. She proposes that we consider the well-documented ways in which Beti adults observe and cultivate children's aptitudes and idiosyncrasies in the context of an expanded wealth-in-people model. As a result of this attention to individual skills, "children are not thought about only in terms of quantities and categories (numbers and sexes), but also as unique composites of capacities" (Guyer 1996: 11). This argument is clearly in opposition to the majority of thinking about African fertility (e.g., Ainsworth, Nyamete, and Beegle 1995; Caldwell and Caldwell 1987); furthermore, it opposes the central tenets of classic socialization theory, in suggesting that children will not—and should not—become predetermined kinds of adults (cf. LeVine and LeVine 1966; Wilson 1951).

And yet, radical or not, Guyer's analysis of Beti social cultivation is clearly right. Contemporary Beti do indeed make lifelong learning a standard practice. This is visible even in the demographic life histories I collected, where women report repeated returns to school, to job training, and to apprenticeships. Indeed, as Mbala Owono explains:

> Everything happens here as if education consisted of one single recommendation: "become who you are." . . . Among the Beti, the central principle that presides over education is stated in this way: "Owog o na enyin, ve menken," which can be translated as follows: to live is to employ oneself in the acquisition of the means to enliven oneself, it is to renew oneself, to change. (1982: 122)

Whether in the form of extended formal training or a simple willingness to always again try something new, Beti society encourages its members to persistently seek out knowledge, both of themselves and of the world.

Much of the visible structure of precolonial Beti social organization is gone now. Villages are rarely home to the members of a single *mvog*, few men clear *esep* fields, and migrations have long since been toward the Ivory Coast and France rather than into unclaimed forest. However, the cultural system of wealth in people and wealth in knowledge on which the acephalous, segmentary lineage society was based does persist. The rights of elders to command the labor and loyalty of juniors in exchange for patronage continue into the present, both in small ways, such as the right to send juniors on errands or interrupt them in conversation, and in large ones, particularly including the nepotism without which the national government could not function. As we will see, these modes of reasoning about persons and values not only persist, but were essential to the emergence of institutionalized inequality in the colonial and mandate periods.

The German Period

When the German government declared the Cameroonian *Schutzgebeit* (Protectorate) in 1884, they had as yet little contact with the Beti. The Duala people of the coast had effectively monopolized direct trade with the Europeans, systematically excluding inlanders like the Beti from whatever material benefits were to be had from the Europeans, and also preventing Europeans from entering the hinterland.[3] The arrival of German expeditions in the Beti regions in the 1880s thus represented not only a political threat, but also an economic opportunity for certain *nkukuma,* that is, village founders and leaders. The German biologist Georg Zenker founded a trading post and research station at the site that was to become Yaoundé in 1888.[4] His notes (1895) claim that he was welcomed there by "Yaunde" people, one of the many transliterations of "Ewondo," the largest and now largely dominant major lineage within the Beti.

The export of ivory and rubber quickly made Yaoundé economically important to the Germans; the import of iron and cloth made it similarly valuable to the Beti (Laburthe-Tolra 1970). In 1895, Major Dominik established a garrison at Yaoundé. In addition to securing trade, the garrison served to reassure other Europeans of the safety of the location: when the Pallotin brothers began proselytizing in the area, they selected a site near the garrison; the first Catholic mission nearby was established at Mvolyé (now part of Yaoundé) in 1901, and a primary school was opened at Mvolyé in 1907. Thus the Beti had relatively early and frequent exposure to German colonials and missionaries.

The Germans sought, first, population stability and administrative control. The legal code for the colony called for a census for orderly governance (Ruppel 1912: 81).[5] It also forbade emigration (889), controlled marriage (27), defined property rights (673–727), and established taxes and tariffs (chap. 3). As a corpus, the laws intended to construct an identified and controllable population from which to extract produce and labor (Kemner 1937), precisely in the ways that Foucault describes as central to the biopower of the modern state (1990, esp. 139–41). Stabilizing the new colony depended both on local alliances and on the effective occupation of key places. Yaoundé was one key place, as a military, religious, and trade center. In 1909, the garrison was rebuilt in brick, and the "indigenous market" was granted a permanent location behind the buildings (Martin 1921). Some, although certainly not all, Beti saw potential for significant economic and political benefit from cooperating with the Germans. The Germans, needing allies in the region, provided access to education, economic resources, and positions of authority in exchange for the continued allegiance of the Beti, who "soon allied themselves with the Germans . . . to work with the administration, traders, and missionaries" (Quinn 1987: 173).

German government policy in southern Cameroon mirrored that in the west of the colony: selecting and strongly supporting a few local allies who would constitute a class of loyal German-speaking Christians. More than other groups in southern Cameroon, the ancestors of the people today called Beti accepted the Germans' offer of asymmetric alliance, incorporating the German officers into systems of wealth in people as rich patrons who would provide protection and financial benefits in exchange for loyalty. And the German colonials appeared comfortable with such a system of patronage: people who demonstrated loyalty to German ways of life were indeed rewarded, for example, with lucrative, newly created chieftaincies. These German ways of life were defined in reference to schooling and Christianity, requiring a close collaboration between church and state, particularly in the domain of schooling. In 1911, only ten years after the founding of the Yaoundé mission, there were 408 Catholic-run primary schools in southern Cameroon; another 8 were managed by the government. Schooling was a key vector to power and prestige, but not without cost: all pupils who completed the curriculum in the twenty-one secondary schools in the colony were required to perform two years of government service (Calvert 1917; also see Ruppel 1912: 264–69).

This government service, which included administrative and military work, appears to have effectively bound some Beti to the colonial government as clients, through the logic of the wealth-in-people system. Patronage depends on loyalty, and withdrawal from a patron is paramount to desertion. Beti loyal to the Germans fought in the losing land war against the British, and some thirteen thousand Beti retreated to Rio Muni with the Germans in December of 1915 (Quinn 1987). Despite the many ways in which German rule was exploitative, a number of Beti wrote to the German government during the era of the French mandate to request that the Germans reclaim the territory (Ngoh 1987), and Woll describes meeting Cameroonians, presumably Bulu-Beti-Fang, "in the deepest virgin forest," who proudly related in the German language their experiences as German soldiers and administrative assistants (1933: 241; see also Bruel 1940).

The German colonial period lasted just over thirty years, but its impact on the socioeconomic landscape was substantial. A generation of Beti grew up with the prospect of going to German schools, working for a German government, and praying in German churches. And in surprisingly large numbers, they did so. The Catholic missions were central not only in transforming religious belief, but perhaps even more in the reshaping of domestic arrangements and everyday practice (Dillinger 1991; cf. Comaroff and Comaroff 1991). By the end of the World War One, the paths to power in Beti society had been extended; founding a *mvog* was still important, but it now stood alongside collaboration with the colonial state. In the French mandate period, the importance of this second path expanded to such a degree that formal employment became almost a prerequisite for founding a family. It is to the French period that we now turn.

The French Mandate

The Germans lost Yaoundé in January 1916, but it was not until 1921 that central authority was reestablished there, under the French commissioner Jules Gaston Henri Carde.[6] Under the League of Nations policy of June 28, 1919, German Cameroon was divided into two mandate protectorates, with most of the country—including the southern forests and Yaoundé—going to the French. The previous capital, at Buea, had been destroyed by a volcanic eruption in 1909, and no adequate substitute had been constructed. Douala, the largest city and major port on the coast, would have been a self-evident choice. However, in March of 1921, France decided to locate the protectorate capital at Yaoundé owing to its salubrious location, malleability, and defensibility (Commissariat de la Republique Française au Cameroun 1923). In 1921, Yaoundé was a small trading post in the hills, lacking much of the infrastructure necessary for a capital. This necessitated a great deal of expensive construction, but it also permitted a capital city to be custom built. Wright (1991) argues that the colonies were the sites of innovation for French utopian architects, the *terra nullis* on which conceptions of order and civic virtue might be enacted. By locating the capital at Yaoundé, the French Service d'Outre-Mer ensured that the mandate territory of Cameroon would be regenerated according to a French model. Douala, with its long trade history, did not offer this possibility. Some French administrators expressed enthusiasm for the project of constructing a French society on Cameroonian soil; for example, one health official argued that "Cameroon is a country for the future. Europeans find vast territories that are very favorable to their installation in this colony" (Martin 1921: i). The hills of Yaoundé, relatively dry and cool, seemed a perfect geographical expression of the neo-European capital that the French hoped to establish. The fact that the Beti had proved themselves able apprentices to the Germans is not mentioned in Martin's account but would likely also have been relevant. The decision to place the capital of French Cameroon in Beti territory ensured that the link between European authority and the Beti, begun by the Germans, would continue. The location of the capital in their region also guaranteed that the Beti would have exposure—and access—to schools, churches, and government jobs.

After the war, however, France lacked personnel and economic resources to invest in Africa and, because of the constraints implemented by the League of Nations, stood to gain much less from investment in Cameroon than in its colonies proper. With few resources and many other places to invest them, French administrators sought ways to manage Cameroon cheaply. They did so by allocating fiscal responsibility for state activities to nongovernmental institutions, particularly relying on the coercive powers of the chieftaincies and on the educational initiatives of the missions.[7] However, among the Beti who had left Cameroon with the retreating Germans were many of those established as native chiefs; since precolonial Beti society was organized without a defined political hierarchy or formalized administration, their absence posed logistical difficulties for the management of the mandate territory. After much deliberation, the French brought back the former German loyalists, including the flamboyant Charles Atangana, who had gone to Germany after the war (Quinn 1987). *Chefs supérieurs,* who reported directly to the French, were reestablished in 1921 according to the German model. At the same time, the lowest order of chiefs, the *chefs de villages,* was institutionalized. An intermediary order of chiefs, the *chefs du groupements,* was added in 1925 (Mveng 1963).

Once the chiefs were reestablished, the French faced two primary problems: assuring that the populace accepted the authority of the chiefs, and assuring that the chiefs were loyal to the central (French) administration. Guyer argues that both of these ends were served by the development of a food requisition system for feeding Yaoundé. She maintains that "food supply became . . . part of a comprehensive plan to create an elite in the rural areas which would mediate the relationship between the state and the people, and which would manage the mobilization of resources for colonial development" (Guyer 1987: 121). Thus the rural elite of inferior and superior chiefs were given power over rural populations through the requisition system, but this authority relied on cooperation with and perceived loyalty to the French. Cooperation and loyalty in this case entailed not only that the chiefs maintain discipline over their subordinates, but also that they speak French and practice Christianity. The requisition system served to provide the chiefs with an economic investment in the mandate government; this, it was hoped, would ensure their goodwill. As in Ijesha, Nigeria, however, the economic benefit that accrued to chiefs seems to have had the additional effect of generating an elite with both rural and urban ties (see Peel 1983). The rural elite that emerged through the management of the mandate territory are now well established; many of today's government officials are their descendants.

The requisition system required rural localities to provide particular types and amounts of food at specified times to the capital city. In addition to putting pressure on the rural food supply, this practice required human labor to carry the produce to the city, as neither mechanized nor animal transport were feasible. The prices paid to the chiefs were set without reference to market principles, and the farmers and porters were not paid for their produce or labor. Without these market incentives, force or the threat of force seems to have been the only method for ensuring compliance. Both recalcitrant farmers and chiefs were submitted to punishment for noncompliance with the requisition system under laws known collectively as the *indigénat* (Guyer 1987; cf. Gaillard 1989). However, as the chiefs stood to benefit more from requisitioning, the punishments fell more heavily upon the non-elite population. As the intermediaries between the mandate government and local populations, the chiefs administered the *indigénat* and were required to mobilize the corvée. Much like Barnes (1986) describes for absentee chiefs in Lagos, this position enabled chiefs to transform the populations over which they presided into clients, that is, into juniors in the logic of wealth in people. As patrons, chiefs could—and sometimes did—protect individuals from the unpaid labor of the requisition system; at the same time, chiefs also demanded what amounted to corvée in their own fields. Patron-client relations, grounded historically in the autonomous extended households of the Beti migration, and mapped onto relations between "native" chiefs and the mandate government, were then mapped onto relations between the chiefs and their people.

The requisition system sought to provide low-cost and reliable food for Yaoundé by excluding the uncertainty and speculation possible in an open-market system. But some of the food supply, such as European specialty vegetables and fruits, remained in the hands of entrepreneurs. These entrepreneurs were again primarily the newly established chiefs, who alone had access to the necessary labor to produce novel foods in any quantity. Through the relationships of dependency implicit in long-standing systems of patrilocal polygyny and those newly constructed by hierarchical relationships with the mandate state, chiefs could command significant labor forces. In this way, some of the chiefs accumulated wealth, although it was the growth of the export economy—particularly cocoa—that enabled chiefs to truly establish themselves as an institutionalized elite.

The Cocoa Boom and Its Social Impact

Yaoundé had been an important trading site since the German period, but its economic significance increased with the arrival of the railroad. In 1927, the Southern Cameroon Railroad reached Yaoundé station. As the end of the line into the rainforest, Yaoundé served as the primary locus for bulking cacao, palm nuts, and ivory for shipping to the coast. In the 1930s, cocoa production increased geometrically, significantly surpassing rubber and ivory in volume and profit (Ndongko and Vivekananda 1989). This transformation was made possible by the activities of the chiefs, who mobilized labor through marriage, kinship, and coercion to cultivate cacao, from which they alone profited. It was therefore largely through the cocoa trade that rural political leaders in the mandate period were able to institutionalize their privilege. The chiefs were in a unique position to leverage this labor: through the requisition system, chiefs had access to some of the little cash in circulation; through their role as middlemen to state power, they were able to coerce compliance with their wishes. Both of these strings to authority enabled chiefs to bind dependent labor to themselves, whether through clientage per se or through polygyny. The strategies of the chiefs to increase their profits from cocoa dramatically shifted the social structure of Cameroon, having an important impact not only on land tenure and inheritance (see Amanor 1994; Berry 1993; Mikell 1989), but also on marriage and the status of women. With the increase in production for a cash economy, the economic value of wives increased. Paradoxically, their economic importance served to disempower women, as fathers and prospective husbands bargained over high brideprices for young girls: "[T]he result was a system of exchange in women which many observers and participants found differed little from servitude" (Guyer 1985: 316). One Beti woman recalled that in that period young women were given in marriage "like sheep" (Vincent 1976: 46). Chiefs were effectively able to monopolize this marriage market: one chief was reported to have had over five hundred wives working on his cocoa farm (Gaillard 1989). Although the French limited the amount of bridewealth in 1922 in an attempt to decrease the control of old men, there is little evidence that this effort was effective (Kuczynski 1939: 157).

In a series of interviews with women who lived through this period, Jean-François Vincent found a significant emphasis on premarital chastity, in contrast to the precolonial period, when women's premarital sexuality was generally accepted. Although premarital virginity could be construed as the almost inevitable consequence of very early marriage, the moral value that Vincent's informants placed on chastity suggests that something more than marriage timing had changed. For example, one woman emphasized the difference between her own premarital sexual behavior and that of contemporary young women:

> My sisters and I were very afraid of our father. Also, we didn't have sexual relations with men before our marriage. My father held tightly to his daughters. By contrast, today parents watch their daughters give birth to bastards! (Vincent 1976: 86)

Another woman that Vincent interviewed concurred: "At that time, a young girl who didn't yet have her period couldn't follow a man, but now the young girls . . . it's something different!" (137). What is striking about these quotes is not only the (perhaps universal) generational politics, whereby older women accuse younger women of moral degeneracy, but also—and perhaps even more—the contrast between this depiction of the cocoa years and Tessman's representation of women's relatively free premarital sexuality in the early years of the German colony. Chapter 6 will discuss these changes in more detail, but suffice it to say that one of the forms of the increasing power of the village chiefs in this period was over young women's sexuality.

This control took the form not only of young, and preferably virgin marriage, but also of large-scale polygyny. The cocoa boom helped to maintain polygamy in the face of efforts by the Catholic Church to eradicate it. Its persistence depended on economic and social considerations, magnified by the development of cocoa cultivation for export. Urban-dwelling men regularly maintained polygynous rural compounds; their wives would grow cacao; from the proceeds of the sale of cacao, men could send their sons to mission schools, ensuring their place in the administration. These urban men thus had access to two sources of wealth—their incomes as civil servants and the labor of rural kin, affines, and clients. These two sources were mutually constitutive, as when money earned in the city was used to pay bridewealth, and income from cacao sales paid school fees. Despite the emphatic protests of the Catholic Church, the pay structure of the civil service also encouraged polygyny by providing allowances for each child born to government employees, regardless of the marital status of the mother. As a result, "all the children of a polygamous civil servant give [him] rights to [financial] allocations" (Froelich 1956: 59). Polygynous men employed in the mandate government were therefore able to draw resources from both rural and urban sources to develop their role as patrons in both contexts. This classic reinvestment of wealth in people provided a strong economic incentive for maintaining polygyny, even for devout Catholics. At the same time, the symbolic value of having many children, especially many sons, provided an ideological underpinning for the practice.

During the early years of the French mandate and the era of the cocoa boom, the inequality between men became increasingly sharp; at the same time, men's control over their daughters and wives also increased. Women's sexuality became more closely guarded as part of a reconfiguration of the relative value of women. Institutional inequality emerged both between men and women, as well as among men. By a curiosity of history,

this extraordinary era—when women were married very young and sometimes against their will—has become the embodiment of "Beti tradition"
for many young Beti, who view the relative sexual liberty of today's youth
not as a return to long-standing social norms, but as an anomaly brought
about by modernity and the recent economic crisis. It is the same kind of
cultural amnesia that makes the reproductive practices at the height of
the baby boom the norm for "traditional" American marriage and childbearing.

Schooling and Catholicism in the French Period

The mandate government expected its chiefs to express their loyalty not
only by delivering goods through the requisition system, but also by speaking French and practicing Christianity. For both of these reasons, the Catholic Church was of central institutional importance in the mandate territory of Cameroon. By controlling land, mounting large building projects,
and employing people in a variety of capacities, the church became a significant economic actor. By providing much-desired education, the church
contributed to the reorganization of the life course of elite men, and the
reorganization of the meaning of eliteness. By assembling large congrega-
tions every week, the church was able both to inform and influence much
of the populace. And as an international bureaucracy of intellectual, committed, and politically effective men, the church rivaled or surpassed the
mandate government. Much of the influence of the church was the result
of its investments in schooling.

The connection between education, Christianity, and elite status that
is evident in Cameroon parallels that described by Kristin Mann (1985)
for Lagos. Mann holds that the urban elite differentiated itself symbolically through the "symbolic capital" of Christian marriage and western
lifestyles. She argues that "how the elite lived was as important for elite
status as what it did. The elite created a distinctive style of life built around
Christianity, Western education, and British manners and customs" (1985:
4). The same applies to southern Cameroon. Privilege and prestige relied not only on the financial benefits that came out of cocoa and chieftaincy, but also on the daily practices of eliteness associated with school
and church. Bayart's model of the "reciprocal assimilation of elites" (1989)
provides a productive framework for thinking about the process through
which these institutions came both to legitimate and to enable social inequality among the Beti. For Bayart, this reciprocal assimilation occurs

when elites from different domains (say, rural "traditional" chiefs and urban merchants) develop a shared repertoire of knowledge and practice through mutual exposure. I would call this a shared set of horizons, which can be shared by people whose relationships to the means of production—and whose *habitus*—differ profoundly. Catholic schools were the key locus of this mutual exposure starting in the German colonial period and arguably extending to the present.

Prior to the war, 204 German Catholic schools had been teaching nearly twenty thousand students in Cameroon (Mveng 1963: 463–64). The French thus inherited a functioning mission school system, which they could not afford to completely dismantle and replace with the secular schools that would have been politically preferable to the representatives of the Third Republic. Instead, the protectorate government focused on replacing the German missionaries with French priests and changing the language of instruction to French. The linguistic difficulties of this transition were eased by the arrival of the Pères du Saint-Esprit, an Alsatian brotherhood. Although the Pères du Saint-Esprit conducted lessons in French, they were able to communicate with educated Beti in German and to use the German-Ewondo translations written by the Pallotins, such as that by Vater Stoll in 1909 (Berger 1978). Also, Alsatians were thought by many Beti to understand their predicament, having also been pushed back and forth between French and German administrations.[8] The Pères du Saint-Esprit were very popular. One of the early fathers, François-Xavier Vogt, is still considered a saint.[9] Recognizing the need for assistance in educating the native population, the mandate government went so far in its collaboration with the missions as to pay them for educating students; any educational institution that conducted lessons in French and followed a government-approved curriculum was eligible for a subsidy (Vernon-Jackson 1968: 260).

Mission schools were important both in providing primary education to a larger number of students than the government schools could serve and in making secondary education available. Catholic secondary schools sent more candidates to the *examen de fin des études* than did government schools in every year between World War One and World War Two (SPECC 1992). What is more, the Catholic missions had a complete monopoly on postsecondary education. The Petit Séminaire at Akono educated many of the major figures in Cameroonian public life, including President Paul Biya and the novelist known as Mongo Beti (*mongo* means "child"). The Grand Séminaire, established at Yaoundé in 1927, remained the premiere educational institution in Cameroon until the construction of the national university after independence. Today, the finest university training is probably offered at the Université Catholique de l'Afrique Centrale (UCAC) at Nkolbisson in Yaoundé, which opened in 1991 under the authority of the Holy See. The reciprocal assimilation of elites through Catholic education continues, only the assimilation now covers Gabon, the Central African Republic, and the two Congos as well.

One of the implications of this near total monopoly of Catholic institutions over education in the Yaoundé region, and particularly over advanced schooling, is the ideological equation of education and Catholicism, especially among the Beti. At least half of the Beti population is Catholic today,[10] and among the Catholics, many believe that God prefers literate people who are able to read prayers, even those that their priest does not know or is unwilling to share. When I asked why she sent her children to school despite the high costs, one woman from the outskirts of Mbeya explained that children who have been to school can read books from many different places. In America, she said, we might know how to pray in ways that Cameroonian priests have never learned; a child who can read will be able to learn those prayers for himself and benefit from their good effects. As in many West African societies, access to secret knowledge is considered a source of power among the Beti (cf. Bledsoe 1984; Bledsoe and Robey 1993; Murphy 1980), and Catholic knowledge is particularly powerful.

The mission schools sought to educate and to convert, both by establishing an indigenous clergy and by providing Catholic instruction to the masses. The Grand Séminaire graduated its first class in 1933, and the Cameroonian clergy has grown steadily since, reaching 885 diocesan priests by 2002. The clergy sought to convert the masses, and to a large degree that meant educating them in lifeways, if not literacy. In many ways, this transformation has been successful. Laburthe-Tolra's magisterial work seeks to explain the origin of the Beti's "global and unconditional Catholicism" (1981: 42), and it is impossible to spend time with Beti people without being struck by their religious devotion. From rosary rings to framed posters of the pope and from verbal expression to the prominence of prayer in time diaries, perceptible signs of Catholic commitment are numerous and powerful. And while we cannot read directly from posters to inner belief states, in terms of understanding social change, posters of the pope may be the more important anyway.

While part of the process of creating a rural elite with allegiance to

France lay in education and—paradoxically for the secular French state—Catholicism, the mandate administration was concerned to create a class of intermediaries, not an overeducated literati. According to a 1929 League of Nations report, the aim of public education, then, was to "train those elements of the population capable of becoming good auxiliaries, efficient in propagating French thought" (cited in Vernon-Jackson 1968: 275–76). To this end, the mandate government founded the École Primaire Supérieure in Yaoundé in 1923, just two years after establishing Yaoundé as the mandate capital. The École Primaire was to form the basis for an urban civil society. As a description dating from 1929 spells out, the three-year program was intended to train

> junior civil servants, clerks, post-office employees and, above all, school teachers. Students with some primary education were boarded in the capital in order to acquire specific skills to serve as intermediaries between the mandate administration and the population. Its scope is limited to the needs of the public service of the territory. (Cited in Vernon-Jackson 1968: 246)

This was to be a small group indeed; by 1929, the school had only 150 students. Yet their education made it possible for the administrative roles of the government to multiply; in 1930, the government decreed that all births, deaths, and marriages must be registered (Kuczynski 1939: 122ff.), and achieving a complete registration of vital events required that each of 122 civil centers employ a literate civil servant. Although the vital registers sought by the French were never fully administered, they are an excellent example of the sort of French thought that was to be propagated. Counting the population and quantifying its movements were both the ends and the means of a functioning, rationalized bureaucracy.

From the end of the World War One until 1960, French officers and priests played central roles in the administration and reconfiguration of southern Cameroon. Education and Catholicism, which had become important in the German colonial period, now became almost essential elements of elite status. The city of Yaoundé itself played a significant role in the reorientation of Beti society in this period, as a center of both administration and education (Franqueville 1987: 585–88). Yaoundé reciprocally assimilated chiefs and sons of chiefs, merchants and civil servants from throughout the Central Province, as they were educated and took communion there together. Thus, the city served as a site in which a new community of Beti elites could be imagined and constructed. This synthetic

ability of urbanity has been noted by Coquery-Vidrovitch in her discussion
of colonial cities in Africa, for she argues that "the city is not only a pole of
attraction, but also a pole of diffusion: it is thus a cultural phenomenon, a
place of the *métissage* of memories" (1993: 11). The Beti memory of themselves, galvanized by their relationship with Yaoundé, constitutes an important part of Beti identity in the postcolonial state. Many Beti today
insist that the chieftaincy is an indigenous institution, and that precolonial
initiation rituals were "Beti schools." Formal education, Catholicism, and
political hierarchy have thus become idioms through which social inclusion is understood. Not only has inequality become institutionalized, but
these institutions have come to appear natural to many Beti.

Independence and *la Crise*

The mid-1940s saw enormous change throughout the French-controlled
territories in Africa. The France-Africa Conference in Brazzaville in 1944
legalized or liberalized local assemblies, political parties, and trade unions.
After World War Two ended in 1945, the mandates became trust territories of the United Nations. The establishment of the Fourth Republic (Oc-
tober 13, 1946) resulted in another round of liberalization, including the
abolition of forced labor and the *indigénat* (Marshall 1973; Rioux 1987).
The next decade saw substantial political turmoil, as numerous new parties were founded and dissolved. In keeping with the already complex history of the territories, the campaign for independence was not unitary. For
example, the nationalist Union of the Peoples of the Cameroons, which
instigated armed resistance against the French and was banned in 1955,
was supported primarily by Bamiliké and Bassa peoples and generally not
supported by the Beti.[11] France granted self-government to the French
Cameroons in 1957 and full independence as the Republic of Cameroon
in 1960.

   The Beti have been central to the functioning of the national government for the past forty-five years, although Ahmadou Ahidjo, the president of the Republic from independence until 1982, was from the north of
the country. Thanks to their high rates of schooling, their physical proxim-
ity, and an acquaintance with formal, western-style governance extending
back to the German period, the majority of government functionaries in
Yaoundé were Beti in the late 1970s (Franqueville 1984), and remain so
today.

Cameroon has had only two presidents since independence, and for twenty-six years of that time (1966–92) was a one-party state. The strong central government has largely benefited the Beti, particularly through schools, employment, and land concessions, and has hence also drawn a great deal of criticism, especially from Anglophone Cameroonians (Fisiy and Goheen 1998: 383; Eyoh 1998: 338). Indeed, people from other parts of Cameroon often accuse a "Beti Mafia" of responsibility for most of the country's problems, particularly government corruption and the relative disadvantage of the Anglophone provinces.[12] And since the ascension of Paul Biya, a Beti, to the presidency in 1982, this rhetoric of Beti political hegemony has grown even sharper.

In the 1970s and early 1980s, the Cameroonian economy was strong. The effects of economic well-being were everywhere visible: falling unemployment, new buildings, extensive European imports. According to one rather fabulous statistic, Cameroonians consumed as much champagne per capita as did West Germans in 1982.[13] Schooling was a major priority of the Ahidjo government, and educational institutions at all levels were built in record numbers in the decades following independence. The number of government employees expanded rapidly, and increased migration into Yaoundé made Beti land valuable (Franqueville 1984).

This rosy picture began to fall apart in 1987 with what became known as *la crise*. Between 1986 and 1993, both household expenditures and the GDP per capita fell more 40 percent, as shown in figure 2.1. The disintegration of the socioeconomic order was felt long after the official indicators of economic decline had reversed. In 1998, many Cameroonians spoke of a generalized distrust caused by *la crise morale*. Cameroon was declared the most corrupt country in the world for both 1998 and 1999 by the nonprofit international watchdog Transparency International.[14] The crisis has also affected education rates; school participation has fallen since 1987. Some 65 percent of children aged seven to twelve were enrolled in school in the Central Province in 2000, down from a high of near 80 percent in the mid-eighties.

In addition to shifts in education, corruption, and prosperity, marriage and fertility patterns have also changed. Many Beti claim that *la crise* has made it more difficult to contract an honorable marriage, as fewer and fewer men are able to assemble the requisite bridewealth. It is clearly the case that women who entered the marriageable ages during or after the economic decline have stayed single longer than did previous cohorts. Some of these women are still likely to marry in the coming years, and

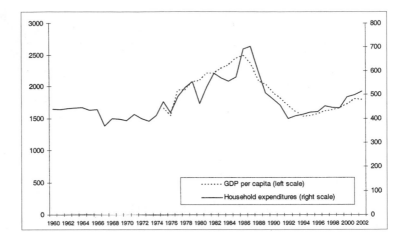

FIGURE 2.1. GDP per capita and final household expenditures in Cameroon in constant 1995 dollars. Data from World Data Indicators Online (http://devdata.worldbank.org/dataonline).

the economic crisis is certainly not the only cause of the change; nonetheless, the difference is remarkable. Whereas some 80 percent of women born between 1960 and 1964 had married by age twenty, fewer than 65 percent of women born between 1975 and 1979 had done so. Figure 2.2 shows the proportion never married by age for these two cohorts: the one group comprising women who were between ages twenty-two and twenty-six and had thus already largely completed the transition to marriage at the onset of *la crise*, and the other made up of younger girls between eight and twelve, who had for the most part not yet begun to move toward marriage. Fertility has also fallen, from a total fertility rate of 6.4 in 1978 to 5.8 in 1991, and then to 5.2 in 1998 (Fotso et al.1999: 43). However, whether these changes should be considered part of a "crisis-led fertility decline" (Eloundou-Enyegue et al. 2000) remains unclear, as there is little reason to believe that fertility rates were higher in the far past.[15] Changes in marriage and childbearing are associated with the crisis, both temporally and in popular representation; whether they are caused by the crisis, however, seems far more doubtful.

The extreme volatility of economic and social life associated with *la crise* extends almost everywhere, from the most mundane situations to the most intimate. To some degree, the forms of radical uncertainty that Cameroonians attribute to the crisis are simply endemic to all poor countries. Still, all of these forms of insecurity or ambiguity are perceived as

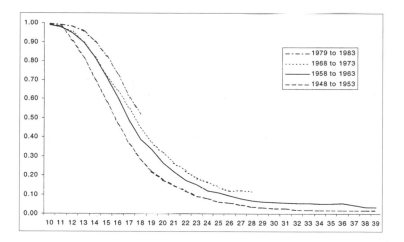

FIGURE 2.2. Proportion of Cameroonian women never married by age in four birth cohorts. Data from 1998 Cameroon DHS.

resulting from the crisis, and in part constitute the lived experience of a "routinized state of crisis" (Mbembe and Roitman 1995). Prices, for schooling, health care, or housing, are unpredictable, as are wages; even government employees are not paid reliably. Most employment opportunities are filled through social networks or kin relations, rather than according to formal skills or job experience; few people have access to formal credit. Busses do not run on schedule. Electricity and running water go out regularly, even in Yaoundé. In the rainy season, roads get washed out, the electricity goes out, and sewers get backed up. Insect-borne diseases like malaria seem to strike more or less at random; the waterborne and sexually transmitted ones, from cholera to HIV/AIDS, only marginally less so. Mortality rates at all ages are high, and death often unpredictable. Associated with these forms of uncertainty is what my informants called the moral crisis, whereby corruption and witchcraft are commonplace, and the values assigned to specific social actions are very much up for grabs. An example is the case of Mme Essele, a woman from a village near Mbeya. Mme Essele was suffering in her marriage, as her husband had taken a much younger second wife, and there was constant conflict in the compound over school fees, pocket money, and the like. Her daughter, by contrast, was doing well. She was a schoolteacher in Yaoundé, and was living with her promising and handsome boyfriend there. Mme Essele went to visit them, and to celebrate her coming the daughter and boyfriend had a goat slaughtered. Back in the village, tales of the goat circulated and inflated. The goat became two goats, a banquet, a feast. Mme Essele's co-wife claimed that the goat was a bridewealth payment for the daughter, and that it should therefore have been given to their husband. Mme Essele, she asserted, had eaten (*adi*) her husband's wealth.

Under *la crise,* claims over all forms of property and privilege have become more contested. For most people, it has become harder to acquire wealth of any kind, and so they struggle more intensely over claims. And this is perhaps particularly true for bridewealth, as the institution itself is under threat. In the past, bridewealth could only have been paid to the father or some other senior man. Today, just as women may be honored with the ritual funerary dance *esani,* which was previously preformed only at the death of a senior man, women may sometimes claim the bridewealth of their daughters. But, as with *esani,* to do so partially usurps the rights of men. The accusation that Mme Essele had eaten a bridewealth goat thus drew into question her wifely submission to her husband, her respect for her husband's authority. The threat to male authority itself is seen by many as evidence of the moral crisis. That this presumed insubordination should be manifested by eating also links it to witchcraft. A spirit-creature (*evu*) induces its human host to eat the wealth of his neighbors, the health of their children, or even his own relatives. Immoderate eating is akin to witchcraft, making Mme Essele a likely witch.

There is some disagreement about what happened to Mme Essele after these accusations. Some people say that her husband paid to have her witched for disrespecting him. Others claim that the co-wife made Mme Essele suffer. Still others assert that it was Mme Essele's own guilty conscience that brought about her demise. Everyone seems to agree, however, that on her way home from Yaoundé, Mme Essele suddenly fell ill. She was not taken to the hospital and died of fever a few days later.

This case, where a goat becomes a plausible basis for a witchcraft murder, points to the dramatic instability of life in *la crise.* Apparently small actions may have monumental consequences. Not only the magnitude, but also the direction of outcomes that follow an event is hard to predict in advance. Uncertainty permeates every plan. This naturalization of uncertainty is strong enough that many people find assertions about futures laughable, absurd. Knowing that I am interested in young women's marital, fertility, and professional intentions, residents of Mbeya sometimes asked me these same questions. How many children did I want? What job would I like to do? What would I do if my husband took a second wife?

These exchanges usually took a familiar form. I'd say I wanted two children, and my interlocutor would ask what I would do if I had five instead. I'd say that I won't have five; I'll stop when I have two. Then my interlocutor and any bystanders would start to laugh uproariously, and tell me that it is God who gives children and "you can't refuse!" Similarly, if I said that I wanted to be a professor, I would be asked what I would do if I had to work in the fields instead. When I would assert that it could not happen, that in America it was impossible that I would be forced to work in the fields, my conversation partner would laugh and remind me that no one can know the future, and that anything is possible in this world. Under the state of permanent crisis, many Beti young people have become habituated into this kind of agnosticism about the future: life is so uncertain that plans are always tenuous, partial, as much a hope as a plan (Whyte 1997).

The Beti began the postcolonial period with especially good prospects and high hopes. But they have been disappointed. *La crise,* marked by widespread economic hardship and corruption, has left many people distressed about the present and fearful for the future. Many aspects of life seem extremely uncertain, and planning for the future is difficult. But there is still hope vested in the children: that they will learn, that they will do better than this generation. It is to children, female childhood, and socialization that we now turn our attention.

Becoming Beti Today

The development of institutionalized inequality through church, school, and government has transformed Beti social organization. Among the most compelling changes is an intimate one, concerning the socially acknowledged stages of human development and markers of status transition. The meaning and markers of adulthood were in flux throughout the twentieth century, and today formal education and communion in the Catholic Church have joined—or arguably even replaced—precolonial markers of age status. Amid this plethora of competing and complementary systems that define entry into adulthood, parents, children, and others are contesting what constitutes a culturally meaningful rite of passage. Among the contemporary Beti, there are not ubiquitous, ordered, and coherent life stages, but rather context-specific statuses that can be differentially occupied by people with certain resources or skills (Johnson-Hanks 2002a). Most important for our thinking about the entry into honorable motherhood, the terms *ngon* (girl) and *miniga* (woman) refer to statuses, rather than stages. What establishes someone's status as a child or an adult is not having achieved a set of life-history transitions, but rather the role that she inhabits in a given social interaction.

The model of piecemeal development, rather than clear-cut life stages, that I am proposing for Beti socialization requires that people be construed as having multiple, partially independent parts—that people are not totally unified, but internally complex. Indeed, Fardon has claimed that most West African societies hold precisely this idea of personhood. West African personhood, he suggests, is always multiple and fragmented: "The West African person was an internally organized composition, but each element of the composition was unlike any of the others and derived from a source initially external to the person" (1996: 19). "Personhood" is therefore both more and less than the person—it extends beyond bodies and is divided within bodies (cf. Reisman 1992). Different elements of this human composition may follow different trajectories at different paces; growing up is therefore not a unitary process. Different skills, habits, attitudes, or modes of reasoning may follow distinct paths, which diverge and intersect.

Contemporary debate in Beti communities about legitimate adulthood focuses largely on women, for whom standards of adulthood have long been radically in flux. Even in the precolonial period, the transformations in the female life course were minimally marked by ritual; a girl's status changed with life experiences such as pregnancy and parturition that were not associated with culturally elaborated rituals or formal *rites de passage* (Alexandre and Binet 1958: 57). The most significant women's ritual, *mevungu,* is not categorized as a rite of initiation either by Laburthe-Tolra (1985) or by Vincent (1976), but rather as a fertility ritual, performed when the game became scarce, since women's fertility paralleled the fertility of the forest (Laburthe-Tolra 1985: 234).[16] Laburthe-Tolra argues that, in counterpoint to *so,* the initiation that served to make boys into men of the lineage, *mevungu* served at once to bind women to their affinal families and to recognize and harness their ambivalent status there. The Beti women interviewed by Vincent refer to *mevungu* both as an initiation and as a rite of purification, an ambivalence that makes sense only if women's social status was defined by life events other than rituals such as *mevungu,* as Alexandre and Binet argue was the case.

According to the vocabulary Alexandre and Binet collected in the early 1950s, an adolescent Beti girl (*ngon*) becomes a "true woman" (*nya ngal*) by losing her virginity, presumably in a licit, although extramarital, relationship.[17] Her transition to being a married woman (*nya minga,* which could also be translated as "true woman") is similarly defined in relationship to sexuality and reproduction, in the sense that these are the fundamental things that are transferred to her husband by marriage (1958: 57). Alexandre and Binet's focus on reproduction in defining the female life course is in keeping with academic tradition: the first birth has been treated by Africanists across the continent as the sine qua non of the transition to female adulthood. In his review of social organization in sub-Saharan Africa, Lesthaeghe argues that "the reproductive function itself is so crucial to both the individual woman and to the two kinship groups concerned that the status of adulthood for women is almost completely contingent on motherhood" (1989: 37–38). But while sex and giving birth are important to Beti adulthood, the determinism of Lesthaeghe's model seems inadequate to describe socialization and the emergence of full personhood among the Beti.

For Beti boys and girls, the progression through age statuses has long been marked in social ways. Life transitions depend not only on biological or ritual markers, but are also gauged "in reference to the responsibilities that the child can assume toward the social group and to his relationships with adults" (Mbala Owono 1982: 131). Growing up means attaining recognition as someone who "has sense" (*mfefeg*) in specific domains (Laburthe-Tolra 1977: 881). The change from childhood to adulthood is therefore not a single moment or even a single trajectory. Children become sensible along several discrete trajectories, simultaneous and non-synchronous. The lack of synchrony in these paths enables parents, children, teachers, and others to dispute a specific child's appropriate place in a developmental hierarchy by emphasizing the importance of one or another trajectory at the expense of the others.

Beti children spend much of their time performing domestic labor, but they also have time for play, particularly in urban households. Both Alexandre and Binet and Laburthe-Tolra have argued that Beti children's play consists of mimicking elders, and that this mode of play prepares them for adulthood. In this vein, Laburthe-Tolra writes that "the essential aspects of education occurred through the spontaneous imitation of adults and elders in the form of games among children . . . boys playing 'war' and girls dancing or playing the flute" (1981: 292). Alexandre and Binet similarly claim that children's games "are to a great extent mixed with the learning of future tasks: little girls play at housekeeping and sometimes with dolls; little boys hunt rats with the bow [and] throw small *assegais* at moving targets" (Alexandre and Binet 1958: 94; as translated in Alexandre and Binet 1985: 120). But it has probably been many generations since these activities could realistically have been imitative. In Cameroon in the 1950s, few men were hunting, and the only armed conflict was the campaign for independence in which few of their fathers would have fought (see Mbembe 1996). Even when Beti children's play does imitate adults, its function as preparation for adulthood seems limited at best. Children often add their own—sometimes very insightful—social commentary to their games, mocking adults as much as copying them. For example, I once observed a group of children playing "wedding," in which the only roles were that of bride, groom, and photographer. A wedding in which the pictures are more important than the officiator, attendants, witnesses, or guests: is this imitation or parody? It seems to me that such games are best seen as polyvalent (Schwartzman 1978), ironic (Raum 1940) and innovative (Deloria 1999), rather than as rehearsal for a taken-for-granted adulthood.

Children's games take place in a context in which they are largely left to their own devices on the periphery of adult society. Parents rarely speak directly to children, unless to assign them a task. Instead, parents talk with other adults *about* children, often in their presence, evaluating their conformance to expected modes of behavior, telling stories about their antics or special skills, or deciding what disciplinary measure should be taken in case of truancy. Childrearing is loose and children are allowed a great deal of freedom; even a child of three or four will be allowed to play unsupervised and to wander quite far from home. My observations, both in Yaoundé and in smaller towns and in rural areas, were basically in agreement with Mbala Owono's description that "children roam and play in the village center, wander in the forest in order to hunt there, or fish in the neighboring stream" (1982: 132). As adults increasingly identify specific children as having sense, that is, as able to conduct themselves in conformity to adult models, these children move further into the circle of adult worlds: entering conversations and performing tasks in work parties with adults. This motion through social space, slow and piecemeal, offers new opportunities at the same time as it demands new responsibilities.

Direct interaction between children and adults is often organized around the management of household labor. In allocating household labor, parents, senior siblings, and other elders benefit from their seniority, as children are charged with a large number of boring, burdensome, or unpleasant tasks. These tasks range from the simple (fetching water, buying matches, sweeping) to the quite complex (preparing food, daily market-ing), and also include child care, work in the fields, and laundry. In theory, these tasks are not only necessary for the household but also can indicate the degree to which a child has gained *mfefeg* in certain domains, or even be used strategically to teach children how to handle new situations. For example, six-year-old Tati, the half-sister of one of the schoolgirls I knew in Mbeya, was sent by her visiting uncle to buy cigarettes from a small stand at the road. When she returned with the wrong brand, he sent her back. When she returned again with too few of the correct brand, he sent her back a third time. By this point, Tati was crying. The uncle, however, considered the lesson a success, because—tears and all—she got it right on the third visit. As young people prove themselves ever more capable, they are assigned more numerous and more difficult tasks. For a capable and diligent child, these tasks can become quite burdensome, despite the value adults place on them. Children's labor is something to which parents have a right, through the logics of seniority and authorship, but it is also a mode of instruction and evaluation.

Beti children can and do manipulate the ambiguities inherent in the multiple scales of mental agility, encouraging and discouraging the impres-sion that they are prepared to take on adult responsibilities in different contexts and at different times. Children in their early teens are particu-larly able to manipulate their status; demanding respect as sensible people at certain times and appearing to lack sense for important work at other times. This is especially significant in terms of their education and train-ing, about which many Beti children have strong feelings. By manipulating the ways in which they are thought to have sense, children are often suc-cessful in persuading parents to provide them with their preferred kinds of training. Whereas most Beti parents do not consider it appropriate to ask children their preferences, thinking children incapable both of hav-ing well-formed opinions and of expressing them eloquently, most parents do spend a great deal of time and energy observing their children, assess-ing their strengths and guessing at their as yet hidden talents. Reasoning from Guyer's model of "wealth in people as wealth in knowledge" (1993, 1996), this kind of strategic, targeted investment in children's natural tal-ents looks like enlightened self-interest. By diversifying their child port-folios, parents are enriching the networks on which they can draw in the future (see Bledsoe 1993). But the benefits do not accrue only to parents, but also to children, some of whom quite effectively manage their self-presentations to lead their parents to make certain choices.

One successful case of this kind of persuasion is Yvette, who in 1998 was fourteen years old and lived with her family in Yaoundé. Clearly on the cusp of adulthood, Yvette played on her ambiguous status as "schoolgirl." She is academically talented, and when she performed well on her exams, her parents decided to switch her from the public school she was attending into a private, Catholic school, where they expected she would receive a better education. Two schools were under consideration: Collège Vogt focuses on math and science, while Collège de la Retraite follows a literature curriculum and has a reputation for being more religiously conservative. La Retraite is also significantly further away from the compound where Yvette lives. Yvette wanted to attend Vogt, and her grandparents wanted her to attend la Retraite. But Yvette said nothing about it. I only learned of her preference in an interview about her plans for school, childbearing, and marriage. Instead of making a request, Yvette enacted her preference. She set out to make it clear to everyone that she did not "have sense" in the domain of cross-town travel; although la Retraite itself might be safe, getting all the way across town would not be. She proved herself "incapable" of getting home by shared taxi from a church concert.[18] She constantly complained of harassment from older men when she left her neighborhood. She even managed to miss dinner one evening, because she got "confused" downtown. Finally, "convinced" that their otherwise talented daughter simply did not yet have sense in things directional, Yvette's parents enrolled her at Collège Vogt. I do not think that Yvette's parents were actually fooled; in fact, it seems likely that they understood precisely what Yvette was doing and interpreted her actions as compelling evidence that she was serious about her intentions. It is also important that what was at issue was her "sense" in one specific domain—Yvette's general skill and reason were not in question, and no one considered her inability to manage a taxi ride a negative indicator of her future success in school.

Beti *mingon* (girls) rarely undergo a coherent transformation of their status to *biniga* (women) across different domains. Instead, life changes are partial and piecemeal; marital or schooling statuses may undermine, rather than undergird, a woman's status as adult based on her work, childbearing, or roles in a religious community. Women's experiences of these processes emphasize contingency and variation. Entry into adulthood is not a single moment or even a single trajectory in contemporary southern Cameroon: adulthood is situation based. It is on the basis of her stock of experience and attributes, organized in a social context, that an individual woman may command the rights of the adult, the respect of others. This has a variety of important implications for how educated women think about childbearing and plan for the future, as we will see in chapters 7 and 8.

*   *   *

Looking back to precolonial Beti social organization, we can trace the increase of institutionalized economic inequality in southern Cameroon over the twentieth century. Dramatic economic inequality has become a taken-for-granted element of Beti social life; a young man can no longer assume that he will in due course become a *mfan mot* with dominion over his own compound, as his forefathers did. At the same time, much of what is considered plausible or desirable has shifted through the evangelization, widespread schooling, and—increasingly—access to the international media. Social status has become similarly variable and uncertain, as Beti life courses are organized in reference to a variety of nonsynchronous timelines, diverse and often very hard to choreograph. What it means to become an adult is changing; honorable adulthood has become more uncertain.

But not everything is new. Some important patterns of social organization remain very much in force. Central among these is the system that Guyer has described as "wealth in people as wealth in knowledge," a means by which value inheres in social relationships and in special skills—and by extension in relationships with people who have special skills. Beti social organization continues to depend on the rights of elders to command the labor and produce of juniors, in conjunction with a heavy emphasis on continued self-improvement through training. Children are loved, but not coddled—from early on they are expected to obey their elders, and contribute to the functioning of the household. In chapter 3, we will turn to how these socioeconomic transformations have affected the Beti honor system, what that system means today, and how it relates to the system of wealth in people.

CHAPTER THREE

The Making of Honorable Women

At the ultimate level of analysis honour is the clearing-house for the conflicts in the social structure, the conciliatory nexus between the sacred and the secular, between the individual and society, and between systems of ideology and systems of action. — Julian Pitt-Rivers, *The Fate of Shechem*

My God, in the midst of our modern world, even if I am an educated woman, teach me to remain a true wife and an honorable teacher of the children who will be born of our love. Amen. — Prayer to be memorized and repeated, from Victor Tonye, *Catéchèse pour jeunes et adults*

As young Beti women memorize the catechism, they learn to entreat God to make them honorable women, despite their schooling and modernity. But in other contexts, they hope that education and modernity themselves will have this power, making them honorable in a new way. Such partial paradoxes and misfits signal both the centrality and the complexity of honor in contemporary Beti social life. While concepts of honor infuse almost all Beti interaction, honor's identifying features are changing rapidly. Whereas in the past, honor applied only to men, Beti women are increasingly considered potential bearers of honor. Whereas in the past, honor was primarily associated with control of land and people, honor is increasingly related to school attendance and church participation. Whereas in the past, honor adhered to visible actions and social statuses, today internal states known only to the individual are considered worthy of honor or shame. In this chapter, I first review the scholarship on honor, seeking theories that shed light on the Beti case and help us to make sense of seeming contradictions and the relationship between internal senses of honor and outward respectability. We then turn to an overview of Beti honor, the essence of which I term self-dominion, and examine what has remained constant about honor—particularly men's honor—in the past century. Finally, we explore the changes in honor that have opened the door for women's growing participation in the honor system.

Definitions: Ethnographic Uses of "Honor"

All ethnographic theory is local, if only because bodies of theory have always been generated out of ethnographic engagements with specific places. In this regard, honor is to the Mediterranean and Islamic Africa what exchange is to Melanesia, or what kinship is to sub-Saharan Africa (see al-Khayyat 1990; Gilmore 1982; Herzfeld 1980; Kressel 1992; Lazaridis 1995; Péristiany 1966; Schneider 1971). In fact, theories of honor are perhaps more local than most. Debates about kinship quickly moved into the Pacific and were transformed in the process, but the focus of theories of honor remains firmly Mediterranean (see Hatch 1989, 1992, for a notable exception). Ethnographers of Africa, for the most part, have relied on concepts such as "status" (Mann 1985), "status groups" (Comaroff 1985: 190), "status elite" (Southall 1966: 348), "prestige" (Clark 1994: 285; Fernandez 1982), or even "prestige and status" (Moore 1986: 154) to describe social formations that might otherwise have been considered systems of honor. I analyze the modes of status ranking among the Beti as "honor" because it shares such a wide range of attributes with the better-known Mediterranean systems, casting the specific differences into clear relief.

Many of the societies that surrounded the Mediterranean in recent history shared a number of structural features, although these similarities exist alongside substantial difference and variability (Herzfeld 1980: 339, 347–48). These societies are—or were—largely pastoral, characterized by conflict over pasture, "remarkable flexibility in social [kinship] organization," and "widespread distribution of decision-making powers" (Schneider 1971: 3–6). The forms of honor represented by these societies are also similar. Beyond the famous male virility and female virginity (e.g., Lazaridis 1995: 283; Péristiany and Pitt-Rivers 1991: 6), scholars have noted the importance of secrecy (Campbell 1974: 192), independence from others (Campbell 1974: 285; Schneider 1971: 6), competition (Gilmore 1982: 191; Schneider 1971: 17), and pride bordering on conceit (Pitt-Rivers 1977: 19). While heeding Herzfeld's call (1980) for culturally specific, linguistically careful research on local forms of honor, we can see in the Mediterranean something of an honor prototype. Not all of the societies show all the characteristics, and certainly not all in the same ways; however, there is a recognizable pattern of some kind. In examining Beti honor, I will use the Mediterranean pattern as a comparison.

Perhaps because the Mediterranean honor complex is so well known, a number of scholars use the term honor without explicit definition, making comparison with other cases difficult. For example, in his 1993 work *Sacrificed for Honor,* Kertzer argues that during the nineteenth century, unmarried Italian women who gave birth were pressured into abandoning their infants in order to protect their honor and uphold the values of the community. But he does not explain what he means by honor, nor whether his usage parallels that of the historical figures he describes. From his usage, we may infer that Kertzer intends "honor' " to mean something like "reputation," in the sense that it depends not on a woman's actions, but on public knowledge and evaluation of them: in describing a set of documentation procedures associated with coerced abandonment, he notes that "in procuring documentation, the woman jeopardized the most fundamental value of the whole system, her anonymity and, hence, her honor" (1993: 46). The equation of honor with reputation, or something like it, is not uncommon. This appears to be the meaning assumed by Boddy in her study of fertility and religious experience in Muslim Sudan: "Should [a woman] become pregnant out of wedlock, whether before marriage or through adultery, her male kin have the right—even the duty—to kill her for so dishonoring her family" (1989: 76). But if honor means nothing more than reputation or good name, then it offers no analytic advantage over these more common terms.

There is good reason to think that honor means something more than reputation. For example, a certain action may be considered honorable although no one else observes it; this implies that one element of honor is independent of public approval or opprobrium. It is to this element that Abu-Lughod seems to refer when she notes that "the ideals or moral virtues of Bedouin society together constitute what I refer to as the Bedouin code of honor" (1986: 86). In order to bring these two meanings together, a number of scholars have interpreted honor as intrinsically bipartite: one aspect of honor is external or defined by society, the other internal or somehow innate (Stewart 1994: 12). At the first degree of interpretation, this distinction appears to apply well to the Beti material: in Camfrançais as spoken by Beti, *être respectable* refers to the external sense of honor, and *être digne* refers to the internal one.[1] There is much analytic purchase in analyzing these two elements separately, and I will do so later in the chapter. But their separate analysis begs the question of the relationship between them: is *dignité* (inner honor) independent of *respectabilité* (outer honor)? Is it its basis? Its prerequisite? Or even its consequence? It would seem that while any analysis of Beti honor must address the distinction between internal and external honor, this distinction must not be pressed too far: in the end, both are part of the same complex.

Three elegant solutions have been offered to the dilemma that, while honor has internal and external aspects, it is in the end a single system. The alternatives each emphasize one of the two components, offering different views on the empirical problem of honor. The first, presaged in Veblen's work and developed ethnographically by Campbell, suggests that honor consists of the right to a certain consideration by others, on the basis of some characteristics or accomplishments. Among the Sarakatsani of Greece, honor

> is conferred as a sign of recognition of the excellence or worth of a person. It becomes the respect or esteem owed to certain persons. . . . From the point of view of the receiver it is whatever raises him up in the eyes of another and gives him reason for pride. In other contexts it may indicate certain qualities or conditions on which the reputation of an individual, or a group, is dependant. (Campbell 1974: 268)

This definition resolves the bipartite problem by bridging a sense of internal legitimacy with the social recognition of that legitimacy through certain (and certainly variable) qualities. In his classic collection of essays on the Mediterranean, Pitt-Rivers makes a similar suggestion:

> Honour is the value of a person in his own eyes, but also in the eyes of his society. It is his estimation of his own worth, his claim to pride, but it is also the acknowledgement of that claim, his excellence recognized by his society, his right to pride. (Pitt-Rivers 1977: 1)

Both of these definitions emerge out of specific ethnographic contexts, but the argument that honor consists of a socially recognized right can also be made on a general level. Based on a comparative analysis of texts from across Europe, F. H. Stewart proposes a general definition of honor as "the right to be treated as having a certain worth" (1994: 21); in other words, honor is a mode of social distinction, a claim to a specific social status, to a position in interaction.

Stewart does not count Veblen's theory of "pecuniary honor" (1899) among his sources, but the similarities are striking. Whereas Campbell and Pitt-Rivers say that honor may entail anything that gives the right and claim to pride, Veblen focuses on how that right came to accrue to the privileged classes. He proposes that conspicuous consumption of time and goods first represented honorable or distinguished characteristics, especially success in hunting and war, and then later came be seen as itself honorable. Thus, conspicuous leisure and conspicuous consumption become admirable even when they do not in fact indicate past efficiency, diligence, or success, but are inherited or even—at the limit—won by luck. Although as history the model is dubious at best, Veblen's analysis of the relationship between privilege and prestige does offer one approach to understanding one part of the system of modern honor among urban Cameroonian women: *être respectable* requires that a woman earn her own money through clean work, dress well and in French metropolitan (*hexagonale*) style, and eventually be married with bridewealth or to a European man. These are primarily pecuniary achievements, yet they are fundamental parts of modern honor.

Elvin Hatch, working on ranking and prestige among ranching families in California and New Zealand, offers a second approach to the integration of "inner" and "outer" honor. Rather than treating honor as a fundamentally social relationship in which one actor owes and gives respect to another, Hatch focuses on the personal—one could say internal—impetus to attain the characteristics, attributes, or accomplishments considered honorable. Thus, while there must be some social consensus about what modes of action are honorable, Hatch's analysis of honor relies on an inner motivation to achieve them. In his own words, this theory

> assumes that the agent's focus is primarily inward upon his or her own sense of self-worth. The underlying motivation is to achieve a sense of personal accomplishment or fulfillment, and the individual does so by engaging in activities or exhibiting qualities that are defined by the society as meritorious. Self-identity resides in the recognition that one's actions . . . are important as judged by criteria that transcend one's personal self-interest. (1989: 349)

Hatch suggests that honor inheres in and is driven by self-perception. The external aspects of honor (rank or prestige), then, follow from an essentially internal desire to lead a life that society will find meritorious. In this way, Hatch's self-identity theory connects to the body of literature in life history, which emphasizes how people use autobiographies to make sense of their lives, to connect and impose order on disparate events, to create a sense of continuity between the past, present, and future, and to construct themselves as able or honorable (Chambon 1995; Hoerning and Alheit 1995; Ochs and Capps 1996). Indeed, Eisenhart has claimed that "building or claiming an identity for self in a given context is what motivates an individual to become more expert. . . . [D]eveloping a sense of oneself as an actor in a context is what compels a person to desire and pursue increasing mastery of the skills" (1995: 4). The argument perfectly parallels Hatch's, substituting skills for honor. The model offers great descriptive advantage: the drive to achieve specific self-perceptions—to be *digne*—appears throughout Beti schoolgirls' explanations of their behavior. And yet the danger of this approach is that treating honor as self-identity means assuming the very forms of subjectivity that we want to understand. The motivation to perceive oneself as honorable may generate social action, or it may be the product of social action, or both at once.

A third, and in many ways more satisfying approach to the duality of honor comes from the writings of Saba Mahmood (2001a, 2001b). Mahmood does not, I believe, intend her analysis of the practice of prayer in the women's mosque movement in Cairo as a theory of honor; nonetheless, it both offers a resolution to the set of partial paradoxes that make honor such a hard problem and applies particularly aptly to the modern honor of young, educated Beti women. Mahmood describes how participants in the mosque movement seek to attain piety, or "being close to God," through the intentional shaping of their desires, actions, and wills; the practice of prayer is thus both the means and the end of religious self-formation. What she elucidates is a pedagogy of sentiment through which members of the mosque movement acquire proper exterior forms through the structured acquisition of specific emotional states:

> The ability to cry effortlessly with the right intention did not come easily to most women, however, and had to be cultivated through acts of induced weeping during salat. Booklets . . . suggest different strategies for the attainment of this state, and women are advised to try a number of visual, kinesthetic, verbal, and behavioral techniques in order to provoke the desired effect. (2001a: 843)

Like Hatch, Mahmood emphasizes that the subject seeks to acquire those habits and attributes that characterize the honorable, or pious, person. In contrast to Hatch's analysis, however, Mahmood does not begin with a fully formed subject choosing between alternative courses of action in a kind of enlightened self-interest. Instead, piety—and, I will argue, honor for the Beti—requires the re-formation of the subject from the ground up; the external becomes both a sculptor and an indicator of internal honor. For Beti women, as for the women in Mahmood's study, "the role of conscious training in the acquisition of embodied dispositions" (2001a: 838) is central to the making of modern honor; women perform physical behaviors associated with specific intentional states in order to cultivate the inclination for those states. Performing the purportedly outward sign of an interior condition develops the habit of that condition, like Pascalian belief that emerges from prayer, but does not initially motivate it.[2]

The Foundations of Beti Honor

Despite common folk histories that trace the Beti to classical Egypt or Greece, there are neither historical nor ecological reasons to classify the peoples of southern Cameroon with the Mediterranean.[3] My argument is merely that the Beti system of status ranking is an honor system, comparable in content and structure to those known in the Mediterranean, and not that the societies as a whole are either similar or related. The Beti share with the Sarakatsani and other Mediterranean groups the close linking of honor with secrecy, independence, and sexuality. But the two systems differ as well. Most importantly, it is Mediterranean families who guard and may lose honor, whereas in the Beti case it is (primarily) individuals. The degree to which Beti honor is individualized is perhaps unique. Not only do all the classic ethnographies focus on family honor, but Hardiman suggests that even among South Asian bandits, honor resided in the family (1995: 116). Thus, while Beti families do have forms of collective honor, the fact that individual honor takes priority makes the case unusual.

Any discussion of Beti honor must begin with the fact that the word *beti* itself indicates autonomy and honorability. *Beti* is the plural form of *nti,* which means "noble" or "lord," particularly in contrast to "slave" (*olò,* pl. *bolò*). Today, Beti is used almost exclusively as an ethnonym, and Nti refers only to the Christian God; it is the standard translation for "Lord," as in Nti Zamba wan, "the Lord our God." In the past, however, these terms appear to have had much wider meanings. Largeau uses *nti* to translate height (1901: 372); Trilles notes that *beti* indicates legitimate customs (1912: 112). Throughout, however, there is a strong sense that being *beti* refers to

being honorable, being righteous, or being independent. In seeking to find
an acceptable translation of the term, Laburthe-Tolra suggests:

> It is likely that the concept most exactly corresponding, although abstract, would
> be that of the "non-barbarian," because the word connotes respectability and
> the mutual recognition of culture. . . . The Beti are the Civilized. (1981: 48)

To be Beti is therefore—by definition—to be respectable, civilized, and
honorable. But what is the constitution of this honor? Although the system of Beti honor has undergone substantial change over the past century,
certain fundamental aspects appear to persist. I term these fundamental
components of honor "self-dominion," which necessarily encompasses autonomy, privacy, and increasingly, self-control, and, for men, also entails
competitive patronage through the system of wealth in people described
in the chapter 2. I use "dominion" in part to emphasize the parallels and
contrasts between the classical honor of men and the newly emerging, still
contested honor of women. We will see that women's honor resides largely
in a set of embodied practices of self-restraint: self-dominion in the sense
of mastery of one's self, of one's own desires, reproduction, aspirations,
timing, and so forth. Women's self-dominion is necessarily corporeal, and it
is achieved through explicit acts of self-formation and especially restraint,
for example, from sex. This self-dominion is the basis and expression of
dignité and *respectabilité;* that is, it is the essence by which women consider
themselves and are deemed by others to be honorable. Men's honor also
rests on a form of self-dominion, but centrally in the sense of maintaining
autonomy from the power of others. However, his honor is also associated
with certain forms of authority over women, as wives or daughters. Thus,
control over women constitutes an important element of the honor of both
men and women, but in different ways.

Autonomy

Whether we call it independence, self-reliance, or autonomy, there is ample
evidence throughout the ethnographic corpus and across time that Beti
place an extraordinary value on the freedom of the individual, and particularly the individual man. In all sorts of domains, it is considered appropriate for people to have unique callings and life trajectories. In his
collection of Beti folk wisdom, Tsala cites the adage "Mendim mè à tòng
mmbàn akóg" (water flows in its own bed) to mean that each person should

recognize and pursue his own path (1985: 219). Some scholars have suggested that this autonomy is the essence of the Beti identity; Ngoa, for
example, translates the name into French as "free men who can defend
themselves" (cited in Laburthe-Tolra 1981: 47). Even the earliest descriptions of the Beti note their love of independence. For example, Largeau
writes that "a self-respecting Pahouin [a man of the Bulu-Beti-Fang] does
not take orders from anyone" (1901: 22). To this day, Beti men are fiercely
autonomous, and perceive any threat to this autonomy as a direct assault
on their honor, in the sense of their right to respect. This self-assertive autonomy resonates, of course, with Veblen's concept of the identity of honor
and superior force. Veblen suggests that "an honorific act is in the last analysis little if anything else than a recognized successful act of aggression"
(1899: 17).

The centrality of autonomy to the honor of Beti men is related, perhaps
most saliently, to the traditional system of social organization described in
chapter 2, in which the adult son would found his own household, over
which no higher political organization existed. That is to say, this form of
autonomy is first and foremost the prerogative of adult men, and any extension to women or children is secondary. Laburthe-Tolra explicitly links
this interpretation of Beti autonomy to male power:

> If the most characteristic political trait of Beti society is its segmentation and the
> independence of the family-fathers and founders-of-villages, which places all
> men on, more or less, an equal footing, it is similarly clear that the fundamental
> form of power is the power to possess women. In this regard, every head of a
> residential unit is *nti,* "lord" . . . that is to say a distinguished man, worthy of
> regard. (1981: 356)

This observation offers insight into several aspects of the Beti honor
system. While the independent, neolocal households of the past century
evoke the similarly independent pastoral households associated with classical Mediterranean honor systems, Laburthe-Tolra suggests that it was
neither the households nor patrilines of the Beti that bore honor. Instead,
it was individual men. Elsewhere, Laburthe-Tolra suggests that even open
adultery on the part of women was tolerated, because the husband's claim
to any children borne by his wives was absolute (1981: 244). Thus, a man's
individual distinction and worthiness of regard was independent of the
sexual reputations of the women associated with him. In addition to elu-
cidating the individuation of honor, Laburthe-Tolra's explanation of male

honor suggests why women's increasing claims to autonomy and an honor parallel to that of men should pose such a fundamental threat to Beti men. As Veblen articulated, as long as male honor consists in large part of "pecuniary emulation" grounded, ultimately, in women's labor, female claims to parallel honor must threaten it (1899: 23, 353–57).

We saw in chapter 2 that growing up Beti is largely associated with acquiring "sense" (*mfefeg*) in a variety of domains of life. Acquiring sense and being autonomous are closely related. Indeed, it is because children demonstrate good sense that their parents cede to them the prerogatives of independence. In Camfrançais, these two elements of sense and autonomy are united in the phrase *être grand(e)* (to be big). Being big is equated with having good sense, and therefore having a right to respect, as suggested by Stewart (1994). In particular domains, "good sense" is cumulative, in that people slowly acquire it over their lives. This does not imply that there is any correlation between domains; a person who has "good sense" in one area may not have it in another; a person who is "big" in one social context may not be so in another. But within a specific domain, consciousness and independence are closely linked. As one of my research assistants explained: "They baptize you when you are a baby. You are not conscious then. When you take communion, you are already big. When you do confirmation, then you are already big." The equation here between good sense—expressed by "consciousness"—autonomy, and adulthood is explicit: first communion and confirmation require individual conviction and autonomous action (Tonye 1986: 107, 115). Being big entails having sense and being autonomous.

Being big is centrally about rights to self-determination and to certain kinds of consideration, based on having acquired *mfefeg* in the appropriate domain. But this right is not accorded without contention. As described by Goffman (1967: 10–11), an individual requires the collaboration of others to successfully claim the identity of someone *déjà grand*. Thus, refusal to accord someone the treatment appropriate to a big person is the same as rejecting their claims to that identity. Large or small, such refusals are met with a furious defense. A large example is that of a priest who had been relieved of his parish duties for disobeying the bishop, and who settled in a town near Mbeya. To the consternation of the Catholic hierarchy, he continued to say mass and even—reportedly—to perform exorcisms. Appearing in his cassock at the weekly market, blessing children and pregnant women, hearing confession and assigning penance, Père LeBon demanded the respect due a parish priest, and he largely received it from a populace thankful for his actions as a generous patron. Unwilling to risk the embarrassment to the church that would have almost certainly followed any reprimand of Père LeBon, the bishop left him alone. At the small extreme, I once had a conflict with the driver of a minibus, and the argument became quite heated. He had taken my bag and put it onto his bus, although another vehicle was next in line to leave. I wanted to take the first bus, but he refused to release my bag. The argument drew a small crowd, amused by the odd battle of wills. With the assistance of another passenger, I managed to get my bag off his bus, which the driver considered appallingly inappropriate. After ten minutes or more of argument, I declared, "I am not listening to you anymore!" To which he cried out, "But you have to listen to me! I myself am already big! [*Je suis déjà grand, moi*]." The informal audience laughed, as his words were belied by the fact that a woman had succeeded in making him angry enough to lose his self-dominion.

The fury of this man's response to a very minor conflict gives an indication of the importance of maintaining honor. A Beti man must actively guard his honor at every turn, since other people's rejections of his claims—if ignored—will eventually undermine his standing. But his fury also hints at the potential for social conflict in the Beti honor system. In order to defend their public honor, men are quick to anger, and even to violence. The most extreme statements regarding this passionate temper must, of course, be read with a moderating mind. But from early on, statements of the ease with which Beti men are incited to anger are plentiful. For example, Georg Escherich, a former plantation-owner, noted:

> In character the Pahouin is not at all disagreeable. His love of wildness and independence, which easily lead him to insubordination, are in and of themselves not faults. He appears to be conflict-loving and eager for war, . . . also vengeful, such that he holds the law of blood vengeance especially holy. (1938: 53)

Escherich had rather peculiar notions of what constituted an agreeable character, and his description is certainly excessive. Nonetheless, he was correct in noting that open conflict in Beti society results from the "love of independence" that runs throughout it. Slights—or perceived slights— to an individual's autonomy regularly met, and still meet, with extraordinary defensiveness (see also Tessman 1913, 2: 241–42). And the connection between honor—in this case through autonomy—and quarrels is not unique to the Beti. Campbell describes much the same pattern among the Sarakatsani of Greece:

Personal and family honour and pride, which are fundamental values of the community, breed a spirit of intense and aggressive competitiveness that sometimes threatens even the relations of unmarried brothers . . . and frequently provokes verbal or physical quarrels between shepherds unrelated by kinship or marriage. (1974: 25)

As in the Sarakatsani case, aggression arises in reference to thwarted claims to honor, not in cases where those claims are successfully pressed. And as in the Sarakatsani case, the overt and explicit jostling for public honor occurs among men. Women may also seek autonomy in certain ways, but not through public demonstrations of this kind.

To allow oneself to be publicly humiliated brings shame (*honte,* or *osòn*). Thus, a self-respecting Beti will vigorously defend himself against verbal or financial abuse: to be tricked in the market, for example, is shameful. One of my research assistants gently scolded me after watching me tolerate being overcharged by a vegetable seller in the market. If you permit people to treat you badly, my research assistant explained, it means you have no self-respect. You have to defend yourself! Similarly, a neighbor explained to me that if a married woman is known to have affairs, thereby dishonoring her husband, no one will respect him, because he has not stood up for himself. After the first instance, he should beat her or throw her out. However, there are some contexts in which self-defense is impossible. In these circumstances, a Beti person is expected to tolerate the abuse with composure. Only a rich man can defend himself against legal prosecution; only a powerful man can defend himself against extortion. No one is expected to refuse the police their bribes, or the national politicians their self-aggrandizing claims of voter support. Although one is expected to defend oneself to the best of one's ability, one is also expected to judge what that ability is. There is something pathetic about a powerful man who permits others to abuse him and also something laughable about a weak man who makes grandiose claims of power. One should know one's place and demand the rights to respect that it entails, but no more.

In certain cases, autonomy must be defended with verbal or even physical force. But this is not to say that very frequent outbursts are honorable, or even tolerated. As with the minibus driver, tempers flare where honorable autonomy is assaulted, not when it is intact. Indeed, the greater value is on self-control. A Beti does not behave carelessly (*n'importe comment*), but rather is poised. We will see later in the chapter that being poised applies perhaps even more importantly, and in a somewhat different way, to

women. For both men and women, this composure is increasingly linked
to the concept of discipline as practiced in school.[4] Self-control may be
demonstrated in slow and deliberate speech, in the careful guarding of
secrets, or in the coordination of life-history events. In certain instances, it
may become frankly infuriating for the foreigner who wants, for example,
to complete an interview. Indeed, Laburthe-Tolra interprets this Beti self-
control as near to arrogance:

> The certainty that the Bënë [a Beti clan] had of their superiority to their neigh-
> bors, which was noted by the first travelers, was expressed by the measured
> slowness of their gestures that must never betray precipitation or the lack of
> self-control. (1981: 305)

Thus, in Camerooon, free men move with deliberate caution because
they can. They are not slaves, whose motion is controlled by someone else.
As adult men who answer to no authority higher than themselves, they
practice self-dominion in the dual sense of controlling themselves and not
being controlled or dominated by another. This extreme self-control, and
the autonomy of action it marks, must be seen in contrast to the radical
uncertainty of most everything else. Today, as in the past, most Beti live
in uncontrollable and unknowable circumstances: from violent weather to
the timing of paychecks, from the arrival of buses to the functioning of
offices. As in all poor countries, death is common, disease more so, and
both are expensive for the extended family. Because these things are perceived as uncontrollable and unalterable, the only honorable response is
to endure them. In fact, the sympathetic response to a story of hardship is
"patience."

Autonomy is the first and most central aspect of "self-dominion," which
constitutes the core of the Beti honor system. In its classic incarnation as
adult independence from authority, autonomy applied only to men. However, as we will explore later in this chapter, women are increasingly able
to succeed in their claims to autonomy. We now turn to the second component of Beti honorable self-dominion: secrecy.

Secrecy

The Beti are extremely reluctant to share nearly any kind of information
with each other. From the trivia of daily life to exam success, marriage
plans, or the details of an illness, Beti vigilantly guard any information that

they consider "personal." Campbell's description of the Sarakatsani might as easily apply to the Beti:

> Secrecy about the family and its affairs is a measure of loyalty and of the internal cohesion of the group. The Sarakatsani are, in fact, extremely secretive. As a matter of policy and habit they never give accurate answers to questions. . . . Information about private family life is denied to all unrelated persons; and with reason, because people are always seeking to find or fabricate incidents of intimate family life to destroy the reputation of others. But secrecy goes beyond the point of mere discretion and becomes an end in itself. A Sarakatsanos declines to give almost any personal information to a non-kinsman, even where it could not remotely damage the family's interest or prestige. (1974: 192)

We will return to the issues of gossip and slander later in this section. For the moment, however, let us focus on the idea of secrecy itself.

In part, Beti secrecy arises out of the dictates of autonomy. Just as an individual guards his right to independent action, he guards his right to private knowledge of those actions and their motivations. Secrecy might thus be viewed as an aspect of autonomy. This interpretation is bolstered by the fact that secrecy is socially distributed following the same pattern as "being big," for children are almost never granted the prerogative of secrecy, whereas adult men almost always are. Thus, children are constantly exposed to public view and criticism: their grades are read aloud and posted in public, their misbehaviors are discussed openly with neighbors, and their personal effects may at any time be investigated by an older relative. Children do not yet have the right to secrecy, as they have not yet demonstrated "sense" in the relevant domains. Successful adulthood, by contrast, is marked by the ability and right to guard secrets of the self, and to a lesser degree of others.

Keeping secrets as an expression of independence is particularly salient in bridewealth negotiations and market transactions. In reference to the Pahouin as a whole, Largeau noted that "their bad faith in their mutual dealings is all too evident" (1901: 15). Similarly, Lembezat described the Beti as "lazy, selfish, [and] distrustful" (1954: 55). A popular song on the radio in 1998 threatened a lover thus: "Si tu me triches, je te tricherai" (If you deceive me, I will deceive you). Indeed, a successful deception meets with relatively little moral opprobrium, as long it is intelligently managed. Over the course of my fieldwork, I heard a number of stories of people who accomplished outstanding fraud, making themselves rich at the expense of gullible victims. Although the storytellers acknowledge that such trickery is immoral, they also recognize it as exceptionally clever. One such story told of a group of people who claimed that the body of a man burned in a national disaster was a kinsman. They were given CFA 30,000 (about USD 60) by the government to bury him. Instead, they took the money and dumped the body in a trash pit. In another case, a man raising money in his village to get electricity lines extended there absconded with his neighbors' money, reportedly to France. Both cases were the topic of extensive conversation over hair-braiding and at the market, and the usual reaction was a combination of dismay and grudging respect at the cleverness and bravado. When I recounted the means taken by urban shysters to get money from me (many of which I admittedly fell for, at least the first time), people in Mbeya laughed and shook their heads. As one woman explained, "In Nigeria they just kill you for money, but we have some pride."

But Beti secrecy is not entirely derivable from the logic of autonomy. It must also be located in Beti understandings of truth and certainty. As I have noted, Beti face extraordinary unpredictability in everyday life and yet believe in a highly ordered world, in which each individual has a calling, or a path; the child is taught to "become who you are" (Mbala Owono 1982: 122). This apparent contradiction is resolved through the assumption that truth and certainty are necessarily hidden, that nothing is what it appears. An open assertion is presumed to be false, as truths are concealed, known only to a few or, in the extreme case, only to God. Beti conceptions of knowability and truth are central to understanding secrecy, and therefore to understanding honor itself.

In Beti cosmology, truth is connected to the supernatural, and duplicity to everyday life. The visible and perceptible is by definition untrustworthy, in contrast to the certainty of the divine. As early as 1913, we have a description of religious oaths as contrasted with common lies: "The Pahouin confront the constant and practically virtuoso lying of their fellow tribesmen through the contrivance of an oath, which stands in a very close relationship to the cults" (Tessman 1913, 2:239). Although we may reject Tessman's moralist tone, it is significant that he describes truth as inherent in religious contexts and falsehood as inherent in everyday contexts. This pattern recurs throughout the ethnography, and conforms to contemporary practice as well.

Consonant with Mbala Owono's description, many Beti assume the divine predestination of life courses. They often employ the French expression "Tout qui doit finir est déjà fini" (Everything that must end is already over), to express that outcomes are always buried in beginnings. But despite being inevitable, outcomes are always hidden and largely unknowable: truths are revealed only slowly. One student who aspired to a career in medicine explained that it was not her own effort, but God's will that would permit her to succeed. When I asked how she would attain entry into medical school, she replied: "I don't know what to do. If God wants it, I will be able to heal people. If he doesn't want it, no matter what I do, I will not be able to cure." Here my interlocutor speaks of life courses as if they were predetermined: what happens is a natural exposition of what must be, for "everything that must end is already over." This is not an unusual trope: Beti often treat people as if whatever they were preparing for had already been actualized. Engaged women are called by their future married names and students by their future titles: I was called *docteur* and the junior seminarians *les abbés;* young women refer to their steady boyfriend, their *meilleur,* as *mon mari* (my husband), without irony or the intention to deceive.

Everyday life is perceived as unpredictable, even random, and its caprices can be observed by even the most casual observer. By contrast, ultimate futures are certain, but knowable only in as far as they are revealed by God. What is of no consequence is therefore perceptible, and what is real is hidden. These equations produce a constant supply of gossip and speculation. Accusations that so-and-so "occupies himself too much with [the business of] others" are traded back and forth; a great deal of time and energy goes into hiding one's own secrets and discovering those of one's neighbors. Gossip is often malicious and based on little evidence. When a white Jeep was spotted in the vicinity of Efok, someone began the rumor that it was from the CIA and that I was a CIA employee, sent to conduct espionage in the village; the Jeep had presumably come to check on me. One young woman tried to console me when I was dismayed that people could think that I worked for the CIA, recounting how she herself had suffered from rumors that she had seduced a teacher. She explained: "Sometimes girls who have complexes talk about you. They tell untrue stories about you. It doesn't mean anything to me, but it can hurt." Thus, honorable secrecy is connected to potentially dishonorable gossip and distrust.[5]

Secrecy is perhaps most important in sexual contexts. Unlike in the Mediterranean honor cultures, the Beti have no cult of virginity of young women per se (Laburthe-Tolra 1981: 234). Nonetheless, there is great emphasis on discretion in sexual relationships, and on women's maintaining a degree of sexual decorum. I will discuss sexuality and its control in more detail in chapter 6, but a brief introduction to it is in order here. Most Beti assume that people need sex, and indeed that most people are sexually active. But sexual relationships must be conducted with extreme circumspection. Young women are expected to hide their relationships from their parents until they are prepared to present a future son-in-law, perhaps with a speech, which one woman explained should begin, "We have been together for a long time, but I have hidden [it] from you." Instead of being perceived as deceptive, this discretion is the mark of young woman's good sense, and therefore of incipient adulthood. Secrecy surrounding sexuality implies autonomy and discretion.

There is some debate as to the precise content of honorable sexuality for women. Although nearly all Beti agree that it is critical for a woman to keep her sexual life out of the public eye, some argue that this can be achieved through discretion alone, while others argue that only the strictest monogamy is adequate. It is interesting that no one in these debates suggests that a woman's sexual life is not the business of her neighbors. One of my informants argued that strict chastity as demanded by the Catholic Church was not feasible, and that girls could maintain their honor by keeping their sexual relations secret:

> The church should come down a little into life, study the youth a little. They should enter into the environment of the youth, because you can say, "No, you can't do this," but when you enter into an environment where your friends tell you that you don't know anything [you will do it]. But if you already have sexual relations, retain your self-respect. Don't recount that you are here, you are there, you are with that girl, that boy. That is what the church ought to ask of the youth.

Thus, secrecy in sexual relationships enables women to retain their honor, despite the disagreements in Beti society about the precise nature of honorable sexuality.

Secrecy also applies to men's management of their sexual relationships. Men are often assumed to need sex more frequently than women, and even to require multiple partners. Male sexual infidelity is thus universally condemned only if it becomes public. As long as an affair is secret, it does not harm a man's honor. Making infidelity public, however, indicates a lack of maturity and respect. One of my neighbors explained:

> If you have a wife at home and you don't care about her at all, you lead another girlfriend in front of her, you do any old thing in front of your wife, how is anyone

going to respect you with that? . . . So, when you have a wife, [you know that] "My wife, she is at home. I respect her." So you have to go do your things very much in secret, so that no one even knows.

Discretion, not monogamy, is thus the measure of a respectful husband.

In order to keep secret their sexual partners, young Beti often introduce their lovers as cousins (*cousin* or *cousine* in Camfrançais). On the whole, however, so common is this ruse that it serves less to mask the relationship than to draw into question all so-called cousins. Since any kind of sexual relationships with members of the same *mvog,* that is patrilateral cousins of any distance, are prohibited, the common usage of the term "cousin" is perfectly ambiguous, referring both to lovers and people excluded as sexual partners. I first discovered this quite accidentally when a friend of mine became furious when he introduced me to a young woman, his *cousine,* and I remarked, "You've sure got a lot of cousins!" He assumed that I was announcing that he was promiscuous (in front of one of his *cousines,* no less!), when all I meant was that he came from a large family.

Secrecy is a key part of the Beti honor complex. People are expected to conduct much of their lives in secret; they hide their own actions and attempt to reveal those of others. This secrecy has two roots: first, it may be linked to autonomy, as the autonomous Beti claims the right to self-determination and privacy through secrecy. Second, the value of secrecy arises out of a more general epistemology in which truth is hidden, and anything that is plainly declared is assumed to be false. Secrecy and autonomy together constitute the basis of the Beti honor system. Although their specific forms have shifted, they have remained central to Beti honorable self-dominion for the past hundred years. We turn now to the ways in which the Beti honor complex has changed over this time frame. These transformations focus centrally on women, Catholicism, and schooling.

The Transformation of Honor since 1900

In its classic incarnation, Beti honor consisted of the right to respect, autonomy, and privacy accorded to a *mfan mot,* a true man. A true man was the head of a household and the founder of a lineage. No political authority reigned above him. Over the course of the twentieth century, the system of social organization to which this form of honor related has been transformed through school, market, church, and state. The honor complex has also changed, and indeed continues to change. As participation in school, church, and state have come to compete with, and even replace, founding a household as the defining feature of adult honor, the content of honor has shifted. The most monumental shifts are directly related to the topic of family formation among educated women. The content of honor has shifted into ever greater alignment with the values of school and church; greater emphasis is placed on an internal sense of honor, and discipline is an increasingly important element of self-dominion. In addition, and perhaps as both a cause and effect of this growing association of honor with religious and school-related values, women have increasingly come to be eligible for honor. The honor of women differs somewhat from that of men, but like male honor, it is premised on self-dominion. The fact that the Beti system of honor remains in transformation means that its attainment is always precarious; the honor to which contemporary Beti women aspire is always an uncertain one.

Internal and External Honor

Beti society has been transformed over the course of the past century, and with these changes Beti honor has been pulled into ever closer alignment with the values of schooling and of the Catholic Church. Indeed, the two systems already had significant parallels. Part of what made possible Beti conversion to Catholicism so rapidly and on such a large scale was the fact that many long-standing Beti beliefs about the nature of the world resonated with Catholic doctrine as taught by the Pallotins. The shifts are more salient—or at least more clearly discernible—in Camfrançais than in Eton/Ewondo. As many young, educated Beti speak French more often and in a wider variety of contexts than Eton or Ewondo, these shifts are very important for the understanding of honor.

In our discussion of the theories of honor at the beginning of this chapter, we saw that a distinction is drawn in the literature between internal and external honor. These distinctions have come to be identified by the Beti themselves in contemporary Camfrançais, but the manner in which the Beti conceive of these two aspects of honor is unique, both in how each sphere of honor is defined, and in what constitutes honorability in each case. *Être digne* (glossed here as "to have self-respect") refers to honor as enduring and intrinsic to the individual. By contrast *être respectable* (glossed as "to be respectable") refers to honor as inhering in social relations, and to social achievements that are cumulative over the life course.

In Eton and Ewondo, these two concepts remain unified as *mfan,* particularly in *mfan mot.*[6] The distinction arises out of missionization, which valorized internal states of being, in contrast to the values of adult male autonomy in the old system. In contemporary usage, *digne* and *respectable* are strongly related: being *digne* is sometimes considered a prerequisite for being *respectable,* and the two are, in fact, sometimes thought to be identical. Yet the distinction is made often enough to deserve analysis.

Être digne refers to an internal state, cultivated through regular practice. Unlike *être respectable,* it does not depend on the control of resources. Socioeconomic class plays an important role in most discussions of *respectabilité,* but even a poor woman can have *dignité.* Many of the visible signs are the same: chastity, reticence, tact. However, there is a strong sense that only she will know, in the last instance, to what degree she is *digne.* In this regard, it is related to the admonitions of the Catholic Church that each is an individual before God, answerable in the last instance to him. Some women decline to take communion, even after the rite of reconciliation, because they consider the priests' penances too categorical and lacking in nuance. We see this explicitly in the words of a student who asserted in catechism class, "I know when I am correct [with God]," and more generally in the explanation offered in an interview by an elderly woman: "I think that if we base ourselves on what the Lord demands, there will be a little more self-respect. It is that manner of wanting to do everything that leads us to debauchery." Fundamental to the notion of being *digne* is the moral judgment of the secret, hidden actions and intentions. Other people may gossip about you, but only you and God will ultimately know whether you are *digne* in your heart.

The link between *être digne* and the church is not accidental, as the concept was inherent to the process of missionization. Although similar values existed in the precolonial period, the specific emphasis on the internal state of righteousness arose in the context of conversion. But the contemporary usage of *digne* in Camfrançais was not borrowed wholesale from the missionaries; its meaning has been transformed to represent one aspect of a uniquely Cameroonian honor system. In metropolitan French, including in standard French editions of the Bible, the first and most common definition of *digne* is "worthy of something," and requires a complement. The first set of examples given in the *Petit Robert,* a standard French dictionary, are: "Personne digne d'admiration. Coupable digne d'un châtiment. Tout homme digne de ce nom. Objet digne d'intérêt, d'attention. Témoin digne de foi" (1972: 482). By contrast, *digne* is commonly used in Camfrançais without a complement. "Elle n'est pas digne" is standard usage in Camfrançais, but nearly impossible in metropolitan French. The loss of the complement occurs commonly in Camfrançais, and in this specific case reflects the semantics of *respectable*, which does not require a complement. In Camfrançais, *digne* is coming to be used in structures parallel to those of *respectable*. The semantics are coming to match the meanings, as the two terms represent complementary aspects of the same phenomenon. Biblical texts offer some basis for the Beti usage of *digne*. Although *digne* almost always occurs with a complement in the standard French translations of the Bible, there are three instances, all in the New Testament, that employ *digne* alone. In 1 Timothy 3:8, the usage of *digne* is perhaps closest to its common form in Camfrançais, referring to a pure heart or righteous character. "Les diacres, eux aussi, seront des hommes dignes, n'ayant qu'une parole, modérés dans l'usage du vin, fuyant les profits déshonnêtes" (Likewise the deacons will be *digne*, not double-tongued, not given to too much wine, fleeing dishonest profits). Here, *digne* is used to express an internal characteristic, ultimately knowable only to God, but measurable through certain external actions.

The Beti usage of *digne* is further developed in local catechisms and religious texts. Whereas in the Bible, *digne* is usually used in its standard metropolitan form, followed by a complement, in Beti religious texts it appears more often alone. In the catechism by Tonye, quoted at the beginning of this chapter, young Beti women are taught to pray "teach me to remain a true wife and a self-respecting [*digne*] teacher of the children who will be born of our love" (1986: 39). This catechism is significant because it is memorized verbatim by all young Beti women preparing for their first communion, a key sacrament in the Catholic Church. They are repeatedly tested on the material in the catechism, and their performance on these oral examinations is critical to their attaining access to communion.

Among the most significant manifestations of local Catholicism is the apparition of the Virgin Mary at Nsimalen, just south of Yaoundé, in 1986. Although the Vatican does not accept this apparition as authentic, many Beti Catholics believe strongly in it, telling stories of how they were healed, or their marriages saved, through the intercession of the Virgin. In fact, the Vatican's rejection of the apparition seems to make it all the more real to ordinary people in Cameroon, who see the Virgin's visit as supporting their claims for an indigenous church, partially independent from Rome.[7] To this day, a small number of young women continue to serve as mediums, communicating to pilgrims and penitents the wishes and advice of the Virgin. In 1989, a local priest published a collection of testimonials, including some verbatim transcripts, from this intensely local Catholic manifestation. At one point, the Virgin Mary is quoted as having said through a medium:

> My daughter, a great punishment will fall on the human race. . . . All of humanity must repent, pray, and do penitence, rosaries and confessions. Many magistrates will die. Free masonry in the churches. For the prelates no longer have self-respect [*ne sont plus dignes*]. (Ketchoua 1989: 62)

This usage of *digne* references the usage from the Book of Timothy cited above. But in this emphatically Beti context, it also resonates strongly with the local honor complex. To have self-respect implies conforming to specific local notions of righteous behavior and faith; the prelates who lack self-respect are not Beti—they are the cardinals and archbishops in Rome, those who reject the apparition of the Virgin, and indeed the autochthony of the Cameroonian church. The fact that the prelates are no longer *digne* indicates that they have wandered far from God, beyond the circle of grace (see Péristiany and Pitt-Rivers 1991).

In 1998, I went to Nsimalen myself. A different clairvoyant met with me and told me the story of Mary's apparition. After praying for some time, she was taken into a trance. At her permission, I recorded the words spoken through her, some of which I reproduce here:

> Receive the peace, the peace of my Son. . . .
> Yes, for my Son is justice.
> He is love.
> Yes, he blesses all of your enterprises. . . .
> Yes, he blesses all that you may undertake in your life.
> Yes, practice love.
> You will have life in abundance.
> Yes, for my son gives it you.
> You will be an honorable woman [*Tu seras une femme digne*].
> Yes, receive the peace.

Through the medium, the Virgin Mary equates the gift of abundant life with having self-respect, being honorable.

Here we see the close relationship between grace and *être digne* as private, internal states knowable only to God, and ultimately attributable to

him. Thus a woman who is not *digne* is not in a state of grace, and is ineli-
gible to take the sacrament of communion. Several women explained that
they do not take communion because of the irregularity of their marital
situations. One woman who has never married in the church because her
husband is Muslim said that although she sings in the choir and the parish
priest has told her to take communion, she will not. "To live that way with
a man, according to the church," she explained, "it is not *digne.*" They are
civilly married and have borne four children together: thus, by standard
external measures, she is a legally married woman and *respectable.* But
because she is not in conformity with the demands of the church, she finds
herself unworthy of the Eucharist. She alone can know where she stands
with God, and she has found herself lacking.

The other part of honor, *respectabilité,* resides in social relations and is
largely comparable to Veblen's concept of pecuniary honor. It is central to
the system of wealth in people, that is, to rights in labor and to respect. It
is cumulative over the life course, such that seniors are more *respectable*
than are juniors. To be *respectable,* you must be discreet, wise, and willing
to give advice. The fact that all of these characteristics relate to having
and dispensing knowledge points to a connection between *respectabilité*
and "having sense." Respectability is associated with status in the context
of some social interaction, rather than constituting an inherent attribute
of a person. Inhering in external measures, *respectabilité* consists of a single metric for all people, ages, and situations. People may be more or less
respectable in certain domains, but the measures themselves do not shift.
What is *digne* varies by context; what is *respectable* does not. Being *respectable* means that people must treat you in certain ways and speak to
you in a particular manner. To be *respectable* is to have achieved specific
milestones relevant to a particular interaction. One of the most significant
of these is marriage. In an interview, one of my close neighbors explained:

> For me, a *respectable* woman is one who keeps her image clean. When she
> passes, you know that this person here has to be respected. And then it is some-
> times good to be called Madame Such and Such. When someone says, "Here is
> Madame Such and Such who is passing," you have weight. But when you are
> free, someone looks and calls you Mademoiselle. Even if you are fifty years old,
> they can't call you Madame. They call you Madame, but you live with whom?
> They are going to say Madame Who? They are obligated to call you Mademoi-
> selle.

The director of the pediatric ward in a major Yaoundé hospital agreed. He noted that you only become *respectable* when you become an adult, and that for a woman, "to be an adult is to live with a man." Respectability, therefore, does not depend on your interior consciousness, but on the actions you commit in public. One man explained: "You can do bad things and still be *respectable.*" However, this is only because others have no proof of your acts; if they become widely known, you will be ashamed (*avoir honte,* or *óson*).

Being respected is associated with achievement, particularly monetary, marital, and reproductive achievement. Bad luck, witchcraft, or the ill will of powerful people can prevent a woman from being *respectable,* but not from being *digne.* Achieving *respectabilité* is therefore not a moral victory, but one of status. One of my research assistants clearly summarized this, using the example of marriage:

> A woman who hasn't had bridewealth paid for her in her village, her mother is not respected. Her relatives are not respected. She herself is not happy. So bridewealth, when someone pays bridewealth for a young girl before marriage, it is a great joy for the family.

Achieving bridewealth marriage, therefore, is a socioeconomic triumph. A bride's reward is respect, the external aspect of honor, and the medium is the money itself. External measures like economic welfare or legal marriage do not validate claims to respectability, but in fact constitute the claims.

As *respectabilité* is more a social than a moral achievement in the Beti honor system, its absence is also a social failure. Thus shame (*honte*) arises both from immoral and from asocial actions. A person can be shamed for failing to follow customary practice. For example, when I asked a young woman with a long-standing boyfriend if they had plans to marry, her answer turned to the appropriate order of marriages within a family, placing her own actions in a larger social context:

> I am not in a hurry. None of my brothers or sisters are married. . . . and according to the norms of the Christian family . . . it would be seen a little badly if you marry before your older siblings. It is not good. It's like if it were an affair of shame, of dishonor. It often creates a climate that is not good. To see her little sister marry before she does, it's a little bit of a sexual precocity that is not

always well viewed here in Africa. Since we are in Africa, we must get married in order.

The shame in this example is tied to the fact that actions have a sequence in which they should occur: the elder children should marry before the younger. But this sequence is not necessarily a moral edict. Shame can be associated, therefore, with nonconformity to either moral or social precepts—it is not necessarily an ethical failure. In Camfrançais, honor has come to consist of two discrete, but related elements: *dignité* and *respectabilité*. These two elements remain connected—for example, they both have *honte* as their inverse. Both *dignité* and *respectabilité* have similar requirements for honorability; both are based on self-dominion, including self-control, autonomy, secrecy, and as we will soon examine, discipline. Ideally, the two exist in a circular relationship; *dignité* leads to *respectabilité,* and *respectabilité*—or actions to gain it—sets the stage for a person, especially a woman, to consider herself *digne.* With these similar definitions of what constitutes honorability within each sphere, the two forms of honor do blend. Thus, for women, timing of life events becomes very important as an indication of *dignité* as well as an achievement of *respectabilité.* The two together show self-dominion, discipline, control, and foresight. But *dignité* and *respectabilité* are disparate also. The distinction between the two has arisen in the context of the Catholic Church, which has emphasized the importance of internal traits as the mark of a true Christian. *Respectabilité* is closest to Beti men's traditional honor system in that both emphasize the external, achievement, autonomy, and control. In the new importance of *dignité,* internal honor is the open door to women's increasing claims to a modern, if uncertain, honor.

The Disciplining of Honor and the Honoring of Women

Concomitant with the differentiation of internal and external honor has been a transformation in honor's markers: over the past century, *la discipline* has come to signify honorable action and *dignité* in a new way. This transformation is linked to schooling, as we will see in chapters 4 and 5. Here, however, I want to briefly introduce discipline as a new element of the contemporary Beti honor system. Discipline, which can be conceived of roughly as acting with control, keeping oneself and one's world orderly, is increasingly emphasized as an element of self-dominion. The value placed on *la discipline,* and the antipathy accorded to its opposite, *la desordre,* makes a strange fit with the rest of the Beti honor system. On the one hand, discipline refers to training in self-control, such as that maintained in school or cultivated through a commitment to prayer and the church. It therefore encourages correct adult behavior. Disorderly conduct implies a lack of self-control, and is therefore shameful. On the other hand, however, discipline contradicts the fundamental value of independence and autonomy. Many contexts—market exchanges, the loading of minibusses, for example—are exceptionally disordered as the result of participants making their own decisions and following their own inclinations. Discipline seems at once the epitome and the opposite of Beti self-dominion, depending on the relationship between the discipliner and the disciplined.

The value of discipline in the contemporary Beti honor system is directly related to schooling, and much of the ambiguity surrounding it derives from this relationship. In school, and especially the elite Catholic schools, children are explicitly trained through discipline. Indeed, some school activities appear to have no other function. Schools with reputations for particularly rigorous discipline are highly valued by parents and students alike. Through school discipline, students are thought to attain self-dominion—they will internalize the discipline of school to become self-disciplined, Christian adults. Thus, although the process of being disciplined is humiliating, its outcomes are extremely desirable: school discipline inducts children into self-dominion. The forms of self-dominion brought about by schools are specific to them. As we will see, schoolgirls (perhaps even more than schoolboys) think of themselves as new kinds of Beti—honorable in new ways linked to education, Catholicism, and indeed modernity itself.

At the same time as the content of honor has shifted, the category of those eligible for honor has expanded to include women. Although women's honor remains somewhat different, and their access to it less certain than that of men, Beti women now participate directly in the honor system. Women's honor differs from that of men in several key ways. There is a loose, but nonetheless salient association of women's honor with *dignité* (rather than *respectabilité*) and hence with explicitly Catholic values and constructs, most notably discipline. Relatedly, while economic independence is prized, women's honor is more closely related to their sexual and reproductive conduct. This clustering is reproduced in that women constitute the majority of practicing Catholics and Catholic-educated women have most strongly claimed eligibility to honor. If the traditional reference for male honor is the *nkukuma* (rich man), the prototype today for honorable Beti womanhood is the Virgin Mary.

The Festival of the Assumption, the day on which Mary ascended into heaven, holds special metaphorical significance for Catholic Beti women. On Assumption Day, many children take their first communion, the ritual that confers religious adulthood. Pubescent girls begin the ritual as children. Then, in white gowns, symbolically compared to the Bride of God, they are momentarily transformed into the Virgin Mother herself. The parents of girls undergoing communion emphasize their similarity to the Mother of Christ: virginal, chosen by God, affirming their relationship to him. After this, they are adults and members of the church. Through identification with Mary, Mother of God, these young women incorporate a strong and positive image of their future childbearing as a moral—even spiritual—act.

These girls have entered the family of the church as adult women in a somewhat different way than have the boys with whom they attended catechism classes. The boys enter the church with Mary as their intermediary, but the girls enter the family of the church by becoming Mary themselves. In parallel, in due course they will become mothers through the transformations of their own bodies, unlike their male partners.

It is the first communion, rather than the wedding, that is employed by Beti women to talk about the intersection of their faith and their gender. For example, the teacher of catechism class at Collège de la Trinité, the Catholic school where I did most of my school observation, explained that it is only at the first communion that a woman meets God as he intended, that is, as an individual pursuing her own path in life. At her wedding, the catechism teacher told me, a woman has been bent to the path of her husband. The virginity of Mary as taught by the church, the teacher explained, represents the fact that Mary knew her own mind; she followed the path that God alone had selected for her. Girls become women through the first communion; at their weddings, they only become wives.

In the precolonial period, women were not dishonorable, but rather were simply without honor. Self-dominion inhered in the status of the *mfan mot* and could therefore not apply to women. But women did not lack forms of prestige entirely. Laburthe-Tolra argues that although women could never attain the independence of men, some women had

> gifts of wisdom and reflection which were also expressed through the telling of stories and the giving of private advice, that could lead people to come to them

to settle disputes; when a woman united some of these qualities with fecundity and a life that was "*digne*," she would receive a certain celebrity. (1981: 386)[8]

But this celebrity should not be confused with the honor of men. Indeed, Laburthe-Tolra's observation comes from a section in which he discusses the contrasts not only between men and women, but also between adults and children, and between free men and slaves. That women could attain renown for their extraordinary talents surely constitutes part of the system of wealth in people as wealth in knowledge described by Guyer and outlined above in chapter 2. Insofar as a woman gained special skills, her mastery would have been valued. But as a woman, dependent on a man, her skills would not have truly been her own. It is critical to remember that in the precolonial period, wealth in people and skills could only have accrued to an autonomous man.

In many ways, women's honor relies more on self-restraint and self-monitoring than does that of men, consistent with the fact that women's honor is more explicitly Catholic, and more explicitly linked to discipline. To be *digne* today, a woman must have an economic independence from men that would have been impossible in the precolonial period. In addition, my informants consistently noted that an honorable woman must practice sexual restraint, which by contrast plays little role in the honorable self-dominion of men. A fifty-year-old woman, an active catechist in a large parish in Yaoundé, explained to me the dual bases of female self-respect:

> I am going to say how Cameroonians interpret this self-respect in women. You first look at the way she manages her sexuality, you can't avoid that. The less you are a sexual vagabond, the more you have self-respect. But that is not sufficient, because there are people who practice a certain chastity but who have a spirit of laziness. So I think that when a woman is decent it means first that she restrains her sexual activity and second that she can earn a living all alone, without waiting for the help of a man.

My interlocutor begins with sexual behavior, which rarely enters into descriptions of male honor. Next, she contrasts economic autonomy with laziness. In her account, women who attain financial independence are morally virtuous. The theme of independence resonates throughout Beti honor, but women's independence from men has an additional edge. Beyond its value as autonomy per se, women's financial independence also buttresses their chastity, or at least their control of their own sexuality, for a woman who is not dependent on a man can resist his sexual demands. Note that the speaker blends *dignité* and *respectabilité,* blurring the distinctions that we uncovered above. The actions of a woman, whether, for example, she earns her own living or is promiscuous, are taken as signs of her internal honor, her *dignité.*

When Beti women talk about honor, self-perception often appears to precede action, rather than the inverse. In keeping with Hatch's self-identity model described earlier, educated Beti women suggest that attaining discretion, financial success, and sexual restraint requires certain forms of self-perception, particularly pride (*fièrté*) and self-respect. Marie-Paule, one of my research assistants, explained why she thought that women educated in Catholic schools were different from those who were not:

> I think that it is a question of self-respect, because women who have done all of their studies in the missionary high schools have self-respect. They are very proud of themselves. And so, because they are proud, they are not dependent. They love to be financially independent from their husbands.

Here, women's self-respect is treated as synonymous with pride. It is this self-respect or pride that prevents women from tolerating dependence. My interlocutor thus views autonomy as the result of self-respect or pride, and not its cause. For a woman to attain external honor, she must first have internal self-respect. Another woman agreed, claiming that "women who have attended the Catholic high schools don't sell in the street. When they sell, it is in a good location, and they are always clean. They cannot reduce themselves to a certain level." Catholic-educated Beti women distinguish themselves by their cleanliness, their industriousness, and their pride.

We cannot leave the topic of women's access to honor without mentioning childbearing. Although Beti social organization is remarkably tolerant of premarital births, many people—especially educated women—have come to view these births as shameful. The principles on which they are judged shameful are related to discipline. Pregnancies, and especially births, that occur too early are perceived as disordered, as indicating the opposite of discipline. In as far as Beti honor equals self-dominion, a loss of self-discipline automatically brings shame. In order to perceive herself and be perceived as honorable, the young educated Beti woman thus seeks to avoid "mistimed" births. This association between early childbearing and shame is extremely significant for understanding the correlation between education and fertility.

The honor system has more varied contours for women than for men. The honor to which Beti women aspire is more directly tied to their sexual conduct, making reproductive practices all the more important. Their honor is more closely tied to the morality of the Catholic Church, and to the woman's own perception of her conformity to Catholic values. The very newness of women's claims to honor makes their honor less certain: the structure of the honor system is shifting, and the guideposts for success in honor have yet to be cemented. In addition to the changing structure of the system, uncertainty is inherent in the emphasis in women's honor on *dignité*, even though this internal worth is also judged by others based on visible, external factors, such as education and career, timing of life events, or where a woman has established her market stand. A woman cannot claim honor through founding a village, nor is acting autonomously assurance of honorability; a Beti woman must develop her sense and status of honor through shaping readings of her actions, attempting to make them consistent with values of self-dominion, from discretion to discipline.

* * *

Beti society is organized around a system of honor. Although this honor system differs from those of the Mediterranean, it has a number of similarities and can productively be compared with them. Beti honor is defined primarily by self-dominion, the autonomy prototypically associated with the *mfan mot*. Thus, Beti honor is essentially individual and not heritable under normal circumstances. Although autonomy and secrecy remain important elements of the Beti honor complex, the contents and extent of the system have changed over the past century. Women, especially educated women, are increasingly successful in claiming honor, although an honor somewhat different from that of men. The content of honor has also been reoriented toward the values of church and school. In this way, the internal elements of honor, or *dignité*, are increasingly salient.

Because educated women orient their actions toward it, the contemporary honor system plays a significant role in explaining the reproductive practices of young, educated women. These women seek to perceive themselves as honorable through discipline and modernity. These values have acquired currency through the church, but also through schooling. Indeed,

Catholic-educated women perceive themselves as distinctly more honor-able than their less-educated counterparts, and attribute their childbearing practices to this difference. Regardless of whether educated women are right to claim greater discipline and honor—and many would argue they are not—the fact that they orient their social practice toward reinforcing their self-identity as honorable in this way is significant to the social and demographic patterns of the Beti. In chapter 4, we will look at the fusion of schooling with this system of honor, focusing on how the social organi-zation of schools selects certain students and excludes others.

CHAPTER FOUR

School in the Social World

School has altered values and perceptions to produce a hierarchy: school education is more valued than traditional instruction; being a teacher is more prestigious than being a farmer; wearing a dress is more dignified than wearing a skin. —Henrietta Moore, *Space, Text, and Gender*

We have seen how inequality has become institutionalized among the Beti over the course of the past century, centrally through schools, the Catholic Church, and the state. We have also noted that although honorable self-dominion, defined by having sense (*mfefeg*), continues to epitomize Beti honor, the same institutions of school, church, and state that have contributed to increased inequality have also instigated significant changes in the content and social distribution of honor. We now turn to schools, specifically to Catholic schools, to investigate in greater detail their role in the contemporary systems of honor and social inequality. We will see that although Catholic schooling is dramatically circumscribed in its distribution, it has come to serve as the prototypical form of socialization for honorable Beti adulthood (cf. Bledsoe et al. 1999: 1). That is, school values paradigmatically define honorable adulthood although schooling is open only to a few. Access to honor, particularly in the sense of *respectabilité*, is thus unevenly distributed by socioeconomic class. In this respect, Catholic schooling has reinforced the partial equation of honor with status.

The links between socioeconomic privilege, education, and honor in southern Cameroon function on multiple levels. This partial equation has deep historical roots among the Beti, as we saw in chapter 2; the title *nkukuma,* that is, the founder-leader of a minor lineage (*mvog*), can be translated as "wealthy man." In the precolonial period, wealth and honor were closely associated, and the honor of schooling arises in part from the refraction of this association through the prism of contemporary society.

The prestige of school-based honorability is also related to its scarcity: access to school, and particularly to the upper grades, is very limited; this limitation alone generates some of the value attached to advanced education (Bourdieu 1984: 133). Finally, schooling has catalyzed a transformation in the definition of honor, as we saw in the chapter 3. Formal education, and especially Catholic schooling, is thought to impart discipline, and therefore self-dominion, above all. As discipline has come to occupy a more central location in the honor system, formal education has gained in significance. Although alternative pathways to honor continue to exist, school has become a privileged site for socialization in honorable self-dominion.

The very centrality of schooling as a locale for developing women's honor makes it hotly contested. Should all girls go to school? How long should they stay? What about the more elite boarding schools? Are they good? Although the proposition that girls should attend some school is no longer controversial, debate continues in some communities about where, how much, and what kind of schooling girls should receive. Before laying out why schooling is desired—so very intently desired—by young women, we need to remember that this desire is not unopposed. A small but vocal and influential proportion of Beti society—especially older, rural men—strongly opposes girls' schooling on the grounds that it makes them too proud, and too much like men. Perhaps paradoxically, the basis of the opposition is the same principle that leads young women to desire education: the idea that women's access to social prestige, and indeed honor, is produced in and through schooling.

At the extreme, the older, rural men opposed to girls' schooling—and particularly Catholic schooling—view it as interlinked with witchcraft, homosexuality, and the rejection of procreation. In particular, these men assert that schoolgirls are at particular risk of *evu,* a common form of sorcery in southern Cameroon that usually possesses only men. In exchange for power and wealth, *evu* "eat" a man's lineal kin. *Evu* is thus consumptive (of people, particularly kin) at the same time as it is productive (of wealth and power). On rare occasions, *evu* may also possess a woman, instilling in her a man's desires (for sex with women) and making it impossible for her—or the women whom she seduces—to conceive.[1] Although boarding school dorms are probably universally imagined to foster same-sex passions and pleasures, it is critical to note that the threat of *evu* to female fecundity is more than nonprocreative sex, represented in the social figure of the "lesbian until graduation." The danger is far greater, for *evu*—or even sexual contact with another woman who is possessed by *evu*—leaves a woman permanently sterile. Thus, girls' education, and particularly elite Catholic education, is viewed by some as endangering their reproductive potential, their very identity as women.

This fear has traction in part because of the symbolic parallels between Catholicism, particularly the sacrament of communion, and *evu*. Both are "put in your mouth" when you are a child by an adult initiate, and through this act of ritualized patriphagy, the initiate enters into a relationship with a powerful, invisible force. In both cases, the relationship is mediated through the acquisition of a body of specialized, secret knowledge, which may bring wealth and power. Powerful men—particularly priests and politicians—are generally assumed to have access to occult powers, if only because they are powerful and successful. When I asked why our bishop did not do more to fight against witchcraft, my favorite "uncle" shrugged and responded: "So how do you think he got to be bishop?"

In addition to the symbolic parallels between Catholicism and *evu*, Catholic boarding schools are thought by certain older, rural men to be particularly dangerous for girls because by treating male and female pupils the same, schools make women resemble men in their comportment, independence, and expectations for life. The girls become too proud, the argument goes, so that they no longer know their place. In this sense, the dangers of *evu* may be almost metaphorical, because of its masculinizing effects. But whether literally or figuratively, schoolgirls are accused of *evu* and school dorms are feared to be rife with the homosexual, antiprocreative sex that can result from women's possession by this strange spirit.

Educated Beti women laugh at these notions, calling them old wives' tales. But they do not dispute the transformative power of schooling. Education *does* change people, they assert, it makes women less willing to bear children indiscriminately, and may even make women more like men. But none of that is associated with *evu*, they argue, and certainly not with anthropophagy or homosexual desires or encounters. School makes women resemble men, they counter, because it makes them rational, modern, and honorable: "people of the future." And "people of the future" is something that most young Beti women very much want to be.

The Value Placed on Education

There is ample evidence in writing, talk, and action that Cameroonians in general, and Beti in particular, place a very high value on formal education.

Newspaper articles declare education as the solution to *la crise,* the basis of social betterment, and even as the most sacred element of the national patrimony (Ntonga 1998; Tchasse 1998). At the height of a national scandal over cheating on the public exams, one editorial argued, "You can amuse yourself with anything in a country, but never in the world did any country fake its diplomas" (Atangana 1998). Cameroonian law declares formal schooling as the "first national priority" (law 98/004 cited in Mana 1998), and indeed school construction was one of the first major undertakings of the national government after independence. The Catholic Church in Cameroon defends its educational mission as "able to give Cameroon valuable citizens" (Ze 1998), legitimating religious schooling on the grounds of serving state interests. In interviews and everyday conversation, Beti call schooling important, even essential. And in fact, parents endure great financial hardship to send children to school; Eloundou-Enyegue (1997) found that even faced with financial crisis, most Beti parents kept their children in school, although they did sometimes shift them to less expensive schools.

In chapter 2, we saw how the emergence of institutionalized inequality among the Beti was linked to formal schooling. But in addition to creating the basis of inequality among Beti, this close interaction with schooling and the state provided Beti with distinct advantages vis-à-vis other groups. As Franqeville (1984) has noted, the majority of the administrative and managerial class in Yaoundé is Beti; this privilege rests on their high rates of education. The Beti are the most highly educated ethnic group in contemporary Cameroon, both in terms of proportion literate and average years of school attended (Atangana-Mebara et al. 1982). And they pride themselves on this fact. Indeed, education has become part of Beti ethnic identity; being Beti, being honorable, and being educated are symbolically parallel.

In exploring the value of education in the Beti honor system, we must ask why schooling is esteemed and in what ways the worth of schooling is convertible into other values.[2] In interviews with schoolgirls, I often asked, "What does it mean to be educated?" The answers to this question touch on many aspects of life, from economics and employment to rationality and fertility. In every case, however, it was clear that to be educated is to be honorable, to be transformed, and to have more options. Thus, even when schooling is valued for the economic prospects it offers, those economic benefits come to their full fruition in permitting a woman to be economically independent and thereby honorable. We will first look at the economic reasons that women value education, and then turn to how women envision the consequences of education on childbearing, rationality, and foresight.

The potential for an independent income is frequently cited by women as an important reason to pursue an education. Schooling, especially in the liberal arts rather than professional schools, is seen as the ideal pathway to good jobs and high incomes: honorable work is defined as clean work, the kind performed by educated people.[3] Despite the dramatic downturn of the economy that has limited the number of white-collar job openings over the past decade, education is still perceived as the means to a better job and higher incomes. To some degree this is accurate: although there are some opportunities for women without formal education to support themselves independently in Yaoundé, in small towns it is all but impossible. The only truly independent women—unmarried or divorced, living without natal kin—that I know of in Mbeya are schoolteachers. As we saw in the chapter 3, independence has long been—and remains—an important part of honorable self-dominion. As women are coming to claim honor, their ability to fend for themselves economically is consequential (cf. Clark 1994). Relatively well-paid work permits economic independence from men: schooling thus enables women to attain one aspect of honor.

The significance of economic independence to many young women is in fact only partially about money; underlying the emphasis on financial independence is a value on independence of thought and action, a personal ability to look to the future. Thus one young woman who had recently left school to marry explained that she encourages her younger sisters to stay in school. Formal education, she said,

> is important in life because you seek what to do tomorrow to live better. Because my husband himself is just doing odd jobs now. Women should also have something to do, that you don't just wait that he gives you five hundred [CFA, about one USD] in the morning, tomorrow another five hundred. . . . So, you yourself need something. That's why schooling is good. Because you search there what to do tomorrow, to have something.

This woman explains the value of school in primarily financial terms: education, she argues, could free her sisters from the need to ask their husbands for pocket money every day. But these financial terms have a strong moral valence; a woman should have work to do, a life and resources beyond her husband's. In earning her own money, a woman fulfills the social expectations of an honorable woman in that she is not dependent on her husband.

The logic of financial independence that holds within marriage is even more powerful when a union dissolves. Most Beti women know of cases in which a man has left his wife and children. Unless the wife is able to support herself and her children, these tales of abandonment become stories of destitution. Thus, some women emphasize that schooling is valuable as insurance against impoverishment should their husband desert them. One woman, who had been legally divorced, lived in large town between Mbeya and Yaoundé. She supported herself and her children as a typist, and reminded any young woman who would listen that had she not gone to school, she would have been stuck with her alcoholic and good-for-nothing former husband. In an interview, a student who had been raised by her maternal grandparents explained how her education could spare her the hardships that her own mother had faced:

> I want to study for my life first. Because you never know. You could involve yourself [with a man], perhaps getting married. After, he ruins you. You would be obligated to return to your parents. So, it is not good. On the other hand, when you work, [you] have your money, if there are problems you can separate. You stay in your place, he stays in his. You rent your house, he stays.

As we have seen, this depiction of the future as dark, unknowable, and likely dangerous is common. But my interlocutor provocatively argues that schooling provides insurance against these dangerous futures—although you never know what will happen, if you go to school and have a job, you are secure. Many women echo this suggestion that schooling enables women to confront unknown circumstances successfully, whether from an economic or social perspective. The value of schooling thus lies partly in its expanding the field of possibility—a woman who has been to school has more options than one who has not, and she uses her greater field of choice to confront the unpredicted more effectively. Schooling is opposed to disorder.

One student explained that she continued her studies not so much to secure her own future, but to provide economic support to her family. These upward "intergenerational flows of wealth" (Caldwell 1982), in which educated children provide economic support for the family that paid their school fees, have often been noted in the West African literature (e.g., Barnes 1986; Bledsoe 1992). Yet the motivation to take care of parents was, surprisingly, seldom mentioned by the women I knew or interviewed. Even older women, talking about their investments in the education of their children, rarely noted that they anticipated a financial return. Many Beti children do indeed provide financial support to their families, but the promise of independent adulthood rhetorically overshadows the repayment motive for educating children. Parents may hope that their children will care for them in their old age, but they rarely attribute choices about schooling to that hope.

Beyond its financial advantages, schooling is valued by young women because it is thought to construct honorable habits and tastes, to cultivate honorable modes of action and reaction. This honorability is understood to be evident in areas ranging from reproductive practices to personal grooming styles. The perception that schooling prepares women to be honorable is especially widespread among women who are in the process of becoming educated. Of course, the perceived relationship between schooling and honorability becomes circular: among women who aspire to education, the actions of educated women are defined as honorable actions, and their tastes are defined as refined tastes. As Bourdieu notes in reference to a strongly parallel case in France, it is therefore "impossible ever to determine whether the dominant feature appears as distinguished or noble because it is dominant—i.e., because it has the privilege of defining . . . what is noble or distinguished as being exactly what it itself is" (1984: 92). But this is a problem for analysts of Beti society, not for its members. Especially for schoolgirls, who see in their education the pathway to privilege and prestige, the equation of schooling with honorable actions and tastes is impeccable.

Since honor is defined through certain kinds of understanding, schooling can serve as the mediator of new, explicitly modern, forms of honor. Another young woman described this explicitly: "When a woman has done a lot of schooling, she knows that it is emancipation that makes girls evolved [évoluées], that they not be like our mothers." In the French colonies, the term évolué had a legal definition: under the Third Republic, certain Africans who were literate in French and demonstrated a commitment to European styles of life could become French citizens, thereby liberated from the corvée and the indigénat. Evolution, therefore, should be understood here in terms of class mobility and orientation to a modern world. It is historically very much the equal of legal emancipation, with the same sweeping consequences. In the Francophone postcolonies, the évolués are no longer a legal category, yet by holding onto the title, schoolgirls are claiming western modernity as part of the honorability that school confers. Throughout the talk of Beti schoolgirls is evidence of the notion that schooling creates rational, and thus honorable, women. One young student explained the relationship between schooling and rational thinking as follows:

> To become educated means to have . . . more good experience in life. For example, to change the rhythm from before, to correct the errors of society. . . . There is a big difference between those who have not gone to school and those who have gone to school. . . . If you are educated, when you want to do something you see if it's good, what it could produce, before you react. You nonetheless foresee the inconvenience before doing something. . . . When you already have experience, you say to yourself for example, "If I do this thing, there will be positive and negative points." If the positive points are superior, you choose the positive. If the negative points are superior, you drop the subject.

We see here how "sense," reflection, and knowledge—long central to honorable Beti adulthood—are being transformed into traits learned only at school. The more that this occurs, the more that Beti honor becomes dependent on formal education. Insofar as something as central to *mfefeg* as the foresight to consider the positive and negative possible outcomes of an action is represented as something that derives from school, then schooling becomes a necessary precursor for honor. As among the Marakwett of Kenya described by Moore (1986), schooling among the Beti is reorienting long-standing systems of value, making book knowledge superior to traditional modes of knowing.

Reproductive practice and the management of childbearing play particularly central roles in women's honor, and they are similarly central to the way that educated women talk about the benefits of schooling. The knowledge, reasoning, and discipline that they have acquired in school should make them different kinds of mothers—both more cautious about having children only under propitious circumstances, and better able to care for children and raise them wisely. Educated young women assert again and again that they, unlike the uneducated, do not bear children "in disorder" or "no matter [which] way" but systematically choose when and with whom to bear a child. Provocatively, this perspective resonates with the educational objectives of the foreign policy and development agencies, which perceive schooling as a route to creating modern citizens who practice low fertility (e.g., Hari 1991). Also like the policymakers, the schoolgirls are clearly self-interested; regardless of the observable effects of schooling on rationality, maintaining the equation of schooling and reason has clear advantages for educated women, who thereby acquire the social capital of rationality in a community that has long valued *mfefeg*. If being rational is the modern version of having sense, then controlling access to rationality is very powerful indeed.

Another young woman I interviewed had left school two years earlier but hoped to return. She explained how she saw the value of schooling:

> There is a very big difference between women who went to school or who are going to school and women who never went to school. First of all, women who are going to school are instructed and so they reflect logically. For example, a woman who went to school cannot have lots of children when she doesn't have a lot of resources, because they showed her at school the inconveniences that could bring. So a woman who has been to school really knows "If I have lots of children and I don't have the resources, that could have this consequence," but a woman who has not been to school, she doesn't know any of that.

Like the student quoted above, this woman talks about weighing costs and benefits, thinking rationally or logically, and acting with foresight. But in her focus on reproduction, the second woman seems to limit the activity of reason. The outcome of reflection is predetermined; the decision is premade: "She cannot have lots of children . . . because they showed her the inconveniences that could bring." In contrast, the first young woman clearly values the ability to think for herself—there is a sense that honor lies as much in the action of weighing alternatives as in the choices that she will eventually make.

It is in this move, from identifying honor in the process of reasoning to identifying modernity in reason's outcomes, that I think we hear most clearly Beti schoolgirls quoting international policymakers and NGOs. That they should do so is not surprising. They are converts to modernity and have learned by heart its discursive styles and key phrases. But it is perhaps ironic that its emphasis on products rather than process should make the quotation conspicuous. For Foucault (1979) as for Weber (1958), the mark of modernity was the move toward the micromanagement of process. For both Beti schoolgirls and policymakers, the modernity associated with schooling entails controlled fertility. But the meanings ascribed to controlled fertility, and the methods envisioned to achieve it, sometimes differ. For policymakers, fertility control is fundamentally tied to concerns about population growth and age structure; it is the outcome (lower fertility) that matters, rather than the process or practice of achieving it. Why education should be associated with lower fertility has long been a "black box" that policymakers have preferred to leave closed, saying simply that "the increase in the education of women and girls contributes to greater empowerment of women, to a postponement of the age of marriage and to a reduction in the size of families" (United Nations 1994, sec. 11.3).

For Beti schoolgirls, the distinction between honorable process and modern outcomes is not so clear, and the process often matters more. It is the practice of reason, rather than the outcome of lower fertility, that defines honor. In their view of the world, educated women manage their fertility as an expression of their developed consciousness and their modern honorability. Schooling teaches mental skills, particularly foresight and reason, which constitute the basis of a modern, rational honorability. Controlled fertility thus becomes an expression of modern honorability, mediated through educated rationality. This is clear, for example, in the social analysis offered by Marlyse, a student in eleventh grade at la Trinité, who began her explanation of the value of school with restrained reproduction. To be educated, she said, means

> to better understand life. Because my cousins with whom I don't get along, those are girls who haven't attended school a lot, who stopped at primary school. And now, they each have at least one child. And when they see me still going to school, and that I don't yet have a child, they detest me. But me, I love them!

Marlyse explicitly identifies early childbearing as both a cause and an effect of school failure. In the case she presents, the distribution of advanced schooling and early childbearing is perfectly complementary. Still, given the certain social validity that childbearing has, it is hard to imagine that all of her cousins experience enough envy and resentment to truly detest her for her alternate path. One might formulate a different hypothesis about the cause of their resentment in reading the rest of the quote. After asserting that they detest her while she loves them, Marlyse continued:

> So, they have a certain mentality. I don't understand. They are brutes! You can sense that they are not transformed. You can sense that they have not been to school, in their manner of reacting, their manner of dressing. So we can say that an educated girl and an uneducated girl are very different.

With her dramatic rhetorical style and frank prejudice, Marlyse focuses on how uneducated women lack refinement in dress, speech, and mental habits. These are the everyday practices that school discipline is to cultivate. Marlyse calls the refinement of these habits and practices "transformation," a term that resonates both with the idea of evolution or maturation and again with classic Beti ideas of acquiring special knowledge and having *mfefeg*. The distinction Marlyse draws between the educated and uneducated woman therefore parallels the distinctions between the colonial elite and the *population indigène* and between adults and children. Finally, Marlyse's insistence that she loves her cousins, even though they are untransformed brutes who detest her, is either a remarkable achievement of Christian charity or else a degree of cynicism worthy of the American presidential election.

Beti women who have attended school, and particularly Catholic school, argue that education transforms not only how, when, and with whom they have children, but also how they raise those children. The assertion that formal education will make them better wives and mothers, more able to raise the men of tomorrow, retains pride of place among traditional arguments for sending women to school (Denzer 1992; Hunt 1990). Thus Annette, an articulate high school student, equates schooling with modern values and argues that this modernity creates better wives and mothers:

> Those who have attended school are already different from the illiterates. Even if she doesn't work, the advice that [an educated woman] gives to her children could make them become the people of the future. Women who have not been to school don't know certain things. For example, those who have not been to school in the village, they will tell you that girls are for marriage, and that you should fear women who go to school too much. . . . While the educated women say that first you must finish school. The child isn't fleeing. You can give birth after[ward]. While the mothers in the village are saying that you need to search for your husband already . . . she who is educated says that the husband comes after. Men are now searching for wives who are educated, wives who have been to school, wives who have something, and wives who can improve their life.

Closely linked to having sense, advising is one important aspect of being a full adult, classically associated with male elders. By claiming that educated mothers will give wise advice to the benefit of their children,

Annette is therefore associating good mothering with classic male honor and then linking both of these to school. Like the opponents of women's schooling, Annette is rhetorically associating education for women with their masculinization, suggesting that school-educated women can give advice like men. Next, Annette notes that educated women think more carefully than do the uneducated, particularly about the pacing and ordering of life events, such as marriage and childbearing. Here again, school provides foresight: education provides a way of preparing for the future that is not available to uneducated women. Finally, Annette ends with the assertion that men, too, have changed. In the final analysis, she concludes that women should go to school because men want educated wives.

It is critical to note that the importance of these claims is not their statistical validity—some are actually counterfactual—but rather the role they play in motivating and justifying the reproductive practices of educated women. That is, these ideologies of school, rationality, discipline, and honor are horizons that educated women employ in navigating the uncertainties of their lives. Women in school often have clear and compelling ideas about their distinct identity as increasingly disciplined, modern, and honorable. This self-identity serves as the basis of their aspirations for the future and orients their actions in reference to schooling and childbearing. Relationships between discipline, modernity, and honor—all credited to formal education—are thus key horizons in the vital conjunctures in the lives of schoolgirls.

Schooling lies at the crossroads of the Beti honor system in transition. The importance of education in part reflects the long-standing idea that honor is found in knowledge and consciousness. Schooling can thus epitomize proper Beti socialization despite being relatively new and not open to all. At the same time, schooling has transformed the categories of knowledge and consciousness, equating the more desirable forms with "modernity," social change, and new choices. For some Beti, schooling has now come to be equated with honorable adulthood; educated women are thus categorically honorable.

Comparing Catholic and Public Schools

Catholic schooling epitomizes schooling in general, and Catholic schools are thought to create most perfectly honorable women out of female students. As a result, the difference between Catholic-educated women and public-educated women symbolically parallels the difference between educated and uneducated women more broadly. It is worth briefly reflecting on the ironic position of Catholic schooling here: Catholic schools, even more than public schools, are seen as promoting family planning and women's autonomy in the household; Catholic schools thus effectively promote the agenda of secular modernity. Beti schoolgirls perceive no conflict between the modern lives of consumer comforts and limited childbearing to which they aspire and the teachings of school and church. To them, the Catholic Church is modernity incarnate.

Throughout my demographic survey, the whole research team met weekly to discuss how the work was going and what we were finding. In one of our group discussions, two of my research assistants disagreed as to what the exact distinction was between Catholic- and public-educated women. Although both of the speakers, and indeed the entire group, appeared quite convinced that the difference was tangible, they had varying interpretations of it. Veronique spoke first, focusing on the disparity in women's experiences and knowledge:

> Women who did not receive an education in a Catholic high school—I can say that these women are also a little naïve in some way. Because already you will find that they give birth to children like that, without limit. Perhaps they don't have enough money [for their children], and then even in their household, there are lots of things that they don't do because they haven't received that education from the religious sisters, so there is really a difference.

While a wide variety of people have told me that educated women have a wider scope of experience and are therefore less naïve than are the less educated, what is noteworthy here is that Veronique applies the same differentiation to Catholic- and public-educated women. The behaviors of which she accuses women educated in public schools—negligence and excessive fertility—are identical to the accusations made of women who have not been to school. The implication is that public education is little better than no education at all, and only Catholic education can successfully impart the honor ascribed to education broadly. When Marie-Paule responded to Veronique, she did not question the merits of Catholic schooling, but only disagreed as to their form. Instead of knowledge, she suggested, Catholic school imparts certain dispositions, particularly pride and self-dominion. We examined her comments in chapter 3, focusing on the relationship Marie-Paule sets up between pride and independence. Now we must attend to the specific role of Catholic schools in fostering this relationship:

> I think that it is a question of self-respect, because women who have done all of their studies in the missionary high schools have self-respect. They are very proud of themselves. And so, because they are proud, they are not dependent.

Marie-Paule emphasizes that Catholic-educated women have a certain comportment that distinguishes them from those with a public education. It is critical to note here that although both Veronique and Marie-Paule have attended Catholic school, neither was exclusively Catholic-educated. Both had also attended public schools. Therefore when Marie-Paule talks about the self-respect of women educated *exclusively* in Catholic schools, it is not self-aggrandizing. She is speaking admiringly of women with an attribute she does not possess, although she has something like it. Here again, Catholic schooling is opposed to public schooling in a form parallel to the opposition between schooling and its absence. Catholic schooling serves as the prototype of good schooling.

The same distinctions of knowledge and self-dominion are visible in the negative case as well. Women who fail to conform to the norms of moral sexual behavior ascribed to Catholic-educated women may have their training itself drawn into question. It is a social syllogism: Catholic-educated women are honorable. X is not honorable. Therefore, X cannot be Catholic-educated. One of my neighbors in Yaoundé was trying to help me locate women to interview. On one occasion she explained that she had found someone who lived nearby, but that this woman was not suitable for my study, because, as she noted:

> It is true that she attended Catholic high schools, but their references are not very good; so, these are low-quality private high schools. I think that her education is of the same value as that in the public high school, because she had multiple boyfriends. It is true that she did not admit it, but in her manner of responding, I understood.

This comment, dense with inference, contains three points important for my argument. First, my neighbor equates low-quality Catholic schools with public schools, implicitly constructing a hierarchy among Catholic schools and between Catholic and public schools, but not among public schools. Second, she infers that the schools attended by the would-be interviewee were of low quality because she had several boyfriends, implying that since good Catholic schools teach sexual restraint, a girl who does not practice sexual restraint cannot have attended a good Catholic school. High-quality Catholic schools are thus by definition effective at social engineering: a misbehaving student is not evidence that the school failed, but that she lied about having attended. Finally, my research assistant notes that she inferred that the interviewee had had multiple boyfriends from her manner of speaking, her comportment. Unfortunately, I did not think to ask at the time what that manner of speaking was.

Catholic institutions epitomize schools for many Beti today, such that the differences between Catholic- and public-educated women parallel the differences between the educated and the illiterate. There are many reasons why Catholic schools are so appreciated. They are often older, as we saw in the chapter 3, and remain more expensive. The most elite schools have difficult entrance exams, and all are known for their relatively stringent discipline. In many cases, they have fewer students per class than do the public schools. But regardless of the reasons, Catholic schools are represented as ideal socialization for Beti adulthood, instilling honorable values and comportment. Catholic schooling is thus esteemed as a locus for the attainment of honor, clarifying why some endure hardship to attend it. Only a few even have the option of striving for the honor reportedly imparted by Catholic education. We now turn to how and why access to schooling is limited and consider some of the ways in which those who are Catholic educated may be preselected to be honorable.

Selection into Catholic Secondary School

The cost, distance, and academic demands associated with Catholic secondary schools make them unavailable to many would-be students. Indeed, part of the high value placed on Catholic schooling derives from its limited distribution. In 1989, more than 34,000 students were enrolled in public schools in the Central Province, another 17,000 in non-Catholic private schools, but fewer than 10,000 in Catholic schools (National Geography Division of Cameroon 1989: planche 15). Although students focus on the role of schooling in transforming them, in making them into honorable women, it is critical to notice that only a limited number of women are able to attend school through the upper grades, and still fewer in the preferred private schools. Schoolgirls are a highly selected group, and many of their characteristics are surely the product of the processes of selection. We will look first at the ways that access to school is limited, then at the processes that lead to school dropout—two key moments of selection.

Entry into Catholic secondary school is limited in a variety of ways. Owing to the high cost of a private education, its students come disproportionately from relatively small families with access to the formal economy. Schools are heavily concentrated in urban areas (although la Trinité is rural); urban children therefore experience less resistance to going to school. A child who goes to a private secondary school may be chosen from among her siblings because of her birth order or because she is particularly talented; many families educate only a few of their children to the secondary level, and educational variation within a family can be substantial. Many scholars have noted the enthusiasm with which Beti parents encourage their children to "become who they are." Beti parents and guardians spend a great deal of time observing children to identify the talents that will be fostered with training. There are thus multiple axes on which students are differentiated from nonstudents; each axis can be formalized into a principle of selection. I focus here on household, institutional, and life-historical selection.

Household-based Selection

Households are differentially capable of paying school fees and are differentially committed to education. Women who come from elite families or those highly committed to education are more likely to attend school—and also more likely to practice limited childbearing—than are women from less advantaged backgrounds. There is a strong and consistent effect of household income on children's school attendance across a range of societies (e.g., Caldwell, Reddy, and Caldwell 1985; Glick and Sahn 2000), probably due both to the parents' greater ability to pay and to the various forms of "cultural capital" that children from such families bring to school (Bourdieu 1984, 1993; Bourdieu and Passeron 1971). More attuned to the educational field than their less advantaged counterparts, the children of the elite find school more congenial, and their teachers provide them more positive reinforcement.

A couple of studies have shown that children from large families are less likely to persist in advanced education than are children from smaller families (see Blake 1989; Lloyd and Gage-Brandon 1992; but see also Montgomery and Lloyd 1999). The inverse association between school attainment and number of siblings could arise through a number of pathways. If the total amount that parents have to spend on children's education is fixed in advance and independent of family size, then children born in large families will simply get a smaller share of the same pie. That leads to an explanation consonant with Easterlin's theory that cohort size significantly shapes individual outcomes(1980). Conversely, if parents select how many children to bear based on their plans for how much education to give each of them, then the explanation for higher academic achievement of children from small families falls more in line with Becker's hypothesis of a "quality-quantity trade-off" (1991). Finally, if the kinds of people who like to have lots of children are also—by some coincidence—also the kinds of people who disregard school, then the proper explanation is a selectivity argument. In fact, most likely all three processes are at work, to greater or lesser degrees at different times and places.

The relationship between household income and school attendance is known from quantitative survey data, but in interviews students focus more on parental commitment to school. Again and again, students insisted that their parents were not well-off but had sacrificed to "send them far." One student, whose four siblings were all attending private schools, explained that she does well because her parents have invested in her education:

> It is because I am always in class. They [the school administration] rarely suspend me [for school fees]. They never even suspended me. My parents always arrange to pay. I wanted to specify that it's not because they have money—it's a sacrifice.

Similarly, Marie, whose story is recounted in chapter 7, bore a child and then returned to school. She explained her ability to continue her studies as the result of her father's attitudes, particularly toward the schooling of girls:

> Because my father doesn't accept bad advice. People say, "No, when a girl does that [gets pregnant], you drop her, you abandon her." He says, "No, she is my daughter. No matter what she does, she will always go to school." Because there are plenty of girls, as soon as you give birth like I did, they [your parents] drop you.

At one level, it is clearly the case that parents differ in their willingness to invest in, and sacrifice for, their children's schooling. On another level, however, it is hard to separate sacrifice from ability to pay. More privileged parents appear more committed to their children's schooling, in the sense that they push their children harder, give them more assistance, and are less likely to withdraw them from school if they fail a grade. Because "help" with school so often has a financial component, it is hard to know how much of what looks—to me as to the students themselves—like parental commitment is simply the differential ability to pay. That said, I will argue that parents' commitment to the education of their children, while difficult to assess and even more difficult to quantify, matters for their children's access to schooling.

Partially independent from income, parental attitudes affect how household values are organized. These differential attitudes are connected to the emergence of the institutionalized inequality described in chapter 2: family "taste," in the sense used by Bourdieu (1984), has powerful symbolic counterparts in attitudes about school. Marie's father cares deeply about the schooling of his daughter, not only as a result of his social and economic position, but certainly in part because of them. Her father is a prominent figure in Yaoundé society, educated, urbane, and well-spoken. He has traveled extensively, and—like many of the Yaoundé elite—has a number of cousins and nephews living in Europe. These things do not uniformly cause Marie's father to want her to pursue her studies, but they are certainly relevant.

Very few households, especially since the onset of *la crise,* have the resources to send all of their children to a private high school. Even when a benefactor, such as a priest or wealthy relative, pays the school fees, most families must choose which children to push into advanced grades. Yet parents generally try to allow all their children to start at schools of equal quality; many families make significant economic sacrifices to do so. The action of differentiation between children within a family comes primarily in rates of attrition. Given that resources are very scarce, many parents will withdraw a child from school for relatively minor infractions (Eloundou-Enyegue 1997). Thus household selection reinforces—and is reinforced by—institutional selection.

Institutional Selection: Grades and Money

Of the many ways that access to Catholic secondary schooling is limited, two are particularly formalized: exams and fees. These structures intersect with the more individual and variable patterns of household-based selection, so that girls who attend school share many important traits not caused by school. It is partly on the basis of these preexisting similarities that schoolgirls construct the idea of a unified community of the educated, characterized by a presumably coherent commitment to honorable discipline.

All Francophone schools in the Central Province follow the same institutional structure (see table 4.1). Most children start primary school between the ages of four and six. The primary sequence consists of six grades (K–5), of which many children must repeat at least one as a result of poor performance. There is no formal tracking in primary school, although there are certainly qualitative differences among schools. These differences are not all in favor of the private institutions. Although classes are often larger there, public schools employ only teachers who are formally trained at the École Normale. Public schools are also conducted exclusively in French from the first grade, while private primary schools may teach in French or in an indigenous language, or both. At the end of primary school is a public exam called the BCE (*brevet des cours elementaires*). Students who pass the BCE are theoretically eligible to continue to secondary school. However, public high schools, locally called *lycées*, will only accept students into the sixth grade (*sixième*) who are under age fifteen: there is therefore only a limited window of opportunity to attend a *lycée*.[4] Most private schools, including Catholic schools, by contrast, do not have age limits.

Unlike at the primary level, there are multiple distinct tracks in secondary education. The most significant distinction is between technical and general education. Technical schools offer job-specific training, as in carpentry, auto mechanics, or tailoring; general schools offer standard academic courses, with no job training. Both tracks are offered by private and public schools. In both the general and technical tracks, secondary school consists of two parts, called "cycles." The first cycle is four years long, and the second cycle is three. At the end of the first cycle is another public exam called the BEPC (*brevet d'études du premier cycle*). According to Père Amerin, fewer than 40 percent of candidates pass the BEPC the first time; however, students are permitted to repeat the year of failed classes,

TABLE 4.1   **Order of grades and exams in the Cameroonian school system**

School	Grade name	Public exam	Approximate U.S. equivalent
École primaire	Sil		Kindergarten
	Cours préparatoire		1st grade
	Cours élémentaire 1		2nd grade
	Cours élémentaire 2		3rd grade
	Cours moyen 1		4th grade
	Cours moyen 2	BCE	5th grade
Collège or lycée, premier cycle	Sixième		6th grade
	Cinquième		7th grade
	Quatrième		8th grade
	Troisième	BEPC	9th grade
Collège or lycée, second cycle	Seconde		10th grade
	Première	Probatoire	11th grade
	Terminale	Baccalauréat	12th grade

and to retake the exam the following year. In my survey of 184 women with some Catholic secondary education, a few women reported trying to pass the BEPC up to four times, and nearly 30 percent of women had taken it at least twice.

The repetition of classes, as we will see later in the chapter, serves as a major filter for entry into the advanced classes. Only parents with both access to some financial resources and a commitment to their children's education will continue to pay school fees for a child who has repeatedly failed. However, as huge numbers of children repeatedly fail their exams and are forced to repeat or leave school, repeating grades becomes the norm. In 1998, I collected the reported ages for students taking the BEPC exam at la Trinité. If they advanced through school without repeating any classes, a student would confront the BEPC at age sixteen. But we see that by the tenth year of school in a moderately elite private school, the modal age is two years behind recommended grade for age, and some students are upward of five years behind. The results are shown in figure 4.1.

Students who pass the BEPC may continue in the second cycle. In the second cycle, students must select a *serie,* or broad topic of specialization. In general education, the available series include philosophy, math, and science. The series are called by letters: "A" signifies philosophy. Some of the series have subseries, such as A4—literature—a nice coincidence, as A4 also refers to the size of paper on which documents are typed. The three grades that constitute the second cycle are named *seconde, première,* and

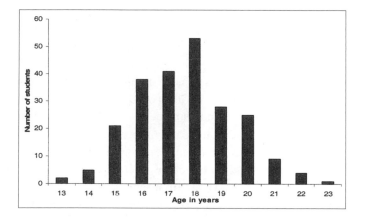

FIGURE 4.1. Ages of students taking the BEPC exam, Collège de la Trinité, 1998

terminale. There is no exam at the end of *seconde*—it is therefore called an intermediary class. At the end of *première,* there is a public exam called the *probatoire,* which qualifies you to enter *terminale.* It is perhaps the most detested of exams, not only because so few people pass it the first time, but also because it has almost no more value than the BEPC outside the domain of school. At the end of *terminale* is an exam called the *baccalauréat,* commonly referred to as the *bac.* Success on the *bac* enables a student to continue at university or to present an application for employment in a variety of formal-sector jobs. Prior to the government hiring freeze induced by *la crise,* many civil servant positions were available to people who attained the *bac.* Today, it retains its appeal as a marker of school success and the pathway to university, although its economic value has somewhat declined. In summary, there are four public exams in the course of a school career through the high school level. In addition to the repetition of classes, each of these exams serves as a gate, limiting the number of students who continue on to the next level.

Alongside exams, the cost of schooling serves as a major structural impediment to acquiring an advanced education. There are many costs associated with entering and staying in secondary school, both legitimate and illegitimate. The illegitimate costs of schooling, consisting of various forms of extortion and graft, are no less real for most students than are the standard fees. The bribes necessary to enter school are often calculated by the family as part of the normal costs, as they are unavoidable. Schooling in southern Cameroon is in fact very expensive. Public and private schools alike charge formal fees, although the rates differ widely. In the second cycle at la Trinité in 1997–98, the fees were CFA 60,500 (about USD 121), up from CFA 55,000 (about USD 110) in 1995–96. These fees are moderate for a private secondary school; the most elite Catholic *collèges* in Yaoundé cost nearly three times as much. Public high schools, by contrast, may charge as little as CFA 15,000 CFA (USD 30) per year in school fees.

In addition to school fees, students are required to buy uniforms and supplies. As we will see in chapter 5, they are encouraged to buy books as well, although they rarely do. In all but the most elite private schools, books are considered a luxury, and classroom instruction does not rely on them. The cost of uniforms varies widely from school to school. Most private schools require students to purchase their uniforms through the school itself, whereas many public schools allow students to have them made privately, provided they match in color and style. School supplies, such as pens and notebooks, vary in price, because few schools require them to be uniform. Students can relatively easily procure an occasional pen from their parents or a local anthropologist; therefore, although students complain about the high cost of supplies, it does not appear to impede school attendance. Finally, all exams have associated costs: public exams and private school entrance exams alike involve a reading fee, which must be submitted in order for the exam to be evaluated.

What I am calling the "illegitimate costs" of schooling are a much more heterogeneous set. They can include bribes given to exam preceptors to assure a passing mark, extra payments to a school headmaster to ensure that a place will be available at the school, and money given covertly to teachers for advance copies of exam questions. While experienced differently by students in different social positions, these costs are simply ubiquitous. Focusing on students, rather than on the system, a Cameroonian newspaper columnist noted:

> Everyone knows perfectly well the illegitimate means that certain of our students use in the public and private high schools to pass into the next grade or to succeed on an official exam. Everyone has heard talk of "Sexually Transmitted Grades" and of the "water" that flowed at such and such an exam. (Tchankam 1998)

These hidden costs of schooling are not optional in any real sense. A student cannot refuse to bribe higher-ups and still hope to succeed in school;

she will not pass. Aptitude and hard work are necessary in addition to, but not as a substitute for, these payments.

The bribes necessary to pass in the school system have parallels throughout the civil service, where they are known as *choco,* a neologism in Camfrançais said to come from the English word "corruption." The highway patrolmen are so well known to demand bribes that they are called "the eat-thousands" (*les mange-milles*). This term is a play on words, since *mange-milles* is the common name of a predatory bird, as well as referring to the one thousand CFA notes that the officials are given to eat in bribes. The Cameroonian public is aware of corruption and generally abhors it; however, few are willing to sacrifice their own welfare to combat it. Thus, one prominent Cameroonian intellectual said in a newspaper interview: "As no one is evaluated on the basis of the results of his work or on his actions, we are constructing a society of bricoleurs, symbolized by the love of easy gain" (Monga 1998).

According to my informants, *choco* rates vary widely. In some schools, a few thousand CFA (a few dollars) will assure you advance copies of exams. At the other extreme, a forged pass certificate for the BEPC can cost CFA 250,000 (USD 500) or more (see also Godong 1998). Another alternative is to purchase an exam certificate from a neighboring country, such as Chad. These certificates are reported to be less expensive than the Cameroonian ones, although I do not know the specific price. One of my research assistants figured that at la Trinité, one should calculate that the 1997–98 school year cost an average of CFA 120,000, taking into account the tuition, uniform, supplies, and *choco*. This estimate, that tuition is approximately half of the cost of a year of school, met with wide agreement among the women I worked with.

Life-Historical Selection

Perhaps the most interesting and difficult processes of selection are those that occur in the life of a specific girl. Over the life course, people draw on assembled repertoires of what is plausible or desirable in confronting new structural constraints; they choose to put themselves into social positions to preclude or facilitate certain anticipated outcomes. A schoolgirl aborts a pregnancy to stay in school; a student accepts a teacher's offer of sex for grades; a parent withdraws a girl from school so that she can help at home: the moments of uncertainty and confusion that precede these acts are what

I call "vital conjunctures." They are durations where the future trajectory in one domain of life—such as schooling—becomes entirely entangled with other trajectories. To sort them out, people mobilize constructed histories and hoped-for futures. The trajectories that come to dominate the decision are not necessarily given in advance, and the conjoining of arenas in which different systems of value apply makes the outcomes unpredictable. Bernstein (1994) warns against historical analyses that treat the contingent endings as inevitable—or obvious—from the beginning. So, too, life-historical selection into or out of school is hard to model because it is so radically and at so many points contingent on life experiences that on their surface appear unrelated to education.

Vital conjunctures are inherently social enterprises; although the subject of the conjuncture may be an individual, actions are almost always shared among several people. Kin groups and domestic units constitute "communities of practice" over which knowledge of, and decisions about, education and fertility are distributed (see Carter 1999; Lave and Wenger 1991). As a young woman approaches a vital conjuncture, members of these communities may contest her preferred options and predicted obstacles; the outcomes of these contestations effectively select her into specific demographic categories. This means that not only the labels and semiotically defined boundaries of demographic categories, but also their specific memberships, are social products. It is not enough to say that some social category, such as the *évolué*, is historically contingent and socially produced. We must also point out that the concrete demography of the category is a social product. Which specific individuals are selected into the *évolués*, over the course of their lives and through a sequence of conjunctures, each of which had an outcome that was uncertain up until it became actual, this too is the result of social form and social process.

Most of the time, the continued attendance of a girl in school might not be up for debate. But occasionally, something occurs that makes her schooling suddenly questionable. Her mother falls ill, and she is needed to help at home. She fails her exams and must retake the class in order to advance. Her family's resources decline so they can no longer afford the fees at the school she attends. The teacher harasses her and asks for sex. She gets pregnant. These kinds of events precipitate the vital conjunctures through which life-historical selection out of school takes place. Depending on how these vital conjunctures are resolved, that is, depending on how the horizons of the honorable and the possible are invoked and applied to the specific case, the schoolgirl will either continue or withdraw.

Failing Exams and Dropping Out

We have seen that there are myriad impediments to entering secondary school. But even for those students who make it into secondary school, the possibility of dropping out is very real and almost always present. At la Trinité, fewer than 50 percent of the students who begin *sixième* eventually graduate, although some may well graduate from another school. The dropout rates are even higher for girls, whose labor is needed at home and whose potential earnings are lower than boys'. Some students drop out because of a compelling event; others have no demographically visible reason. To stay in school, girls must be highly motivated to endure its rigors and to succeed on the public exams. Staying in school also requires complex social maneuvers to elicit the support of kin (see Rowlands 1994: 156). The life trajectory that leads a girl through school might be punctuated by the drop in the price of cocoa, which makes school fees too expensive for her family; the birth of a sibling, which necessitates her labor at home; the largesse of an aunt in the city who agrees to foster her and pay her school fees; or her own pregnancy.

In southern Cameroon, dropping out of school is intertwined with grade repetition and school transfer. Although specific instances of leaving school may be immediately predicated on a specific cause, such as financial troubles at home, grade repetition is a frequent contributing factor. Even in cases of pregnancy, adult kin decide whether to continue supporting a student based on her past academic success. A pregnant girl who has always succeeded in school is far more likely to persuade kin to continue paying her school fees than is a girl who has repeated many classes. Although students generally say that they left school for lack of resources, parents cite the ineptitude of their children at school as the primary reason for withdrawing them. But it is critical to note that students who fail only one or two classes are not usually pulled out of school entirely; the first response to failure on public exams is to change schools. In association with repeating grades, many Beti students circulate through a variety of different schools; many students will, over the course of their academic lives, attend both Catholic and public schools.

Although some students do fail in the intermediary classes, most school failure is associated with the public exams. As we touched upon above, public exams serve as gates, restricting entry into more advanced classes. In my survey of 184 women, we observed significant differences in the progression through exam classes on the one hand, and the intermediary classes on the other. Figures 4.2 through 4.5 depict progression through the two exam classes (*troisième* and *première*) and two non-exam classes (*quatrième* and *seconde*). In these diagrams, the width of the lines indicates the number of women who reported following the indicated trajectory— the thinnest lines are for ten or fewer women, the thickest for more than a hundred. The students enter on the left of the diagram and follow one line each year. Thus, a young woman may enter and in that first year pass the grade and progress to the following class, at the bottom of the diagram. She contributes only one year of data to the diagram. Another young woman may enter, repeat the grade, drop out for one year, return to repeat again, and then pass the grade at the end of her fourth year. The total number of women entering and then finally passing each grade is indicated at the left and bottom of each chart.

In figures 4.2 and 4.3, we see the strong effect of public exams on grade progression. Both of these diagrams show that many students repeat at least once and some repeat many times. A small minority of students repeated the *première* four times, although none of these students succeeded in entering *terminale*. The average number of years spent in each of these grades slightly exceeds two; students who pass these classes in a single year are treated as exceptional by their classmates, and these diagrams indicate that they are exceptional indeed. Students who always succeed on exams risk both accusations that they have used occult powers to succeed as well as becoming victims of the occult themselves. We note that in both of these exam grades nearly one third of the students never succeed in advancing to the next grade: the exam is a major hurdle.

Figures 4.4 and 4.5 show the quite different story that emerges in the intermediary classes. No one repeated either of these grades more than twice, and the vast majority passed them the first time. The eventual success rates are also much higher than in the exam classes. Over 90 percent of students entering *quatrième* eventually enter *troisième,* and over 80 percent of those entering *seconde* eventually enter *première.* Note also that there is an additional pathway on these diagrams: a small number of students withdrew from school at the end of these intermediary grades although they had succeeded in them; when these students returned to school, they did so in the succeeding grade. This trajectory does not exist at all in the exam classes, where everyone who gains entry into the succeeding grade enters it directly. Success in the exam classes is thus organized differently than success in the intermediary classes.

What these diagrams do not show is the movement of students between different schools. At age fifteen, the young women in my survey had attended an average of 2.8 schools; by age seventeen that number had risen to 3.2; and by age twenty, it had attained 3.8. A significant proportion of this school transfer is the consequence of exam failure: when students fail a grade, they are likely to switch schools. Figure 4.6 shows the mean (square) and full range (ends of bars) of the number of schools attended as a function of the number of grades repeated. The fact that some students repeat a grade several times and then drop out—eliminating them from the risk of either repeating any more grades or attending any more schools—should work against our finding any association between these two variables. Nonetheless, an association is visible: the increase in the average number of schools attended by number of grades repeated is nearly monotonic. The graph also shows that the number of schools that the women in my study attended over the course of their lives is high. Eighteen women, that is, about 10 percent of the sample, had attended seven or more different schools before graduating from high school or dropping out. Data collected by sociologists of schooling in the United States indicate that such frequent school transfer may be harmful to learning (Warren-Sohlberg et. al. 1998; but also see Lee and Burkam 1992). In Cameroon, however, my data indicate that the students who transfer often go on to complete school, because transferring schools serves as an alternative to dropping out of school in the face of failure on public exams.

Students transfer schools when they fail for three main reasons. First, schools are thought to be largely responsible for a student's exam preparation, so that if a student fails, part of the blame should be assigned to the school. Second, even if the instruction at the school is blameless, the school social environment may be seen as inconsistent with studying. This is one of the reasons that the Catholic schools in small towns, like la Trinité in Mbeya, are popular among Yaoundé parents: without the amusements of the city, the students have no choice but to study. Finally, students may be embarrassed to return to school in the class below their former classmates—it is uncomfortable, even though grade repetition is common.

One of the effects of high rates of school transfer is to create, in some schools, different subpopulations of students. At la Trinité, for example, there is one group of students from Mbeya and its environs for whom school transfer is not an option. If la Trinité fails to meet their educational needs, or they are excluded from the school for any reason, these students generally drop out of school entirely. In the best of circumstances, for these students la Trinité truly offers a step up and out of rural disadvantage. In

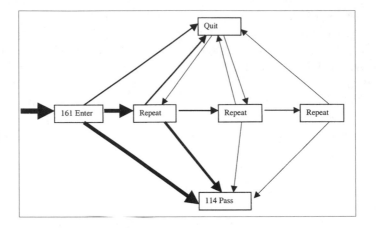

FIGURE 4.2. Student progression through *troisième*

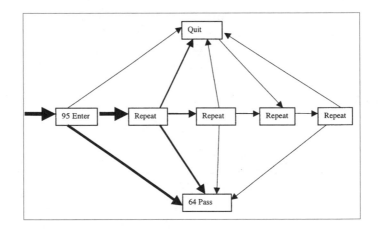

FIGURE 4.3. Student progression through *première*

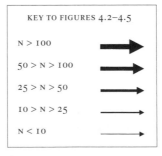

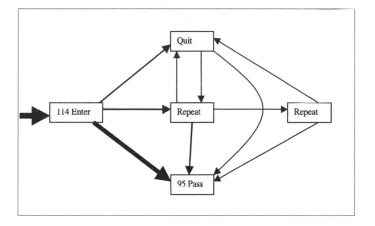

FIGURE 4.4. Student progression through *seconde*

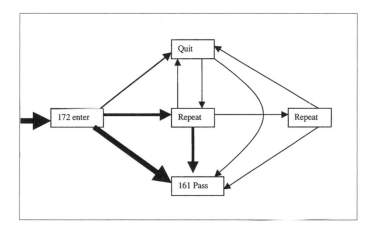

FIGURE 4.5. Student progression through *quatrième*

the worst of circumstances, it is an expensive, frustrating exercise for a couple of years before they return to farming. At la Trinité there is also a second group of students, largely from Yaoundé or other urbanized areas, who have transferred in from other schools. The local students accuse these city dwellers of "academic tourism," there only for amusement. Although these visitors regularly attain higher pass rates on the exams, they are perceived as "dangerous troublemakers" by many of the local students.

The conflicts that develop around academic tourism are intense and easily perceptible. I conducted an interview with a student in *première*

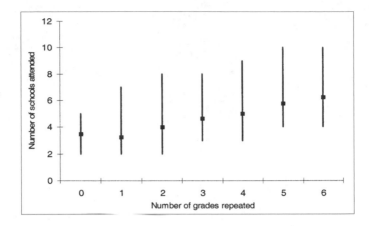

FIGURE 4.6. Mean and range of number of schools attended by number of grades repeated

who had attended la Trinité since *sixième*. She lived with her natal family just outside of Mbeya, and all of her siblings had also attended the local Catholic school, although she had attained the highest grade level so far. She noted that certain members of her study group from the previous year were no longer at la Trinité. When I asked where they had gone, she answered that they just wanted to get a "change of environment." I asked her opinion about changing environments, and she replied:

> Changing environment and changing schools each year is not good. It is often bothersome. There are often students who come here. They do one or two years. These are the students who have already done the tour of schools. They are disorderly, and they come here to get a little refuge for themselves in the country. That is what I say to myself.

There is very much the sense here and in the speech of many rural students that school transfer is a sign of disorderly conduct. Yet, in as far as school transfer is an alternative to school dropout, these disordered students are the ones who eventually leave school with a degree. For their part, the urban students consider the local, rural students provincial, even naïve. They perceive their own experience in multiple schools not as academic tourism, but as the only way of overcoming exam failure.

Exam failure, grade repetition, school transfer, and school dropout are both tightly related and extremely common in the schools of southern Cameroon. At every public examination, a significant proportion of students fail. Failing exams requires students to repeat grades and leads some students to transfer to other schools. The widespread pattern of school transfer means that many students will experience both public and private education in a variety of milieus. For students who are unable to repeat classes, for financial or other reasons, exam failure often leads to dropping out of school entirely.

*   *   *

Schools are thought to impart honor to women through two central mechanisms: by making it possible for them to be economically independent, and by inculcating them with honorable habits and ideas. Catholic schools are often portrayed as exemplars of schooling more broadly and are thought to epitomize proper schooling and training for Beti adulthood. The high value placed on schooling, and especially of Catholic schooling, is in part maintained through the difficulty of attaining it. Children who persist in school have overcome substantial structural impediments, in the form of exams and high costs, including the illegitimate costs of *choco*. As places for the inculcation of honorable habits and ideas, schools are thought to impart the skills and tastes of the elite. Yet they are also places inhabited primarily by students who are already elite. Children who are selected to attend secondary school, and most particularly to attend Catholic secondary school, are largely from families with money, power, and status. Furthermore, students are often privileged vis-à-vis their own siblings, as they have been chosen by their parents and other adult kin as worthy of support. Consistent with other aspects of Beti childrearing, siblings often receive very different levels of schooling investment from their parents.

The processes of selection into and out of school create a school community that shares a variety of traits in addition to the experience of schooling itself. Thus, schooling per se is not the sole cause of schoolgirls' distinct practices in reference to marriage and fertility, but is also a marker of shared history and experience. At the same time, it is crucial to attend to the fact that educated women consistently point to their schooling as the basis of their honorable discipline. That is, although educated women constitute a highly select group, they insist that their shared practices are the result of their schooling. In explaining educated women's motivation to delay marriage and socially recognized motherhood, the fact that they perceive this delay as an indicator of their educated, disciplined, modern honor is critical. In fact, the interplay between classic selectivity effects and the ongoing evaluation of schools as places of honor may provide a more adequate explanation.

In this chapter, we have looked at the place of schooling in society at large, arguing that although Catholic schooling is circumscribed in distribution, it has come to serve as the prototypical form of socialization for honorable Beti adulthood. This role stands in a somewhat uneasy relationship to what goes on inside the classroom, where the production of honorable adults is assumed to take place. We will now move inside the school, exploring how and what students learn. Is there something in the experience of schooling itself to which educated Beti women are referring when they speak of their own discipline and honor? And if so, is it to be found in the curriculum, in interactions with teachers and administrators, in the act of learning itself, or elsewhere? How, in short, do Cameroonian classrooms work?

CHAPTER FIVE

Learning Honor in School

Fathers used to take their children to school as they might lead sheep into a slaughter-house. Tiny tots would turn up from backward villages thirty or forty miles up-country, shepherded by their parents, to be put on the books of some school, it didn't matter which. They formed a miserable floating population, these kids; lodged with distant relations who happened to live near the school, underfed, scrawny, bullied all day by ignorant monitors. The books in front of them presented a universe which had nothing in common with the one they knew: they battled endlessly with the unknown, astonished and desperate and terrified. — Mongo Beti, *Mission to Kala*

For most students, the world described by Mongo Beti (1958) is long since gone. The Cameroonian fathers who today enroll their children have, for the most part, themselves been to school; the world presented to students in school looks increasingly like the one they already know. Many students now come to school having been raised with the socioeconomic benefits, and arguably the daily habits, attributed to the educated in the popular imagination. Nonetheless, school continues to been seen as transformative, capable of making its students into honorable men and women, instilling in them self-dominion, improving their chances for a respectable, white-collar job, and giving them the means to a direct connection with God. Again and again, in a variety of contexts, educated women repeat that school transformed them, cultivated their habits, endowed them with modern honorability. Scholars, too, have considered education to be transformative (Goody and Watt 1963; LeVine et al. 1991), although in different ways and for different reasons, and much of the literature on the association between education and fertility assumes that education matters because of the concrete knowledge and skills that it transmits. In this chapter, we look at what happens inside school. How is time organized? What knowledge is transmitted? How do schools discipline students, and to what effect? I will argue that schools are neither as disciplined as Beti parents hope nor as effective at communicating content as western demographers imagine. Instead, much of what happens in southern Cameroonian schools is boring, confusing, or frustrating.

Both parents and students assert that the excellence of Catholic schools lies in their discipline: their ability to control their students, maintain order, and, ideally, inculcate the postures of self-control that will carry the effects of school discipline beyond the schoolyard and after the final exams. When parents say that a school has discipline—"Il y a de la discipline là-bas"—they mean that the classrooms are quiet, the rules are clear, and the students follow them. Punishments should be severe and administered without hesitation; the knowledge that this is true should induce compliance. Students should study intently. There should be no disruptions or distractions. If necessary, rules may be arbitrary and even trivial: rules against colored pens, hair extensions, and polished fingernails fall well within the parameters of "discipline" as locally construed. According to parents, the regular application of strict timekeeping, rules, and punishments will cultivate self-dominion in students, as they first learn to submit to authority without question and then eventually incorporate the practices imposed by school into their own dispositions, mastering their own actions as the *maîtres* mastered them before. "Habit is second nature" the saying goes; schooling should create self-controlled natures by forcing submission to controlled habits.

The view that discipline enters into the student through repetition, culminating in the child's being able to reproduce both the outward forms and the inner intuitions of self-dominion reflects Beti socialization generally, as we saw in chapter 2. Children acquire *mfefeg* through repeated practice, enforced by parents and other elders, who assign them unpleasant tasks as pedagogical exercises. However, school is not merely a large-scale replica of the training children receive at home. Unlike schoolteachers, Beti parents seek to observe the innate characters of their children, to identify potential undeveloped talents. Unlike parents, teachers spend much of the day in direct engagement with children, addressing them explicitly and responding—in some way—to their questions. Schooling may be increasingly seen as the prototypical preparation for honorable adulthood, but that does not mean that all other forms of socialization are coming to imitate it.

Educated Beti women use the term *la discipline* to express an idea close to Bourdieu's concept of habituation; students explain that school imbues them with habits and attitudes, developing in them an ordered set of inclinations. These are the "systems of durable, transposable *dispositions*, struc-tured structures predisposed to function as structuring structures," that Bourdieu calls the *habitus* (1977: 72). The *habitus* is both structured (by repeated experience) and structuring (of new action). Bourdieu's model applies well to the approximate consensus among Beti regarding the "so-cial capital" of school-based discipline.[1] Rather different from Bourdieu's representation, however, is the explicit, conscious manner in which Beti students approach the reforming of their *habitus*. In attending secondary school, girls intentionally seek to be made disciplined, modern, and hon-orable women; this is hardly the "practical knowledge not comprising knowledge of its own principles" that the *habitus* classically constitutes (1977: 19).

As Beti discipline is partially self-conscious, we need to consider cases of the intentional and explicit remaking of character alongside Bourdieu's concepts of the *habitus*. The most monumental explication of these issues is Foucault's *Discipline and Punish*. Although much of the historical ar-gument does not interest us here, we may focus on Foucault's analysis of the making of docile bodies in disciplinary institutions from the late eighteenth century onward, and more specifically on what Foucault calls the "modality" of making disciplined subjects, the "uninterrupted, constant coercion, supervising the processes of the activity rather than its result . . . exercised according to the codification that partitions as closely as possi-ble time, space, and movement" (1979: 137). This ongoing process through which disciplined subjects are made evokes an intentional, and insidious, application of the principles of *habitus* to the project of constructing docile bodies, and through them, a disciplined institution. But Foucault's theory of disciplinary institutions is more somber still; the uninterrupted making of disciplined subjects does *not* produce generative dispositions that are the basis of innovative social action, but rather "prompt and blind" obedi-ence (166). Thus, Foucault portrays disciplinary institutions in which those who discipline act with intention and forethought to produce precisely the opposite in the subjects of their disciplinary practice.

Between the largely unconscious and generally consensual *habitus* of Bourdieu and the more explicit, albeit coercive, disciplinary practices of Foucault, must lie some theoretical middle ground through which to ap-proach the Beti material. For this, studies of missions, colonial schools, and religious education offer some of the most compelling models (e.g., Keane 1997; Miescher 1997; Starrett 1995). Analyses of missions and colo-nial schools have been forced to take account of how people were remade in ways that straddle awareness and unawareness, coercion and willing participation—precisely the ambivalences that exist in Beti students' submission to school discipline. Thus Hanks explains that the missionization of Yucatán relied on the concept of *policia cristiana*, which sought "to instill ways of perceiving, experiencing and behaving, rooted in the little details of social life and disposition to reproduce them" (2000: 3). Although this process was highly asymmetric, it did not and could not proceed without the partial collaboration of certain Mayans. The evangelization involved domination, but not in the manner described for disciplinary institutions by Foucault. Instead, we see a "blending [of] collusion with domination in a volatile and sometimes baleful mix," whereby the subjects of reformation intentionally sought to cultivate in themselves a new set of Christian intuitions, habits, and inclinations (Hanks 2000: 36; see also Comaroff and Comaroff 1991: 19–27). Mahmood's analysis of the practice of prayer in the women's piety movement in Cairo, introduced in chapter 3, resonates with Hanks's interpretation of colonial conversion. It is in the central "role of conscious training in the acquisition of embodied dispositions" (Mahmood 2001a: 838) that self-cultivation in southern Cameroonian Catholic schools, in the Cairene piety movement, and in seventeenth-century Yucatecan missions parallel one another.

And yet, despite the poetic appeal of school discipline engendering self-dominion in its subjects, there is something ironic or even farcical about the practices of discipline at la Trinité and other schools I visited. Students spend much of the school day unmonitored; classes have little academic content; there is a sense of the haphazard interrupted occasionally by the rigid observance of form. Insofar as school discipline is about subjugating students to humiliation and boredom in turn, these schools are highly disciplined. But that is not, I think, what most Beti parents have in mind. In any event, when teachers insult students, demean them, or leave them waiting while attending to other matters, they are resorting to methods used widely outside of schools. As powerful elders, teachers are to some degree the patrons of their students, worthy of respect and even obedience. Just as children demonstrate their readiness to be considered sensible adults by accepting their place and conforming to their role, students can only earn the right to school knowledge by passing through the trials of being junior and thereby dominated.

I begin our exploration of what happens in schools by setting the stage, describing the physical and temporal structure of schools. From there, we will move to a closer examination of the specific forms through which students are required to submit to their schooling, including waiting for teachers, taking dictation, and being punished. These are the activities that come closest to disciplining students in the sense that parents hope for; we will interrogate in what ways they are disciplining, and to what ends: for parents, schools instill self-dominion, whereas for policymakers, they teach content. We will turn next to the content of classroom lessons, particularly as it relates to reproduction. What are Catholic schoolgirls taught about childbearing and motherhood? Which of the many things that they attribute to their schooling can we actually trace back to the classroom? Finally, we will explore how different the experience of schooling is for girls and boys, relating these differences to the gender-specific forms of honorable adulthood discussed in chapter 3.

The Schools and Their Teachers

Not only the economy, but also Cameroon's instructional system is in crisis. In May 1998, the Ministry of Education declared an emergency, asserting that education levels were slipping dangerously. It responded by publicly inflating the scores on the *baccalauréat* to ensure that Cameroon's national pass rate would not decline vis-à-vis other Francophone African nations (Anon. 1998; Atangana 1998; Azébazé 1998; Malkal 1998; Mombio 1998; Nouwou 1998). This well-publicized grade inflation was almost uniformly condemned outside the ministry. Educated people, especially, argued that the basis of school success must be academic achievement alone, and that by inflating results, the ministry had "annulled" the exam (Tagne 1998). Students in the affected graduating class wondered whether their success was "true" or merely the result of an administrative sleight of hand, and the faculties of several departments at the National University in Yaoundé threatened to suspend admissions. The public debate—in newspapers, on the radio, and in bars—assumed a baseline in which education was richly focused on content and treated the 1997–98 school year as an unfortunate aberration. But looking inside the classroom, it is difficult to view its activities as primarily academic, or its scholarly content as of foremost importance. In all the schools I visited, disruptions to learning are legion. At la Trinité, noneducational activities occupy nearly half of scheduled classroom time, of which there is already little. The desirability of schools as preparation for an honorable adulthood appears to be reflected only minimally in the curriculum. More important are the forms of self-identity practiced in school; although these forms differ fundamentally for men and women, self-dominion is central to both. To begin to understand how women in particular might credit their Catholic schooling with teaching them self-dominion, let us take a closer look at the form and content of their education.

Like most Francophone secondary schools in Cameroon, la Trinité is administered by a principal, a vice-principal, a surveillant general (chief disciplinarian), and a vice-surveillant. The surveillant is responsible for most grave disciplinary matters: he suspends students for the nonpayment of fees, investigates absences, and metes out punishments. The principal and vice-principal are responsible for the curriculum and staff. The teaching staffs of public and private schools in Cameroon differ considerably. The public school faculty is tightly regimented: its members are state employees, and are required to have completed a degree at the École Normale Supérieur in Yaoundé. The faculty at private schools show significantly more variation: some private school faculty members are trained and licensed teachers, but others are not. Public school teachers are better paid, on average, than those in the private schools, although even the public school salaries are low. That parents should esteem private schools above the public although public school teachers generally have better credentials and higher pay seems contradictory. Of course, the same is true in the United States. In both contexts, private school students are more heavily selected by social class, the classes are smaller, and the threat of suspension or expulsion more convincing.

Given the low salaries for teachers, many public school teachers have secondary jobs giving lessons in private schools, commuting during the day between two institutions. At la Trinité, there is often quiet tension between the nonlicensed teachers who teach full-time at the Catholic school and the licensed state teachers whose primary appointments are in the public schools in nearby towns, and who teach only one or two classes at la Trinité. As in most public schools, the teachers are predominantly male. Two of the three female teachers of the advanced grades teach classes that are outside the central curriculum for the public exams.

At la Trinité, the teachers are overwhelming laity: in the upper secondary school, the only member of a religious order is the teacher of catechism.[2] Even "Education in Life and Love," which covers relationships, sexuality, and contraception (as well as how to wash linen and what "dry cleaning" means) is taught by a lay teacher. Like students, teachers are generally presumed to be Catholic. Also like the students, there is relatively little effort to check on their attendance at mass or compliance with church teachings. For most of the teachers, I know nothing more about their private views on the church, *la crise,* or Cameroonian politics than do the students. The exceptions are the three women, all of whom I interviewed, and one of whom befriended me. Mme Ngah is an eloquent, deeply intellectual woman who takes her profession seriously. Teaching high school has made it possible for her to continue to read and think while fulfilling the aspirations of conventional Beti womanhood. She has four children and lives with her husband in Mbeya, one of the few teachers to do so. Mme Ngah has great faith in the power of education to transform lives—as it did her own—even as she worries about the lassitude of her students and the difficulties of really motivating them to work.

Schoolrooms are spare at la Trinité: they are mostly built of cement and open directly onto a covered cement walkway. Beyond the walkway is a packed-dirt yard with occasional acacia trees. As in every school I visited, the classrooms at la Trinité contain nothing other than a blackboard, wooden benches and desks, and a table for the teacher. Classes in public schools are as large as eighty students; the largest class at la Trinité had fifty-six students. Groups of students in the same grade and series are taught together and remain in the same classroom all day. The teachers of specific subjects rotate through different classrooms. As the teachers rotate, there is always some time between classes when the students are left alone. Teachers are rarely prompt to arrive in class, and indeed they may not come at all. Each student has a regular, assigned seat and usually shares a bench and a desk with another student. In the primary school and first cycle of secondary, seats are assigned in the classroom by merit, those with the best exam scores sitting in the front row, and those with the worst in the back row. In the second cycle, the teachers arrange the students as they see fit, either by grades or by some other mechanism. Each class has a prefect, elected by the class at the beginning of the year, who is responsible for taking attendance and recording disruptions.

I will call a group of students who share a curriculum a division. Thus *seconde A* refers to the division, defined by a series (A) and a grade (*seconde*). A large school might have two or more classrooms assigned to each division, but la Trinité has only one class of each division. The series are courses of various curricula; series A focuses on philosophy and language arts, for example, and series C on math. In the second cycle, each division officially meets for approximately thirty-two hours of class a week, with the number of hours devoted to each subject varying by series, according to a system set out by the Ministry of Education. The divisions have different course schedules each day to accommodate the many subjects. Table 5.1 shows the number of hours per week devoted to each subject in two divisions: *seconde A* and *seconde C.*

Thus, students in both series will be examined on the *probatoire* in the same eleven subjects; the differences between the curricula concern emphasis, not inclusion. The scheduling is complicated as the teachers move between divisions, and each division has one or more hours of unscheduled and unmonitored time during the week, officially for study hall, but usually consisting of barely constrained disorder. Classes are held Monday through Friday, with no classes scheduled on Wednesday afternoon. On Saturday morning and Wednesday afternoon there are sometimes *travaux dirigés,* a kind of special study session directed explicitly at preparing for the public exams, and for which teachers are paid extra.

The school calendar and grading cycle is elaborate, and testing constitutes a significant proportion of school time. The school year is divided into trimesters, and each trimester is divided into three *séquences,* each lasting three weeks. Students take one exam in each subject in each *séquence;* these exams typically require an entire class period to complete, and often a second class period to return and discuss. At the end of each trimester, classes are suspended for a week of final exams. In classes such as civics and "Education in Life and Love" (EVA), which meet for one hour a week, students will therefore have six hours of class per trimester in which to cover new material, assuming no national holidays or similar interruptions. School holidays, however, are numerous. In addition to the fourteen annual bank holidays, schools regularly take an extra day off between two public holidays (*font pont*); thus, if Thursday is a religious holiday, classes are also cancelled on Friday. Altogether, la Trinité had 121 scheduled days of instruction in 1997–98.

The elaborate examination apparatus is the sole basis for student evaluation; neither homework nor class participation is graded or recorded. And these exam grades are very public: results are read aloud in class; seating in the lower school and first part of the second cycle is according to test scores, séquence grades are announced at a school assembly; annual and national results are publicly posted and read on the radio. As in France, the exams are graded, without a curve, out of twenty points; a score of ten points or higher is passing. The questions are a combination of short-answer and essay. In French, for example, students are generally given a passage from a work that they should have read as part of the curriculum.

TABLE 5.1 **Hours devoted to lessons per week, Collège de la Trinité, 1998**

Subject	Seconde A	Seconde C
Assembly*	I	I
Biology	2	2
Catechism*	I	I
Chemistry	I	2
Civics	I	I
English	4	3
Education in Life and Love (EVA)*	I	I
French	6	4
Geography	2	2
German	4	2
History	2	2
Math	4	6
Physical Education	2	2
Physics	2	4
Total	33	33

*Not evaluated on public exams

First they respond to two or three short questions, and then they write either a commentary or an analysis.

Most of the students at la Trinité have similar family backgrounds, as we saw in chapter 4. At CFA 60,500 per year (about USD 121 in 1998), the tuition is prohibitive for many families: students are either from relatively well-to-do families or are talented enough at school to attract a sponsor to pay their school fees. But significant distinctions also exist. The most important of these is the division between students whose parents reside in Yaoundé and those from the district surrounding Mbeya itself. While the students in the lower school are nearly all local to the town, nearly a third of the students in the second cycle come from Yaoundé. Most of these students explain that their parents decided to send them to study in the country, away from the temptations of city life. (As we've seen, this decision is often, although not always, the result of failure on one of the public exams.) These students live in rented rooms or in the dormitory; they have pocket money and are relatively little supervised. The difference between local and city-dwelling students is poignantly felt: the two groups rarely socialize and largely perceive themselves as having different temperaments and habits. In contrast to the urbanites, students whose families live in Mbeya or in small neighboring villages perceive la Trinité as a route out of the village and toward the educated, urban elite. These students have both lower academic aspirations and lower rates of success on the public exams than the urbanites. They sometimes come from families in which they are already the most educated person. The urban students, by contrast, see la Trinité as a convenient step in an educational trajectory, a place where they will be able to study without temptation, and thereby succeed on the exams and return to Yaoundé. The differences between these sets of students are significant within the school, but from the outside all Catholic secondary students are perceived as members of a single educated elite.

The Central Province of Cameroon has achieved near gender equity in school participation in the lower grades. At the higher grades, males continue to outnumber females, although not to the same degree as in northern Cameroon. This numerical inequality is not evenly distributed over subjects. In the higher grades at la Trinité, male students dramatically outnumber female students in the math and science series, while females constitute the majority of philosophy and language arts students in *terminale* and *première*, but not in *seconde*.[3] The fact that the scientific and math series are dominated by male students mirrors the pattern of college majors in the United States (Frehill 1999; Jacobs 1996; Turner and Bowen 1999). Table 5.2 shows the numbers of students enrolled in each of the seven divisions of the second cycle in 1997–98. The total ratio of male to female students in the second cycle is less that two to one, but this ratio is the average of some highly male-dominated divisions with a few divisions that approach parity or even have a slight surplus of girls.

Students in all secondary schools, both public and private, are supposed to wear uniforms, and in most schools students will be sent home for not wearing their uniforms. At la Trinité, however, the school changed its official uniform twice between 1995 and 1998. Because official uniforms are expensive and can even be hard to come by (many parents have a local seamstress simply copy the uniform as closely as possible), enforcing the rule would have excluded a large number of students. As a result, during the time of my study, the school administration permitted those students who did not yet have the new uniforms to attend classes in street clothes. Hairstyles continued to be rigidly controlled, however, and students were routinely sent home for unacceptable hairstyles, particularly the long, free-flowing braids locally called "Rasta." Girls are required to wear their hair tied or braided close to the head, and boys are required to have their hair cut short. These dress codes serve not only to standardize the appearance of students within school, but also to make them recognizable outside: students are identified with their school and expected to conform to its modes of disciplined practice even beyond its physical boundaries.

TABLE 5.2 **Gender distribution of students by division, Collège de la Trinité, 1998**

Class	Male students	Female students	Male students per female student
Terminale A	15	17	0.9
Terminale D	37	8	4.6
Première A	22	25	0.9
Première C	13	2	6.5
Première D	31	14	2.2
Seconde A	20	12	1.7
Seconde C/D	24	13	1.9
Total	*162*	*91*	*1.8*

Experiencing School Structure

The structuring of space, time, and material culture described above has important consequences for what happens at school, but the consequences are not always transparent. The discipline that parents so intently want for their children appears sporadically and somewhat arbitrarily. Teachers differ enormously in their classroom styles, and that variation matters a lot for how—and even what—students learn. A couple of examples of what assemblies and classes feel like will serve as empirical touchstones for our discussion, demonstrating key aspects of school life.

Monday Assembly

School assemblies at la Trinité take place each Monday morning at eight o'clock in the packed-dirt yard separating the two classroom blocks. These assemblies serve both to submit students to regimentation—consisting here of nearly an hour of standing in formation in all kinds of weather—as well as to dispense information and instructions. They always follow approximately the same format. The following description is compiled from my observations of nine such assemblies.

About five minutes before eight, students gather in the yard. Each division stands together in lines, the shortest students in the front. The front of each line is marked by a small stone on the ground. The students are boisterous as they line up, and many small disagreements break out over who is taller, particularly in the younger classes. Once all are assembled, the students of the drum-and-bugle corps march in, their stilted choreography underscored by the old and ill-tuned instruments. It feels farcical,

and some of the watching students laugh. When the band finishes, the
principal leads the students in prayer. Next, the surveillant general drills
the students in standing at attention and marching in place, calling out
"Attention! Prenez la stance!" After a few minutes of marching drill, a
color guard of students (identified by gloves and sashes) raise the national
flag with ceremony; their earnestness is also considered ridiculous by the
other students, whose laughter punctuates each heel-spin and bow. Then
the principal gives a brief talk that is part sermon, part lecture, usually emphasizing the importance of hard work in school, and which once a month
consists of the results of the monthly exams. Next the surveillant general
gives formal announcements of the week: when school fees are due, which
different classes have special programs, and the like. He then repeats the
standing and marching drill. At the end of the drill, the band starts again
and the classes march off—lowest grades first—toward their classrooms
to begin the day.

The weekly assembly can be read as ritual performance, as mimesis, or
as convention and routine. Although stylized, "characterized by a higher
than usual degree of reflexivity, [and] . . . calling attention to the rules
of their own enactment" (Kapchan 1995: 479), the assemblies are at the
same time numbingly repetitive, such that some of the older, male students
talk about the assembly as something to disrupt if possible and ignore if
not. The pseudomilitary forms—marching in place to the drill calls of the
surveillant, the color guard, and drum-and-bugle corps—seem most like
farcical imitations of colonial forms, both to me and to the many students
who laugh at the pompous performance despite the punishments that the
surveillant metes out for this disrespect. And yet, this farce fails to have
the creative, paradoxical, culturally redemptive consequences that Stoller
(1984) ascribes to the Hauka in Nigeria, or Argenti (1998) to the Air Youth
in Cameroon. Whereas the Air Youth use mimesis to "appropriate . . . a
foreign and often violent modernity and thereby remodel or transform it
into a highly aestheticized politics of performance" (Argenti 1998: 265),
the students at la Trinité enact the weekly assembly out of obligation. The
assembly, with its replication of military, colonial, and nationalist forms,
is the creation of the school staff, and particularly of the surveillant general. And he sees absolutely nothing theatrical, humorous, or mimetic in
the marching he demands. For the surveillant, there is only zero-degree
interpretation.

As the habitual initiation of the school week, the assembly serves as a
symbolic frame for all other school activities. But students spend most of

their time in the classroom, and it is therefore centrally in classrooms that a school *habitus* is made. We look now at the classroom experience. The following passages are excerpted from my classroom field notes during my first week of informal observations, before I had started the formal measures.

French in Seconde C

The teacher arrives to a class of noisy teenagers. He is an older man. The students—both male and female—call out "Fresh Boy!" in English. I ask why, and am told it is because he has just had his hair done. Indeed, his hair is short and tidy. He does not respond to these catcalls, but smiles. A boy calls out that "Vous méritez une petite!" [You deserve a girlfriend on the side!]. Janette explains to me that this is "parce qu'il est très branché" [because he is very fashionable, literally, "plugged in"]. The teacher laughs and responds that he won't take one, because "les filles ne sont pas mûres" [the girls are not yet ripe]. This elicits a great deal of laughter and appreciation, expressed by drumming loudly on the desks. Between all of this joking, erasing the board, etc., it takes about ten minutes to get class started. The teacher then passes back the exams [from the last sequence]; reading out the grades as the students come forward to fetch their papers. For example, "Mbella Natalie, 9 of 20." The teenage students do not make this particularly efficient; they are talking or doodling, and are not quick to come when their names are called. Students who did not take the exam then present *billets d'excuse* [excuse cards from the surveillant general] if they have them. Marie-Claire explains that they will therefore not fail the sequence.

The correction of the exam, of which the topic is French grammar, consists of the teacher reading the questions and correct answers. Occasionally, students protest an answer. They are overruled in every case. There is quite a bit of other background conversation going on. At one point I count fourteen of thirty-seven students in the classroom chatting. Once the corrections are finished, a good eight or nine people, all but one of them boys, surround the teacher to get their grades raised. He sends them back to their chairs without looking at their exams. Later, two more girls and another boy approach; they, too, are sent back to their chairs. Part of this argument is about copying errors: the exam questions were written on the blackboard and students had to copy them down. Some students made spelling or grammar errors in their copying, for which he graded them down. They find this unfair, and one student insists that she could not see the board, and so had to copy from a neighbor.

At the end of the corrections, he writes the topic of the next lesson [the subjunctive] on the board, telling them to copy. I count six separate conversations going on. However, some students do copy as requested. The teacher reads the lesson from a sheet of paper, sitting at the chair behind his desk. Two girls (opposite side of the room) have turned around completely in their benches to talk, but since they are not too loud, the teacher ignores them. At the end of the hour, the school "bell" rings—it is a loud speaker attached to a boombox playing loud, scratchy pop music. This inspires some stomping of feet with the rhythm, which the teacher ignores. He packs up his papers and leaves the room.

Both the contrast between formality and familiarity and the extremely low density of educational content are striking here. The focus on formal, even ceremonial procedure in the returning of exams and the dictation of new material is framed by extreme informality in the form of sexual joking between teacher and students. Juxtaposed against the general noise and disorder, the formality of the teaching methods is remarkable: the dictation is highly stylized and repetitive, and the exams are returned in an elaborate and inefficient format that requires each student to come to the front of the classroom alone as their name and exam grade are read aloud. This formality could be interpreted as precisely the school discipline that parents and students so intently want. Like the hollow regimentation of the weekly assembly, the correct observation of form in the classroom might be seen as a means of cultivating correct habits. Under this interpretation, the students tolerate the breach of their privacy in the reading of their grades because it is a necessary part of the process of attaining honorable self-dominion. But the insistence on protocol could also be viewed as a substitute for discipline or, more accurately, an imitation of discipline. In *1984*, Orwell attributes to one of his characters the idea that "if you keep the little rules, you can break the big ones." Similarly, the vacant formality with which exams are returned obviates the disciplinary practices that could in fact cultivate the self-dominion for which parents send their children to Catholic school.

In the French class described above, formal classroom activities are introduced by what appears to be their opposite, the sexually suggestive teasing that begins the class. Teasing is common in classrooms at la Trinité, both between students and teachers and among students, and it was also common in the other two Catholic schools I visited. Although sex between female students and male teachers is widely purported to be common, sexual joking in the classroom is surprising. Teachers' ability to discipline their students rests in part on their position as respected elders, parallel to fathers and uncles. Sexual joking in the classroom thus crosses generational lines as well as hierarchical ones. In addition, sex between teachers and students—even if frequent—is always at least moderately illicit, being considered a form of corruption, coercion, or illegitimate exchange. To joke about it implies substantial familiarity, or even reciprocity of perception. And it is perhaps this familiarity that makes the teasing understandable. By joking with teachers, students assert the status of self-dominion that is denied to them during the core of lessons. The structuring of school activities as hierarchical and disciplinary relies in part on a basic consensus between teacher and students; students take on the outward forms of school discipline because they are convinced that by so doing they will effectively attain the desirable status of the educated, honorable person.

Teasing can thus serve to reframe school discipline as essentially collaborative, and to reframe the student—particularly the male student—as an equal participant in the classroom activity. Through their joking, the boys are able to establish themselves as interchangeable with the teacher, if only for the duration of the joke. For girls, however, the joking is not necessarily inclusive. The teacher refers to the female students in the third person—"les filles ne sont pas mûres"—presumably talking with the boys about them. He claims that the girls are not yet mature enough to take as (casual) girlfriends, suggesting that if they were, he would do so. In this way, the teacher treats the female students as marginal participants in the classroom, not as "legitimate peripheral participants" (Lave and Wenger 1991), but indeed as only marginally legitimate ones.

Along with the dichotomy between formality and informality, the French lesson in *seconde C* demonstrates a scarcity of educational content. The class is very slow to start, and during the correcting of the exam, the students are largely uninvolved. Many are chatting, none are taking notes, and the teacher is providing all the correct answers himself. When the class moves to new material, both the dictation format and the low level of class participation inhibit learning (see Pelissier 1991). Thus, in addition to the fact that students have relatively little class over the course of a year, the density of educational content in class is low. The value of schooling does not appear to lie in the content of the formal curriculum, as there is just so little time and effort dedicated to learning that curriculum. Some classes, however, show more emphasis on the traditional curriculum than others.

Math in Terminale A

Before class starts there is a public announcement given by a male student about a Catholic-centered social event to take place on Saturday evening. People laugh and say that they are not going to participate. The teacher arrives calmly and promptly begins dictation. His style throughout is chalk and talk—he calculates equations rapidly, pausing slightly for the input of the class, which is given en masse and on which he does not rely to continue. Students copy his work, although the glint on the chalkboard makes this difficult from one side of the classroom. The day is not too hot, making concentration somewhat easier.

There are a number of small conversations going on. Some of these appear to be topical, as when one student explains a certain step of the solution to another, but others are clearly not. These conversations are predominantly among neighbors, and as seating in this class is largely gender-segregated, the conversations are too. The back of the class is primarily male, and also the source of most disruption when such occurs. However, two girls are chatting near the window, and are reprimanded. A boy from the back row calls out "Ce sont les filles de la brousse!" [They are girls from the bush!]. Instead of scolding the boy, the teacher adds "On peut rester au village et ne pas être fou!" [You can stay in the village without being crazy!]. General laughter breaks out among the boys.

At one point, a female student indicates that she does not understand. The teacher smiles condescendingly and says, "She still doesn't understand the basics. Let's start again." He redoes the problem, still smiling, but I find myself feeling badly for her. The line between useful and disruptive interjections is sometimes thin; for example, one boy asks a very long and complex question which does not appear related. It is tolerated and tersely answered, but does not generate further conversation. Another boy interjects a wisecrack which the teacher co-opts to continue the class. The class ends promptly with the bell.

In contrast to the teacher in the French class, the math teacher, Mr. Atangana, is young and charismatic. He attended the École Normale Superieur and lived for some time abroad. He comes from a family of talkers, and loves words—especially elegant, fanciful and dramatic ones. While I enjoyed his classes for this very reason, his elaborate vocabulary and rapid speech made some of the students very uncomfortable.

Several recurring aspects of the school experience are apparent in my description of his class. First, boys and girls have very different experiences in the classroom, particularly with male teachers. In this math course, girls are made to feel unwelcome both by the male students and, in part, by the teacher. Although most of the disruptions come from boys, the girls who were talking are subjected to direct and significant criticism, from which boys are mostly spared. Boys' disruptions are largely tolerated, even in one case actively incorporated into the lesson. Girls' questions are answered, but in a way that may leave them feeling condescended to or inferior. The difference is all the more noteworthy since this class took place in a literature and philosophy division, where female students make up the bare majority of the students. Notice also the ways that teasing and joking come into play here. Joking occurs predominantly between the teacher and his male students, and it sometimes serves to advance the pedagogical project. Boys' interjections, therefore, are validated as part of classroom activity. Finally, information in this classroom, as in the previous example, flows from teacher to students. The teacher solves problems on the board, expecting the students to follow. Their participation is essentially limited to copying.

These classroom vignettes serve as a backdrop for discussing what students learn in school. We now turn to the modes of school discipline, emphasizing both its importance in the external valuation of Catholic education and its centrality for all other kinds of learning in the school.

Learning School Discipline

The aspects of the school experience that are shaped primarily by school officials—chiefly the surveillant general, as the principal plays little role in the day-to-day running of the school—are largely focused on demanding that students submit to authority and to the institution. This domination is most colorfully demonstrated in the weekly assembly and in forms of punishment that include humiliation and sometimes also physical discomfort. These overt ways in which the school elicits submission constitute part of what parents call *la discipline,* although arguably only a small part. More important are the everyday practices of administrative control, the small observances of protocol that, as we saw in the French class in *seconde C,* allow teachers and students to reenact this magical discipline, as the Cameroonian state reenacts elections and certain priests reenact the missionization with every adult conversion. Parents hope that school discipline will induct their children into honorable self-dominion; however, the path from submission to self-dominion is neither straight nor unobstructed. It is as much in the breakdown of discipline as in its application that students can acquire the self-mastery that makes Catholic schooling so desirable.

Instruction relies heavily on dictation, through which students are trained to submit to authority. Outside of instruction itself, students spend most of their time waiting for their teachers or being accounted for, whether by taking attendance, filling out registration forms, or paying school fees. These kinds of accounting take far more time than I would have expected, averaging about 7 percent of the school day. We will see that there are three central activities to which students must learn to submit: waiting, taking dictation, and public disgrace. These are forms of discipline, in the sense that they subordinate students to the rhythm and activity of the school, requiring submission rather than reflection, even if—as is clear with waiting—they do not entail the "uninterrupted, constant coercion" that for Foucault defined the making of disciplined subjects (1979: 137). At times it seems that the content of the Catholic school discipline that parents vaunt is completely irrelevant: it is the hardship itself, regardless of its form or cause, that allows school to produce "the people of the future."

Waiting

While students seek to cultivate honorable self-dominion through their submission to school discipline, specific skills acquired through that learned submission may prove very helpful outside of school in their own right. This is particularly clear in the case of waiting and patience. The long delays that students learn to endure in school exist in multiple domains of life, from traditional funerals to interactions with state bureaucracy. And students do spend much of their school time waiting: teachers are often late and sometimes completely absent, interruptions are legion, and administration and punishment are slow and public. Over the course of an average seven-hour school day, students spend an hour and a half waiting for the teacher to begin class, and nearly another hour waiting during classroom interruptions, punishments, or administration. Learning to wait— to be patient—is a significant part of learning school discipline. Table 5.3 shows the distribution of activities during the 110 hours of scheduled class time at la Trinité that I observed and recorded minute-by-minute in the spring of 1998.

The categories listed here are mutually exclusive; I developed them after some dozen hours of open-ended observations in the classrooms.

TABLE 5.3   Use of classroom time, Collège de la Trinité, 1998

	Activity	Minutes	Proportion
Academic activities	Dictation	1,053	0.16
	Elicitation	1,059	0.16
	Lecture	1,122	0.17
	Questions	264	0.04
	Testing	726	0.11
Subtotal		*4,224*	*0.64*
Nonacademic activities	Administration	462	0.07
	Interruptions	528	0.08
	Waiting	1,386	0.21
Subtotal		*2,376*	*0.36*

"Dictation" means that the teacher is speaking slowly and repetitively, with the explicit intention of having the students write what is said into their notebooks. During dictation, most students do indeed copy verbatim. "Elicitation" refers to class contexts when the teacher encourages or elicits participation from the students, posing questions or asking for their opinions, and the students take turns responding. "Lecture" defines when the teacher speaks freely, either explaining or elaborating ideas in the dictations. During these sessions, very few, if any, students take notes. "Questions" refers to when the students ask questions of clarification or additional information and the teacher responds. "Testing" includes interim quizzes and monthly evaluations, but not the formal compositions at the end of each trimester, which are not counted as instructional days in my calculation. Testing is classified among the instructional activities, although in fact students are often waiting during time devoted to testing, as most students finish before the time allotted runs out. "Interruptions" are all those situations in which someone disrupts the flow of class for a nonacademic reason, whether a couple of students get in a fistfight or the surveillant comes to suspend students for the nonpayment of fees. "Administration" refers to situations in which students are being accounted for in some formal way, such as taking attendance, recording the payment of school fees, or passing out uniforms. Finally, "waiting" refers to situations in which the teacher is either not present at all, or is present but is in no way engaged with the students. For example, one teacher who taught at both la Trinité and a public high school would sometimes bring exams from the other school and correct them at his desk during class time, leaving the students sitting before him to wait.

This time-use distribution shows how much of a student's normal day is spent in noninstructional activities. Assuming perfect attendance, students would spend some 77.5 out of the 121 scheduled class days engaged in instructional activities. At 6.5 hours of class per day, this comes to a total of just over 500 hours of instruction, distributed over twelve subjects, over the course of an academic year. Waiting alone accounts for 21 percent of scheduled classroom time, the largest single activity. Given that students are also often waiting during interruptions, administration, and—to a lesser degree—testing, students spend more than a third of scheduled classroom time learning patience. Always, students are waiting for teachers, and not the reverse. This conforms to the pattern throughout the social organization of southern Cameroon that you wait for those of higher rank. In offices, service places, schools, and missions, who waits for whom signals domain-specific rank.

The hours of waiting in school also provide a space for students to practice specific modes of interaction. Although not taught by teachers, these forms of social intercourse are closely linked to education, as they are developed by students and transmitted in school (see Thorne 1993). These forms also differ significantly for boys and girls. In the absence of teachers, boys bully girls, tease them, interrupt their conversations, and physically hassle them. This bluster and bravado conforms to external expressions of male honor. Girls, for their part, endure these invasions with composure. Just as male presumption indicates high status, evoking the mastery of the *mfan mot* over his compound, female poise in the face of hardship indicates gender-appropriate honorable self-dominion.

Taking Dictation

According to the time-use data, classroom instruction consists of dictation, lecture, and elicitation. These three activities are not, however, equally valued by students as part of their education. Although each occupies approximately the same amount of classroom time, lecture and elicitation are considered substantially less important than dictation by students. During dictation, most students are quiet and attentive; they listen to the teacher, and transcribe his or her words carefully. During lecture and elicitation, by contrast, students are largely inattentive, and almost no one takes notes. Among the reasons for the importance of dictation is the absence of textbooks.

Although textbooks are produced and sold in Cameroon, almost no one buys them, and they are rarely referenced in class. Students and teachers have different explanations for the fact that students do not purchase textbooks. Students regularly explained to me that they could not afford them, and that they were anyway unnecessary, since the teachers dictate everything of importance. But teachers disagree. One teacher argued with his class about their dependence on dictation and their lack of initiative. He declared that "knowledge is a sacrifice!" and advised them to study at home. They countered that they did not have any books and therefore could not study at home. The teacher told them to buy books that were for sale in a nearby town. The students then said that they had no money, to which the teacher responded that they ostensibly had enough money to buy fashionable clothing, and they should rather spend their money on books. Some of this discussion was lighthearted, for indeed many students do make an effort to study at home, using their notebooks or whatever materials they can find. But for teachers, the absence of authorized texts remains a key marker of the "bush" conditions under which they are obliged to teach, and from which most of them hope to escape one day.

Whatever the reasons that students do not buy textbooks, the public exams nonetheless test on material provided in the books. Teachers must therefore provide the same material in another form. The form is verbatim dictation, which effectively replaces textbooks as the primary instructional material and modality. Students are expected to take impeccable dictation, and they are critiqued on the accuracy and standardization of their notes during repeated daily checks, as well as on their mastery of the content during examinations. Students are criticized on everything from their handwriting to the precision with which they copy the teacher's chalkboard style. In English class, a teacher noticed that some students were not double-underlining the section headings as he had done on the board. He told them to rewrite their notes, announcing, "If you do not copy, it means you are making fun of me!" Here we truly do see Foucault's attention to "the processes of the activity rather than its result" (1979: 137).

Teachers approach dictation in different ways. Some write out the dictation beforehand and read it from papers or small cards. Other teachers compose the dictations in situ, choosing the words for the next phrase while waiting for students to transcribe the current one. But all are introduced in the same way. The teacher will move from lecturing, that is, talking freely about the subject at hand, to dictation with a standardized phrase, commonly "Nous prenons!" (We take!)," or "À la ligne!" (On the line!). This transition has dramatic effects on the appearance and noise level of the classroom; students who have been looking out the window, chatting with a neighbor, or resting their heads on the desk will sit up and begin to write. Although lecture, elicitation, and questions all technically contribute to the mastery of the explicit curriculum, it is really in the dictations that students attend to the material and try to learn it.

Some teachers insist that students have standardized classroom notebooks, so that the dictations can be identical in form, as well as content. Many types of notebooks are sold, yet only one variety is acceptable. It consists of thirty standard pages folded in half and stapled together with a cover made of colored paper. The most rigorous teachers, like Mr. Atangana, require students to have a separate notebook for each subject and two pens: one blue and one black. This entails a minor financial burden and a more important one of organization. A student who had not yet bought new notebooks was using a single one, borrowed from his sister, for multiple subjects. When the biology teacher saw the various notes commingled, he snatched the notebook and, pinching it between thumb and forefinger like a dirty Kleenex, told the class that he would allow no such "notebook of cocoa purchases" in his classroom. Equating the student's lack of appropriate class materials with the social status of a farmer, the teacher called into question the young man's legitimacy as a student. Teachers regularly equate village residence with a lack of education, a lack of intelligence, or even the right to *become* educated. They use the terms *villageois* (villager) and *brousse* (literally, "bush," meaning not the city) as insults, insinuating that their students lack education, modernity, and even honor. This usage both reflects and reinforces the notion that schooling orients its students to the lifeways of the urban elite; although students whose parents are cocoa farmers constitute two-thirds of the upper grades at la Trinité, they are treated as the exception, whose habits will have to be corrected to the urbane norms of the teachers.

The attention given to the notebooks themselves and to the precision of dictation evokes the practices of the classic disciplinary institutions (Foucault 1979). By taking and memorizing verbatim dictation, students learn both a stance toward knowledge and a stance toward authority. "Knowledge is an object to be received through proper channels, not only learned but earned" (Bledsoe 1992: 191); neither the information nor its proper owner should be questioned. This attitude sits awkwardly with the demands of self-dominion, and some teachers find it disturbing or out of place. The dynamic young math teacher Mr. Atangana, whose class is described above, regularly contrasted what he perceives as the "sheeplike" passiveness of the students at la Trinité to the more outspoken class in the capital where he had done his practicum. "They write without understanding what they write," he complained, "they have no real interest in the thing." Mme Ngah was particularly concerned about the girls who tolerate both the teasing of classmates and the disrespect of male teachers. "You have to fight [se battre] to succeed," she admonished them in class one day, "especially you girls; no one is going to take you in hand." And yet, the common forms of instruction encourage precisely the passive attitudes toward learning that Mme Ngah and Mr. Atangana find objectionable. Students are disciplined into a passive acceptance of instruction, and even into a patient acceptance of not being instructed, for example, when the teacher simply fails to appear for the lesson, leaving the class waiting under the tin roof in the sun.

Public Shame

It is not only in calling them villageois and brousse that teachers insult students. Teachers commonly use insults and humiliation both to punish students and to remind them of the long road that they have yet to traverse before attaining honorable and educated adulthood. Teachers publicly contradict students on even trivial matters, call attention to their mistakes, and insult them in front of their classmates. They punish students by making them kneel in the front of the room, read their incorrect answers aloud to the class, or make them sit on the cement floor for the duration of the lesson. For a particularly serious disruption, a group of upper-school boys were sent to kneel in the gravel in front of the classrooms of the lower school, making them the symbolic inferiors of the younger students, who looked out the windows and taunted them.

Verbal derision can be directed at individuals or at whole groups of students. Teachers call students animals, idiots, and insane. When a student gave a poor answer in English class, the teacher responded: "Sit down, you are not normal!" To another student who answered a question in Francanglais, the same teacher said: "We'll have no country English!"[4] Teachers also criticize whole classes, for example, threatening students with the fact that Europeans think badly of them, and that their poor behavior conforms to these negative stereotypes. One teacher said: "They say that the black doesn't know how to listen. Do you want them to be right?" Another said: "There are people who believe that Cameroonians are savages, and you behave as badly as savages. I do not accept that." Of course, these examples may have been chosen for my benefit, or—alternatively—my being in the class may have made the threats more compelling. In either case, however, teachers relied on public shame to bring order to their classrooms.

The use of public shame is only partially successful, and when necessary it is supported with more serious action. In one case, a group of boys were quarreling in the back row of a French class. When the quarrel began to disrupt class, the teacher asked who had been making noise. No one confessed, so the teacher instructed the entire back half of the class to kneel on the floor next to their desks. He left them that way for a while, and then asked again who had been causing the trouble. When still no answer came, he threatened that everyone who was kneeling would be suspended from school unless someone reported who had been making noise. This threat was sufficient for one student to break ranks. The person named then flew into a fury, and he attacked the boy who had told, hitting him and calling him a very ugly racial and sexual epithet. The fight grew into a conflagration, and the teacher went to find the surveillant general, who sent about half the boys in the class into the courtyard for a punishment I did not see. The teacher then lectured the remainder of the class—that is, those who had not been involved in the physical altercation or the disruption that lead to it—on the dangers of insolence and self-importance. There are many people who have gone to school, he said, who are now selling palm wine in the village market. Having obtained a place in secondary school does not mean that you are safe; many will still fail. He concluded with the assertion: "If you behave like animals, you will be expelled!" With that, and another twenty minutes of class time remaining, the teacher left.

Students tolerate the regular humiliations in various ways. Girls learn, most of all, to endure insults with composure. Boys, by contrast, often resist the domination of the teachers more directly. They may refuse to complete a task set as punishment or resist being scolded by a teacher by directly insulting him. The fact that they get away with these forms of outward defiance, even some of the time, is somewhat puzzling, given the importance that parents place on discipline and the degree to which students can be dominated, if teachers so decide. I am left to think that there is a kind of complicity between some male teachers and male students, which permits boys a little space of self-dominion (in contrast, see Willis 1977). When one young man walked casually into his classroom during a lecture, the teacher scolded him for entering without permission. The teacher told him to return to the door and wait until he was recognized. The student walked back to the door, went out, and kept on walking, not to return for the rest of the day. These different responses of young men and women to classroom discipline through humiliation resemble other gender differences in interactive style, as will be discussed further below.

It is somewhat ironic that the social capital of the educated elite is won through submission to forms of discipline that appear to be honor's opposite. But when we recall how often Beti socialization relies on submission to elders, through which children demonstrate that they possess the "good sense" to someday become elders themselves, then school discipline looks rather more familiar. It is also clear that the submission required—especially of boys—is only partial. Teachers permit a fair amount of backtalk, wisecracking, and general disorder as long as students do not go too far.

Curriculum and the Acquisition of Elite Values

The subjugation of students critically frames the learning that takes place in Cameroonian schools. As we turn to focus on what is taught, I concentrate on what teachers actually say, rather than on what is in the Ministry of Education guidelines because, as we have seen, dictation constitutes the primary basis of instruction, and the curriculum matters only insofar as it is told to the students. Some scholars have assumed that the content of education accounts for the lower fertility of educated women (e.g., Caldwell 1980: 226–29). Having observed classrooms, however, I find this hard to believe. Although reproduction is a regular topic of classroom talk, the messages are contradictory and sometimes downright wrong. Students are, however, habituated into a standardized set of attitudes toward consumption, family, and state: they are instructed in elite values strongly supporting theories of modernization shared by NGOs, international aid organizations, and the Roman Catholic Church. The attitudes and values probably matter very much for reproduction, although they are not part of the formal curriculum.

There is a significant effort among the faculty at la Trinité to make the curriculum more "relevant" to students by making it more applied. At a round table on school failure held as part of the festivities for the Festival of Youth, several teachers argued that students fail primarily because the curriculum is too theoretical and therefore not interesting to the students.[5] My own observations are quite to the contrary. The content of classroom instruction is largely practical, or at least practicalized. Nearly all of the examples in the sciences come from daily or professional life: one biology teacher explained snail morphology by describing what snails look like when one prepares them for eating. Another noted that in order to catch fish, you have to know that they swallow their food whole. A physics teacher used a lengthy example of repairing televisions to talk about electron motion. Even much of the material in French and history is prefaced with a note about its application to daily life.

One of the corollaries of this constant process of making school knowledge "relevant" is that much of it is strongly ideological. The ideological content of course material arises most powerfully when the line between fact and opinion is heavily blurred, and when ideology-laden examples are selected to demonstrate an essentially nonideological point. The topics often revolve around country, family, and fertility. For example, the fact that Cameroon is "an underdeveloped country" into which certain forms of "modernism" have not yet penetrated is repeated often, as is the centrality of *la crise* in everyday life. Teachers reiterated the importance of education as a practical solution to Cameroon's "backwardness" or its "submission" to France. While these attitudes have no direct bearing on reproduction, I would argue that they are in fact far more important for demographic change than are the lessons on contraception described below. It is in thinking about themselves as moral agents in a modern state that Beti women have come to assert an honor of their own, and it is women's honor that makes possible new forms of reproductive practice.

I was not able to observe catechism at schools other than la Trinité, but there, at least, it was the one class that was consistently and surprisingly theoretical. Not only does the second-cycle curriculum focus almost exclusively on Bible readings and a mastery of the liturgical calendar, but its lessons were presented in remarkable abstraction from everyday life. Sister Margarite spoke rarely of the morality or immorality of specific actions, and made only the most general appeal to lead a life in Christ. With incredible consistency, she avoided any topics as specific as polygyny, premarital sex, abortion, or the use of contraceptives.

Whereas morality and information about fertility is missing from the catechism, it is covered in many other subjects. Reproduction itself is discussed in nearly every subject: in biology, students learned about human fertility, including information on the period of fecundity; in EVA the teacher discussed the psychology and physiology of pregnancy; the economics of population growth was the topic of a civics class. Sexuality is also

often used to illustrate lessons about other topics, from language to biology. EVA, specifically, addresses what kinds of reproductive actions are legitimate or moral. The liberal curriculum for EVA, written by a Canadian
priest, covers premarital sexuality, sexually transmitted infections, and a
full range of contraceptive methods. Like all course material, however,
its realization depends entirely on the teacher, and the instructor of EVA
at la Trinité had strong opinions about contraception. Two class sessions
were devoted to the physical risks associated with contraceptive pills. The
teacher noted that pills can cause bleeding, miscarriages, even permanent
sterility, and furthermore, that taking them makes a girl uglier. Periodic
abstinence, by contrast, was presented as natural and safe. Yet if a student
wanted to rely on periodic abstinence as a method of contraception, the
information provided in class would be completely insufficient.

The second of three classes on contraception was devoted to a discussion of periodic abstinence. The hour-long class consisted primarily of administrative tasks and the efforts of the teacher, Mme Abega, to get one
of the students to draw a basic graphing space on the board that could be
used to record daily temperature.[6] Twenty-five minutes into class, she had a
workable graph with straight lines and clearly labeled axes, but there were
still no data represented on the graph, and the axes had no units recorded.
At that point, Mme Abega explained awkwardly that a woman should take
her temperature every day for one month and make a mark on the graph
for each temperature. After doing this for a month, she asserted, a woman
will know when she is fecund. Any questions? Mme Abega asked, and a
male student put up his hand to say that he should not have to learn this,
since it would never affect him. Before Mme Abega could answer, another
boy said that, indeed, he should listen, because he might marry a woman
who has not been to school, in which case he will have to instruct her. Next,
a female student asked how you know from the temperature when you are
fecund. Mme Abega said that this is an important question, but not one
that can be answered right now, because "we want to understand the basic principles first. . . . We will talk about the details another time." To the
best of my knowledge, however, the teacher never did answer the young
woman's question; she certainly did not do so in the rest of that class, nor in
the subsequent one. After taking those questions, Mme Abega turned her
attention to some administrative work and covered no more content that
day. If in 1997–98 attention in la Trinité's upper secondary to the methods
of periodic abstinence was thin, AIDS was not covered at all.

Fertility is both a frequent topic and a contentious one, as different teachers approach it from widely varying perspectives. One position, presented most clearly by Mr. Ebene, associated family planning with infanticide on the one hand and genocide on the other. In a civics class on the Cameroonian population, he asserted that "we are not numerous enough" and that some young women are now dumping their babies in the trash because they "have no love in their hearts." Abortion was just the same as infanticide, he argued, and taking contraceptive pills the same as abortion. Finally, Mr. Ebene equated motherhood with serving in the military, asserting that "the women must also defend us!"[7] Even the French teacher, who above we saw garnering compliments for his fashionable haircut, found reason to argue against condoms in particular and fertility limitation in general. "Why did France lose the colonies? Because we were more numerous!" he asserted, eliding World War Two, the constitution of the Fourth Republic, and the fact that Cameroon was not a French colony. Then to conclude he added, "They [the French] gave out hoods [condoms] too freely!" At the other extreme, Mr. Zogo argued that high fertility persists in Cameroon because of "backward" cultural patterns that must be changed for the country to advance. Zogo claimed that high fertility is a national problem, since "the poor do not have the resources to rear and educate their children." In an analysis that could have come straight out of an international development pamphlet from the 1980s, he went on to argue that excess fertility inevitably leads to crime and more poverty, creating a vicious cycle of poverty and high fertility. Mme Ngah offered a similar perspective. During a history class, she declared: "It was necessary to limit births. Why? Because of the lack of resources." A variety of perspectives on reproduction are thus part of a Catholic secondary education. On the one hand, childbearing is portrayed as a moral obligation, particularly to the state; on the other hand, there is a strong ideology that parents should not bear children they do not have the resources to support.

Sometimes partially conflicting perspectives are presented within a single class. One of the more compelling teachers, Mr. Mfan, lectured on Malthus and demographic change. He argued both that Cameroon's population was failing to reproduce itself and that fertility among young Cameroonian women was excessive. Although not directly contradictory, these two positions are in tension with each other, a tension that was not lost on the students. Mfan's argument that the Cameroonian population was shrinking did not make any mathematical sense, but went like this: the population of Cameroon is about sixteen million, and therefore the country has about eight million women. The median age at childbearing is twenty. Divide eight million by twenty, and you will get four hundred thousand: the anticipated number of births. But there were only three hundred thousand births reported last year. Therefore, Cameroon's population is failing to reproduce itself.[8] The lack of births, he suggested, is the result of economic development, since rich men reject sexual relationships: "They have better [things] to do than think about that animal instinct," he said. But while overall fertility is too low as a result of economic development, Mfan noted that adolescent fertility is dangerously high. Cameroonian girls, Mfan argued, begin bearing children at age fourteen, "because if a woman reaches eighteen without giving birth, one starts to worry," and this undisciplined fertility is the rightful "object of dark predictions." Given the complexity of classroom "messages," any model of demographic change that rests on students' acquiring straightforward information in school simply cannot stand.

Not only fertility, but also sexuality and heterosexual relations slip into classroom talk. In demonstrating the use of the simple present tense instead of the present continuous for verbs of being in English, Mr. Ngono joked that some boys "from the bush" try to impress girls by saying "I am loving you." But, he explained, "the girls are smart, so they answer, 'No, I am refusing you!' " In a biology class devoted to the anatomy of birds, the teacher pointed out that male birds can only copulate at specific times during the year. He then went on to joke with the male students that this is different from human males, who are always able and willing to have sex. About humans, he laughed: "He says to himself, 'Good, I've got some money. I'll go find some!' " Like the joking we saw above about the unripeness of girls, this kind of sexual teasing offers boys and girls different modes of incorporation into the classroom. In addition, certain attitudes toward sex are normalized by their inclusion in teachers' instruction. Males are portrayed as being the sexual initiators, females, when portrayed at all, as resisting males' advances.

A couple of classes become loci for ongoing conversations about gender, sexuality, and childbearing. Mme Ngah, an exceptionally capable, well-educated teacher and the only female teacher in the core curriculum, maintains a dialogue with her classes about work and motherhood. In a philosophy class, she alleged that for a marriage to be successful, the wife must cook for her husband. She continued: "But you are free now, because of modernity. You can even give the keys to the kitchen to your little boy.

But there! That means divorce!" Many of the girls in the class protested, arguing that if a woman has a career, she can hire someone to cook. But Mme Ngah held fast, insisting that wives must always cook. A young woman in the front row rejoined, "But, Madame, *yoyettes* don't cook!" This interaction, where an ideological program is not only raised but debated in the classroom, is rare. Mme Ngah, more than any other teacher on the faculty, encourages discussion and tolerates dissent. But even when teachers do not permit debate about fertility, sexuality, and heterosexual relations in the classroom, the fact that these topics are raised may form the basis of personal reflection and reevaluation.

Gender Work

As we have seen, teachers partially collaborate with male students in excluding female students from legitimate class participation. When teachers are absent, the classroom becomes even more clearly the domain of boys, in which girls are an entertaining distraction. However, these facts must not obscure what is most central about gender in school, which is its relative equality, or at least its integration. Most contemporary Cameroonian schools are gender-integrated, and boys share benches with girls throughout the school day. For many students, full-day interaction with young people of the opposite sex is imaginable only in school, for at home and elsewhere, males and females inhabit very separate realms. The constant and direct exposure to unrelated members of the opposite sex creates an environment in which students develop and learn new forms of gender identity and heterosexual relations, forms with significant consequences beyond school. What is more, students are formally equal in the school context, comparable to that of the church, regardless of their sex. Although this formal equality is often undermined by the practices of teachers and administrators, it is at least discursively available as legitimate grounds for social action. In the historical process through which Beti women are coming to claim a modern honor, their position as men's equals in school and church plays a critical role.

Standards of self-dominion apply somewhat differently to men and women, but for both sexes they are associated with composure, restraint, self-mastery and—perhaps most of all—schooling. Thus one young woman who had come from Yaoundé to attend la Trinité explained that she refused to have a boyfriend in Mbeya because the local boys were poorly educated. She noted that she could date "perhaps guys [who are] a little more educated, but here I have never seen a guy who is poised. The guys from here behave as if their youth was a time to amuse themselves aimlessly." In this quote, my interlocutor suggests that educated men should carry themselves with the same composure and restraint that is believed to characterize educated women. However, this opinion is not universal. Male and female students in fact experience schooling in very different ways, and they learn very different modes of social engagement there. The variations between male and female engagement in school can be partly predicted by the dissimilarity in male and female honor; for Beti men, honor is measured in part by their visible domination of social interaction (recall, for example, the minibus driver in chapter 3). Even among the educated, male honor requires a kind of overt authority largely missing from female honor. Thus male students, as honorable men in training, learn a somewhat different discipline than do their female classmates.

Gender socialization is not part of the explicit curriculum and is only partially under the control of school authorities. It is deeply contradictory, such that its obvious elements—like boys' verbal aggression toward girls—work in the opposite direction of the equally powerful fact that the girls are nonetheless there, seated alongside the boys, taking the same exams, and sometimes earning superior grades. In part, teachers' lack of control over the learning of gender roles arises from the fact that the students of a division are always together, whereas they are with any specific teacher only a few hours a week, and they are often without any teacher at all. But teachers also collude with the gender dynamics that students introduce, ignoring them and therefore enabling them to continue. Explicit gender relations between students can be reduced to simple principles. Boys overtly assert themselves, invading the privacy and person of most girls and of any boys unable to defend themselves. Girls try to endure these invasions with composure, ignoring them when possible and minimizing their effects when not.

Boys actively and effectively dominate classroom space, time, and discourse: they speak more loudly and more often and harass girls into submission. Boys use loud interjections to claim the classroom for themselves, calling out snide comments on the lesson or a nickname—often an insulting nickname—for another student. When a girl speaks in class, boys interrupt with critical comments: "But the women are bothering!" or "She is always talking!" An attractive girl in western attire, regardless of her sexual conduct, is called *ephesse* (Eton for "prostitute"). Very few teachers effectively suppress these interjections and brief interruptions. Boys who use them can therefore assert their interpretations of classroom activities without rebuttal. The gender inequality in the classroom is accentuated by the fact that the vast majority of teachers are male; male teachers are far more indulgent of boys' pranks than are female teachers. Male teachers also elicit legitimate classroom participation from boys much more often than from girls, while female teachers are more evenhanded.

The boys' interjections are not all directed at girls. Some are general exclamations, some directed at other boys. Even teachers, as we saw earlier in the chapter, are teased. Looking at common nicknames, we can see how interjections directed at boys differ from those directed at girls. Nicknames can be either complimentary or insulting, but are much more commonly the later, particularly for girls. Table 5.4 lists some nicknames and their explanations, starting with those used for men and boys. Fewer girls have nicknames, their nicknames are more consistently derogatory, and they are more often used for many students, rather than being specific to one.

With the exception of "Kimbo," none of the nicknames given to girls are based on personal talents or habits in the way that so many of the boys' nicknames are. The first two of the only four that I recorded can indeed be used to refer to almost any girl, given that the context is fitting—that is, that she is doing something noticeable or unusual, such as walking into class late. Also, very few girls have nicknames at all. I asked a male student why, and he offered, "The other girls don't have nicknames because they behave well." But this is clearly beside the point; there is little evidence for any relationship between girls' behavior and their being subjected to boys' sometimes hurtful interjections.

Girls' response to nicknames and the general harassment that they receive at the hands of their male classmates is something like forbearance. Only rarely do girls respond to the name calling, and even then they do not respond in kind. Girls repeatedly explained to me that the only way to deal with interjections is to ignore them, the same advice that they gave me about men hassling me in the market or on the bus. Indeed, female honor through self-dominion is strongly focused on patience and endurance, and schoolgirls practice these traits not only during long periods of waiting and in response to boys' heckling, but also in reaction to teachers' behavior. In reference to classroom material with which they disagree, girls use a similar tactic; instead of overtly disagreeing with the instructor, they memorize the dictation for the exam but refuse to believe it. During one civics

TABLE 5.4 **Nicknames, Collège de la Trinité, 1998**

Nickname	Given to	Explanation
Male		
Abraham	Student	After the biblical character, because "he knows a lot."
Armstrong	Student	Like Louis Armstrong, he plays the trumpet.
Bad Colour	Teacher	"Because he is too black."
Chercheur	Student	"Researcher," because he is always studying.
Diouf	Student	Resembles Abdou Diouf, the former president of Senegal.
Dombolo	Teacher	A popular dance from Congo Kinshasa, because he once did it at a party.
Negatif	Administrator	"Because he is it!" That is, he is perceived as having a negative character.
Nicombarga	Student	A (now deceased) musician from Douala, who limped in the same way.
Pfilsen	Student	The brand of beer he prefers.
Popo	Administrator	"Papaya" in Eton, but no one knew why.
Za Morano	Student	After the Chilean soccer player.
Female		
Ekus	Many students	"Purchase" in Eton, the term that is increasingly used to refer to bridewealth.
Ephesse	Many students	"Prostitute" in Eton; by far the most common nickname given to girls.
Impressio	Three new students	Name given to new girls who are thought to be attractive or impressive.
Kimbo	Student	A television character who is tall and slender, like the student.

class, the teacher said that women are important for the cohesion of the family but play no political role. Everyone copied this into their exercise books with no debate, but when I asked several girls about it afterward, they pointed out that women are now in the government and gave me the names of three women ministers at the national level. This attitude is precisely the kind of submission for which Mme Ngah was scolding them when she said, "You have to fight to succeed." From the perspective of the schoolgirls, fighting would *prevent* them from succeeding; it is by never actively resisting that they are able to have some space for themselves in school. Girls at la Trinité generally seek to retain their partial autonomy by never overtly asserting it; they do not contest the visible domination of men, but evade it.

To formalize the question of gendered classroom participation, I devoted nine classroom hours to recording incidences by gender of three behaviors, which I label contributions, disruptions, and retreat (see table 5.5).

TABLE 5.5   **Gender distribution of classroom participation, Collège de la Trinité, 1998**

	N (person-hours)	Contributions (rate)	Disruptions (rate)	Retreat (rate)
Males	198	29 (0.15)*	34 (0.17)	15 (0.08)
Females	121	11 (0.09)	4 (0.03)	19 (0.16)
Total	319	40 (0.13)	38 (0.12)	34 (0.11)

*The first number represents the total number of events; the second (in parentheses) the rate per person-hour.

"Contributions" are utterances that contribute to the pedagogic project of the class, such as asking a pertinent question or answering an elicitation. "Disruptions" are utterances that detract from the pedagogic project: name calling, wisecracks, and loud conversation. "Retreat" includes all forms of visible nonparticipation, such as resting your head on your desk or sleeping against the wall.

We see that boys are more active than girls in all three categories (i.e., more likely to act and less likely to withdraw), but the difference is by far the most pronounced in the domain of disruptions. These are the interjections with which boys often belittle girls, calling their legitimacy in the classroom into question. It is also interesting to notice that student participation in the educational project is quite limited overall. Counting only positive interjections, we have forty cases of legitimated talk by students over nine hours: less than five instances per hour, or about one contribution per student per day.

While both Beti girls and boys learn discipline in school, they do so in very different ways. Because of the preponderance of male teachers, male teachers' tolerance of boys' mischief in the classroom, and systems of gender relations that extend far beyond school, Cameroonian Catholic schools are far more hospitable to boys than girls. Both boys and girls learn to wait and to subject themselves, at times, to others' authority. But in the classroom, boys practice dominating interactions. The interjections we have seen here resonate with the vociferous claims to male honor in Cameroonian society at large. Girls, by contrast, practice endurance, tolerance, and patience: markers of self-restraint and female self-dominion among the Beti.

Before leaving the topic of gender in the classroom, I would like to return to the basic fact that the girls, however much they might submit to unequal treatment, are there at all. Comparatively, they are even there in large numbers. Some 40 percent of Beti teenage girls now attend at least one year of secondary school, to be contrasted with about 8 percent of girls in the Northern Province of Cameroon. And this simple fact matters hugely for how gender relations in school translate into gender relations more broadly. In response to my question of what it means to be an educated woman, one (rather obstreperous) young woman explained:

> It's a woman who has done class, no? . . . Because normally, a woman is equal to a man. So if a woman is educated, in my opinion it's the same thing. There is no difference. Like when you came to us; a man could do the same thing. . . . Take me, for example, I am educated. I went to school. So I can say that it is normal for a woman to go to school, because the woman is equal to the man.

She argues here that women can attend school just like men because the two sexes are equal. However, the primary evidence that the two sexes are equal comes from schooling itself. It is in large part because young women now attend school equally and alongside young men that they are able to claim formal equality with them. The only other site in which women have such visible and significant equality is in church participation and the reception of the sacraments, grounded in the doctrine that all are equal before God. Thus, Catholic schools are among the key loci of Cameroonian women's liberation and the radical transformation of Beti social order. The sometimes extraordinary force with which schoolboys seek to assert themselves over girls must be seen in this light. Although they are often successful in shutting girls up in the short run, the very fact that they have to do so points to the ways things are changing.

*   *   *

In exploring what happens inside schools, we have looked at the daily practices that constitute the honorable discipline that parents and students so strongly ascribe to Catholic education. We have seen that much of what happens inside the classroom only partially conforms to the image of regular, systematic discipline, cultivating honorable self-dominion in its charges. By contrast, much of what matters about formal education is outside the curriculum, and even outside the control of teachers and administrators. The gender equity implied by coeducation is arguably more important than all the exams and punishments together, as students are habituated into a standardized set of values of "modernity" and equality, values as much in keeping with the worldviews of international corporations and international aid organizations as with those of the Roman Catholic

Church. In chapter 6, we examine the heterosexual relationships in which educated women participate. These relationships constitute the immediate context for reproductive practices, starting with the use of contraception. We will see that many of the forms of interaction and self-perception that educated women practiced in school come into play in their sexual relationships.

CHAPTER SIX

The Secret Politics of Sex

Free love, in the boldest sense of the word, reigns [between puberty and marriage]. The girl may give her affections to whom she wants, when she wants. She must only observe the religious doctrine that forbids sexual intercourse during the day, and the social doctrine that forbids it between blood relatives. Otherwise there are no boundaries. — Günther Tessman, *Die Pangwe*

For almost a century, western ethnographers and historians have drawn attention to the relative sexual license of the Beti, particularly for unmarried women. Alexandre and Binet, for example, write of the "sexual freedom" of adolescent girls (1958: 52), and Laburthe-Tolra refers to "the famous sexual liberty of the 'Yaundes' that so struck the first observers" (1981: 234).[1] Some in the Beti intelligentsia have strongly disputed the validity of these interpretations, arguing that foreign authors have unfairly depicted Beti social life as highly sexualized, or even sexually obsessive. To counter the sexual lens of classical ethnographies, Cameroonian authors often offer alternative accounts of Beti social practices. For example, Mviena (1970: 12) and Tabi (n.d.: 15) both interpret the ritual *mevungu* as oriented only to procreation, without sexual content or connotation.[2] There is, of course, nothing new about western scholars representing African sexuality as excessive or out of place. And most Beti—educated or not—are well aware of the politics of being represented as chaste or unchaste to a western audience, which they associate with the Catholic Church and anti-AIDS campaigns. Several educated men asked me to write a rebuttal to Laburthe-Tolra's claims about Beti sexuality, a rebuttal to be read by people in America and France who are assumed to have negative stereotypes about the Beti. Yet not all Beti, or even all Beti intellectuals, concur with the position of Mviena and Tabi. Some have, to the contrary, contributed to the representation of Beti society and culture as unusually sexually permissive. For example, Ombolo's remarkable book *Sexe et societé en Afrique noir* (1990) moves between ethnographic description, psychoanalysis, and semiotics to portray the Eton as creating and inhabiting a world defined by sex.

Contention surrounds not only "traditional" Beti practice, but also the changes that have occurred in sexual practice. The women interviewed by Vincent (1976) almost all claimed that sexual practice in their own youth (mostly in the 1930s) was more restrained than at the time of Vincent's research in the early 1970s. In my own experience, both this attitude and its opposite are widely held: some people suggest that premarital sex and pregnancy were less common in the past, while others argue that people were more "promiscuous" before the wide-scale conversion to Christianity at the beginning of the twentieth century. Jane Guyer has told me that women married very early during the cocoa boom, as young as eight years old, and she holds that the practice of mandatory bridal virginity during those decades was an anomaly associated with these young ages at marriage. Over a shorter time horizon, data from the Demographic and Health Survey (DHS)—nationally representative surveys of women fifteen to forty-nine years of age on matters of reproduction and infant health—suggests that the median age at first intercourse has increased slightly in recent decades, from 15.6 years among women born between 1949 and 1953 to 16.3 years among those born between 1974 and 1978.[3] Of course, these disparate facts and opinions are not necessarily in conflict: nonmarital sexuality for women may have been common in the late 1800s, become less tolerated during the colonial occupation and growth of cocoa cultivation, only to become again more widely practiced and accepted since independence, with both ages at marriage and ages at first intercourse rising, the latter more slowly than the former.

Sex and romance are—perhaps everywhere—compelling, focal topics of teenage girls' conversation and fantasy, as well as the immediate context for pregnancy. In southern Cameroon specifically, sexual relationships play a significant role in defining modern honor, especially for women. Educated Beti women construe their romantic and sexual engagements as one element differentiating them from uneducated women. These women describe themselves as "modern," "disciplined," even "rational," and therefore less likely than the uneducated to bear children outside of marriage. Indeed, the cultivation of this self-discipline that shapes honorable sexuality and controls reproduction tops the list of benefits that young women ascribe to formal schooling, and constitutes important evidence of their claims to a modern honor. But these seemingly distinct lines of rationality and control that are central to honorable sexuality and modern honor get very blurry in the actual course of educated women's sexual lives.

According to the young women I came to know in Mbeya and Yaoundé, honorable women have children while still young, stay in school, and marry prior to having children. And yet these three expressions of control and modernity and honor are fundamentally incompatible. While any two can—in theory—be achieved, their joint attainment will necessarily preclude the third (Johnson-Hanks 2004). What is more, the three social goals are not clearly ranked, such that women are willing to forfeit the less important goals in order to have the more important ones. Nonetheless, my interlocutors identified all three as central components of a proper female life course. All three are actively sought, and gossip about "women who have gone astray" usually focuses on their failure to attain one or more of these goals. As a result, every educated woman will necessarily have strayed in some way. Their honor is uncertain not because it is difficult to fulfill the dictates of a demanding standard, but because the category itself—still in flux—is internally contradictory. Thus the exploration of sexuality, schooling, and childbearing among young Beti women becomes an exploration of the context in which these young women must make choices whose consequences cannot be known in advance, in an attempt to invent and inhabit the honor of the modern woman.

Sexual behavior and its cultural construction are pivotal to understanding how educated women manage the entry into motherhood in a manner they consider honorable. In this chapter, I offer a partial description of the sexual lives of young, unmarried Beti women, and especially of those still in school. It will become clear that sex is accepted as common but is also required to be discreet. It is understood to be a healthy and normal practice but is nonetheless often fraught with distrust. Although much of the symbolism of sex has deep local antecedents, it would be wrong to see this as a description of Beti sexuality over long sweeps of history. In almost every domain of their lives, educated Beti women are required to find new ways of being and bringing together partially incompatible identities: sexuality is no different.

"Le corps a besoin de beaucoup de choses"

Raised in a Methodist household in a small, American town, my own attitudes toward sexuality are most fairly described as prudish. Perhaps more
than anything else, this made me feel like a stranger in southern Cameroon, where my interlocutors' views and experiences—although far from
uniform—were systematically different from my own. For the most part,
my friends and acquaintances held the position described by Laburthe-
Tolra: that sexual desire is natural, inevitable, and very powerful, that both
men and women require regular sexual activity for their health and welfare, and that entry into sexual life constitutes an important element of normal adolescence outside the parameters of marriage (see Laburthe-Tolra
1981: 237). Most of the educated women I interviewed considered nonmarital sex and concurrent sexual partners (at least for men) acceptable,
assuming reasonable discretion. This is not to say that the young women I
knew have sex all that often, for they do not. What matters is that the duration of abstinence not extend too long. The importance of sex for health,
in this perspective, is physical—like exercise and good nutrition—rather
than emotional or psychological. When educated women emphasize that,
through the practices of self-cultivation and schooling, they have acquired
the moral self-mastery to refrain from sex at the wrong times and under
the wrong circumstances, it is sex as a fundamental physical need that they
are abjuring. They restrain their eating and sleeping as part of the same
ethical practices of self-dominion.

During my research, both men and women expressed concern about
my well-being, on the grounds that my extended abstinence was neither
healthy nor normal. Even casual acquaintances suggested that I should
take a lover, if only temporarily, and that the consequences of doing so
would be minor. As one woman whom I met on a bus clarified: "Il ne faut
que faire le cache-cache" (You just have to keep it secret). The range of
opinions on this topic was informative. Some people thought that I required a lover, going so far as to volunteer a brother or cousin, and considered my assertion that I preferred to wait for my partner back home
frankly naïve. Sometimes exasperated and sometimes amused, people
pointed out that *he* had surely taken a lover in my absence, and I would
only be reciprocating. Others thought that I was more clever: they were
convinced that I *had* a local lover, but that I was so discreet that no one
knew about it. This imaginary man was the subject of great speculation:
Was he white? African? Was he rich? Did he work for the government?

There was no point for me in disagreeing; denial—like silence—was considered evidence that their claims were true. But suspicion that I was an adept hider of sexual secrets was also the more flattering position, to the degree that Claudette (whose experiences are recounted in chapter 7) offered to befriend me by explaining that she believed *both* that I was not working for the CIA *and* that I really did have a lover in the capital city. Others were not so generous. One late afternoon, sitting on the wooden benches that constitute Mbeya's most popular bar with some of the high school teachers, the conversation turned to my sexual abstinence while conducting fieldwork. One of the teachers reasoned that white women were just different than Cameroonian women, that we had different physical constitutions (an explanation that I had cultivated in explaining my vegetarianism). Another suggested that my problem was racism: that I rejected black men. The third started down a list of potential partners in town, asking what I found objectionable about each one in turn. In part, of course, they were teasing me; my discomfort offered an afternoon's amusement. But they were also genuinely trying to understand.

Later, recalling the conversation and observing my emotional reaction to it, I was struck by how the alternative explanations that the teachers had offered for my unwillingness to take a lover in my partner's absence applied only to me. How would they have accounted for a similar decision by a Beti woman? I started to ask women whose husbands or partners were away what they did, how they managed. Some I knew had a "little guy" on the side. On the other hand, Nanette explained that she had indeed remained faithful to her fiancé, who had been away for nearly a year, despite the pressures of her friends and of her body:

> I have girlfriends who say, "No, you can't stay like that [without a sexual partner]. You also have to look. No one will know." I say that it depends; each person is different. . . . Of course, the body demands. Sometimes you have to do certain things. So I say to myself that you have just have to tolerate [it].

The ambiguity of Nanette's conclusion—does she mean that you have to tolerate the unfulfilled physical demands or the breach of your own standards of self-restraint?—was not clarified. Later in the conversation, I asked more directly, "So when the husband travels like that, the wife will also search [for a lover]?" Again she demurred, "Ça dépend de tout un chacqun" (literally, "That depends on every one each," or more colloquially, "Everyone is different").

The idea that both women and men require regular sexual activity comes up in all manner of contexts, extending even to debates over the accuracy of national statistics. In conversation, Beti men frequently volunteered that there are significantly more women than men in Cameroon; because both men and women need regular sex to be healthy, this superfluity of women requires men to have multiple sexual partners—otherwise some women will be constantly frustrated, even turning to prostitution for satisfaction. Men's estimates of the imbalance between the sexes varied from two to ten times more women than men.[4] Many people appear committed to these estimates: given a conflict between the national census—which shows, of course, that about half of the population is female—and their intuition of an excess of women, people generally assume that the census is wrong. Some of my male interlocutors explained that the prefects just filled out the forms randomly to get money from the government; others said that people were afraid or ashamed to admit how many unmarried women lived in their households. A pharmacist from a nearby town asserted that the birth records for the province show that only 36 percent of newborns were male, and that in his town, this ratio surely held.[5] A teacher recounted that the original census figures revealed that the country had three times as many women as men, and that the government changed the numbers because of the embarrassment, and also the risk to national security, if neighboring countries knew that Cameroon was full of women without men to defend them.

The joint perceptions that women have a physical need for sex and that Cameroon has too many women are regularly used to explain why polygyny is necessary. Yet in the face of widespread schooling for women, some men worry that even the polygyny solution will be insufficient to absorb all of the women into legitimate marriages and domesticate their potentially socially disruptive sexual desires. One young unmarried man, himself completing high school, explained that most of the "surplus" women are not suitable for marriage: "Given that there are many more women than men, that causes problems. Because the women don't leave school. They get educated and so the men are afraid of them." Linking a perceived surplus of women specifically to the recent expansion of schooling, this young man draws an argument against female education: it disrupts a nuptial regime that relies on early and universal marriage for women.

A corollary of the assumption that women, like men, need regular sex is the belief that women enjoy it, or at least that they can or should. The Beti never practiced excision,[6] and the central female rite, the *mevungu*, is described by Ombolo as oriented toward "the exaltation of the beauty and majesty of the sexual organ of the woman" (1990: 348). Although, as we will see later in the chapter, there is a great deal of secrecy surrounding the identities of nonmarital sexual partners, unmarried educated Beti women often talk quite freely among themselves about their sexual pleasure or frustration. Women often described being "overcome" by sexual passion, or explained how they had chosen to stay with a particular boyfriend because of his sexual aptitude. One woman explained that she left her previous boyfriend because he was unable to satisfy her sexually. She concluded by saying: " 'To make love' is an expression that I find is misused. You have sexual intercourse. When you make love that means that you attain another dimension; it means that both partners are satisfied. But it is rare to make love. But to have sexual intercourse is common." In this way, sex is separated from potential marital relationships; women may pursue it for its physical pleasure, choosing at least some of their partners for their sexual abilities.

Although many women talk about the importance of sex for health, and most agree that mutual satisfaction is important, there is little consensus on how easily sexual gratification can be attained. Some women explain that pleasure is easily attainable with the right partner, while others think that to be satisfied depends more on the woman's own mindset. Claudette explained that from her perspective, there were different kinds of sex: sex for love, for desire, and for "kindness" (être gentille). This last kind of sex—where the woman gives sex as a gift to her male partner—may be reciprocated with some other kind of gift on the part of the man. As with all forms of gift exchange, the line here between generalized gifting and market exchange for formal compensation constantly risks breach and requires active maintenance (see Malinowski 1984: 96). In some contexts and for some people, the line does not exist: the interpretation that sex is something that men take from women, and for which women should justly be compensated, is also culturally available in Cameroon, as we will explore further below (see also Calvès 1996). Few of the young, educated women who shared their stories with me would, however, go so far as to agree with Laburthe-Tolra's assessment, made on the basis of masterful ethnography primarily among senior Beti men, that "the sexual act is conceived as an aggression" (Laburthe-Tolra 1981: 351). Still, while heterosexual desire is perceived as healthy and inevitable, there is also a sense in which its fulfillment is dangerous; some women demand physical pleasure from their sexual partners, but few expect trust.

"On ne mange pas le macabo chaque jour"

Although sexual instincts are presumed to be strong in both men and women, men are thought to be particularly susceptible to their influence, and—as a result—to be particularly likely to have several sexual partners at once. At the same time, sexual restraint plays a far less central role in male honor than in the honor of women, so that a young man notorious for seducing women may be seen as rambunctious, rather than sexually incontinent. To some degree, this whole set of interrelated assumptions resembles those found in the United States, and perhaps in most places: coarse jokes about untamed erections or men's inability to wield both a brain and a penis at once are common in the female-only company of kitchens and hair salons. What is at least somewhat specific to southern Cameroon is the degree to which women tolerate men's *acting* on these widely assumed inclinations. To a striking extent, young and educated Beti women abide a partner's affairs as long as they are discreet, and older, less educated women are arguably even more tolerant. This should not be interpreted to mean that women find men's multiple simultaneous relationships desirable, or even really acceptable, but rather that they tolerate them because they see little other choice. Indeed, young women spend substantial time with friends discussing the causes of and possible remedies for male roving. Throughout an afternoon and evening of domestic chores, braiding one another's hair, and eating dinner, groups of young women find ample time to analyze and reanalyze men's sexual habits. While some women claim that it is simply impossible for men to be faithful, others argue that men should be able to control themselves, but seldom do.[7] Regardless of whether they *could be,* most Beti women are adamant in their assertion that men never *are* monogamous. While I do not have data on men's actual sexual practices, men's talk about their conquests would lend credence to women's accounts (cf. Calvès 1996: 174).

Beti women state emphatically and consistently that Beti men always maintain multiple sexual relationships, both within and outside of marriage, and that a wise woman simply learns to tolerate it. Nanette, whose thoughts about her own abstinence are quoted above, explained how she coped with her fiancé's presumed infidelity: "He is doing his professional training, and I am here waiting. I tell myself that he is faithful. I know that a man cannot remain faithful, but I tell myself that to avoid making too many problems for myself." A similar sense of the impossibility of male abstention comes from an interview in which I asked a twenty-two-year-old student about her hopes for the future. What kind of a man would she like to marry? She replied:

> I would like to marry a man who doesn't look at other women too much. But that is impossible here in our place. When you are married, do not think that you are the only one. Give yourself an idea that before you there were others and after you there will be others still.

Whether in talking about their current boyfriends or even about dreams for future husbands, Beti women generally assume that they cannot expect fidelity from men. Men will simply always have relationships with multiple women, some legal and socially legitimated, others in secret.

Although Beti women vary in their willingness to accept infidelity, in general it is silently tolerated, especially if the man continues to fulfill his economic obligations to his wife or steady girlfriend. What she will not tolerate is for her husband to reveal his extramarital affairs, or—worse yet—to bring his lover into his wife's house. This insult asserts that he has no respect for her, for her honor, or even for his own. One woman who was recently married explained that she hoped her husband would hide his inevitable infidelities from her. "I will perhaps get angry in the case that he brings his women into my house. But in the case that they go elsewhere to meet, we won't have any problems." If a man openly brings other women into his house, it is thought to show grave disrespect for his wife. One woman called it "an act of disdain." When a man respects his wife, he will protect her from knowing about his affairs, but he will probably have them nonetheless.

Even to bring a girlfriend into the house of his patrilateral kin who have contributed to the bridewealth for another woman is shameful, although it sometimes happens. A man I knew in Yaoundé, Jacques-Marie, was married with bridewealth. His young bride remained in his natal village while he worked in the city. He stayed with a cousin of his father, eating with the family and contributing to the household. When Jacques-Marie began inviting his city girlfriend to stay the night with him, everyone ignored her, behaving as if they had never seen her. The relatives expressed neither surprise nor curiosity, and they were not directly impolite; the young woman was simply invisible to them. This is the same mode of avoidance that parents use with children's sweethearts before they are formally presented. They may see them regularly over years and yet will say that they do not know who they are, or even know their name.

One day, I wanted to take pictures of all the people in the household that Jacques-Marie calls home when he is in the city, passing my camera around for people to take the pictures, so that I could be in some of them. One was to be of me, Jacques-Marie, and his girlfriend, whom I had come to know a little bit and liked very much. When I got the film back, I was there, clear and in the middle of the picture, Jacques-Marie standing next to me at the edge of the frame, his arm reaching out of the edge of the picture, into the space where the girlfriend had been standing. She was cut off, just a little bit of her foot showing at the bottom right.

When I asked men why they so often had multiple partners, I was surprised that they neither appeared offended, nor asserted that they were indeed faithful to their wives or girlfriends. Instead, most men had articulate reasons for their diversity of sexual partners, based on some combination of Beti "tradition," western psychological theory, and biblical exegesis. Some of the justifications were elaborate, but the most common was a simple adage in Camfrançais: "On ne mange pas le macabo chaque jour" (One does not eat cocoyams every day). Cocoyams, along with yams and manioc, are tubers that constitute the mainstay of the diet in southern Cameroon, particularly in rural areas. The implication is not that cocoyams are undesirable—to the contrary, many people prefer their slightly waxy softness to dry manioc—but only that any food has its place alongside others. Food and eating serve metaphorically both in Eton/Ewondo and in Camfrançais not only for sexuality, as here, but also for violence, power, witchcraft, and corruption. A person possessed by *evu* "eats" his relatives; a politician who has embezzled money "ate" it (*adi*). In contrast to many West African languages, Eton and Ewondo make no distinction between the healthful, productive eating that metaphorically represents normal social reproduction and the dangerous, destructive eating of witchcraft (pace Rowlands and Warnier 1988). Procreative sex, sex for pleasure, abuse of power, and witchcraft can all be called *adi*.

Although eating metaphors are broadly applied, this particular adage does not apply to women. My repeated question as to whether women are supposed to eat cocoyams every day usually met with laughter, then silence. But one woman explained why men's more overt escapades were tolerated, while those of women must be kept a dark secret:

We say to ourselves that when a man is unfaithful it is not so bad, but when it's the woman it is bad. Because here in Africa we know that the man is born for polygamy, that's it. Because we Africans say that children are wealth. So we say to ourselves that a man can have as many wives or women as he wants. But there is no polyandry in our place. So the man can deceive, but not the woman.

Asserting that polygyny resembles "deception," my interlocutor might well have concluded that polygyny is as unacceptable as deception; instead, she concludes that deception is not so bad after all. Polygyny is acceptable because "children are wealth," and because of its similarity to polygyny, men's deceit in having sex outside of their marriages (in which the man would normally have no rights to any children conceived) is also acceptable.

Polygyny poses one of the most consistent conflicts between Catholic doctrine and practice and what is considered "African custom" in southern Cameroon: men who are polygynously married are refused communion by most priests, and the affront is deeply felt. In 1996, a catechist from a rural parish explained to me why the church was wrong to consider polygamy a sin in Africa. After carefully reading the Old Testament, he concluded that God's word prohibited a man from having two wives under the same roof; a reasonable prohibition, he felt, as the wives would almost certainly argue. Indeed, it is considered a grave dishonor to force two wives to share the same house; in cases of polygyny, each wife must have her own roof, her own door. In Europe, he explained, men could only afford one house, and therefore were rightly prohibited by the church from having more than one wife. But in Africa, a man can build many houses, and it is therefore fully in keeping with God's law that he be polygamous. Another man had a provocative interpretation of biblical ethics: "God told us 'multiply yourselves,' and we want to do as he tells us. But if your wife does not give birth, what are you going to do? You have to take another wife." That the arguments are phrased in terms of Catholic theology, even while opposing canonical Catholic practice, points to how deeply Catholic doctrine infuses the daily lives of many contemporary Beti. In many domains, proper social action is at once traditionally Beti and Catholic, and the points of partial contradiction between those two systems seem striking only to the (Protestant, American) outsider.

The fact that men have multiple partners is so widely accepted that it makes for good comedy. Jean-Pierre and Annette, students at la Trinité, have a running joke that they are married. In fact, they are classificatory cousins, that is, members of the same *mvog*, and therefore forbidden to each other as sexual partners or spouses, making their innocent joking

relationships both safer (because so impossible) and more naughty (because so forbidden). One evening, Jean-Pierre took another student—a
neighbor and friend—by the hand and declared that he was going out with
her for the evening. Annette played the part of the offended wife, crying
loudly that her husband was cheating on her. To calm her, Jean-Pierre's
sister assured Annette that "the woman of the house is more beautiful
than the one you go out with," a common expression used to assuage jealous wives. Annette conceded that this was true, saying that when you have
your house and legal marriage, even if your husband goes out with other
women, you are the one who has won, because you are his wife "at the
bank and in heaven." Few women in Mbeya have official bank accounts
and few men have the kinds of pensions for which legal marriage would
matter. It is therefore provocative that Annette uses these signs of the
privileged modern economy as the conditions under which male philandering is acceptable. In reality, Beti women with and without access to
bank withdrawals accept that their husbands have affairs.

The fact that men and women are thought to control their libidos differently is just a small part of the perceived complementarity between men
and women. Countless aphorisms reiterate that woman is not man; she
cannot do the same things, talk the same way, or have the same feelings.
This clear distinction by gender is replicated in all kinds of domains; even
as women come to attain honor, it is not the honor of men. Young women
are regularly admonished by their elders that marriage relies on the differences between the sexes. For example, the fifty-seven-year old Mme
Mbene advised me on how to succeed in my future marriage:

> From the beginning you must have certain bases. You establish your marital
> home on certain bases. Already the wife must respect her husband, because
> that is the problem. You must understand that a man is not a woman. Because
> there are certain things that you must allow the man to do. In brief, it is nature
> that imposes it on us. You can't do anything about it. There are just certain
> advantages that men have over women.

The naturalized difference between men and women will be familiar
to many readers, working in Central Africa or not. So, too, will be the notion of innate male advantage. But an important part of her meaning—
that the wise wife will allow her husband a certain amount of freedom to
take lovers, or spend money on palm wine, while she focuses on raising
the children—is perhaps less familiar, albeit no less clear. When I asked

what "certain things" we must allow men to do, Mme Mbene exclaimed, "Whatever! [*N'importe quoi!*] What he wants! If he doesn't bother you too much, you just have to tolerate [it]." There are, of course, marriages that do not follow this pattern, even unions where the woman appears to have the upper hand, and the husband helps her with household labor. Among educated city residents, such marriages might even be considered modern. But in the village, that is a dangerous and ludicrous kind of witchcraft, a potion called *tobassi* (literally, "Sit down!"), which when put in his food induces a man to behave like a woman, to sit down while his wife stands upright.

The Commodification of Sex

While Beti men are often accused of philandering, Beti women are accused of having too much interest in material gain in relationships, of seducing men for financial benefits. For most people, the two problems are related to each other and to *la crise morale*. Both are thought to result from the duplicity and disloyalty that have come to permeate Beti social life as a consequence of the crisis. This is not to say that people explicitly believe that men were faithful and women uninterested in physical comfort before the crisis; rather, they attribute these failings to the crisis without any clear belief or opinion about how things worked before.

A number of people (albeit mostly unmarried men!) expressed horror at what they saw as the increased monetization of sexual relationships: contemporary women demanding money and gifts from their men, so that men without money are unable to secure a steady girlfriend or wife. This accusation entails the claim that women cannot be trusted, and that they will take advantage of you if you let them. One young man explained that he was not yet married because "the women of today marry men according to their [financial] resources." As he was poor, he said, he could never find a wife. Another man expressed a similar sentiment: "Even feelings are materialized today. If a woman is with a man, it's to get something." The moral distinction between spheres of emotion and material gain resonates with western categories (Hochschild 2003; Zelizer 1994), but for this young man to attribute the commodification of sexual relations to modernization or the economic crisis seems somewhat paradoxical. With bridewealth, women's allegiance and sexual fidelity was always materialized (although arguably not commodified); what has perhaps changed is that young women are viewing their adolescent boyfriends as potential marital partners, and so evaluating them in that way.

In fact, many women do expect some financial benefit from their relations with men. But this doesn't necessarily mean that their primary motivations are economic ones, nor does it mean that they are untrustworthy as partners. Instead, many Beti women measure a man's commitment to a relationship by the frequency and extravagance of his gifts. In southern Cameroon there is an apparently long-standing equation of male commitment to a relationship with his financial investment in it. Bridewealth, for example, is sometimes described as demonstrating the depth of a man's love for his wife, and some women proudly report how lavishly their husbands "paid" for them. A man who does not give clothes, pocket money, or presents to his female partner thereby indicates that his intentions are not serious, and that the relationship is unlikely to lead to marriage. Although giving such gifts does not constitute a promise as such, women usually interpret a man's generosity as an indicator of his qualities as a potential spouse.

Even if a relationship is not likely to lead to marriage, many Beti women treat gifts from the men they are dating as an intrinsic aspect of the relationship, or as their right: women explained that they "don't give men love [meaning sex] for free." If a woman fails to receive gifts from her lover, she is likely to be teased by other women. One student at la Trinité explained that she never asks her boyfriend for anything, not even travel money. The other female students, she said, find this flatly ridiculous: "My friends say to me: 'What do you want with that? You show everyone that you are with a boy and you don't even ask him for little bit of money?' But that isn't part of my habits." One of my research assistants was similarly the subject of derision by other women, because she continued to date the man she loved although he was poor. She never received expensive gifts, leading her friends to point out that since she was pretty, she should find a more obliging man. Among the women I knew in Mbeya and Yaoundé, at least three ideas about sexuality and exchange coexist in awkward tension: that men and women both enjoy sex, and it should be separate from exchange; that men "take" sex from women, who should therefore be compensated for it; and that sex should be embedded in a broad range of exchanges, which include women giving cooked food and men giving cash and presents. All three of these representations were used to some degree to justify or explain particular relationships, and all three were subject to disagreement and debate.

It is important to note that these critiques about the increasing commodification of sex are sometimes put forth by women as well as men.
While bridewealth is considered by older Beti women as a form of gift
that a man makes to a woman's family, many younger women (and some
younger men), insist on calling the practice *ekus* ("purchase" in Eton); they
argue that bridewealth is merely a socially legitimated form of prostitution. Arguably bridewealth set a tone for what women now expect from
men, although these lines between bridewealth and seeking financial gain
from men are not yet well drawn. It is nonetheless apparent that between
men's fears of women's seducing them for financial gain, and women's assumptions of male infidelity, heterosexual relationships are fraught with
mistrust and potential danger.

Kinds of Heterosexual Relationships

Young, educated Beti women have a variety of relationships with boys
and men. Some are kin, others acquaintances from work or school, others friends, and still others lovers or potential husbands. Of course, these
categories may and do overlap. Kin are likely to be classmates, and school
friends may become lovers or possible husbands. School serves as a key
locus for the transformation of heterosexual relationships. As we saw in
chapter 5, the fact that students spend the entire day with unrelated age-
mates of the opposite sex is remarkable; school is the only context in which
Beti adolescents have these experiences: although those who do not attend
school have some opportunities to spend time with unrelated members of
the opposite sex, such opportunities are quite limited. Most chores and
forms of entertainment in Beti villages are sex-segregated (farming, laundry, swimming in rivers, etc.), and those that involve members of both sexes
remain largely segregated by patriline (such as the seating at life-cycle rituals). A notable exception is mass; this is, however, only once a week, or
in some of the small villages far from main roads, once a month. For some
people, the habitual daily practice at school of sharing space and time with
unrelated people of the opposite sex will not be replicated for the rest of
their lives.

Many of the relationships among students derive their emotive power
from relationships outside of school. In one instance, a girl at la Trinité
was being harassed in the schoolyard by some boys; her classificatory
cousin came to her defense. In another instance, a teacher tried to get

two half-siblings to collaborate on a project. But their mothers, co-wives of a wealthy local man, had an ongoing conflict, and the students refused to work together. On the other hand, sometimes ties forged in school come to constitute the basis of significant relationships outside of school. Anyone of your same *mvog* is a classificatory cousin; however, almost no one knows all of the members of his or her *mvog.* In one case, a boy and girl who were school friends learned that they were members of the same *mvog;* their friendship became the basis for searching out the specific ancestral tie and reasserting their kin relationship. In this segmentary lineage society, kinship ties may follow sentiment, rather than the reverse.

Among the schoolgirls at la Trinité, it is common to have nonsexual friendships with boys, some of whom are cousins. Women call these male friends "plain friends" (*amis simples*). Some of these relationships are quite warm and include the familiar exchange of food or other resources, frequent visits, and a lot of joking—some of which may be sexual although, or because, the relationship itself is not. Simple friendships constitute a particularly important part of social life among students from far away, who live alone in rented rooms during the school year. Several girls who resided in the privately owned block of cement and corrugated iron known as the Foyer de la Grande Famille regularly cook together, sharing the meal with their "plain" male friends. The boys often, but not always, contribute by buying the ingredients. This situation is a clear break from tradition, in which cooking for a man expresses a woman's sexual relation to him, even constituting an important part of the marriage process. Some working women in Yaoundé hire someone to clean and to cook for the children, but nonetheless insist on preparing their husbands' food themselves, and when a schoolgirl brought cooked food to one of the teachers at la Trinité, the scandal that ensued ranked well above that of the Monica Lewinsky case, which hit the local news a few months later. Nonetheless, the young women in the *foyer* laughed when I asked about the sexual implications of their cooking for the men, saying that this cooking was collective, that the boys were like their brothers, and that sisters can cook for their brothers without anyone interpreting the relationship as sexual. Plain friendships are by definition platonic; however, they also differ substantially from friendships among girls (or among boys, presumably), most significantly because they are not reciprocal. For example, no boy ever cooked for a girl at the *foyer.*

Simple friendships can demand significant investments of time, money, and energy. By contrast, relationships with boyfriends are sometimes much less demanding, and certainly much less public, than are similarly named relationships in high schools in the United States. Particularly in urban, educated circles, it is considered quite normal for high school students to have boyfriends, with the presumption that some of these relationships will lead to marriage after the girls complete school. But decency demands that these relationships be kept very private: a Beti woman is rarely seen with her boyfriend, and even then she demonstrates little affection for him. Although Beti youth—particularly those in the city or residing in rented rooms at school—participate in a variety of social events, they almost never do so in couples.[8] Even in the city, couples do not go to parties together or share food in public; such actions would become the basis for extensive and perhaps vicious gossip. On a number of occasions I attended social events where I knew that two of the guests were romantically involved; they never came or left together, and while at the event hardly spoke to each other.

Educated Beti women have sexual relationships of several kinds, many of which have distinct names. Some of these names are quite stable, although the details of the classification differ somewhat by neighborhood and school.[9] For boyfriends of approximately a girl's own age, and those who might become husbands, there are two basic terms. *Le meilleur,* or "the best," refers to a very significant boyfriend, used almost synonymously with fiancé. It implies that one's friends and even classmates will also know about the relationship. *Le petit,* or "the little [one]," indicates a less important boyfriend. This can mean either a recently acquired boyfriend or one of minor significance, including the second boyfriend of a girl who already has a *meilleur.* In either case, he is not someone with whom a girl currently has long-term plans. Her parents are not likely to know about him, nor are her classmates. Schoolgirls also give both kinds of boyfriend a variety of sweet nicknames, such as *la hanche* (the hip), *mon B,* and *café noir* (black coffee).

There is a third important category of male sexual partner among Beti schoolgirls, usually called the *cou-plié,* or "the folded-neck." These are older men with money. Classically, they are already married, have children, and have no intention of formalizing the relationship with the girl. However, some of these relationships endure for years, and some schoolgirls are very fond of their *cou-pliés.* It would be unfair to consider these relationships exclusively as an exchange of sex for money, although that is certainly part of what is going on. In general, the man provides the girl with money for clothes, school fees, and the like; normally he starts doing so before they begin sexual relations, and as a result some girls call these men their "benefactors" (*bien-faiteurs*). Similar relationships have been noted throughout Africa; in particular, the Anglophone literature on "sugar daddies" is pertinent to the *cou-plié* phenomenon (Bledsoe 1990b; for a fictional account, see Emecheta 1979).

Finally, a fourth category of sexual relationships must be acknowledged. Some Beti schoolgirls are coerced or forced into sexual relationships with teachers, priests, and other men of power. Gossip about these coercive relationships is extremely common, but I do not know whether the phenomenon itself is as widespread as is commonly believed: such data are notoriously difficult to collect, and I did not explicitly ask about coerced sex in my questionnaire. But regardless of the frequency, the consequences of these relationships are sometimes tragic; in 1997, the sister of one of my informants died from hemorrhaging following an abortion when the genitor of the pregnancy, who had reason to keep it secret, prevented her from going to the hospital. In another case, a beautiful young woman whom I knew in Yaoundé assented to a sexual relationship with a man who threatened to have her brother expelled from seminary if she refused. Although it is difficult to collect reliable data on the distribution of coercion and sexual violence, women recounted chilling tales of compulsion or intimidation by social superiors with disturbing frequency.

Marriage and Its Multiple Forms

Most Beti women, educated or not, hope to marry. As one informant explained, "It is the desire of all women! Even if she only manifests it internally, if she doesn't show [it] on the surface, she still thinks of that." And indeed, these hopes are often fulfilled, although not necessary at young ages: data from the 1998 DHS show that by age twenty-six, about 50 percent of Beti women have been married, and this figure rises to some 90 percent of Beti women over forty. Perhaps paradoxically, the relatively high ages at first marriage result at least in part from the importance that educated women place on marriage, not on a lack of interest. Few men are seen to have the characteristics that make a good husband, and women prefer to wait rather than make a mistake. They also wait to "observe" the habits and character of any specific man—he may be the one, but it is only though careful study that one can know. But what kind of marriage are women waiting for? Like so much about life in southern Cameroon, the meaning and form of marriage are changing. A variety of different domestic arrangements are now called marriage, and women married in different ways may have substantially different rights and obligations as a consequence.

In the classical ethnographies (especially Ngoa 1968), as well as in the concept of "proper marriage" held by the older women I interviewed in 1996 and 1998, a man's first marriage should ideally be contracted according to specific guidelines. Once a young man has begun to clear forest on his own behalf, he is ready to marry. Senior men from the family of the young man come to the father or paternal uncle of the bride-to-be, expressing an interest in the girl. After some deliberation, the two families agree on the bridewealth, and on the time horizon over which it should be delivered. Although in some cases, the couple would already know each other and indeed could have been lovers for some time, when the two families agree on the bridewealth, the young man's nighttime visits to her compound become an open secret—not formally citable, but largely assumed and the legitimate topic of humor. On some appointed date, the young man and his family will come in procession, bearing gifts for the family of the bride. A senior man of the groom's lineage will make a request for the girl, saying something like "Our son saw your beautiful little chicken, and we would like to ask you to give it to us." The bride will remain hidden while her father or his representative evaluates the gifts against the previous agreement. If all is in order, a celebration of eating and drinking will follow, and afterward the bride will travel to the home of the groom, most likely to the compound of the groom's father, as the young man cannot really establish a fully independent household without a wife.

In the subsequent days, the young bride will be given a supply of pumpkin seeds, called *ngwan,* ideally from the field cleared by her husband. Depending on tone, *ngwan* means pumpkin seed, moon, adolescent (marriageable) girl, and menstruation: a symbolically coherent set of concepts.[10] *Ngwan* grows best (and, ideally, only) as the first crop on newly cut, virgin land. As we've touched upon, clearing this *esep* is an essential part of a young man's transition to honorable adulthood. Not only is it the prerequisite for marriage and a first stage of establishing an independent compound, but it is symbolically important: for example, it does not have the same social effect if it is hired out. Clearing *esep* is also the most intense physical labor that Beti men perform.

Receiving the *ngwan,* the young bride will begin a laborious process of cracking each seed and removing the soft kernel inside. She may be assisted by the groom's sisters, but not necessarily. Some older women describe this task—which can take weeks, depending on the quantity of *ngwan* and the bride's speed in cracking—as the loneliest time they ever experienced. The new bride then grinds the kernels on a low stone mortar. These mortars are long and narrow, with rounded ends; in order to grind, a woman hikes up her skirt and crouches over one end, holding the stone tight between her thighs. A sexual reading of these mortars is not at all foreign to rural Beti women, who call their grinding stones "my husband," nor is it foreign to young men, many of whom, watching through spaces in the wattle-and-daub of the kitchen walls, find women's grinding to be frankly erotic. The ground pumpkin kernels are blended with water and spices, wrapped in banana leaves, and steamed over a fire. This is now *nam ngwan* (the dish of *ngwan*), and it should ideally be the first meal that a bride prepares for her husband. From then on, he will eat what she prepares, rather than eating from his mother's cooking pot.

Nam ngwan is the essence of conventional bridewealth marriage. Not only is it extremely labor intensive—an attribute that many women express as the basic nature both of local food and of honorable marriage—and, similarly, sensitive to the skill of the cook, but it also shows the partnership of the man and the woman. For *nam ngwan* to be successful, the labors of the man and woman have to be coordinated and reciprocal: the man clears the field and "plants the seed" while the woman gestates and cooks (cf. Delaney 1991).

Young, educated Beti women now often say that they hope for a "modern" marriage, by which they mean a marriage that is monogamous, based on love, and eased by financial security. But in addition to the various attractions that modern marriage may have in and of itself, many women argue that modern marriage is the *only* option now, because a true, proper bridewealth marriage is no longer possible, as the gendered reciprocity based in *esep* and *nam ngwan* has been lost. Men no longer work, women say, and so they have nothing to offer in bridewealth. Underlying these assertions are basic issues of resources: the decimation of the forest and the economic crisis. Nearly all the hinterlands of Yaoundé have long been cleared of virgin forest, and the secondary clearing of a fallowed field is often done by women. Except for felling, adult men do as little farming as possible, lest they be seen as victims of *tobassi*. Men's role in food production has thus significantly declined, and the gendered exchange of labor formalized in *nam ngwan* no longer holds.

With the decline of *nam ngwan* and traditional bridewealth marriages, some modern girls argue that a woman's obligation to prepare the traditional, labor-intensive dishes has gone as well. As many young women explained, today the woman cooks and the man just eats. Recall also the dialogue in Mme Ngah's philosophy class recounted in chapter 5, in which she said, "But you are free now, because of modernity. You can even give the keys to the kitchen to your little boy. But there! That means divorce!" And the student's reply: "But Madame, the *yoyettes* don't cook."

The teacher begins by equating modernity with changing gender roles, and particularly with changes in who may cook. But since women regularly give cooked food to the men with whom they are having sex, the wife's giving up the keys to her kitchen might be read as refusing sex. The student sees the relations differently. Modernity should offer women freedom from the "irksomeness of labor," in Veblen's brilliant phrase (1899). For this student, the modernity of the *yoyettes* is expressed in a life of consumer comforts shared with a devoted husband. Canned and prepared foods, along with the chance of hiring domestic help, mean that the modern woman might lead a life of relative ease. Thus, modern marriage replaces with shared leisure the labor exchange that characterized traditional bridewealth marriage. In this way, marriage remains both a central social aspiration for young women and a partially economic institution, even as its forms are changing.

With the former clear line of bridewealth marriage eroding, today Beti women in a variety of domestic situations might call themselves "married" (a problem with interpreting data from the DHS, which do not specify which event is meant by "marriage"). Three ceremonies—the bridewealth, legal or civil marriage, and Christian marriage—each confer specific rights and obligations on the bride and groom. Performed together, these three make *le tout,* or the total set of binding marital transitions. They are the most desirable and honorable kinds of marriage. In addition to these three binding ceremonies, three other transitional events—the onset of cohabitation, the formal presentation of the groom to the parents of the bride, and the engagement ceremony—might also be considered forms of marriage. Women who are living with men to whom they are engaged, for example, will almost always say that they are married, and often other people will also refer to them this way. Each of these six marital transitions has a specific character; although all might be called "marriage," what they entail is quite variable. Some have their roots in Beti tradition, others were brought by missionaries and colonists, and still others are contemporary Beti innovations. Data show that couples marry in a wide variety of ways, entering one or more of these types of marriage at differing paces and in differing orders. While most Beti women marry, many women are only ever married in one or a couple of ways, skipping or dropping some ceremonies altogether. As cohabitation is relatively easy, and civil marriage is mandatory for the legal recognition of the union and protection of the children, these two transitions are quite common. At the other extreme, church marriage is difficult to coordinate, extremely expensive, and rare. Marriage is thus very common for Beti women, but *le tout* is relatively rare.

Of the marriage transitions, coresidence is perhaps most visibly in a state of flux. In the past, it appears that couples only cohabited after the celebration of the bridewealth. Today, coresidence is often the first marital transition; some educated Beti women even talk about coresidence as a form of "trial marriage." Coresidence is preferably neolocal, particularly if the young couple can afford to reside in a large town or even in Yaoundé, but it may also be patrilocal. Coresidence with the woman's consanguines, however, appears to be impossible. For the most part, couples who are cohabiting without having undergone any other marital transitions are young, and most cohabitations do lead to other forms of marriage within a couple of years, although there are exceptions. The oldest woman in my sample to be cohabiting without undergoing any other marital transitions was thirty-eight at the time of the survey and had been living with her partner for seventeen years. There are only fourteen instances in the data of a couple cohabiting and then breaking up.

For a couple to begin living together, they should preferably have undergone some formal and public ceremony. At the very minimum, this could be the *presentation aux parents,* the formal presentation of the potential husband to the woman's parents. A relatively new phenomenon, as it is only really performed when the bride's parents have not been involved in selecting the groom, it is most common among educated youth in Yaoundé, and indeed was rarely practiced in rural areas before the mid-1980s. Whether a lavish or a simple affair, the *presentation aux parents* is almost always stressful for the young couple. One woman recounted that when her sister presented her boyfriend to their father, the father kept pretending that he didn't understand why the young man was there, and kept asking him to explain himself, more and more loudly, as more and more kin and neighbors came to see. "She wanted to die!" was the commentary. The presentation is a formal statement of the intent to marry, but it is not binding except insofar as the bride's kin can exert moral suasion, which explains the father's attempt to gather witnesses.

The *demande au mariage,* or formal engagement, used to bc a distinct celebration, sometimes enacted when the bride-to-be was still a young girl, or even before her birth (Guyer 1984: 16). The two families come together and share a lavish meal, at which the groom's family may give gifts to the bride's family, and especially to her mother. At the engagement, the two families ceremonially agree on the amount of bridewealth to be transacted, and usually on an approximate calendar for its delivery. At least since the onset of *la crise,* the celebration of the formal engagement is often collapsed into the bridewealth, the *demande* being celebrated first and the bridewealth later in the day, or else the *demande* portion is dropped altogether.

Although no longer including the presentation of *ngwan,* bridewealth continues to be an important marriage practice, if only symbolically. Bridewealth retains much of the grandeur and propriety of "real marriage" (*mfan aluk*), and even educated state functionaries still want to be married with bridewealth. At the same time, as mentioned above, some young people have come to think of the bridewealth as excessively traditional, even degrading to women, going so far as to call the ceremony *ekus,* or "purchase," rather than by its traditional titles *mevəg* or *nsuba.* Yet, even among those calling bridewealth *ekus,* most aspire to be married in the full suite of rituals, including bridewealth. This is no more contradictory than when American feminists want to be married in a white dress, walked down the aisle by their father: it may symbolize gender roles of a passed or rapidly passing era, but the ritual itself matters nonetheless.

Ideally, the gifts of the bridewealth should be given all at once, on the day that the young woman is taken from her parents' home. Whether or not *mfan aluk* was regularly contracted that way in the past, it serves as an ideal against which guests and potential in-laws evaluate present-day ceremonies, and failure to arrive with all the promised or anticipated goods may have substantial consequences. In 1996, I attended a bridewealth ceremony that nearly fell apart for exactly this reason. The young couple had been living together in Yaoundé for several years. The woman, Anne-Sophie, worked for a government agency, supporting her husband, who had been unable to find employment in the city. Anne-Sophie's family resented the match and had pushed the groom's family to agree to an opulent bridewealth. By the day of the celebration, the groom and his agnates had not yet assembled everything promised, but the ceremony began anyway, and they gave over casks of palm wine, bottles of whiskey, plantains and goats, boxes of cigarettes, and a substantial amount of cash. When it became clear that something—I never did learn what exactly—was missing, Anne-Sophie's father tried to call off the rest of the ceremony, demanding that the groom's family return another day to pay the rest. An argument broke out, and the senior men from the two families withdrew to discuss. Eventually, it was Anne-Sophie herself who persuaded her father that she wanted to be married, and that the few things were not worth the trouble of arranging another ceremony. By the evening, the mood was festive, and members of both families danced together.

The civil marriage is the only legally binding marriage rite, and it is thus important for the protection of children in cases of polygyny, desertion, and contested inheritance. When a man dies, his kin often try to claim his belongings; a woman who has been legally married has a stronger claim to keep the house and goods. For the few men with pensions, civil marriage allows their widows access to those funds. The civil marriage involves relatively little ceremony; it consists of both marriage partners signing a legal contract, which stipulates whether they are marrying under the monogamous or polygamous regime.[11] It is witnessed by a vested civil servant and may be conducted either in the municipal building or at the site of a bridewealth or church wedding. Today, civil marriage is usually transacted on the same day as either the bridewealth or the nuptial mass, although some women are married either first, or even only, à l'état civile.

Church marriage is by far the rarest marital transition and is usually the last one that couples make. What is called church marriage may be either a full nuptial mass or a blessing of the marriage within the context of a mass, but it is always accompanied by an extremely sumptuous party that, ideally, continues until dawn, with food, drink, and dancing. The social obligation to spend lavishly on this celebration makes church marriage exceptionally expensive. Many young women view the religious ceremony as the capstone to a happy marriage, rather than the beginning of a union; a church wedding seems an appropriate celebration of the enduring union, perhaps even once the children are grown. The ritual is also made less common by the requirements of the Catholic Church, both real and imagined. A nuptial mass may be performed only when both spouses are baptized and confirmed in the church and neither has been previously married. Although the blessing of the marriage may be performed for couples in a variety of situations, polygynously married men and divorced men and women are still excluded, and many couples who would be eligible hesitate to ask, embarrassed to explain their situation or afraid that the priest will turn them away. Together, the cost and exclusiveness of religious mar-

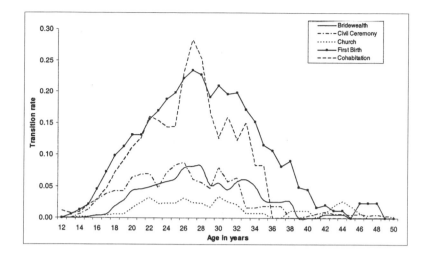

FIGURE 6.1. Age-specific transition rate for four marital events and first birth

riage, combined with the common perception of a church ceremony as the fitting culmination—rather than initiation—of true marriage, mean that relatively few couples are married in the church.

Since the DHS data do not distinguish between different kinds of marriage, my analysis of the relative distribution of marital events relies on the smaller sample of my study. I gathered data on all six transitions, but since the presentation and engagement are less important, and the diversity of event sequences is already substantial, I analyze only cohabitation, bridewealth, civil ceremonies, and church marriages here. As suggested above, the data indeed show that some transitions are more common than others. All of the 184 women in my survey reported having had at least one sexual and romantic partner. Of these, 139 had made the transition to at least one form of marriage by the time of survey, but only 19 had completed all six transitions. The steps that women take to become married are illustrated in figures 6.1 and 6.2. Figure 6.1 charts the age-specific rates of each marriage event. Figure 6.2 graphs "survival" in the pretransitional state for the four critical marital transitions. This can be thought of as the proportion of women at each age who have *not* undergone the relevant transitions; more precisely, it is the proportion of women in the synthetic cohort who would not have transitioned by age, holding the age-specific transition rates constant.[12] The two figures show essentially the same data, but in two different ways: the transition probabilities reveal

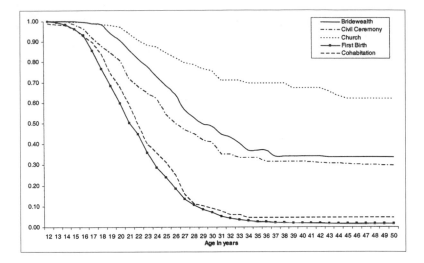

FIGURE 6.2. Cumulative survival by age in pretransition state for four marital events and first birth

the ages at which women face the highest "risk" of marrying; the survival data demonstrate the consequences of that distribution of risks.

Figures 6.1 and 6.2 reveal several important aspects of marriage among educated Beti women. First, cohabitation and bridewealth are common, while church marriage is rare, as seen by the fact that the transition probabilities for cohabitation and bridewealth are higher, and the cumulative survival in the pretransition states lower, than for church marriage. Second, the ages at which women enter the different types of marriage differ only slightly. This is seen most clearly in figure 6.1, where the greatest likelihood of transition into all four forms of marriage occurs at similar ages, but at very different overall levels.

It is not only the timing of marriage rituals that vary among contemporary Beti couples, but also the sequence of those transitions. Although there is a preferred sequence, that sequence is not always followed. For example, civil marriage comes before bridewealth in some life histories, at the same time as or even after that traditional form in others. Also, since many couples do not complete all four transitions, and two, three, or even all four transitions can be completed at the same time, the possible pathways through the marital transitions are numerous.[13] A sample of 184 women is thus far too small to offer any leverage on the problem of sequence with full histories; however, if we look only at the possible marital states—rather than at all the transitions—there are only sixteen possible situations and our sample is sufficient.

This method reveals both significant variability and some clear trends. Of the sixteen possible states, eleven in fact occurred: no one was married in the church before being legally married (eliminating four theoretically possible states), and no one married in all three ways without also living together. Cohabitation is by far the most common first transition: 94 of the 139 women who had made at least one marital transition lived with their partner before marrying in any of the ritual ways. Bridewealth and civil marriage both also occur alone, in 21 and 33 cases respectively. Throughout, the order of bridewealth and civil marriage appears almost interchangeable: while 33 women were married with bridewealth and lived with their partner before making any other transitions, another 29 were married civilly and lived with their partner. Substantially fewer women were married in two rituals before ever cohabiting: 13 married according to church and state, while 14 married with bridewealth and a civil ceremony before ever living with a partner. When women completed three transitions, the civil service and cohabitation were always among them. More postponed the church marriage (32) than the bridewealth (17). By the time of the survey, 19 women had completed all four transitions.

These counts of how many women ever spent time in each combination of marital states offer an imperfect picture of the processes of marriage, because it ignores the transitions. Women who performed only one transition at a time are counted in each of their intermediary states, whereas those who jumped from no marital transitions to all four at once (actually only two women, but the point still holds) are counted only once. Nonetheless, the patterns are revealing. Although cohabitation without any marital ritual is broadly considered dishonorable, it is by far the modal pattern. Civil marriage, which is eventually completed by the vast majority of couples, occurs almost as often after bridewealth as before it. Church marriage never occurs before civil marriage, and therefore only very rarely before couples begin living together. But the most striking fact remains the remarkable diversity. Even without accounting for the lesser events of the *presentation aux parents* and the *demande au mariage,* women who answer they are "married" may be in any of eleven different states, each of which entails somewhat different rights and obligations. *Le tout,* the complete set of major marital transitions, remains desirable, but it is only at older ages, after a number of worldly accomplishments, that most women can hope to achieve it.

Managing the Dangers of Sex

Heterosexual relationships in southern Cameroon may take many different forms, from short-term, friendly affairs to serious courtship and one or several types of marriage. Through all the variation, however, we see that while Beti consider sex necessary for normal health and development, heterosexual relations are often strained and distrustful. These relationships nonetheless constitute the immediate context for vital conjunctures involving pregnancy. Indeed, in addition to its potential transformation of a young woman's schooling trajectory, a pregnancy may be a turning point in a relationship, inducing a young man to either marry his girlfriend or abandon her. Some Beti men told me that they suspect their girlfriends of trying to get pregnant in order to entrap them; however, most unmarried schoolgirls that I knew were trying very hard to avoid pregnancy. In keeping with their self-identity as disciplined, honorable, and modern, most Catholic-educated women seek to postpone socially recognized motherhood until they have attained a subjectively appropriate configuration of life events; averting a mistimed pregnancy is the first line of defense against what they perceive as mistimed motherhood. We will examine in detail what makes motherhood mistimed in chapters 7 and 8. Here we focus on how it can be avoided. Younger women seek to avoid mistimed motherhood through periodic abstinence (also known as the rhythm method, fertility awareness technique, or natural family planning), while older women who are mothers tend to be more accepting of other types of birth control as well. By contrast to the widespread acceptance of reproductive management, the use of condoms to avoid AIDS is almost entirely unacceptable.

For about a decade, contraceptive methods have been widely available in Cameroonian clinics. In Mbeya itself, the family planning section of the Catholic hospital had a supply of condoms, sponges, pills, and IUDs in 1998; at the public hospital in Yaoundé, the range of methods also included Depo-Provera. All of these options are technically available to everyone, even unmarried women, and the services are not expensive: two months of pills, for example, cost CFA 500 (about USD 1: the price of two small cokes). Condoms are sold everywhere, including in the small stands that sell soap, matches, candy, and batteries. Educated women are quite familiar with the range of birth control methods; many could name five or more types. They also know where these methods are available; almost everyone noted that contraception can be acquired at local clinics, and some women also knew that pharmacies in Yaoundé carried some methods.

Despite this knowledge, use of the so-called modern methods is relatively limited. In the 1998 DHS, nearly 42 percent of educated women, and 19 percent of all women in Cameroon reported that they were currently using some form of contraception, but fewer than half of them were using the so-called modern methods available in clinics and pharmacies. Only 6 percent were using condoms, and those who did listed fear of pregnancy rather than fear of AIDS as their primary motivation. The majority of all women using contraception reported using periodic abstinence.[14]

There are many reasons why Cameroonian women rely so heavily on periodic abstinence, but here I will focus on the reasons that apply particularly to unmarried, educated Beti women. Certainly, many are embarrassed to go to the clinics, even in the city, because they do not want to be seen as sexually available. In addition, most have grave concerns about the safety and potential side effects of hormonal and mechanical methods of contraception. Although they want to avoid pregnancy, most young Beti women are unwilling to employ any method of contraception that they perceive as invasive. Contraceptive pills, IUDs, and Depo-Provera are all considered potentially harmful, or at least likely to cause weight gain and bad skin. I was often reminded of Naomi Rutenberg and Susan Watkins's informants in Kenya, who asked whether contraceptives would "rhyme" with their bodies (1997: 97). Students do not invent these concerns themselves; the sexual education instructor at la Trinité was quite explicit that pills were dangerous, claiming at one point that they could cause permanent sterility. One of my informants explained which contraceptive forms she found acceptably safe:

> Taking the pill, I find that ugly, bad, whatever. That will come to change your body, the way your body works. So it's not useful to take the pill. What I find good is abstinence, also condoms. But the diaphragms and the IUD, I don't like.

Other students were less tolerant, finding condoms as unacceptable as the pill or the IUD. While I was in Mbeya, a rumor was circulating about a couple who had used a condom that was the wrong size. The condom came off during intercourse and made its way into the young woman's bloodstream. It circulated through her blood before making its way to her heart, which it enveloped and smothered, killing her. This might be read as a morality tale on the deathly consequences of casual sex—the kind of sex during which people use condoms. But it is also a story about the dangers of contraception itself. Many people suggested that contraception, like AIDS, was an invention of the whites designed to limit African populations for nefarious, if unknown reasons. The idea that pills could cause permanent sterility was believable because it fit into a theory of fertility control as an insidious weapon of neocolonialism.

The concept that AIDS was unleashed intentionally on Africans by cynical or wicked westerners was widely held in Cameroon in 1998, so much so that it convinced me finally to avoid the topic altogether. Already I risked being mistaken for a spy; a spy with a genocidal mission was an identity I was unwilling to take on. The French acronym SIDA was said to stand for "Syndrome Imaginaire pour Décimer les Africains," and many people expressed the opinion that its aim was to terrorize Africans into avoiding sex. The idea that condoms would be an effective or useful strategy to protect yourself from AIDS struck most young people as ridiculous. They reasoned that if condoms are too dangerous to use to prevent the known risk of pregnancy, then certainly they are too dangerous too use against some potentially imaginary disease that—if it exists—was created by the same people who make condoms. The only person I interviewed who expressed any concern that she herself might contract AIDS was Marlyse, the young woman who explained in chapter 4 that she loved her uneducated cousins despite the fact that they were "brutes." Marlyse argued that it was more dangerous to use condoms than to just accept the risk, as no one had presented any evidence that condoms themselves did not carry the disease. For her, sexual abstinence was the only path: she planned to become a nun. Setel's call for a "moral demography" of AIDS, which attends to the ways that "various actors produce knowledge about the locations of bodies (migration), their status (morbidity and mortality), and the consequences of reproductive action (fertility)" seems appropriate here (1999: 56).

Because of their association with illegitimate sex, their limitation of physical pleasure, and their rumored dangers, condoms have few supporters among the women I knew in southern Cameroon. By contrast, periodic abstinence, or natural family planning, usually called *le calcul*, receives both general acceptance and widespread use. Explicitly taught to both boys and girls in Catholic schools under the program "Education in Life and Love," periodic abstinence receives both official support from the church and broad social sanction. In part, the popularity of natural family planning can be attributed to the fact that it is the only means of family planning officially condoned by Rome since the 1968 encyclical *Humanae Vitae*. However, I hesitate to attribute too much causal force to the encyclical, as Catholics worldwide have long ignored it. Fehring and Schmidt (2001) found that 70 percent of American Catholics were using contraception in 1995, of which only 3 percent was periodic abstinence. In both Brazil and the Dominican Republic, countries more heavily Catholic than Cameroon, over 60 percent of women reported using "modern" contraception in the most recent Demographic and Health Surveys. Of the 79 percent of Italian women using contraception, only 5 percent were using periodic abstinence in 1995 (Castiglioni, Zuanna, and Loghi 2001: 212). There appears to be nothing particularly Catholic about using periodic abstinence or about avoiding other methods of contraception. In addition, we have seen that many Beti Catholics consider other aspects of the catechism "negotiable," including the condemnation of nonmarital sex, polygyny, and even abortion (United States Catholic Conference 1994: 565, 411, 547). Although official church sanction of periodic abstinence does ease its acceptance by Beti Catholics, that sanction alone does not explain the overwhelming preference for the method. As in many Catholic communities around the world, many Cameroonian Catholics consider their faith and religious practice to be antithetical to blind obedience to the Vatican.[15]

Periodic abstinence is preferred by young, educated Beti women not only because it is safe, free, secret, and accepted by the church hierarchy, although those are all good reasons for its use. In addition, its form—of repeated, structured sexual continence—conforms perfectly to local notions of honorable self-dominion. Managing a calendar and abstaining from sex for certain durations seems the perfect enactment of modern female honorability, combining a school-learned technology, self-discipline, and some amount of female autonomy within sexual relationships.[16] In order to abstain effectively, the young woman needs to be able to manage not only her own, but also to some degree her partner's sexuality; therefore the relationship itself must have some of the characteristics of the "modern" marriage to which so many educated women aspire. By contrast to something like Depo-Provera, which is entirely outside the woman's control and makes no demands on her, periodic abstinence appears frankly modern: like the school bell and the ecclesiastic calendar, it is a technology for the management of time and the manipulation of bodily practice through time.[17]

"Il ne faut que faire le cache-cache"

Both inside and outside of marriage, a woman's management of her sexuality—and perhaps especially of its public perception—is central to her honor. For an educated woman postponing marriage and waiting for the right man, this management can prove delicate. Young women hold themselves to a rigorous code of discretion regarding their feelings, actions, and the identity of their partners. The efforts of young women to maintain their own privacy is equaled only by the efforts they dedicate to ascertaining the sexual secrets of others: an arms race of mutual sexual espionage. Given the assumed importance of sexuality for human health, this extraordinary discretion may seem peculiar. Indeed, sexuality occupies a curiously ambivalent place in Beti social life: always assumed to be rampant and always hidden from public view. But in practice, these apparent contradictions—that sex is common and healthy and yet must be kept secret—coexist, uniting in a cohesive code that, when followed, serves as a marker of Beti women's honor.

At its most essential, the honor of keeping sexual secrets requires only that women prevent neighbors, classmates, and others from knowing with whom they are sexually involved, particularly if they have more than one partner. Thus, parents generally believe that their daughters have boyfriends and consider it an indication of the girls' good sense that they keep them secret. As was discussed earlier, women do not socialize with their boyfriends in public. Schoolgirls' may discuss their partners' sexual abilities, but in anonymous terms. I was originally very interested in the social and demographic characteristics of boyfriends, that is, their age, education, lineage, and so forth; however, it quickly became clear that even these questions made women very uncomfortable, seeming too private for tape-recorded interviews. In general, women were more willing to tell me whether they had had sex the night before and, if so, whether they had used condoms, than to tell me even very general information about their boyfriend's identity. Women must be discreet in their affairs.

The secret politics of sex, the honor of discretion, extends past keeping secret the identities of lovers to more active "protection" of one's partner. Both men and women are expected to protect their partners through secrecy, but the term applies differently to members of the two sexes. While men are admonished to keep their affairs secret from their wives or steady girlfriends, women are more often reminded of the importance of keeping their lovers' or husbands' secrets from *other* people, and respecting their privacy. Most centrally, a woman should refrain from gossiping about her fiancé or husband's income, his family, and his sexual performance.[18] Thus, men are called to protect their wives or girlfriends from painful knowledge, while women are called to protect their husbands or boyfriends from potentially embarrassing gossip. A man protects a woman from knowledge about himself; the woman protects the man from others' discovery of the knowledge she has of him. In this way, both partners' honor may depend on their collusion in keeping his dalliances out of the public eye: ideally, he should prevent her knowledge of them, but if she finds out, she should avert everyone else's gaze so that no one knows she knows. Thus, sexual propriety occurs largely at the second and third degree; it lies in managing others' knowledge of your knowledge, or in shaping their beliefs about your beliefs about their actions.

At an extreme, a devoted woman will prevent anything negative about her male partner—whether concerning his temperament, income, or sexual competence—from being known. One example: I was helping a student from la Trinité prepare for the English section of the *probatoire*. She had brought a set of practice questions, which she had answered at home and we were checking over. At issue was the response to the following multiple-choice question:

Choose the best word to complete the sentence:

Abiba loves her husband; therefore she can _____ his arrogance towards her.
(a) tolerate (b) hide (c) suffer (d) reject

The student had chosen "hide," explaining that a wife who loves her husband will protect him from public accusations. For Beti women, honorable discretion in sexual relationships includes tolerating infidelity and even "arrogance" from their men, and in keeping them secret. For Beti men, by contrast, honorable secrecy consists centrally of hiding their own philandering.

In addition to keeping their sexual relationships strictly outside the public gaze, Beti women practice discretion in their dealings with their partners themselves. Nowhere is this clearer than in the cultural model of mutual observation. You should not introduce a boyfriend to your parents, I was told, until you know that you are going to marry him. And that decision takes a very long time: most women say five years. The reason that it takes so long is that you must observe each other to see whether your habits and temperaments are truly compatible, since after marriage you have to tolerate each other (*il faut se supporter*) no matter how ill-matched you may be. One woman explained why Beti women are slow to marry:

> Marriages after two months—you meet someone and after two months you marry—that never lasts. I think you need at least five years. The people who are in a big hurry, they can do three years. But for three years someone can hide his true face from you. You have to have five years of experience, that way you will really know each other. You are going to know who is who.

Because men are inclined to hide their true faces from their lovers, a woman must be very circumspect with her sexual partner. One woman described sexual relationships as "the complete lack of trust," a position that other women shared, if less poetically. Sermons, newspaper articles, and even folklore emphasize the mutual deception of men and women. In urban legend, even women's attire becomes a tool in trickery: under the ample *caba,* a woman who had taken money from her husband wrapped herself in thick layers of cloth, so that when he beat her she only laughed. The abundance of her, soft and jiggly under the loose dress, along with her laughter, so excited her husband that he gave up beating her and made love to her instead. In the summer of 1998, a priest in a large Yaoundé parish gave a series of sermons on the "war between the sexes," describing it as the fundamental danger to Christian marriage: men and women fight all day and have sex all night, he explained to a laughing congregation; they never know each other except in the dark, which is to say, not at all.

Ombolo offers a helpful framework in arguing that among the Beti "social conduct in reference to sexual reality" is based on three fundamental principles, which he names "realism, respect, and discretion" (1990: 168). We have already discussed some attitudes that could be appropriately categorized according to these principles, such as the older woman who advised me to respect my husband, understanding that he will do things according to his own nature and that I should accept them. Discretion arguably both expresses and facilitates realism and respect. For example, the husband who is having an affair: his wife may realistically assume it will happen, but still he should be respectful and practice discretion, just as she will respect and try to protect his privacy, and help to maintain his secret. Or in the case of the student whose parents presume she has boyfriends: her discretion shows respect for her boyfriend and her parents, allowing her parents to be both realistic and respectful of her actions. Everyone politely helps to hide and ignores in their turn the reality that all believe exists. The honor of sexual behavior depends on everyone's secrecy and their discretion.

*   *   *

Relations with men are an important context in which young, educated Beti women enact the code of honorable self-dominion. Beti sexual relationships are characterized by extreme discretion, as many believe that "the exhibition of sentiments is a brazen behavior resulting from shameless temperaments" (Ombolo 1990: 171). But with this discretion comes mistrust: women accuse men of infidelity and men reciprocate with accusations of women's financial motives for love. There is a sense in which Beti sexual relationships are always ambivalent. The source of great pleasure, they are also domains of intense suspicion, and sometimes even malice.

This often perilous domain of heterosexual relationships serves as the immediate context for vital conjunctures involving pregnancy. Women's expectations in heterosexual unions—that men will not be faithful, that sex is part of relations of exchange, that a woman must respect her partner's privacy and protect him from gossip—constitute some of the critical horizons to which women orient their actions in navigating these conjunctures. Educated Beti women, for the most part, attempt to manage the timing of pregnancy, bringing pregnancy into alignment with other life events, especially marriage and formal employment. They do so using periodic abstinence, often with remarkable success. But even when carefully practiced, periodic abstinence will sometimes fail, resulting in a pregnancy that was not intended. In chapters 7 and 8, we turn to the discussion of particular vital conjunctures arising from schoolgirl pregnancies. I focus on these pregnancies, locally construed as out of place, not only because they represent a common experience among educated women, but also and more importantly because they represent the structural contradiction that lies at the heart of modern honor in southern Cameroon.

For an educated woman trying to establish her modern honor, no single, clear trajectory is offered. The partially acceptable alternatives include postponing marriage and childbearing, whereby a woman may persist in school and bear her children later within marriage, but at the risk of being considered infertile. The only way to bear a child before "getting old" while still staying in school is to give birth while still a student; many women follow this path, dropping out temporarily and then returning to school.

However, it is nearly impossible to combine this path with the aim of bearing a child within marriage, because—as we will see—the limitations on being a married student are substantially greater than on being a student-mother.[19] By contrast, to bear that early child within marriage, a young woman will have to leave school. Thus, the problem is not simply how to achieve some stable category of honorable educated mother, but rather how to construct a possible space of honorable modern motherhood out of the partially conflicting values that are available.

This kind of uncertainty is a very common feature of contemporary life, from Yaoundé to Shanghai to Chicago. But in poor countries, particularly those that—like Cameroon—have seen a vast widening of the horizons of possibility at the same time as a shrinking of concrete opportunities, the uncertainty becomes a true dilemma. The crux of the problem is this: given the unpredictability of life in *la crise,* even if a young woman were able to select which compromises she would be willing to make—say, accepting the shame of nonmarital motherhood in order to stay in school without being branded as infertile—she can have no confidence that her compromise will succeed. After all, for these plans to succeed, someone must pay her school fees, she must pass the exams, and a pregnancy must come when she wants and not before, and later a viable husband must show up with the bridewealth. Making modern honor thus requires that these young women be willing to take what comes and make the best of it, to make "contingency plans" (Bledsoe 2002) and to revise them as rapidly and radically as necessary, in short, to live in uncertainty.

CHAPTER SEVEN

Vital Conjunctures

Much of the terminology used to describe unwed pregnancies was that of honor and shame. Illegitimate children themselves were referred to as "figli di colpa," children of guilt. Protecting the honor of such women and their families meant placing tremendous emphasis on secrecy. . . . If marriage was not possible, an affront to a woman's and her family's honor could best be expunged by keeping the pregnancy secret. — David Kertzer, *Sacrificed for Honor*

We saw in chapter 6 how educated Beti women postpone first pregnancies, particularly through the use of periodic sexual restraint. Significantly, it is not pregnancy per se that they are trying to avoid, but rather a dishonorable entry into the social category of mother. At issue is not time in some absolute sense, but contingent social timing. Equating the honor of motherhood with its synchronization with marriage and formal employment, educated Beti women seek to postpone entering motherhood until these other situations coalesce. Kertzer (1993) has argued that in nineteenth-century Italy, premarital pregnancy brought grave dishonor because premarital sex itself was disreputable, and pregnancy an indisputable index of such illegitimate sex. In southern Cameroon, by contrast, premarital sex is widely tolerated or even assumed. The problem with premarital pregnancy is not that it indexes premarital sex, but that it puts a young woman into a contradictory situation where her status is ambiguous, her reproduction out of place.

When an unmarried schoolgirl in southern Cameroon realizes that she is pregnant, the possible futures that she envisions shift suddenly and dramatically. One day the girl takes for granted that she will finish school; the next day catches her in a tumult of confusion and worry, as she searches for some indication as to what the future might hold. What she once assumed to be inevitable now appears contingent. What she once thought impossible suddenly becomes an intensely real concern. In other words, the unintended pregnancy instigates a vital conjuncture: a duration of lived time with many possible outcomes, each of which suggests a radically different future.

The pregnant Beti student finds herself facing four prototypical possible futures. The vital conjuncture continues as long as two or more of these remain possible and imaginable future trajectories, and it ends when one takes on the fullness of actuality, displacing all others in the "future perfect" she imagines (Schutz 1967: 67). The student may marry the genitor of the pregnancy, drop out of school, and take up the identity of a married adult woman. She may give birth alone and keep the child, joining the ranks of the young, unmarried mothers who work in the small phone centers, hair salons, and market stalls in Yaoundé, Obala, and Mbalmayo. She may give birth and then send the child to be raised by someone else, usually a relative, and return to school. Or the woman may abort the pregnancy and remain in school. Of these options, becoming an unmarried working mother is cited by students as the least desirable, although it is not rare. Each of the other three, by contrast, has its partisans: some women assert a preference for one option, and others prefer another. But more important, depending on the particular circumstances of the vital conjuncture that the pregnancy initiated, one or another option may appear more viable. The trajectory that a young woman follows often results from a kind of judicious opportunism (Johnson-Hanks 2005), in which she selects an available means to one of a variety of desirable ends, rather than seeking to optimize the chances of achieving a specific, predetermined end by whatever means possible.

In this chapter, I introduce Claudette, Marie, and Nathalie, three Beti women who have faced vital conjunctures due to mistimed pregnancies. Their stories illustrate the nature and structures of vital conjunctures. In each case, we will see that uncertainty pervaded the duration of the pregnancy and beyond. Each would-be mother struggled to make sense of her options and weigh her values, looking to certain edges of meaning, or *points de repères,* which I call the horizons of the conjuncture. Although the three women we meet here ultimately resolved their vital conjunctures in different ways, in the midst of the conjunctures they nonetheless oriented themselves to similar horizons. Like landmarks or navigational beacons, the horizons provided visible structures in the uncertainty of the specific conjuncture. And akin to my father's principles for sailing in unfamiliar waters (like "red, right, returning" and "never tack into kelp"), the principles of honorable motherhood gave Claudette, Marie, and Nathalie a way of understanding the relationship between their own situations and the horizons. Thus, while their stories and outcomes are different, their arrangements of alternatives are similar.

In chapter 8, I will focus on these shared horizons; here we will explore the conjunctures themselves, along with the organization of the social field in which they occur. Honorable motherhood, fundamental to the three stories here, serves more as a principle of action than a specific goal that can be conclusively attained. Like *mfefeg* (having sense), motherhood is not a set life stage, but rather a status that can be accepted or denied in specific social interactions. This malleability of the status of mother allows some women to relinquish claims to their children through informal adoption, which—similar to abortion and rapid marriage—can rectify dishonorable timing, bringing a young woman's socially identified reproductive status back into line with her actions in other domains.

The malleability of motherhood and the possibility of relinquishing claims to children also belie a concern common among Beti schoolgirls that they will have to leave school for good if they become pregnant.[1] Observed statistically, bearing a child does not necessarily mean the end of a young woman's education. In fact, many educated women persist in school after bearing a child because the birth itself does not necessarily commit them to the full suite of social identities entailed in "motherhood." Local representations of common experience do not accord with observed practice here. My informants conflate childbearing and social motherhood in their talk, but in their actions, they make a clear and consistent distinction. Socially identified motherhood does indeed exclude a young woman from further schooling. Childbearing, however, can only force a girl out of school by inducting her into social motherhood, and this induction is far from automatic.

Foresight, Timing, and Honor

The pregnancies discussed in this chapter were both unforeseen and mistimed, by which I mean that they were not part of the future vistas imagined by the women prior to their occurrence and that they were not well coordinated with other life transitions by local standards. Mistimed births occur too early in a sexual relationship, too early in a schooling trajectory, or too early in a career. As we will explore more fully below, educated Beti women have strong ideas about what constitutes a proper context for childbearing; pregnancies that happen before these contexts come together are "mistimed," a judgment on which most Beti would agree, given the would-be mother's situation. In contrast, whether a pregnancy was "unforeseen" depends on the mother's own expectations: did she envision pregnancy with this man at this time as possible or imaginable? Whether she wanted to be pregnant or not, had she considered it as a feasible outcome? Because it depends on these questions, whether a pregnancy was foreseen cannot be subject to social consensus, but only determined by the mother herself. Still, the attributes unforeseen and mistimed are associated: mistimed pregnancies are more likely to be unforeseen, but they are not necessarily so. A pregnancy may be foreseen but mistimed, or unforeseen although well timed.

I have said that the honor of Beti motherhood rests centrally on its timing. In fact, the honorable timing of births mirrors the two-part structure of Beti honor itself. The distinction between mistimed and unforeseen births parallels that between *respectabilité* and *dignité:* the former in each set depends on broad social consensus and rests on pecuniary concerns. Well-timed births require that the mother have finished school, found employment, and gotten married. Time here addresses socially recognized events and visible life-history coordination. In contrast, whether a birth is foreseen—like whether a woman has *dignité*—can be known in the end only to herself and God. This is the timing of private self-dominion, the cultivated habits that constitute women's uncertain honor. In both cases, the former and latter term share an uneasy alignment. Ideally, a woman is *respectable* because she is *digne;* her births are well timed because they are foreseen: the shared, social attributes should serve as indices of the internal, dispositional ones. And yet, things are never so simple.

"Unforeseen" and "mistimed" are my terms for rather vague local categories. Standard demographic surveys, by contrast, ask whether past births were "wanted." In the Demographic and Health Survey protocol the question reads, "At the time you became pregnant did you want to become pregnant then, did you want to wait until later, or did you not want to have any (more) children at all?" Wanting to be able to calibrate my data against that of the DHS, I used essentially this same question in the pilot phase of my survey, asking whether births were *voulues.* The question was nondifferential: with only two exceptions, mothers called every pregnancy "wanted." Perhaps I should not have been surprised, as there are strong psychological incentives to say that you wanted your child (Klerman 2000). Bankole and Westoff (1998) found that Moroccan women interviewed twice three years apart tended to recast as wanted children that they originally had called unwanted (see also Bongaarts 1990). Yet, even taking this ex post facto rationalization into account, the absence of variation in women's responses about whether their children were wanted concerned me. It was my chief research assistant, Melanie Eboa, who suggested what I now believe to be the correct interpretation: in saying that all of their children were wanted, women were expressing that they, in the abstract, wanted all the children that God saw fit to send them. There is something ungrateful, or even sacrilegious, about saying that you did not want your child in a context where "children are from God." Thus, women were not talking about specific pregnancies, Eboa suggested, even though the survey question tried to elicit such answers. Instead, women responded that they wanted pregnancies and childbearing in general.

As a group, my research assistants then suggested the term *prevu* (foreseen), as potentially distinguishing pregnancies that constituted part of the woman's horizons prior to its occurrence. This did produce differential results, and we used it to the exclusion of *voulu* in the main survey. It is *prevu* that I translate as "foreseen" throughout the chapter. This is its most conventional meaning, but not its only one. In referring to pregnancies, the most accurate translation of Beti women's usage of *prevu* would rather be something like "imagined as plausible." Pregnancies that are foreseen thus may or may not have been actively desired, but they were at least imagined. For example, schoolgirls with steady boyfriends who are contemplating marriage and having children together at some point in the future but unexpectedly find themselves pregnant earlier than desired would likely call their births foreseen, even though they were unplanned, and perhaps mistimed. Unforeseen first births to Catholic educated women are common. Sixty-three percent of first births reported in my survey were retrospectively characterized by the mother as unforeseen. With increasing parity, the proportion of births called unforeseen declines, although it never goes to zero, a pattern that parallels the distribution of abortions.

Although distinguishing foreseen from unforeseen pregnancies remains closer to Beti women's own classifications of their experiences, the dichotomy suffers from several of the same drawbacks as the more traditional distinction between wanted and unwanted. Both are attributes of births assigned by the mother in a retrospective interview, inviting all of the kinds of revision, selection, and elision common in personal narratives that "shape how we attend to and feel about events" (Ochs and Capps 1996: 21).[2] That is, both distinctions are necessarily subject to change as a woman reformulates her history in the ongoing living of it, and these changes cannot be captured by collecting a retrospective fertility history. Both sets of terms allow for only two characterizations—foreseen or unforeseen, wanted or unwanted—erasing great variation and sliding scales of anticipation. Both involve the sleight-of-hand in moving from conceptions to births: my survey question asked whether each birth was foreseen, but obviously it is pregnancies that are foreseen or unforeseen. A better approach would be to interview women about their reproductive intentions, expectations, and aspirations before they became pregnant, and then to follow them forward through time. But that will have to wait for a future field project.

Jane and Peter Schneider have explored how honorable parenthood in early-twentieth-century Italy became increasingly dependent on child numbers. Respectable people did not bear children like "rabbits" or "mice," but practiced sexual continence to limit their family size (1996: 262). The honor of parenthood in southern Cameroon depends similarly on restraint, but restraint in timing, rather than numbers. Educated Beti women treat appropriate timing of childbearing—especially in relation to other events such as marriage, schooling, and career—as the marker and maker of honorable female adulthood. We have seen in previous chapters that this control of fertility is part of the very definition of what it means to be educated, and especially Catholic-educated; educated women do not have children "in disorder" or without thought of the consequences. Instead, they practice foresight, weigh options, and seek to manage their reproductive timing. Such reasoning characterizes honorable action, even in the absence of stability in the world that would make rational choice possible. Educated and honorable women attempt to control their reproduction through contraception, especially periodic abstinence, so that they may coordinate their childbearing with school completion, marriage, their own careers, and financial stability, because to do so constitutes them as disciplined and therefore honorable.

Honorable Beti motherhood today requires that the stage be appropriately set for a child, with house, husband, career, and possessions already in place prior to the pregnancy. As with schooling itself, the value placed on this temporal coordination reflects both pecuniary honor and the cultivation of honorable dispositions: the timing at once indexes honorable self-dominion and enables honorable consumption. Marie, whose story is recounted below, underscores this point. In response to my inquiring whether she intended to have more children, she stated:

Oh no! Not right away. I have to work first. Marriage, that's after. I have to work before having children. Even before I have children, I have to have a house. I have to perhaps have saved a certain sum. My child must not lack anything.

Marie here conflates childbearing and marriage, answering my question about her childbearing intentions with a statement about her marital plans. The idea that the first birth should come in the context of marriage is widely held, if rarely practiced. Women often talk about childbearing and marriage as if they were the same, and assert that both should follow the establishment of a career, as we can also see in the following quote from an interview with another woman attending la Trinité:

If I marry, that doesn't mean that marriage is the most important thing. Marriage can come later, in last place. After I already have everything, everything that I want. After I have a job, a furnished house, and everything. It's there that I can start to think about marriage, about children, and all that.

In addition to the association of marriage with childbearing, this speaker notably views economic welfare as her own responsibility, rather than the responsibility of her future spouse. She implies that marriage and childbearing are the prerogatives of a successful woman, of the woman who already "has everything," rather than being the basis of female adulthood.

The honorable woman has children who are well provided for, as with Marie's anticipated child, who must not want for anything. Such definitions of honor are at once expressions of normative expectations, personal aspirations, and motivations for present action, as young women seek to choreograph the circumstances necessary to enable good timing, whether by returning to school or marrying. Another woman focuses on the moral requirement to be able to take care of the child you bear: establishing an economic career before beginning a childbearing career is not only about having "everything," but about fulfilling basic parental obligations:

You have to educate your child well. You can't give birth now, even though you have nothing for putting that child in the world with. That's being cruel; that's calling the child to suffer. Before giving birth you first need a job.

The importance of employment for childbearing is seen as so great that even women who say that all other things are in the hands of God insist that childbearing must follow the establishment of a career. Take, for example Annelise, a generally voluble young woman who on the day scheduled for our interview did not feel like talking. In response to nearly all my questions, she claimed ignorance:

> JENNA: Do you have an idea what sort of man you want as a husband?
> ANNELISE: The sort that God will send me, I will accept him. These are things of God—one cannot understand them. . . .
> JENNA: And for the number of children that you would like?
> ANNELISE: You can propose, but God dispenses. So you could propose to have only one child, . . . but in some way, it is God who gives children. If he gives you one hundred, you just take them!

But when it came to the timing of children, her position changed. Suddenly Annelise had emphatic opinions:

> JENNA: And so if tomorrow you find yourself pregnant, that would be fine with you?
> ANNELISE: Oh no! I must first be stable. One does not make children just to make them. You do not make children who will come [to] suffer, or so that you cannot be there for their education. You only make children when you are good and ready.

Honorable motherhood for educated women in Cameroon rests on coordination of life events; an honorable birth occurs in coincidence with marriage, after schooling is complete and a career established. The honorable mother can independently provide for her child's welfare and education. When these bases for motherhood are not secured prior to a pregnancy, a mother-to-be has several options for attempting to maintain her honor. Abortion, of course, involves preventing the birth altogether, while relinquishing claims to children is based on postponing entry into the social category of mother. Third, a woman may—if the circumstances are right—recast her mistimed, unforeseen pregnancy into the form of legitimate maternity through marriage. It is critical to recall that whether a woman pursues one or another of these alternatives depends as much on which is possible as to which she would prefer. Vital conjunctures can be reasoned only from immediate context, and not from abstract ideals. Before turning to the case studies that illustrate each of these alternatives, we will explore the options in more detail.

Abortion: The Lesser Shame

Abortion is illegal in Cameroon, considered a mortal sin by the Catholic Church, and highly stigmatized in Beti society. Nonetheless, it appears to be quite common, at least among the young, educated women I interviewed. Confronted with the potential dishonor of mistimed motherhood, many young women choose abortion. Abortion remains shameful, and yet it is widespread, because under certain circumstances, it is the lesser shame.

Shapiro and Tambashe (1997) have shown that abortion and contraception are alternative fertility control strategies in Kinshasa, with the most highly educated women using contraception instead of abortion, and moderately educated women doing the opposite. The pattern in southern Cameroon looks different. The women in my survey who reported having had abortions had indeed tried to prevent pregnancy, but were unsuccessful. As we saw in chapter 6, the vast majority of contraception use in southern Cameroon, particularly among the educated, is periodic abstinence based on the standard method of counting fertile days. Although fertility awareness methods can be effective, they are very demanding, and few couples can achieve the "ideal use" associated with 95 percent effectiveness. Johnston and Hill (1996) estimate that on average periodic abstinence only prevents about 50 percent of pregnancies. Although there is unfortunately no good data on effectiveness of contraception specific to southern Cameroon, it is probably safe to say that despite their concerted efforts to manage fertility carefully, plenty of young Beti couples face the problem of unintended pregnancy.

Despite the legal ban, clandestine abortion is available, and women do avail themselves of it. There are four major sources of abortion. Some licensed medical doctors provide surgical abortion in a clinical setting after hours. Some nurses and even medical technicians conduct abortions in their own homes, largely relying on western pharmaceuticals, although sometimes resorting to crude surgical techniques. There are also ritual specialists who use a combination of indigenous herbs and prayers to induce abortion, cure infertility, and perform a variety of other reproductive cures. Finally, there are abortion specialists, particularly in the poor neighborhoods of Yaoundé, who employ a combination of western pharmaceuticals, percussion, and the insertion of caustic substances into the vagina to cause abortions. Most women learn about providers from friends, schoolmates, or relatives, working through their social networks to identify and gain access to specialists.

The range of methods used by the relatively untrained abortion specialists in poor neighborhoods includes the frankly gruesome and hazardous.
One of my informants gave the following description of a local method employed to induce abortion, mentioned by several young women, although
none had used it:

> You kill a mouse; you put the mouse in water and close it in a bottle. You keep
> it. It rots, the mouse—imagine the stink! And then it is that water there that you
> return to the girl, and she douches with it. You see with all that, the stomach is
> ruined.

This method works by causing an infection in the uterine lining (metritis),
which can indeed "ruin the stomach." Septic abortions can result in severe
illness or shock and are among the leading causes of maternal mortality
(Cunningham et al. 2001:877; Rana et al. 2004). Another woman described
how she was given henna (*verni houssa*) mixed with quartz dust to eat;
a third had inserted bark soaked in bleach into her vagina. How these
two remedies instigate abortions I am not sure, although the women both
reported that the techniques had succeeded.

For safer methods, access to services is limited by economic and social factors. Medical doctors and ritual specialists, considered high-quality
abortion providers and in some cases very well trained, usually charge high
fees: one woman said that she paid CFA 400,000, about USD 200, for a
hospital abortion. This is about seven times the cost of a year's tuition in
a public high school, or twice the price of tuition at la Trinité. In addition,
doctors and ritual specialists are quite selective about their clients, preferring to treat women they already know, or women who are introduced to
them by close associates. Although their position makes sense—their business is both lucrative and illegal—the practice makes women's access to
safer abortions contingent on her social network (see also Rossier 2002).

Abortion appears to be common in southern Cameroon, despite the
parallel facts that it is illegal, often dangerous, and vigorously opposed
by the Catholic Church. Just *how* common I do not know, but I have a
few clues. The 1998 DHS does not ask directly about abortion, but it does
ask whether a woman has ever experienced a *grossesse improductive*. The
DHS translates this as "terminated pregnancy," using "terminated" in the
sense that the pregnancy ended without producing a live birth, and not
necessarily suggesting that the woman herself took action to end it.[3] The
single question lumps together stillbirth, miscarriage, and abortion, and all

are probably underreported: miscarriage may occur so early that a woman does not know that she was pregnant; events that happened long ago may be forgotten or repressed; women may be unwilling to talk about painful or potentially embarrassing experiences with an interviewer. As regards abortion, the impetus to underreport is even stronger, given the legal situation and moral opprobrium. Still, data with a known bias are probably better than no data, at least as a starting point.

Figure 7.1 graphs the proportion of women by age who reported at least one nonproductive pregnancy for each of three groups: the entire DHS sample (all educational statuses and regions), the subset of DHS data that most closely approximates my own sample (women who attended at least some secondary school and reside in the province that encompasses Mbeya and Yaoundé), and the women included in my own small-scale but more in-depth life-history survey. In the DHS, educated, southern Cameroonian women are more likely to report having had a terminated pregnancy than are women in the sample as a whole, and the difference grows with age. My own data, which are not representatively sampled but are probably more accurate for the select population, give estimates that are significantly higher than the DHS at young ages, although almost certainly still lower than reality for the reasons stated above: 44 percent of all women, including 34 percent of women who have never given birth, reported that they had experienced at least one pregnancy loss or abortion.

While the DHS asks only about "terminated pregnancies" as a category, the life-history interviews that I conducted distinguish between different pregnancy outcomes. These outcomes are about evenly distributed between induced abortions on the one hand and miscarriages and stillbirths on the other: sixty-one abortions and fifty-six miscarriages and stillbirths. Although the total numbers are small, this implies that abortion occurs at relatively high rates: 26 percent of my respondents reported having induced at least one abortion, and nearly 7 percent reported having induced two or more. Eleven percent of all reported pregnancies, and 25 percent of first pregnancies, ended in abortion; about 10 percent of all reported pregnancies resulted in involuntary fetal loss. Since the proportion of involuntary fetal loss varies only moderately across populations, averaging around 15 percent of clinically recognized pregnancies (Ellison 2001: 35), it is clear that even the estimates in my survey are too low. Nonetheless, even these low estimates correspond to a total abortion rate of 0.39, and a crude abortion rate of 23 abortions per 1,000 women aged fifteen to forty-

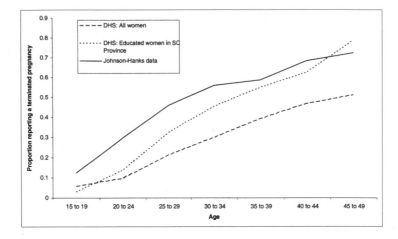

FIGURE 7.1. Proportion of women by age who report having lost at least one pregnancy, Cameroon 1998

four per year.[4] Data from the Alan Guttmacher Institute (2002) indicate that the crude abortion rate in the United States has varied between 16 and 29 per 1,000 women over the thirty years since *Roe v. Wade;* using indirect methods, Henshaw and others (1999) estimate crude rates around 35 abortions per 1,000 women in central Africa as a whole.[5]

Why are practicing Catholics having abortions? Why, in particular, are Catholic schools putting in place structures of opportunity and constraint—such as forbidding visibly pregnant girls from attending class—that make abortion more attractive? It seems deeply ironic that abortion should play an important role in making Catholic education available to young women, in much the same way that the Catholic system of infant abandonment described by Kertzer (1993) seems ironic. Yet internal contradiction and unattainable expectations appear rampant in reference to sexuality and reproduction, particularly of adolescents. When conservative politicians in the United States advocate abstinence-only sex education and oppose the distribution of condoms, when they advocate parental notification and waiting periods for abortion and yet oppose no-fault infant surrender policies, the irony seems just as strong. Making contraception unavailable increases abortion rates, and making early abortion unattainable increases the preponderance of late abortion (Johnson et al. 1993; Joyce and Kaestner 2001; Stoyanova and Richardus 1999; Sugar 1991). There was no formal discussion of abortion in the EVA courses I attended or the annual syllabus that the teacher showed me. In contrast to sex and reproduction, abortion drew little attention from other teachers at la Trinité. And yet every woman who described to me a specific instance of mistimed pregnancy addressed the question of abortion, if only to say why she had rejected it as an alternative.

Abortion occupies a strange place in Beti women's negotiations for honor: although nearly everyone asserts that abortion is reprehensible, over 25 percent of first pregnancies reported in my survey ended in abortion. Although abortion is portrayed as blameworthy, in certain conjunctures it is forgiven, or even encouraged, as a means of avoiding yet graver dishonor. For example, at its most extreme, an ill-wrought entry into socially recognized motherhood when a girl leaves school with no prospects for marriage or employment constitutes an almost irremediable dishonor. Thus, although less desirable than averting pregnancy, a discreet abortion may be preferable to delivering a child for a woman without a stable partner. While no one supports abortion in the abstract, given the specific range of alternatives feasible in a given vital conjuncture, abortion may be the least unattractive option, less bad than marriage to the wrong man or the desperation of dropping out of school and single motherhood. In the routinized uncertainty of contemporary southern Cameroon, people are constrained to act under the principle of judicious opportunism. Rather than selecting specific goals and maximizing the likelihood of attaining them, people cultivate a range of alternative strategies and seize promising chances as they appear. Sometimes, abortion offers a promising chance, and—like other promising chances—it is then quickly seized.

Malleable Motherhood

Abortion is not the only means by which educated women can postpone their entry into the social category of mother. Indeed, giving birth does not define someone once and for all as a mother. Just as we saw in chapter 3 that the titles *ngon* and *miniga* are negotiable and context-dependent, so too is motherhood malleable. Thus, birthing—even if it is unforeseen or mistimed—does not unilaterally create honor or dishonor. Instead, a mistimed birth can be recuperated by the mother after the birth. By marrying the baby's father, a young woman can reset the socially perceived timing and circumstances of her transition to motherhood. Or by relinquishing her rights to the child, distancing herself from the birth, and returning to school, she can sometimes effectively postpone that transition: she can give birth without becoming a mother.

As perhaps everywhere, common talk in southern Cameroon equates childbearing with childrearing. Beti women interchangeably use *infanter, accoucher,* and *donner*—all vernacular expressions for childbirth—to mean "attain the social status of mother." But if we examine the systematicity of action, rather than explicit, normative statements, the social category of motherhood is indeed separate from actual childbirth. Thus, just as pregnancy can either be claimed and made public or hidden from view and in effect erased from a girl's life history through abortion, so too can birth. There are arguably two kinds of first births: some constitute the initiation of a socially recognized reproductive career, while others do not. More accurately, these two are the extremes of a continuum, and specific births initiate a woman into socially recognized motherhood to a greater or lesser degree, rather than completely or not at all. Beti motherhood is a social role, rather than a coherent life stage (see Johnson-Hanks 2002a), which makes possible partial transitions and incomplete affiliations. In the space between the fact and the recognition of birth is a second option for schoolgirls facing mistimed, unforeseen pregnancies: they may relinquish their claims to their child.

As throughout West Africa (Page 1989), Beti children are often raised by people other than their biological parents, either for part or all of their childhood. Of the 431 children born to women in my survey, fewer than 60 percent were living with both parents at the time of the survey and another 22 percent were living with their mothers only. More than 35 percent of the children had lived away from both parents at some point in their lives. Bledsoe has examined how Mende parents use fosterage to smooth the costs and reduce the risks of childbearing, placing children with relatives who may offer particular skills or resources, and managing the flow of children of particular ages and sexes through the household over time (Bledsoe 1990c; see also Bledsoe and Isiugo-Abanihe 1989). Many of the same phenomena take place in southern Cameroon: childrearing takes place in a variety of constellations, from a single mother raising her own children or a couple raising theirs, on one end of a continuum, to temporary fosterage with other members of one's family, to the far extreme of a mother relinquishing any claims to the child. This last possibility is somewhat specific to—and specifically important for—young, educated women. Although relinquishing claims to children lacks the flexibility and fluidity that makes fosterage so appropriate for managing reproduction under uncertainty, as one of a suite of strategies it can be very important.

As may not be surprising given the number of unforeseen first births, a number of young mothers are not ready to raise their children. They may have school to complete or desire to continue on a career path; the child's father may be unsuitable or unavailable as a husband. In these cases, young mothers usually first turn to their families for help. The mother's own mother, her sisters, or her cousins may step in and take over responsibility for the child.[6] Frequently the young mother remains actively involved in her child's life. Many people at Mbeya told me of a young woman who had recently graduated from la Trinité who had a child in the summer before her last year of school. All through that last year she walked home at lunchtime to breastfeed her infant, under the care of her own mother. Similarly, Mina, the young woman who took me to see the clairvoyant at Nsimalen described in chapter 3, had a three-year-old daughter. The child lived with an aunt in Yaoundé so that Mina could complete high school, and Mina traveled to the city to see the little girl nearly every weekend. Like Mina, most unmarried mothers retain ties with their children, even if the day-to-day care is done by others. Unmarried fathers, by contrast, are often absent from their children's lives. Although children born within a bridewealth marriage belong to the lineage of the father, men's claims to children born outside of marriage are subject to negotiation. While some fathers actively care for their children—bringing gifts for the layette or participating in the child's rearing—others are completely absent.

Few unmarried mothers relinquish their claims to their children, thereby giving them over completely to be raised by others, such as the family of the biological father—in which they are outsiders and have no standing. But some do, and the consequences are powerful. The closest thing in Cameroon to legal closed-book adoption, relinquishing claims to her child removes the biological mother from the child's life. She is no longer identified as mother, either in respect to her child or, unless she has other children, as a social identity. In contrast to the strong opposition by many Beti to abortion, there is no public outcry regarding the abdication of rights in children, except in extreme cases where the abandonment itself constitutes a form of abuse, or more dramatically, infanticide.[7] An educated woman who bears a child too early is not confronted by an evangelical effort to persuade her to raise the child herself. Relinquishing claims to children may be emotionally difficult, but—like abortion—it can also erase the shame associated with a birth that does not take place in the proper context. Thus, this practice more often occurs among younger, educated women experiencing unforeseen first births. By abdicating her rights to a child, a young woman can retain, at least partially, the social status of a girl (*ngon*), despite being a biological mother.

Statistical versus Social Norms

Viewed through statistical quantification or the analysis of practice, motherhood appears malleable, indeed reversible. This fluidity stands in sharp contrast to common local representations of birth and its consequences. In talk, educated Cameroonian women treat motherhood as synonymous with marriage and as inevitably leading to dropping out of school. Yet, neither representation accurately portrays what happens to most women. Such disjunctures between local representations and measurable actions, or between ethnographic and demographic data, provide a productive point of reference from which to interrogate both. The point here is not to show that one—the range of observed outcomes or the local perceptions and expectations—is more real or more important. Rather, I am interested in the contrast between the two ways of perceiving the consequences of pregnancy.

The Myth of Marriage

Although educated Beti women regularly emphasize the importance of being married before giving birth—even asserting that this practice distinguishes them significantly from the uneducated—nearly all the women I interviewed who had borne a child had done so outside of marriage. The statistical norm of nonmarital childbearing stands in sharp contrast to the social norm. This contrast between discourse and practice is, however, complicated by the multiplicity of kinds of marriage. As we explored in chapter 6, there are six potential elements of contemporary Beti marriage: the presentation of the man to the woman's parents, the formal engagement, cohabitation, the bridewealth, civil marriage, and the nuptial mass. A significant proportion of Beti women will never complete some of these marital elements, particularly the mass. But even recognizing these various kinds of marriage, the puzzling fact is that marriage and childbearing, represented as a coherent whole, in fact occur separately more often than they occur together. The tie between marriage rites and births is more complex than is commonly acknowledged.

In chapter 6 we saw that educated Beti women make the transition to a first birth earlier, on average, than they make most marital transitions. By age twenty-one, approximately 50 percent of the women in my sample had had a first birth; however, it was not until age twenty-seven that the same proportion had been married with bridewealth (see figure 6.2). The analysis in chapter 6 treated each transition separately as a function of age. Examining the transition to marriage specifically in relation to the timing of the first birth reveals more about their intersection. Women who have a child are more likely to marry than are women who do not, and in particular they are more likely to live with their partner. Although few women in fact marry with bridewealth or in a civil ceremony before bearing a first child, nearly everyone who bears a child subsequently marries. Figure 7.2 comprises scatter plots of the age at first birth and age at each of four marital events for the subset of women who have completed both events. Thus, a woman who has completed all five events appears as a point on each of the four graphs, whereas a woman who has borne a child and lives with her partner, but has never been married in a civil ceremony, church service, or with bridewealth is represented only by one point in the lower right-hand graph. Women who have never borne a child are not included in any of the graphs.[8]

Figure 7.2 reveals two things of interest. The association between age at first birth and age at each kind of marital event is positive but weak, except for cohabitation, which shows a tighter clustering. In addition, the strength of the association between first birth timing and marital timing does not appear to be closely related to the age at the events, except, again, for cohabitation. Women who have a child at young ages appear neither more nor less likely to marry at the same time as the birth than are women who begin childbearing later. For cohabitation, however, it may be the case that women who have children at the youngest ages—that is, as early teens— are more likely to begin cohabiting at the same time.

Because the age at first childbearing does not appear to matter for the strength of the relationship between the timing of childbearing and the timing of marriage, in figure 7.3 we discard age to look more closely at the transition to marriage in the temporal window around the first birth. Figure 7.3 graphs the proportion of women who have not yet married in each of four ways as a function of time relative to the first birth. Obviously, therefore, only women who have had at least one birth are represented

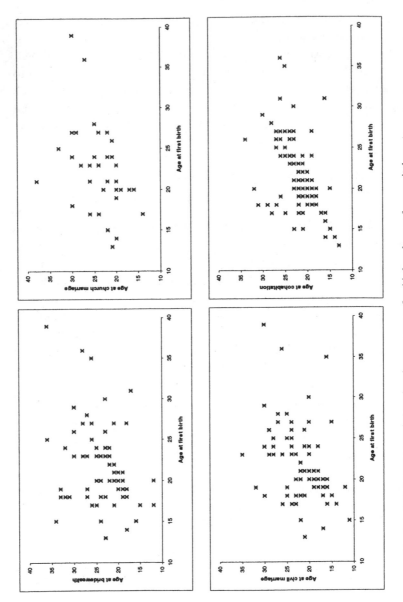

FIGURE 7.2. Association among married mothers between age at first birth and age at four marital events

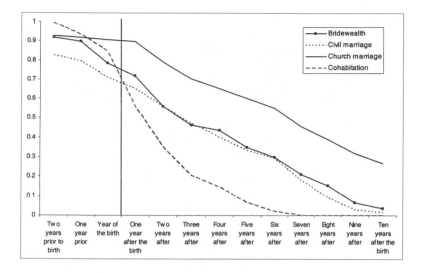

FIGURE 7.3. Proportion of mothers who have never married in each of four ways, by years after first birth

here. This figure is calculated in essentially the same way as figure 6.2 in the previous chapter, except that the reference here is time relative to the birth, rather than chronological age. The graph shows that as of two years prior to the birth, over 80 percent of women had never been married in a civil ceremony, and over 90 percent of women had never cohabited, married with bridewealth, or married in the church. By one year after the birth, the proportion married in church has changed hardly at all, whereas a significant number of women have begun to live with their partners or have married in a civil or bridewealth ceremony. Cohabitation is often closely associated with childbearing: a majority of new mothers begin to reside with a male partner, usually, although not always, the father of the baby, within two years of the first birth, and practically all have done so within seven years of the birth. By ten years after the birth, essentially everyone has married with bridewealth and in a civil marriage. Church marriage occurs late and rarely.

While my informants emphasized that educated women should postpone childbearing until they have married, few actually do. That said, marriage often comes soon after a first birth, and almost always comes within ten years of it. Contrary to popular perception, marriage is more likely to be a consequence of childbearing than its precursor.

The Myth of School Exclusion

The common equation of birth with the social category of motherhood reveals itself in the widely held belief that bearing a child will end a mother's
schooling career. Just as the statistical norm of nonmarital childbearing
contrasts with the social norm that educated women should bear children
within marriage, here local representations and demographic practices diverge. Exploring this disconnect between local assumptions and statistical regularities gives further evidence that motherhood is an elastic status,
which can be accepted or rejected in specific interactional frames. Bearing
a child does not always definitively end a school career in southern Cameroon. Rather, the data imply that the locally perceived conflict between
schooling and childbearing applies only to births that make the biological
mother undeniably recognized as a social mother. Women's strategies for
attaining honorable childbearing are multiple, and many of them centrally
include continued schooling even after childbirth. Data from the demographic life histories make clear that the substantial majority of first-time
mothers continue on the schooling path that they were following prior to
their pregnancy: those who were out of school stay out, and those who
were in school either continue or return. This effect is even stronger in
the case of unforeseen births. Several authors have noted that the fact of
young mothers dropping out of school may account for some significant
proportion of the education-fertility correlation (e.g., Fuller and Liang
1999). But my data imply that the causal paths are more volitional, and
more interesting.

According to my survey data, as mapped in figure 7.4, a majority of
the young women who were in formal secondary school at the time they
became pregnant completed at least one more entire year of formal education at some point after the birth, either immediately or later. Of 139
mothers, 58 were in school at the time of their first pregnancy. Of these, 33
dropped out of school in the year of the birth. Yet 17 of these dropouts later
returned to school, and 25 new mothers remained in school for at least one
additional year following the birth. So of 58 women who were in school,
42—that is, over 70 percent—completed more schooling after the birth.
On the other hand, of the 81 women who were not in school at the time of
their first birth, 50—that is, over 60 percent—had not returned to school by
the time of the survey (although some may well return later). Childbearing, therefore, does not single-handedly determine schooling trajectories:
childbirth is a vital event, but it is only one part of a vital conjuncture.

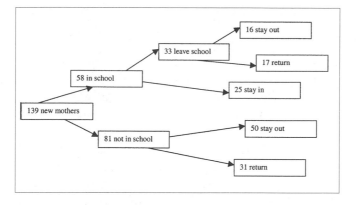

FIGURE 7.4. School participation following first birth. Only formal schooling is included here. Women who returned to professional apprenticeship, to correspondence schooling, or to private tutoring are classified as "never returned to school."

One of the most compelling facts about these data is that so many women returned to school after a birth, although many of these returns were delayed by several years. Many studies that have calculated high rates of school-leaving associated with childbearing have failed to look at the possibility of later return to the classroom because they have used too narrow a temporal diameter, examining only school attendance over the course of a year. That said, the rates of return are surely much higher at schools like la Trinité than elsewhere, because the institutional policies are more lenient. Unlike public schools, la Trinité allows women who have borne children to enroll in school, and has no official age limits for specific classes.[9] Both of these policies expand the options available to young mothers to return to school.

Some new Beti mothers do cease schooling, usually as a result of two interacting factors. First, they may prefer marriage to the genitor of their pregnancy over schooling, particularly if he appears promising as a husband, or if they already were dissatisfied in school. Second, new mothers may find it logistically impossible to continue in school if they do not have financial support or acceptable child-care options. This second logic is much stronger after a second or third child. Whereas by abdicating rights in first children, women can effectively postpone socially recognized motherhood, Beti women with two or more children are almost inevitably classified as mothers. In fact, it is only after a second child that the rates of those who permanently drop out of school become substantial. Of course, women at higher parities are also, on average, older. Age and parity therefore work together to decrease the likelihood that women with several children will persist in school.

My survey data show that two years after the first birth, most women remain primiparous, but by four years, most have gone on to have a second child. However, even ten years after the first birth, there remains a small minority of women who have never had a second child. The progression from parity two to higher parities is slower and smoother than the progression from parity one to parity two. Keeping in mind this distribution of women by parity in the ten years following a first birth, let us turn to the relationship between parity and school enrollment over these same years. Figure 7.5 shows the proportion of women at each parity enrolled in school in each of the ten years following her first birth. Data on school enrollment for women with two or more births are missing for the first couple of years because no women had yet achieved those parities. But note that in all years for which we have data on multiple parities, women with only one child are enrolled at significantly higher rates than are women with two or more children. However, the difference between enrollment rates for women with two children and those with three or more children appears to be much less significant.

These data imply that the locally perceived conflict between schooling and childbearing applies not to all births, but only to births that undeniably define the biological mother as a social mother. This transition may occur with her first birth, but women may also postpone entry into this status until the second birth, through fosterage or by relinquishing their claims to that first child and returning to school. Thus, returning to school serves both as a measure and as a constituent of a young woman's identity as a girl (*ngon*). Returning to school provides the young woman with a context in which she is not a mother, but an adolescent. But as figure 7.5 indicates, at the second and higher-order births, women become less able—and perhaps also less willing—to postpone their entry into socially recognized motherhood. Schooling and childbearing are neither mutually exclusive nor strictly ordered; the one-time mother again becomes a girl when she dons the school uniform.

Unforeseen first births to schoolgirls demonstrate how life events following a birth retrospectively shape its interpretation and define its character and social consequences. A schoolgirl who relinquishes claims to her child and returns to school following a birth may experience relatively

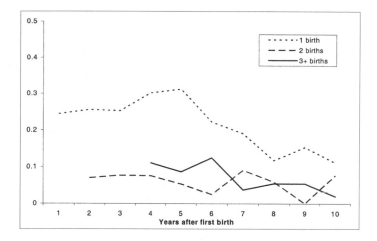

FIGURE 7.5. Proportion of women enrolled in school by parity

little change in her status; her identity as mother is intentionally erased in school contexts. Although her classmates may know that a student is a biological mother, she is unlikely to publicize the fact, especially if her relationship with the father has disintegrated. Beti girls who bear a child and then return to school frequently wait many years before bearing a second child. By contrast, when a couple marries following an unforeseen birth, the child is regularly retrospectively recognized as legitimate; parents often particularly dote on such a child as the seal of their relationship. In this case, the mother often quits school and bears a second child after a relatively short interval. Note here that the conjoining of marriage and childbearing is extremely powerful—a first birth may not force a woman out of school, but a first birth and a marriage almost certainly will.

Young, unmarried Beti women try to avoid pregnancy, managing relationships and the timing of sex, particularly as long as they are in school. Sometimes, however, they nonetheless confront an unforeseen and mistimed pregnancy. When this happens they enter a vital conjuncture, where possible future outcomes are multiple and no preferable pathways clearly visible. Navigating out of a vital conjuncture, you do not select a path from some given set of alternatives—usually, there aren't any—but rather, you must forge one, using whatever resources fall into your hands. This forging, which I have called "judicious opportunism," relies on the rapid and radical revisions of "contingency plans" (Bledsoe 2002). This flexibility enables educated Beti women to navigate the vital conjunctures of unintended pregnancy, as is clear in the story of Claudette.

Claudette

A slender and very pretty young woman, Claudette has a reputation in her Yaoundé neighborhood as being both hardworking and a flirt. My impression of her changed significantly as I came to know her better. At our first interview, I found her flippant, almost callous. But by the end of my fieldwork, I respected her as fearless and persevering, ready to take on great difficulty to achieve her aspirations. Claudette recounted the vital conjuncture described here over the course of three interviews in April and May of 1998.

Claudette was born before her parents were married, their first child. As her mother was still in school, Claudette was sent to live with her maternal grandmother in the village for a few years. By the time Claudette was ready to start kindergarten, her parents had married and were living in Yaoundé. They sent for her, and she spent the next eight years with them. As she was the eldest child in a relatively elite household, Claudette benefited from an excellent education, including Catholic boarding school from the age of twelve. Although she did well in school, the constrictive living conditions and the poor food of boarding school were difficult for her, and she changed schools several times.

At eighteen, Claudette transferred to la Trinité after having failed the *probatoire* at another school. Her parents wanted her to live in the dorms, but Claudette resisted: she wanted to rent a room privately. As she explained: "I knew that since I had already paid the first installment at the secondary school, my parents could not leave that money. So I wanted to force them to accept that I go rent a room. They said that I was too young." Claudette strove valiantly to have her way, but her parents eventually won this battle. In her depiction, and in keeping with local concepts of adulthood, her self-dominion as an autonomous adult was manifested through opposition to her parents. This opposition recurs throughout Claudette's story about her experiences, as does the fact that, in the end, her parents always win.

Soon after arriving at la Trinité, Claudette began to date another student, Alphonse. He quickly became jealous, possessive, and indiscreet:

He loved me so much that everyone at the secondary school knew that he was my boyfriend. That is to say at every moment, angry and really too jealous, he insisted that we be together. . . . Because he didn't want anyone else to come talk to me. . . . My schoolmates fled from me already, because whenever one of my schoolmates approached me, just like that to talk to me, it was necessary to check first if he wasn't nearby.

That so many people at school knew of the romance—particularly when it was yet so new—made it unusual. As we saw in chapter 6, discretion demands that sexual relationships—and even potential sexual relationships—be expertly hidden from view. Most of the time, couples will attempt to avoid even being seen in public together, to the degree that schoolyard gossips may cite the observation that a certain girl *never* talks to a certain boy as potential evidence that they are romantically or sexually involved.

Claudette's boyfriend not only allowed the relationship to become public, but he lacked the self-dominion to master his temper. Although men regularly react to attacks on their honor with vehemence, Alphonse angrily prevented Claudette from having even harmless interactions with classmates. By failing to distinguish insult from innocence, Alphonse demonstrated a lack of good sense, of judgment, and therefore of legitimate claims to honor. In telling the story, Claudette emphasizes his lack of discretion as a serious shortcoming: because he lacked good sense, he made their relationship public; because he lacked self-dominion, he reacted angrily to innocent situations. His lack of discretion becomes, in Claudette's telling, a moral flaw, arguably a tragic one. Tragic because— like Dante's gluttony—it is born of too much love. As much as Claudette may express contempt for Alphonse's lack of judgment, she is also proud of it. She won from him not just love, but devotion; as inappropriate as his actions were, in her view they resulted from the blindness of love.

Eventually, the intensity of her boyfriend's attachment made Claudette feel claustrophobic; the relationship grew rocky. One evening, she was visiting a friend and Alphonse could not find her. She explained: "He looked for me throughout the city, throughout the city, everywhere. He arrived in a place, he tried to describe me; they told him that they had seen me passing like that; he followed me." When he found her, he was furious and beat her. Then his violence became a pattern: to keep her home, out of view of potential rivals, Alphonse would hit her, or threaten to. Claudette's schoolwork began to suffer, but she managed to pass her classes and sit for the public exam. At the end of the school year in May, they broke up and Claudette went back to Yaoundé to her family.

When Claudette arrived home for the summer holiday, her mother noticed a change in her. Although she had always been slender, Claudette had become yet thinner and less inclined to eat, rejecting even her favorite *pommes frites*. Her mother, a nurse in obstetrics, suspected pregnancy, and asked her to get a test. Claudette obliged her mother, feeling certain that she was not pregnant. But the test came back positive. Claudette was shocked. Her mother was furious and enlisted all of her paternal aunts to persuade her to abort. No one told Claudette's father. Although he may well have known about the pregnancy, he did not admit to knowing.

Claudette explained that she resisted the idea of abortion from the first moment because she wanted the baby and thought she could manage. Although her mother insisted that keeping the pregnancy would require Claudette's moving to the household of the baby's father, Claudette planned to keep the baby herself: she was afraid of Alphonse, particularly of the possibility that he might beat the baby as well as her, and was unsure whether his family would protect her. Claudette developed a plan for how she would bear the child while continuing school: she would get a tutor for the first trimester and start classes again in January. She did not know how the finances would work out, but she knew that she would be able to get by (*se debrouiller*). Her mother was adamant that she end the pregnancy, and her aunts supported abortion as well. In their kitchens, Claudette's mother and aunts said that she had to stay in school, that she must not bear this man's child, that she must abort the pregnancy.

Amid all of the kitchen talk, another man announced that he wanted to marry Claudette. He was an officer in the army and someone she had known for a long time. He offered to adopt the baby and pay Claudette's school fees. As we saw in chapter 6, the fact that he would have paid her school fees is not exceptional. Women regularly expect that their boyfriends and husbands will express their commitment to the relationship in monetary ways. Adopting the child, on the other hand, would have been very unusual. Women rarely bring into a marriage children conceived with other partners because they say it causes too many problems. Claudette's child, however, was not yet born and could have been raised as if it were the biological child of its adoptive father.

Claudette explained that she considered the possibility of marriage quite seriously, but in the end she did not accept the proposal because she did not believe that her suitor loved her:

> He said to me, "I'll be a big man." He said to me, "I'll be a big, honorable man. With the work that I do, I need a wife like you, because you are the sort of woman that you want to present to everyone." . . . I said to myself that I'd be like a piece of furniture. You see a little, when you want to decorate a house, you take a piece of furniture, you put [it in your house], good. If you find that it is attractive, you leave [it there]. . . . I said to myself now that he has already done everything, now he needs a piece of furniture.

Claudette eventually decided that she could not be a decorative accessory to this man's career. Not only would it be demeaning to marry a man who did not love her, but it would also be dangerous. Claudette explains that one only keeps furniture that one finds attractive, suggesting that when it no longer is pleasing, it may be set aside without consequence. Married like a piece of furniture, Claudette would have been vulnerable to her husband's whims to pay her school fees, the maintenance money for the house, and for necessities for her child. From a practical perspective, what matters about Claudette's decision not to marry the military man is that it eliminated the only feasible option for her to rear the child without her parents' help—help that, given her mother's opposition to and her father's ignorance or denial of the pregnancy, seemed unlikely.

With the discovery of her pregnancy, Claudette clearly entered a vital conjuncture. At stake was her future itself: Would she continue in school? Would she marry? Would she become a mother now? And if so, would she be able to portray her motherhood as honorable? The vital conjuncture is a unit of social description defined by uncertainty and possibility, of paths considered, but not taken. This uncertainty is palpable in the story of Claudette's first pregnancy. But the narrative also indicates points of reference, horizons that orient action and motivate choices, such as the importance of love for marriage, and of marriage for childbearing.

Of course, our interview, and with it Claudette's description of events and the metaphor of furniture, came well after the fact, once the outcome was clear. It is hard to imagine her wavering back and forth, wondering whether she wanted to be like furniture or not. Instead, the metaphor is a kind of backshadowing, representing the now obvious as having been inevitable at some point in the past. Whereas backshadowing makes for terrible history (see Bernstein 1994: 17–19), it gives the personal recounting of a life history a reassuring inexorability. The uncertainty and range of possible outcomes present in the vital conjuncture of Claudette's unintended pregnancy are analytically important to me, trying to make sense of vital rates and the role of cultural expectations in accounting for them. For Claudette, however, the uncertainty is retrospectively erased, like memories by an accident.

Before Claudette had made a final decision about marriage to the army officer, Alphonse reappeared. She had not seen him since they broke up at school. He asked how she was doing, and professed to miss her terribly. She tried not to tell him about the pregnancy, but he insisted that she tell him what was happening, and she conceded. When she told him, he was angry. He accused her of trying to entrap him, and declared that he did not believe that she was actually pregnant. The next time they spoke, he asked her to abort the pregnancy. Claudette recounted that she had learned that the year before their relationship he had gotten another schoolgirl pregnant, costing his family a great deal of money; she reasoned that Alphonse feared that another pregnancy would permanently cost him his parents' support and thereby his chances for an education.

For at least a month, Claudette felt deeply conflicted and saw no paths out of her dilemma. No one wanted her to keep the baby, but she still couldn't bear the thought of giving it up. Her mother persisted in the position that Claudette would have to move in with the genitor (whose identity the mother did not know) if she kept the pregnancy. Seeing— and wanting—no prospect of that, Claudette considered her alternatives. When I asked how she endured that period of indecision, she answered that she had prayed a lot, mulling over and over the same facts, trying to find some alternative interpretation of them. I picture Claudette during those weeks like a modern-day Mary, "pondering these things in her heart," while she tried to imagine some possible way to continue the pregnancy.

While Claudette tried to think her way through the vital conjuncture that faced her, her mother arranged for a medical abortion, made an appointment for Claudette, and paid the first third of the fee. But when her mother gave her cab fare for the doctor's appointment, Claudette instead went to see Alphonse in order to persuade him to help her resist her mother's plan. At first, he refused, but over the course of the conversation, Claudette persuaded him.

Because he was always like that. Much too hard with me! Too strict! He said no, he didn't want a baby—it would ruin everything. But when I said that I would go with somebody else, just take the baby over to someone else, then he said okay.

With Alphonse's promise of financial and emotional support for herself and the baby, Claudette returned home feeling triumphant. Her mother, however, insisted that his words meant nothing—nothing had changed, and the pregnancy still had to be aborted. Exhausted by the family conflict, Claudette went to meet with the doctor. He said that it was too late to perform an abortion, since the pregnancy was in the sixth month already. Relieved, and believing that her mother would be forced to relent, Claudette returned home. But her mother paid more money to ensure that the abortion would take place anyway. Claudette refused to return to the doctor, but her mother threatened to tell her father about the pregnancy if she did not go. Between the threat of her father's wrath and her complete isolation in wanting to continue the pregnancy, Claudette saw her possible futures narrowed to one, and her vital conjuncture ended.

Claudette recounted quietly that her mother brought her back to the doctor and he gave her something "hot" (meaning strongly alcoholic) to drink. She was dizzy and faint as she lay down on his table. Numb, terrified, and exhausted, Claudette closed her eyes and listened—to the clock, to the doctor's shuffling, to the humming lights. He "scraped everything," she recounted, and then she began to bleed. The pregnancy was far enough along that she would have to deliver the now-dead fetus.

When Claudette returned home, she went into labor. Her bedroom was just off the living room of their small cinderblock house, and she fought to keep quiet through the pain. The labor lasted all night, from eight in the evening until five the next morning. In the morning, the sheets were drenched in blood, but the pregnancy was over. Her aunt washed the sheets and disposed of the fetus, while Claudette slept. In the days following the abortion, Claudette said, she was violently ill. She couldn't get out of bed, couldn't eat. Her father began to be concerned about her health and suggested that they take her to the doctor. Concerned that she would be discovered, Claudette set about to get well:

I did everything I could to eat. As soon as I ate I vomited, but I forced myself to the point where I finally ate. So as soon as I ate, I could get up. It's true that it was too hard, but I told myself "I have to cure myself."

Her strength returned, and a couple of weeks later she started school again. As of ten months after the abortion, Claudette had not told her father about the pregnancy, and she had not seen her former boyfriend since the day he agreed to support the child that never came to be. She was not dating anyone and was enjoying focusing on her studies.

Marie

Marie was born in 1978 in Yaoundé, the eldest of eight children. Her style of self-representation contrasts with Claudette's. Where Claudette is confident and confessional, Marie is restrained. Whereas Claudette talks about her feelings, Marie portrays the events that led to them. Overall, Marie's story reads as if seen through a glass darkly. But that is how she talks, and it is therefore part of her story.

Marie's father was a high-level civil servant. Her mother, who had left secondary school for marriage, stayed home with Marie and her siblings for more than a decade. Although bright, Marie struggled in the different Catholic schools that she attended. A recurrent illness, *mal aux nerfs,* forced her to repeat several classes, and she changed schools four times before the ninth grade.[10] When her parents' marriage grew rocky, Marie's mother returned to her natal village, leaving the children with their father in the city. This choice was not extraordinary: the children of a bridewealth marriage belong to the lineage of the father, and should stay with him. But since they resided in the city, Marie's father did not have the usual assistance of adult female kin for the household or the children. Suddenly, Marie was the senior woman in the household, and her labor at home seemed more important than her continuing her education—particularly given her relatively poor performance in school:

> It was very hard then. And in ninth grade I couldn't succeed. So my father took me out of school. At home there had been problems. Dad and mom didn't get along any more. He chased her out, and mom left during the year. We stayed alone with dad. And me, I was the oldest.

Although this might have meant the definitive end of her formal education, Marie returned to school after a year of keeping house. This kind of intermittent schooling, where young women (and less commonly, young men) alternate between the classroom, the work force, and the home, is quite common in southern Cameroon, as we saw in chapter 4. Leaving school is not a definitive transition, and some high school students are in their mid-twenties. The fluidity and variation of schooling trajectories conforms to long-standing Beti values of constant self-improvement that we saw in chapter 2; it also points to the significance of formal schooling in the contemporary socioeconomic climate, even since the onset of *la crise*.

When Marie returned to school after a year, she attended a public school for the first time. Although public schools do charge fees, they are much lower than the Catholic school fees, making public schools accessible to students from a wider range of family backgrounds. As we explored in chapter 5, the fact that public schools are more accessible is one of the reasons that many Catholic-educated Beti consider public schools disorderly and their students too worldly; they represent public-educated girls as corrupting influences who can lead Catholic girls astray. Marie's description of her experience conforms to this stereotype:

> At the public high school, I am there in class, and the others are outside [in the hallway], and I didn't understand. It was a new thing for me. And so with adolescence and puberty, I started to do like the others. When you arrive in the public school, you have friends who already know too much. They tell you, "No, you can't stay like that! You need to [do this], you need to [do that]." I went with the first boy who came along. Unfortunately I fell pregnant.

When Marie told her father about the pregnancy, he was angry. Marie had obligations for the welfare of her younger siblings as long as she was in her father's house. Her pregnancy not only made it harder for her to fulfill her obligations as caretaker for her siblings, it also placed a significant economic burden on her family.

> [The pregnancy] didn't please my father, and . . . he was right, because first of all I was the oldest. I had to look after my little brothers, and then I was like the mother of the house. So he couldn't bear it.

Even for a high-level civil servant, an additional, unforeseen child represents major costs—especially in an urban context. And Marie's pregnancy marked a departure from the future in which her father had been investing, that of an educated woman well married.

Marie's father insisted that she go to live with the genitor's natal family, that is, in a small town about an hour outside of Yaoundé. In ordering her to join the genitor, Marie's father was suggesting that he viewed her pregnancy as a decision for marriage, implying that she would leave school permanently to take on the social role of a married woman and mother. Although she had not planned to marry this young man, and did not want to live with his family, Marie explained that she obeyed her father because, as she says above, she believed that his judgment was fair. Marie felt obligated to accept her father's opinion and do as he told her to try to ameliorate the situation.

As soon as she arrived, Marie was unhappy in the household of her potential in-laws. Nonetheless, Marie made it clear that she saw herself as a young wife married into the compound, although no marriage rites had been celebrated. As I have previously stated, Beti frequently use assumed future titles to refer to individuals in the present. Marie referred to members of the household by affinal kin terms, signifying not that she was actually married, but that she perceived herself to be moving toward marriage. Marie explained that the hardships she suffered were, in part, normal difficulties inherent in the role of a young wife and daughter-in-law:

> It was *hard*. Because they are Manguissa [an ethnic group closely related to the Eton]. A Manguissa man, he can love you, but his mother can never accept [you]. Even if your husband loves you, his mother cannot. You cannot talk anymore. She makes decisions in the place of your husband. And because [my own parents] didn't teach me to revolt, I was obligated to keep quiet.

Marie represented her difficulties as inevitable for any young woman, particularly one who was well raised, that is, raised not to revolt. But her difficulties were all the more pointed because her potential in-laws were members of one of the many rapidly growing Protestant sects in this heavily Catholic area.

> In the home of the genitor, let's say the father of the baby, there they were in a sect, called "The Way." . . . They were in it. But their manner of doing [things], it didn't please me. Because, say someone comes like that to you. He sees the pen. He tells you, "The pen, it isn't good for you. Me, I take it." He leaves with [it]. He takes [it]. He comes. He sees the pocketknife. If he says, "No, it's not good!" he leaves with [it]. It didn't please me.

Marie's description of the physical intrusions she suffered in this house are at once literal and metaphorical. She had nothing of her own: not a pen, not a pocketknife, not her own space, and not even her own voice. The choice of pens and pocketknives as examples was coincidence; both objects were in view as she spoke. But the principle holds regardless of the objects.

Throughout this time, Marie felt dispossessed and silenced. And throughout, the justification given for her suffering was that it was for her own good; as she was now the mother of a newborn, her place was with the family of the genitor. She herself was ambivalent: Marie wanted to be a good young wife, an honorable young wife, but she also didn't want to be a young wife in this situation at all. As she explained:

> But as I was in a house where I had to submit myself to the people who were there, they made me do their lessons at their school. It was twelve days I sat and heard them. They teach you that what is in the Bible, you must see it in a different manner. Finally, I joined in [the sect].

The lack of emotion as Marie spoke, in marked contrast to Claudette's flamboyant style, was poignant. Serious, diligent, and calm, Marie seemed like an unlikely candidate to join a sect. That in the Manguissa house she could have been so far from the stable woman I saw sitting before me made the story compelling, even as she recounted it in perfect calm. Marie emphasized how she allowed herself to be overwhelmed by her potential in-laws in the attempt to conform to her role as a young wife: in her portrayal, she submitted herself to their school and converted to their religion. Thus, in Marie's narrative, she was intending to spend the rest of her life as a wife in this family. She had left school, was caring for her infant full-time, and was actively yielding herself to the disciplines of her potential in-laws.

At this point, Marie's future appeared again certain, the conjuncture closed. Religion, residence, motherhood were aligned in a single direction. Marie was transformed, perhaps unhappy, but certain. And for several months, that was how it stayed. But as the time passed, Marie felt herself increasingly unable to submit to her potential in-laws and particularly to their religion. She was "tormented" in the night, and would cry for no reason during the day. The parish priest sought her out and talked with her over several months. Marie returned to the Catholic Church, and then to her natal home as well. She equates the homes of her two fathers to explain how her reconversion led her to return to her family. She describes how the solace she found in praying the prayers she knew from childhood reminded her of herself, of her past, and led her to return to her previous life.

> It was much later that the parish priest . . . opened my eyes. When he opened my eyes, I said "No. That voice there was not the best. Better that I return to the house of my father." I went back. I began to pray the Hail Mary and the Rosary. I saw that I was better, because I wasn't so tormented anymore. Better that I stay in the house of my father than to set off, to go looking elsewhere. After a certain time there, I saw that I couldn't stand [it]. I had to leave them.

Seven months after joining the household of the genitor of her pregnancy, Marie returned to her father in Yaoundé. When Marie returned to her natal house, she left the infant with its father's family, weaning it quite suddenly and quite young—less than four months old. By leaving him with the father and his family, Marie relinquished her right to claim him as her child. Weaning an infant so young would have been met with wide social opprobrium, at least in the short term. However, leaving the child at all would have the longest-term social effects. In the intervening years, Marie saw her child rarely, and was not generally identified as his mother.

The vital conjuncture ends with Marie's return to her natal family, for at that point the questions about her future and identity are again laid to rest. The moment of envisioning various possible futures because of the pregnancy and birth closed, and her trajectory—for the time being—is clear. Again a member of the Catholic Church, Marie reentered Catholic school. In 1998, she was completing twelfth grade and aspired to continue at university.

Nathalie

Nathalie, slender and bright-eyed with a whip-sharp wit, is the sixth of seven children. Her father died when Nathalie was only three, her younger brother still an infant. After his death, Nathalie's mother left Yaoundé to return to the village Nkongmesse, bringing the four younger children with her. The oldest three stayed with relatives in the city, continuing in school and then on to work. Throughout her childhood, Nathalie moved back and forth between Yaoundé and Nkongmesse, attending school off and on in both places. She did well, but not exceptionally well, and cobbled together the money for her school fees from her older siblings and other relatives, refusing a series of men who offered to pay her school fees but whose expectations of repayment she distrusted. She came to la Trinité from a school in Yaoundé, where she had failed the *baccalauréat*. Living in a rented room in the cement-block Foyer de la Grande Famille, Nathalie kept to herself more than most, rarely participating in the collective outings and social gatherings of the other young women in the foyer in the first months of 1998. Her boyfriend, Michel, a serious young man from Yaoundé, visited occasionally.

I came to know Nathalie well over those first few months. Like me, she was a stranger in Mbeya, lonely, and wanted someone to talk to. I appreciated her stealthy sense of humor: a quiet tone of voice and soft smile would frame a perfectly ferocious insight into the habits of her neighbors and classmates, such as how one young man "dolled up" his seduction techniques, or how a young teacher "cracked like manioc" when the students opposed him. Soon after my arrival, I suspected that she was pregnant, and by mid-March I was certain. The baby was due in August. Although la Trinité accepts students who have had children, like most schools in southern Cameroon it prohibits visibly pregnant women from attending classes. Nathalie hoped to keep the pregnancy secret long enough to complete the school year, or if not secret, at least disguised and thus deniable.

We first talked about the pregnancy in her room; I asked whether she wanted to marry Michel, and whether he would recognize the baby. The question drew a long silence. Finally, Nathalie explained that he had offered to marry her, but her mother had told him to wait patiently (*patienter*): she did not want to accept the bridewealth. We talked for a long time that evening, about possible options and solutions. Maybe his parents could talk to her mother? Maybe her older siblings could intervene? Nathalie wanted to know what I would do if my parents refused an offer of bridewealth, and whether I knew of any safe means of abortion. I wanted to know if she really loved Michel, and what she wanted in her heart of hearts (a phrase that it turns out does not translate well into Camfrançais). Overall, I am afraid that my advice was not very helpful.

A couple of weeks later, I asked Nathalie if she would be willing to be interviewed on tape. She was, and I asked her to retell the story of her romance with Michel.

> He was already very patient with me, because he was my tutor. We met by co-
> incidence like that and he offered to help me study. So he helped. He was very

kind. Some people tease me, like I was telling you before. They tease me because he doesn't have any money. He can't always be bringing presents. He can't pay for much. But I don't approve of that! I don't think that you should be following money. If you love someone, that's enough.

To Nathalie, the problem was not that Michel didn't have money, but rather the opposition of her family and the problem of his religion: he is a Jehovah's Witness. Of particular importance was the question of baptism. Whereas the Catholic tradition is to baptize infants, Jehovah's Witnesses reserve baptism for people old enough to make their own decisions.

He is very certain that he loves me. He says that I should not make problems for myself about the baptism. He says it is not important. But I think that it is important nonetheless! Jesus baptized babies, didn't he? But [Michel] says that we should only think about . . . the love we have for each other.

Nathalie hoped that Michel would convert, or at least allow her to raise the baby as a Catholic; her family, however, thought that Michel's beliefs were too dangerous, and his ethnic group (the Bassa) too deeply associated with sorcery to be trusted. From the perspective of the family, there were five pieces of evidence that Michel was a sorcerer: he comes from a *tribu* that they associated with sorcery; the relationship emerged suddenly and advanced rapidly; he insisted that she come live with him, even before the baby was born; he wanted Nathalie to stay home with the baby, rather than continuing her studies at the university when she passed the *bac;* and he refused to promise to baptize the baby at birth. The second was perhaps the most serious. Nathalie had gotten pregnant before they had ever been introduced to Michel, and now she was talking about marrying him. Her brothers especially found the suddenness suspicious, and contrary to the methodical slowness that characterizes honorable Beti social action. Nathalie was a smart girl, a reasonable girl, a girl with good sense. To accept a man so quickly, without having had time to observe him, seemed to indicate that she had been transformed, such as by the evil work of a sorcerer.

I never met Michel, but his insistence that Nathalie marry him quickly and against the wishes of her family seemed deeply strange to me as well. I recounted to Nathalie all the arguments that other young Cameroonian women had given me for the importance of long engagements and of waiting to see the "true face" of your partner. "Watch carefully!" I encouraged her, feeling as if I understood the importance of that advice better than I had before. Nathalie herself had no clear explanation for why she had not waited.

> I don't know what took me. It was just a sudden impulse [*coup de tête*]. Sometimes it happens that you act without even knowing why. You just make an action, and then you see what happens next. It was like that. I didn't really decide to be with him, or not to be with him. . . . It was just a sudden impulse.

The sudden impulse was not only to have sex with Michel, but to then also plan to have the baby with him. Nathalie figured that she could finish the year at la Trinité, pass her exams, and then take care of the baby. Living with Michel, she reasoned that she would be able to attend some professional training after a couple of years, once the baby was a little older.

Of course, the desirability of this plan depended both on Nathalie passing her exams and on her mother accepting the bridewealth, so that Nathalie and Michel could be properly married. The first of these was uncertain, and the second downright unlikely. As the semester progressed, Nathalie was deeply fatigued, having a hard time concentrating, and not doing well on her schoolwork; her passing the June exams seemed increasingly in doubt. And the discussions between Michel and her family stalled entirely. But he was determined to marry her regardless, and he began buying things for the baby. Each time Nathalie visited Yaoundé to see the doctor, Michel tried to persuade her to stay with him and bring her belongings to his house. If the family was hesitant to accept the bridewealth, at least Nathalie herself could make a decision to marry him. Even as she assented—leaving her things at his house, having him accompany her to the doctor, Nathalie worried about her siblings' opposition and that Michel's religion might harm the baby. They had reached a complete impasse, but Nathalie did seem to want to be with Michel. Michel insisted that her family was needlessly creating obstacles, and that they should marry nonetheless.

Despite the official rule against being pregnant and attending classes, no one seemed to mind that Nathalie stayed in school as her pregnancy became more visible. She was not expelled, as she feared, but stayed through the end of the year. The pregnancy was hard, and she was exhausted a lot of the time. Still, she persisted, finished her coursework, and retook the *bac*. After the exam, Nathalie moved into Michel's house in Yaoundé. Her family was distraught that she would be living with him in the weeks or months leading up to and including the birth; they wanted her "home," either with her mother in Nkongmesse or with one of her older siblings in Yaoundé. They were particularly concerned about what would become of the infant's placenta, and whether Michel would use it for some kind of sorcery. Nathalie, however, was calm. She was praying a lot, she explained, and was confident that everything would be fine.

In many ways, this vital conjuncture was unusual. From the perspectives of Michel and Nathalie's family, there was no uncertain, ambiguous range of possible futures, no need to struggle through a variety of alternative prospects, no need to look to the horizons to navigate an honorable outcome. For each, the necessary outcome was clear; it was just that the two necessary outcomes were opposite. Michel wanted a rapid civil marriage followed by a proper bridewealth as soon as he could afford it, whereas Nathalie's family wanted her to come home, away from the potential sorcerer, and continue her studies at the university if she could.

For Nathalie, by contrast, the surprising pregnancy with this new man seemed more like a conventional vital conjuncture: the range of possible futures was vast, and she was uncertain which to pursue, or what the implications would be. For a while, it seemed that Nathalie might be able to combine all of them: she hoped to find a way to attend university once the baby stopped nursing, and that Michel would allow her to baptize the baby. Having completed high school, a legal marriage to the father of her first child would be a respectable transition to motherhood.

But then we learned that she had failed the *bac* a second time. To complete school, rather than dropping out, Nathalie would have to return to class in the fall: money, child care, and domestic politics all made that prospect difficult. Still, Nathalie was philosophical. Concerned that I would be disappointed in her, she sent me a note about the exam:

> I do not wish to wear the uniform of a schoolgirl anymore, as I am already too grown-up [*grande*]. But there are night classes, and I can study on my own in order to take the exam again next year. I will continue. Do not be worried.

Nonetheless, I was worried, as was her family. If Michel was worried, I never heard anything about it. His apparent indifference infuriated Nathalie's older brothers even more. They had paid her school fees for so many years and she was so close to finishing with the *baccalauréat*, permitting her to attend university or get a decent job. The brothers were furious both because they believed that the pregnancy itself had caused her to fail the exam that year, and because Michel showed no interest in reenrolling Nathalie in school in the fall, so that she might take the exam a third time the following year. As the opposition of Nathalie's family solidified, the prospects for a bridewealth marriage declined.

Knowing Nathalie during this time taught me a great deal. At twenty-three, she was remarkably calm in the face of some monumental realignments in her expectations for the future. But also simply observing the process of living through the vital conjuncture as it happened rather than hearing about it later changed my understanding of what uncertainty means and how it works. For much of the summer of 1998, nothing perceptible was occurring that would change the horizons of the conjuncture or make the possible future resolutions of the conjuncture clearer. The pieces were all in place, and yet no solution appeared. All that Nathalie could do was to sit with the problem, pondering it, but without any new information. In this sense, vital conjunctures are durations outside of normal time, parallel to the standoffs described by Wagner-Pacifici: "[W]hile we normally associate contingency with fluidity, I need to conjure up a different image of it, an image more bumpy and prone to stops and starts, both frozen and leaking at the same time" (2000: 6). For Nathalie, the seven-odd weeks between the news that she had failed the *bac* and the due date for her baby were both frozen and leaking: she could not move forward and gain clarity on what the future would hold, and yet time advanced, bringing the unforeseeable future ever closer. At one point she explained that she felt as if the whole situation could not be real:

> And then I have the impression that it is a dream, like when you wake up all of a sudden and are trying to know if everything that has occurred . . . really occurred, or if it was only a dream. Because I just can't believe that this could happen, with the exams and everything. Of course anything can happen in this world. But it still feels to me like a dream.

Nathalie gave birth to a healthy baby boy in early August and took him to Nkongmesse. After about six weeks with her mother, she returned to Michel's house in Yaoundé. I left Cameroon while they were in Nkong-messe, but kept up—off and on—with the family in letters. Nathalie did not return to school, or even to night classes that year, although she still planned to return at some point. She and Michel were married in a civil ceremony in the fall, but they had little prospect of either a church wedding or a bridewealth ceremony. Her siblings never visited Nathalie in her new home, as they continued to believe that Michel was a sorcerer. They did not approve of her marriage or wish to appear that they approved, and they were all somewhat concerned that it might be dangerous to visit his house.

In one sense the civil ceremony closed the vital conjuncture, clarifying Nathalie's future path as a married woman and mother, and almost certainly ending her trajectory as a uniform-wearing schoolgirl. On the other hand, the conjuncture lingered half open, as Nathalie continued to imagine that she might one day return to night classes or professional training. Her resolution of the impossible conflict between bearing a child young, bearing children only within marriage, and staying in school—like those of Marie and Claudette—was imperfect, her claims to honor uncertain.

*   *   *

When educated Beti women employ contraception to postpone entry into motherhood, it is not the act of birthing itself that they are chiefly seeking to manage. Instead, educated women are attempting to synchronize the timing of their entry into the social category of "mother" with other life-history transitions, particularly marriage and employment. Contraception, abortion, and abdication of rights in children thus constitute parts of a single logic: that of delaying motherhood. As a result, only very specific pregnancies are likely candidates for these practices. We have seen throughout that these are pregnancies that occur too early in reference to other life transitions, especially regarding school, work, and marriage. The choreography of vital events defines their legitimacy, as the temporal management taught in school exemplifies honorable self-dominion.

While the specific conjunctures related to an unintended pregnancy are particular to a life, the horizons against which they are interpreted are shared widely. By tracing the horizons, the principles against which alternative futures are evaluated, women's actions in negotiating vital conjunctures become more coherent. We turn to these horizons in chapter 8, showing how local representations of demographic patterns, systems of value, and interpretations of events together work to generate population rates, even as those local representations of demographic patterns remain irreconcilably at odds with the patterns themselves.

CHAPTER EIGHT

The Horizons of Honor

The horizon is a sort of background defined in relation to the foreground of actualized meaning. . . . It is not that people are making knowledge de novo at every moment but that the background of what is already known is revisable according to the purposes at hand. —William
Hanks, *Language and Communicative Practice*

W hen Marie, Claudette, and Nathalie found themselves pregnant,
they judged their own actions and prospects in light of a shared
set of horizons, a "background defined in relation to the foreground" of
their vital conjunctures (Hanks 1996: 166). An educated, modern, honorable mother will have worked first, and so can provide her children with
a good home and education. She will have a profession and resources.
She will be married to an honest man of good standing. The honorable
woman will plan for her children, master her own desires, and manage her
reproduction to correspond to these requirements of resources, career,
and husband. The fact that Marie, Nathalie, and Claudette's own pregnancies and prospective births fell outside the expectations of honorable
motherhood both shaped their understandings of their possible futures
and demanded their immediate action. The three young women looked
to an uncertain future to see dishonor looming, and not so distantly. As
we saw in these three cases, vital conjunctures are times of great risk and
possible transformation, when taking no action is not an option. In a vital
conjuncture, as in the standoffs analyzed by Wagner-Pacifici (2000), doing
nothing has potentially explosive consequences.

Marie, Claudette, and Nathalie were forced by their mistimed and
unforeseen pregnancies to completely reevaluate their options. As their
spheres of possible action shifted, their lives were no longer on predictable
trajectories. Their futures became suddenly uncertain. Once obvious paths

disappeared in a mass of underbrush. Disoriented, the young women evaluated their different opportunities against the conjunctures' horizons, that
is, the culturally mediated notions of what is possible or desirable. Like
the horizons of speech and face-to-face interaction analyzed by Hanks
(1996), these social horizons remain tacit and almost imperceptible until
they are contravened. It is only when life trajectories come into question
that people reflect on them. It is only in the throes of a vital conjuncture
that people focus on aspects of the background of common knowledge,
turning to it for orientation.

The quantifiable outcomes of vital conjunctures, such as we observe in
demographic surveys, reveal little about the structured opportunities and
impassioned actions that produce them. We saw in chapter 7 that abortion
is common, although it is reviled, and that educated women bear their first
child more often outside of marriage than within it, although they stead-
fastly assert the opposite. Horizons offer a way of framing the relationship
between these local meanings and population rates—not of reconciling
them, as they are often irreconcilable—but of thinking at the intersection. Horizons are locally perceived borders of possibility, risk, and aspiration; these borders orient action in vital conjunctures, translating local
values into population facts. The horizons of a conjuncture are part *doxa*,
part contingency (see Bourdieu 1977: 164), offering provisional answers
to questions like, What might be the outcomes of this conjuncture? What
should they be? What should be feared? And what might be hoped for?
Horizons are thus not alternative possible futures of a specific conjuncture, but basic principles of orientation that apply to many conjunctures.
They are the *points de repères* that indicate possible directions, not distinct goals. Horizons provide people facing vital conjunctures with common ways of reasoning and reacting. Because they are shared across conjunctures with dramatically different structures and consequences, these
cultural horizons offer more regularity and interpretability than do the
outcomes visible and measurable after conjunctures close.

As we have seen, the fragile modern honor of Beti women implicates
economic, educational, sexual, and religious domains: legitimate reproductive action therefore rests on legitimate action in spheres distant from
reproduction. But while the interrelations between reproduction and economics or religion may be unusually dense here, the phenomenon of
interconnectedness applies widely to vital conjunctures. By calling the
background image of expected futures into question, vital conjunctures

necessarily juxtapose hopes for marital and professional futures, expectations about reproduction and religion, and standards of sexual and educational practice. You cannot make a decision about your marriage only
in reference to marriage, because somehow everything else suddenly becomes also implicated. Faced with a vital conjuncture, whether you should
accept a job suddenly becomes contingent on the stability of your marriage, whether you should marry becomes contingent on your political
commitments. This intermixing is characteristic of all vital conjunctures,
but for a Beti woman facing a mistimed or unforeseen pregnancy, the tendency toward conflation arguably becomes even stronger. The possible
outcomes of the conjuncture—marriage, dropping out of school as a single mother, abortion, or some relinquishment of claims to her child—are
themselves all-encompassing, and what is at stake is not only the reproductive outcome. At stake are the woman's claims to an emerging, uncertain
honor, her rights to respect as a person of position, her sense of self.

I have said that the horizons are the available background that orient
action and make it meaningful. Should not honor, then, be among the horizons? Yes and no. On the one hand, the precepts of modern honor clearly
belong to the horizons, along the "sliding scale of typifications from the
fully saturated . . . to the relatively schematic and vague" (Hanks 1996:
166). Honor does the social work of horizons, serving as an orienting meaning, available to cast present action into a history of connotation and de-
notation. But horizon as I use the term here is not only a cultural product, but also a unit of social analysis. I seek to identify horizons as they
are lived, partially in order to use them to analyze reproductive action.
And in this latter sense, modern honor is not a horizon, because—perhaps
paradoxically—it is too vast, too fundamental, too all-absorbing. For my
usage here, honor is both the landscape and the compass, too vague and
ubiquitous to be included among the articulable horizons that organize
action in the conjunctures.

In this chapter, I explore the horizons that are common to mistimed
pregnancies for schoolgirls and reflect on how these horizons apply to the
case studies recounted in chapter 7. As the available but not necessarily evoked background, the list of horizons could be limitless. For a Beti
woman facing a mistimed birth, however, only a small number play consistently important roles. I focus on three, each of which was critical to
the vital conjunctures faced by Claudette, Nathalie, and Marie, and to the
trajectories that they forged. Horizons take the form of available images,

meanings, or stories, whereby one thing is equated with another, or one interpretation preferred. I name the horizons here after the figures they often elicit—images of unknown individuals who embody the warnings or enticements proffered by the horizons. These almost mythical figures are not explicit roles that the pregnant schoolgirl might occupy or encounter. Rather, these figures represent aspects of a culturally available background, characters that recur in the telling and retelling of exemplary tales.

The Murderous Abortionist

Abortion is often a tempting option for young educated women facing mistimed pregnancies, as it offers the chance to erase a threateningly shameful situation, to return to a previous trajectory, and to postpone the entry into motherhood until a more honorable context emerges. These potential benefits of abortion, however, are calibrated in relation to its potential dangers. Although no one knows how severe abortion-related mortality and morbidity actually are in the region, most Beti women believe abortion to be extremely dangerous, probably with good reason. Deaths due to botched abortions appear regularly in the public media, and stories of such deaths circulate even more commonly as gossip. The compelling stories of specific women—cousins or classmates—who died or were rendered infertile by abortion are often recounted. As described in chapter 7, many abortions are in fact performed in unhygienic circumstances by undertrained technicians.[1] Although doctors, nurses, and trained traditional herbalists all perform what are likely quite safe abortions, it is the figure of the vicious abortionist who sometimes kills schoolgirls out of negligence or malice that young women first envision.

Young, educated Beti often name physical danger as the first reason to avoid abortion. A woman who had borne her first child two years prior was telling me how she had been uncertain as to whether the baby's father would support them. I asked if she had considered abortion, to which she answered: "There, that's hard. Because that can lead far. You have to look at all the sides. You want to abort, but you have to also see if you can lose your life there." Similarly, a student recounted that she and her boyfriend avoided pregnancy by using periodic abstinence, as she had learned in school. She then went on to explain that if she got pregnant despite their attempts to the contrary, she would not abort because of to the dangers.

We take precautions [against pregnancy]. That must not even happen. There must not be a history of aborting. Me, I can't. If [I do get pregnant], I will give birth, but we do everything we can to avoid it from happening. Because my mother says that her daughters must never abort, never and that's true, because there are girls who die. You see a girl who is pregnant. She goes into the *sous-quartier*. They give her some cooked leaves. Afterwards, you see that she has an infection and it's over, because they don't have the money to go do [the abortion] in the hospital.

In addition to the possibility of a woman losing her life through a substandard abortion, Beti women weigh the risk of other illness or permanent sterility against the potential benefits of abortion. Abortions are believed by many Beti women to be one of the leading causes of infertility, itself a major problem here. One of my research assistants explained: " [Abortion] can destroy certain organs in the body. Afterwards, she becomes sterile." In this way, a woman who aborts resembles a woman possessed by *evu*, witchcraft tied to disordered female sexuality that causes infertility (Vincent 1976: 58). Even when abortion offers a chance to resolve a difficult situation, its physical dangers demand attention. Some women, like Claudette, have abortions nonetheless. But they cannot avoid the shared background that equates abortion with physical harm. Although her abortion was performed in a clinic by a medical doctor, even Claudette's account emphasized the blood, the pain, and the lack of basic humanity of the abortionist, who first refused to perform the late-second-trimester abortion, but changed his mind when Claudette's mother offered him more money.

The figure of the murderous abortionist not only portrays abortion as gravely dangerous, but also evokes its immorality. With her flagrant disregard for life—the fetus's and, in many cases, the mother's—the abortionist who embodies the first horizon represents abortion as a depraved act. The equation of abortion with moral depravity may partially result from Catholic missionization, replacing earlier, more fluid notions of the beginning of life and process of ensoulment. As Gable (1996) notes regarding the Manjaco of Guinea-Bissau, the Beti of the colonial era did not regard fetuses as human until the ancestral soul was incarnated in the baby's body at birth, and even after birth, the baby was seen as partially dwelling between two worlds, easily inclined to return to the world of spirits from which it was not yet fully detached (see also Ngumu 1977). In Laburthe-Tolra's magisterial work, the only reference to abortion is in the context of one jealous wife's attempt to prevent the birth of her co-wife's child, a potential competitor to her own child, and in the process killing the co-wife herself (1981: 426). This tale could be read to mean that abortion is literally murderous or, to the contrary, that—except in drastic circumstances—it lies within the domain of women's ordinary reproductive practices. These practices fall generally outside of Laburthe-Tolra's work (he does not discuss contraception at all, for example), so his general silence on abortion does not necessarily mean that it was absent. Regardless of the historical duration of a moral opposition to abortion, today it clearly corresponds to the position of the powerful Cameroonian Catholic Church. While the church in Cameroon has softened its stance on a number of issues, most notably extramarital childbearing, it continues to hold a very strong line against abortion. Abortion is the topic of sermons and catechism lessons, and ending the practice is one of the primary goals of the Action des Jeunes Catholiques in Cameroon, the national branch of a worldwide Catholic youth organization. An active member of this group, Magdalene was explicit about her opinions on abortion: "It is a crime against humanity, a great crime that we youth must now combat. And in light of the methods [of contraception] that are already available, youth must not abort freely." Focusing on the possibility of using contraception, Magdalene locates abortion in a network of practices surrounding the management of fertility within sexual unions where consensus can be reached and effective methods employed to ensure pregnancy avoidance. But in the same breath, she emphasizes that abortion is a collective moral crisis, taking abortion entirely outside the domain of the couple, and of contraception, to make it a public concern.

The public nature of abortion sometimes means that moral opprobrium does not fall on the young woman alone. A fifteen-year-old boy recounted a story that had circulated in his school, where both of the young participants had been students. In this story, the moral burden of abortion lies not on the would-be mother, but on her parents and the family of the genitor, who together gave her no option but to abort.

> There was boy who got a girl pregnant and then fled. . . . His parents knew about it. . . . Suddenly one morning the parents of the girl came [to the household of the boy], but the boy and his mother had already left. The girl had no choice but to get rid of the pregnancy, all the more so because [her] parents didn't want the baby. . . . When the parents don't want the baby, that means that in the religion it is a mortal sin, because it's like you killed someone. So I don't tolerate that.

The sin here results from the parents' desires rather than from the young woman's actions; the immorality attaches to intentions rather than outcomes, and to the adults assumed ultimately responsible rather than to the young people whose lives are most directly affected. Thus, although my interlocutor does not tolerate abortion, neither does he blame the schoolgirl. As abortion takes on its most public and social face, it may become more easily justifiable, as the blame is shared.

Reflecting on Claudette's story, it appears that her resistance to an abortion did not arise from fear of the possible physical dangers; nonetheless, her representation of the doctor still draws on the figure of the murderous abortionist, and her account of her long, bloody night and subsequent frailty still evokes abortion's dangers. In part, Claudette had less to fear than do many women, as her mother had the social and financial means to arrange for a relatively safe medical abortion. But Claudette and her mother were influenced by the danger of social recrimination—mother and daughter together strove to keep both the pregnancy and the abortion secret—and of moral failure. Although Claudette did assent to the abortion, she described in detail how she prayed throughout the ordeal, seeking guidance as to how to proceed. When sin rests on intentions as much or more than on actions, recourse to prayer constitutes one of the myriad actions oriented to the immorality of abortion in the vital conjuncture of an unforeseen pregnancy.

Despite a background in which abortion is dangerous, its dangers do not explain entirely why some young women reject abortion. Horizons offer certain available meanings, culturally accessible interpretations of what-is-going-on-here-now, but they do not exhaust them. Even when visible, measurable actions and outcomes appear to follow one or another principle embodied in the horizons, their actual causes may be altogether different. For example, Marie explained that she refused to abort her mistimed, unforeseen pregnancy out of respect for her mother. She had many offers of assistance, and probably could have arranged for a relatively safe abortion. But parents, especially mothers, play critical roles in young Beti women's evaluations of the chances they face, and Marie—like Claudette—did what her mother wanted:

No one wanted me to abort. Even [my father] didn't, in keeping with the teachings of my mother. Abortion, you must not do it! She forbade us, no matter what should happen, to do that sort of thing. I thought of her, because there was so much temptation. Everyone came to give me things, saying, "Take this, take this!" And I said no, because if my mother hears now, since when she knows that I was pregnant and then they say that I had aborted, that will not please her. I kept the pregnancy.

Nathalie's mother was also opposed to abortion, but I think that played a less important role in the partial resolution of that conjuncture. Instead, Nathalie really did engage in judicious opportunism, grasping onto a promising chance for marriage when no other viable opportunity for retaining honor materialized. She did not have the social ties or economic resources for a safe abortion, and she was unwilling to relinquish her child and return to school. Like most Beti schoolgirls who find themselves pregnant, Nathalie, Marie, and Claudette had to create a path for themselves to traverse a patch of unknown territory where no trails had been staked out, or where the previous trails had become overgrown. Despite the figure of the murderous abortionist whose disregard for life and health makes abortion both physically and morally hazardous, abortion can sometimes open up a path out of harm's way.

The Fallen Schoolgirl

While abortion may lead to moral sanction, infertility, and even death, the alternative of carrying a mistimed pregnancy to term has perils as well. Chief among these is dishonor. Given the centrality of good timing and self-dominion in characterizing women's honor, it is not surprising that giving birth as a schoolgirl is shameful. Schoolgirls often give birth with none of the external requirements for respectable motherhood in place: no marriage, no house, no career, no possessions. Alongside the notable absence of these forms of pecuniary honor lies the visible sign of temporal disorder. Schoolgirls who bear an unforeseen child have strayed from the tenets of self-control and foresight that constitute educated women as a class apart. Without remedial action, they face the loss of their identity and place in the community of the honorable elite. In popular representations that circulate freely enough to become part of the taken-for-granted background, girls who give birth while still in school and without prospects for marriage are reduced to the base level of the uneducated. Their lack of self-control equates them with the villagers who never learned to count their cycle (*calculer;* literally, "to do arithmetic"), and they risk dropping out of school and even abandonment as a result. One woman explained:

> You see, when you are a student and you conceive, when your friends leave for school you are ashamed. You are obligated to hide yourself. Even when you give birth, you even go to the village. You go to give birth in the village so your friends don't see you because you are so ashamed when you are young and you give birth, especially with a schoolboy, since schoolboys flee.

It is not premarital sex, nor even premarital pregnancy here that elicits shame, but the fact of giving birth when one is young and unprepared (Johnson-Hanks 2002b); even more, the shame arises from the fact that the schoolgirl must relinquish a project already in motion. We saw in chapter 3 that although Beti women readily and regularly assert that the future is known only to God, they simultaneously treat as already ful-filled processes that have been initiated and publicly recognized. Engaged women are called by their future married names, and junior seminarians are called parish priests. This distinction means that a public declaration of intention—such as enrolling in seminary—represents a commitment, an assertion of will. To fail in achieving your will can always be read as a fail-ure of self-dominion, even if it cannot be read only that way. Abandoning a trajectory you have visibly begun risks being, itself, shameful. Therefore, when my interlocutor draws a sharp line between the girl and her school friends, because they are continuing on the path that the pregnant girl has left, she is pointing out a first kind of shame.

Like many of my informants, the woman quoted above notes that giv-ing birth is particularly shameful when the genitor of the pregnancy is a schoolboy, "since schoolboys flee." This represents a second kind of shame, and the girl's abandonment marks a second failure: she has failed not only at being a student, but also at being a wife. Off track for achieving any of the life transitions that make childbearing honorable, the fallen schoolgirl is bearing children "in disorder," ideologically equated by ed-ucated women with the uneducated. By leaving school, returning to the village, and failing to marry, the iconic fallen schoolgirl fails to achieve a class-specific model of motherhood, whereby childbearing belongs with a Christian marriage and to an economically well-situated woman (cf. Mann 1985).

In the first instance, the figure of the fallen schoolgirl is about the fra-gility of pecuniary honor, and the ease with which it is lost. These stories are regularly recounted for both didactic and dramatic purposes, some-times by women who have experienced them personally, but also by others. Compelling and often tragic, these tales constitute salient sources of Beti women's knowledge and belief about the effects of schoolgirl pregnancy. At one of our weekly debriefing sessions, one of my research assistants recounted a story she'd heard in the course of her work:

> I talked with a woman in the market yesterday. She was born in 1956. Her father was a very faithful Christian. He had two daughters. . . . Since she was the youngest, he wanted to give that daughter to God. He brought her to a congregation in Edea. Starting in kindergarten, she lived with the nuns. She did all of primary school there, and even secondary until eleventh grade. When she got to eleventh grade, she met a boy when she went to her parents' house on the weekend. . . . She says she doesn't know what took her. The first time she saw that boy is the first time she slept [had sex]. She says she doesn't know and she regrets. She slept with the boy and she got pregnant. She left [the school] in about April when she felt that it was serious. . . . She says to me, "I tacked up my habit on the entry gate and I turned my back. Until today I cannot look. When I pass by there, I don't look, because I am ashamed of what I did. Me, I wanted to be a nun, but life wanted something else [*la vie a voulu autrement*]."

Aside from the dramatic appeal of a pregnant woman running off in the night, her habit nailed to the front gate of the novitiate, flapping in the wind, this story evokes the full richness of the figure of the fallen schoolgirl. She acted without forethought, getting pregnant with a stranger who will not marry her or help raise the child.[2] Like the girl described above who must flee to the village to bear her child, she is too ashamed to see her classmates again. Insofar as women's uncertain honor is connected to school discipline and the moral authority of the Catholic Church, shame is equated with their opposites: a lack of education and the careless sexual behavior attributed to non-Christians.

Horizons are manifested in the kinds of stories people recount and the metaphors that they employ, but also more explicitly, in reasoning through alternatives and the consequences of those alternatives. The background image of the fallen schoolgirl—her financial problems, her social isolation and disrepute—emerges rapidly into the foreground, apart from any specific case of pregnancy, as schoolgirls talk about the perils of adolescence. One young woman, born and raised in Mbeya, explained that through education, women had a chance to attain a good life:

JENNA: What do you mean by that, "a good life"?

ELISE: To have a good life? Well, since I am still a student that will depend on

    my behavior. I might be able to get there, but also I might not. . . . If I give
    birth now, and I give birth to a bastard, that is to say, a baby who doesn't have
    a father, there you go: I will have problems.
    JENNA: What kinds of problems?
    ELISE: For example, if the baby needs some clothes, I might even have to sell
    beignets by the side of the road. And with that rhythm, I will not be able to
    go far. So [a good life] means if I respect myself. It means that . . . I will not
    fail [*manquer*] like that.

Here we see again self-respect preventing dishonorable action, in this
instance symbolized as much by selling beignets in the road as by the
nonmarital birth itself. Feldman-Savelsberg (1995) has analyzed the meta-
phoric mapping of cooking outside the marital, domestic compound onto
extramarital sex in Bangangté. Although that equation is not so automatic
for young Beti women as for Bangangté, cooking on the street for the
consumption of strangers is still an effective image of the ruined woman,
unprotected by a man and unable to maintain an honorable concealment.

    An important part of the figure of the fallen schoolgirl as viewed by
educated women is the claim that schoolgirls are different from other
women, both as they have more refined claims to modern honor, and
as they may and should follow somewhat different principles of action.
This sense of distinction works perhaps most clearly with reference to
abortion. Schooling, arguably uniquely, constitutes in the minds of some
a sufficiently central value to justify the risks and dangers of abortion.
Despite the demographic evidence that childbearing does not necessarily lead to leaving school, the common perception of a trade-off between
schooling and childbearing serves to make schoolgirl abortion defensible,
or even compelling. As one man explained: "Because if you are still in secondary [school] you can say that you abort because you are afraid of losing
your studies," whereas later, this justification can no longer be invoked.
Thus, while abortion is generally seen as immoral and therefore shameful,
the value of managing the timing of reproductive events in reference to
other life domains such as education can overshadow that potential shame.
Abortion is thus selectively acceptable in the context of enabling a woman
to complete her studies and assure the coincidence of childbearing with
marriage and graduation.

    While certain types of contraception are viewed as positively honor-
able, and discreet abortions are often forgiven, for Beti schoolgirls such
as Marie and Nathalie who continue unforeseen pregnancies, the specter

of a ruined reputation and irremediable dishonor lurks close at hand. At the base of the dishonor is lack of self-dominion in the form of inability to control one's body, but the shame is built of dropping out of school, failing to secure the proper career and stability before bearing children. The social hazards of giving birth as a schoolgirl clearly informed the actions of Claudette, Nathalie, and Marie. The secrecy around Claudette's pregnancy was in part to protect her honor from even the suggestion of behavior unbefitting a student. And her abortion emerged as the best option for protecting herself in the long term from the social dangers of childbirth: abortion could save Claudette from the greater shame of childbirth, allowing her to remain in the community of schoolgirls. Similarly, as Marie weighed her options and assented to join the genitor's household as her father requested, she did so in reference to the fear-inducing horizon of an unplanned, disorderly, and therefore shameful entry into motherhood. For a time she did not see her place in the community of educated women pursuing careers, and she sought to make an honorable motherhood through marriage instead. In ultimately renouncing her motherhood and returning to school, Marie illustrates a common trend, as shown in chapter 7: returning to school is more common than permanently dropping out, contrary to local assumptions. When women who have borne children return to school, they subvert part of the figure of the fallen schoolgirl. Still, it is a hazardous path. Marie largely sidestepped the dangers by relinquishing claims to her child. And Nathalie, in seeking to coordinate schooling and secure a bridewealth marriage around the time of her child's birth, attempted to counter directly each element of the danger threatening pregnant schoolgirls. Though she failed in some respects, Nathalie did achieve at least a degree of one of the more powerful remedies for the shame of mistimed motherhood: marriage.

The Glorious Bride

Despite rising ages at marriage and the increasing proportion of educated Beti women who can get by without a husband, most would agree with my informant who explained that

> [marriage] is the obligation of every woman. To be married and have children. To create. It is the desire of every woman! Even if she only manifests that on

the inside, if she does not express it openly, she still thinks of that. She would want in any case, no matter what, to found a family.

If the schoolgirl who drops out without prospects inspires pity, or a shiver of fearful recognition, the magnificent bride—happy, lucky, successful—inspires admiration. Nearly every woman I interviewed wanted to marry, and many spoke with something near reverence about the sanctity and majesty of marriage. Women aspire to both the role of bride and the status of wife and mother, enthralled by gown and party and gifts, as well as by the serious role of a woman "with weight," called by her married name, respected and therefore content. This enchanted view of marriage is reinforced by the almost magical power of marriage to both legitimate a birth and deem the mother honorable. To say that a good marriage can retrospectively reformulate an unforeseen pregnancy as a proper birth is perhaps too weak. Schoolgirls have constantly to justify why they are so dramatically postponing marriage, and particularly childbearing, and therefore rapid marriage does not only retrospectively legitimate the birth, it also resolves the problem of extended spinsterhood. Whereas dropping out of school early represents a humiliation according to the horizons assumed by schoolgirls, marriage and childbearing define proper womanhood in the background accepted by a far broader swath of contemporary Beti society.

As we have seen previously, many women associate childbirth with marriage, referencing them together or even conflating the two. Although the significant majority of educated Beti women are not married by any definition of marriage at the time they bear their first child, there is a strong assumption that marriage and childbearing belong together, that marriage should follow pregnancy closely, or better yet precede it. It follows that pregnancies of married women are perceived as different, and treated differently, than pregnancies of unmarried women. The case studies themselves may offer the clearest insights into this horizon that women facing mistimed pregnancies use to make sense of their options. Despite the differing paths that Marie, Nathalie, and Claudette choose, all three women considered marriage as a solution to the potential shame that faced them if they entered motherhood unprepared and outside of the appropriate contexts. To each of them, marriage offered an opportunity to secure at least one element of honorable motherhood.

Claudette's mother insists that if she keeps the pregnancy, Claudette will have to live with Alphonse. Similarly, when he discovers that she is pregnant, Marie's father sends her to live with the family of her child's genitor. We have seen that in southern Cameroon, cohabitation is regularly viewed as a precursor to more formal marital rites. Thus, Claudette's mother and Marie's father are both suggesting that childbearing is only justifiable in the context of marriage, and they are willing—at least in the first instance—to force that interpretation on their daughters. For the young women, at issue is not only the question of marriage per se, but also the figure of the glorious bride, the horizon in which marriage is a magnificent transformation in a woman's life. The prospects that Claudette and Marie faced for real marriages did not at all conform to this background expectation; the proposed marriages were perhaps even more antithetical to the young women's visions of their futures as honorable modern women than their pregnancies were. Their refusals of these specific marriages were—in part—reaffirmations of the ideal of marriage, reassertions of the notion that they, having been to school, should and would marry well.

Nathalie, also, oriented her action in the vital conjuncture of her unforeseen pregnancy to the horizon embodied by the glorious bride. Chief among her concerns was the legitimacy of her marriage in light of her mother's refusal to accept the bridewealth. As the iconic bride is married with "everything," meaning the civil, church, and bridewealth ceremonies, Nathalie's choice of a partner who was neither Catholic nor acceptable to her mother made it difficult for her to bring her marriage into honorable alignment. Even Nathalie's concern about baptizing her baby related, albeit indirectly, to the legitimacy of her marriage. Although many Cameroonian priests will baptize babies born outside of marriage, they usually resist listing the father on the baptismal certificate, preferring to list only the mother and the godparents.[3] When her legal husband, Michel, was listed on the baptismal certificate, Nathalie considered it evidence that her marriage was acceptable to the church, even without the church wedding.

When we look at premarital pregnancies, we find significant variation in the tenor and character of the relationships between the pregnant women and the genitors. This variation has significant consequences for what women perceive as the possible or probable outcomes of carrying the pregnancy to term, and thus for decisions about abortion and relinquishing claims to children. Women who are married, or who see their relationship as likely leading to marriage, are more likely to continue mistimed pregnancies. Claudette clearly wanted to continue her pregnancy, and attempted to make this possible through her relationship first with Alphonse and then with her other suitor. Her decision ultimately rested on weighing her desire to continue the pregnancy against her reluctance to be a wife "like a piece of furniture": her prospects for marriage deeply influenced her decisions regarding childbearing. Marie's case similarly underscores the importance of marriage in shaping decisions about motherhood. Had she completed more formal marriage rights with the father of her son, her range of options would have narrowed; a married woman cannot claim the status of schoolgirl. The same is seen in Nathalie's case, although she was more than ready to leave school: marriage was the best of her conceivable alternatives.

While marital pregnancies or births conform to local concepts of proper womanhood, pregnancies arising from unions that do not hold the promise of marriage are considered problematic, likely candidates for abortion or adoption. The pregnancies of both Claudette and Marie belong into this category. Nearly all of the abortions reported in my survey were to unmarried women, regardless of the definition of marriage being used. No one reported aborting after having married in the church; only two women reported having aborted after a civil marriage, and only three women reported having aborted after completing the bridewealth marriage. In the rare cases where married women did terminate pregnancies, the abortions were almost always the result of medical necessity. Several women in the survey reported that they had suffered ectopic pregnancies: these women vacillated between calling the requisite surgery a miscarriage and calling it an abortion. One woman in the survey explained how she was forced to have an abortion when she learned that she had contracted a sexually transmitted infection from her husband. He had taken another lover and not told her about it. Nonetheless, after receiving treatment for the STI, she is trying again to conceive.

In this vein, one of my research assistants asserted that abortions are sometimes the result of sexual infidelity. Focusing on the tie between the birth and the love relationship between partners, she noted, "[Abortion] could happen to [any young woman] if perhaps she cheats. If she goes out with another guy who isn't her current boyfriend. Then she has no choice but to remove [the pregnancy]." Here, my research assistant echoes the idea that births solidify relationships, placing the decision to terminate a pregnancy in a web of interpersonal connections. A similar opinion was expressed by an obstetrician, who noted that educated Beti women will often abort a pregnancy if the genitor ends the relationship. "The child shows the bond," he explained.

Claudette's and Marie's stories conclude in very similar ways. Both women leave the period of the vital conjuncture outwardly unchanged. Because of Claudette's clandestine abortion, and Marie's relinquishment of claims to her son, both women reject the shift to the status of mother and maintain their identities as schoolgirls. Both can remain on a path to future honorable marriage and motherhood. For Claudette, motherhood is preventable, and for Marie, motherhood is erasable; they are left with clean slates, on which they can try again in the future to draw an honorable motherhood. The horizon of the triumphant bride, weighed against other models, called out to them more from the future than the present; they postponed motherhood, gambling that they would later be better able to replicate their ideal.

Much of the difficulty faced by educated women in trying to forge some form of modern honor lies in reconciling the prestige and passion of marriage with the necessity of schooling. As evidenced in our case studies, although they desire marriage someday, many young educated Beti women also hope to postpone it. Marriage is the older honor, its value endorsed by senior rural men as much as by young, urban women. Indeed, educated women's tendency to delay marriage and motherhood is the subject of grave social opprobrium from elders and others. Early marriage makes advanced schooling very difficult. Women need to delay childbearing and marriage in order to stay in school and pursue formal-sector employment, or certainly the popular representations suggest that they do. At the same time, there are strong social incentives to commence childbearing early, and many schoolgirls suffer intense pressure from their families to bear a child. Women who have not borne a child by age twenty are routinely brought to ritual specialists for infertility treatments, regardless of whether they have been intentionally managing their fertility to avoid pregnancy.

Educated Beti women begin childbearing both relatively late and—usually—outside of marriage. In the eyes of many Beti, the delay gravely contravenes honorable social practice. But as the grounds of honor shift, educated women are able to claim a new legitimacy for their actions: their births are delayed as an expression of honorable discipline. When educated women say, for example, that "when you have even a minimal education, it is not likely that you will conceive young, because you will think, you have been to school," we must remember that early childbearing is a value that has, until now, held almost sole sway in the majority of Beti communities. By casting their delayed childbearing as disciplined waiting for marriage, educated women transform their potentially shameful nulliparity into a badge of modern honor. By asserting that they are postponing children in order to have them in marriage, educated women are able to justify time-out-of-place. By casting postponement as a part of the horizon of the glorious bride, schoolgirls can legitimate new forms of reproductive practice against an older and more widely accepted background. Thus, educated women's valorization of disciplined timing is not a reiteration of recognized social ideals, but a justification for a new set of reproductive practices. This justification relies on new reservoirs of value in discipline, in schooling, and in a locally conceived modernity that are increasingly entering into the honor economy.

These differences point out another important way in which women's honor remains uncertain. The horizons to which educated Beti women look to interpret an ongoing vital conjuncture are, as yet, under construction. This is one of the first generations of mass-educated women, and the background against which their actions are set sometimes seems disjointed or contradictory. Their habits and expectations were, to some degree, formed in another field: they have *hexis* without *habitus*. Constructing a new background is slow and painful, and sometimes results in strange contradictions. As we have seen, educated Beti women claim that they are distinguished from uneducated women by the fact that they bear their children intentionally, and only inside of marriage. However, the demographic data indicate that more than half of educated women bear their first children outside of marriage, and even that they are *more* likely than uneducated women to have premarital births (Johnson-Hanks 2003).

Any project that attempts to take on both ethnographic and demographic data will be rife with disjunctures of this kind, where the two kinds of information do not "tell the same story" under the available interpretations. Demography and ethnography do not give alternative perspectives on the same facts—they instead tell us about related, but distinctly different kinds of facts. Thus, the integration of the demographic and ethnographic data cannot be one of simple aggregation. Happily, it is in the apparent contradictions, rather than in the easy merging, that the most interesting demographic anthropology can happen. For example, Bledsoe (2002) capitalizes on a disjuncture of this kind to develop a radically new approach to thinking about health, reproduction, and time in West Africa. In Cameroon, the disconnect between self-representation and demographic events offers a smaller window, and my conclusions are less far-reaching than Bledsoe's. What is important is that the self-descriptions not be read as straightforward assertions of established cultural ideals,

which the demographic data then show are not fulfilled. Educated women's claims about their reproductive restraint are instead part of the
process of fashioning a form of modern honor. Their assertions are claims
about the legitimacy of new horizons, alternative backgrounds against
which the foreground of the reproductive and marital delays might make
sense, not simple restatements of accepted ideals.

Educated Beti women's claims about the disciplined timing of their
births should not be mapped directly onto the demographic data about
marriage, contrary to the specific assertions of the women concerned. Instead their claims of disciplined timing serve to justify these births in a
different frame, for in addition to occurring largely outside marriage, these
births occur an average of nearly three years later than do first births
among women with no education. To the delight of international family-
planning policymakers and the fascination of young demographic anthropologists, educated women in most developing countries not only bear
fewer children, but they also bear them later. This same delay is the central
issue in educated women's claims about waiting for children until they are
married. Although the demographic and ethnographic data do not support each other neatly, they do converge around a few issues: delay—the
management of time—is a central one.

In vital conjunctures, possible futures are evaluated and negotiated; in
the case of a first pregnancy, the possibility of future attainment of honorable motherhood is a key goal to weigh heavily. Women who have already
given birth have different goals, different horizons shaping future possibilities, than do women who are just entering motherhood. Especially first,
but also second, pregnancies are thus different from higher-order pregnancies in the local logic of managing a vital conjuncture. At least for an educated Beti woman, navigating a first birth is centrally about its timing—or
sequencing—in reference to the multiple temporalities of her life course.
Women seek to enter socially recognized motherhood when they are already married and formally employed. Contraception can prevent or postpone a first pregnancy, but when it does occur, the abdication of rights in
children and abortion can ensure that the timing of motherhood is appropriate. The fallen schoolgirl can be recast as the triumphant bride.

*   *   *

Throughout the developing world, educated women begin bearing
children later then do uneducated women; in Cameroon, the differential

amounts to about three years. But what does this demographic fact mean, and how can we explain it? I have tried to motivate this "certain calculable frequency" (Weber 1978) with structures of meaning, showing the relationship between social and demographic patterns, explaining the life-historical processes through which the statistical correlation of schooling and childbearing arises in southern Cameroon, and focusing on why educated women wait so long to bear a first child. The answer to this demographic question necessarily implicates social relationships and culturally mediated aspirations. We have seen that educated Beti women postpone their first birth as part of a larger project of seeking to synchronize socially recognized motherhood with marriage and formal employment; they view this temporal coordination as an expression of their own modernity, discipline, and honor, traits that they ascribe to their schooling. Educated Beti women are acutely aware that their schooling differentiates them from other women; they assign great significance to this difference and seek to accentuate it in a variety of ways, including through their reproductive practice. The social identity of the educated woman in southern Cameroon is inextricably tied to her reproductive restraint; restrained childbearing in this sense is defined primarily by the management, the timing, and the context of first births, epitomized by educated Beti women's insistence that they bear children only after getting married and finding formal employment. This emphasis is all the more remarkable because Catholic-educated Beti women are in fact more likely than the less educated to bear their first child outside of civil or bridewealth marriage. Their explicit claims run contrary to the demographic data, but are nonetheless critical to understanding these data. Although they are not often able to postpone childbirth until its ideal context emerges, educated Beti women still construe their own honor as dependent on the synchrony of motherhood with other transitions into social adulthood.

The equation of restrained childbearing with modern honor is recited and rehearsed in schools, in the households that send girls to school, and among school friends in the *foyers*. It is primarily habits of behavior and perception, rather than a specific curriculum, that is meaningfully learned in the secondary schools of southern Cameroon. This empirical conclusion resonates with the work of Bourdieu (1977, 1984) and others who argue that social action should be understood through the habituation of everyday practices. One of the most important facts about southern Cameroonian classrooms is also one of the simplest: unrelated boys and girls spend much of their day together, engaged in the same spheres of activity. Curriculum per se is comparatively insignificant in southern Cameroonian schools, where most of the school day is spent on activities outside the formal curriculum: waiting for the teacher, being counted, accounted for, and disciplined. These activities play a constitutive role in social practice more broadly; they inscribe in students the attitudes, orientations, and habits associated with the educated. This school *habitus,* based on certain conceptions of order and discipline, largely constructs educated women's self-perceptions as bearers of modern honor, and it is this self-perception that generates the statistical facts.

Uneducated women are also concerned to conduct themselves in an honorable fashion, and educated Beti women are not necessarily any more disciplined than are uneducated women. But the fact that educated Beti women explicitly and repeatedly claim that they have more of these traits than their uneducated counterparts in fact plays an important role in their decisions to delay childbearing, regardless of the veracity of these claims. Herein lies the balance between honestly listening to our informants and agreeing with them. By proposing that educated Beti women's self-perceptions—or precisely, their aspirations for certain self-perceptions—inspire them to postpone childbearing, I am not proposing that these self-perceptions are necessarily right, only that they are consequential. Whether these self-perceptions should rightly be classified as ideology, belief, or common sense, they orient and motivate reproductive practice. The young Cameroon women who shared glimpses of their lives with me sought, above all, to be *filles dignes* and *filles modernes;* they sought to manage the vital conjunctures that they confronted in such a way as to conform to this self-perception. In the last instance, people do not obey norms or fulfill the dictates of rational choice; instead, they seek to perceive and represent themselves as certain kinds of people. That is, "claiming an identity for self in a given context is what motivates an individual to learn" (Eisenhart 1995: 4), or indeed to act. The significance of these claimed identities lies in the orientations, motivations, and aspirations for the specific courses of action that they generate.

In these last two chapters, I have sought to apply the model of vital conjunctures to specific life crises among educated Beti women. Vital conjunctures are a unit of social description that should have wide applicability to analyses of life-history, social structure, and population-level outcomes. Vital conjunctures are structures of possibility that emerge around specific periods of potential transformation in the lives of one or more participants. These vital conjunctures are the periods when seemingly established futures are called into question, when women must employ all their skills and patience to manage durations of radical uncertainty. As socially structured configurations of what could—or should—be, vital conjunctures resemble the conjunctures that Bourdieu describes as the context of practice. In Bourdieu's practice theory, the conjuncture "is constituted in the dialectical relationship between, on the one hand, a *habitus*, understood as a system of lasting, transposable dispositions . . . , and on the other hand, an *objective event* which exerts its action of conditional stimulation" (1977: 82–83). Vital conjunctures share this dual quality; they, too, are the locus of intersection between structured expectations and specific, lived contexts. But not all conjunctures are vital ones. Vital conjunctures stand out as the moments when transformation is possible or imagined, when futures previously construed as inevitable or impossible are suddenly up for grabs, when the objective conditions that form the basis of the *habitus* become, perhaps, changeable. In these moments, I suggest, orienting principles become clear, because they become the basis of debate. Vital conjunctures are analytically central to a study of the social causes of demographic facts.

Educated Beti women use a variety of techniques to synchronize their reproductive careers with other temporal patterns in their lives. These techniques serve primarily to delay entry into socially recognized motherhood, rather than to speed up the parallel trajectories of schooling and employment. Socially recognized motherhood refers to more than just childbirth; it is a social status. Beti women delay socially recognized motherhood through contraception (especially periodic abstinence), abortion, and by giving up certain children to informal, but permanent adoption. Since motherhood is a social status, not a biological state, this giving up of children—which I have called "relinquishing claims to children" in the context of a wealth-in-people model of social organization—serves nearly as well as contraception as a means of motherhood postponement. Periodic abstinence, abortion, and the relinquishment of claims to children are best understood here as alternative means to achieve the same goal, means that are selectively available at different moments and to women with different social resources. Thus, contraception, or even contraception and abortion, do not exhaust the methods by which families are planned; reproduction cannot be reduced to births. Contraception, abortion, and the relinquishment of claims to children are strategies with a similar *telos*, but requiring different resources and social networks, and potentially usable under different circumstances. Although in general, educated women say that contraception is preferable to abortion, and abortion preferable to abandoning a child, in a given context, different logics may came to the fore. For example, Marie, who left her infant son with the family of the genitor when she returned to her own family, explained that since she had already borne a child and therefore knows that she is fertile, no husband will be able to repudiate her. Thus, the outcomes can be variable while the principles of action remain cohesive.

Among young, educated women such as Nathalie, Marie, and Claudette, pregnancy might be considered the prototypical vital conjuncture. It inevitably raises questions about the future path of the life of the subject; it alters her range of options and brings them into sharp relief; it casts much that seemed certain into doubt. And the vital conjuncture of pregnancy offers unique analytic purchase on the transition to female adulthood in contemporary Cameroon. As I have argued, pregnancy among Beti schoolgirls inevitably unfolds with the specter of shame and the hope for modern honor as defining features of its horizons. As we have seen, the specific conjunctures are unique combinations of lived history, specific configurations of opportunities and dangers from a broad range of life domains. But the horizons that educated Beti women and their families use to navigate through these stormy waters are not unique or particular. The horizons are the largely shared expectations and aspirations of what is possible or desirable, mythical figures evocable from the shared background. By focusing on these horizons, we can come much further toward understanding the social causes of the demographic facts. The horizons of a conjuncture are not the choices themselves that players face, but rather understandings or information that help them make choices about futures, and perhaps even make possibilities visible or invisible. The horizons that are most relevant may change over the duration of the vital conjunctures, as certain imagined futures are made impossible and other alternatives are opened up. Thus, the uncertainty of the conjuncture carries with it a temporal dimension—understanding the forms of uncertainty requires following the conjuncture through its temporal arc. The horizons of a vital conjuncture hold the key to its interpretation in another way as well: although the conjunctures appear idiosyncratic or individual, the horizons are part of the *doxa* that binds a community of practice. Although the specific alternative futures viewed from a given conjuncture are indeed new, the *habitus* that saw them in *this* way and oriented to *these* horizons is sedimented history. Without the structured systems of value typified in the horizons, the demographic data are incomprehensible, because the demographic outcomes are merely the residua of practices oriented to the horizons of various conjunctures.

Both anthropologists and demographers have studied reproduction, although with remarkably little coordination. The vital conjuncture may offer a means to achieving such interdisciplinarity. For when we begin to conceptualize our data through a model of vital conjunctures, dramatic things happen to the way we study reproduction. The frame of analysis is no longer the event, but rather the social process of establishing "what is to be done here now?" Whereas vital events happen to individuals, vital conjunctures are distributed over social groups. Whereas events are discrete and conceptually instantaneous occurrences, conjunctures have variable duration. Whereas events are outcomes in themselves, conjunctures may have multiple outcomes over different time frames. Thus, vital conjunctures are the place where social processes result in demographic events; it is here that we can observe the social causes of demographic facts.

Concomitant with the departure from an event-based model is the move from actuality to potential, for vital conjunctures are defined in part by their horizons, their structured spheres of possibility. Analyses of vital conjunctures inevitably include what might have been, but was not—as we saw in Marie's temporary religious conversion, and in Claudette's consideration of the marriage proposal of the military man. This is the "possibility that things might proceed otherwise" (Bourdieu 1981: 99) that makes the actual outcome only one part of the social system to be explained. In these futures that might have been, experienced as horizons at one point in a vital conjuncture, we can capture some of the "adequacy of meaning" that Weber demands, for these alternative trajectories, locally understood but never actualized, trace out a territory that grounds the demographic events. In an analysis of vital conjunctures, we need to ask what kinds of futures are imagined, hoped for, or feared, and how these orientations motivate specific courses of action. The vital conjuncture is therefore a unit of social description that emphasizes both the shared structures underlying action and the population-level outcomes of that action. It promises to integrate demographic patterns with social patterns, providing—perhaps—a method for more adequate explanation.

As Cameroonian schoolgirls become mothers, they seek to coordinate a whole range of events and statuses in keeping with their aspirations for modern honor. As they navigate vital conjunctures defined by an unforeseen pregnancy, a marriage proposal, or failure on the *baccalauréat,* these young women orient their actions to the horizons of the possible or imaginable, the *points de repères* that guide social life. The contexts of marriage and motherhood consistently figure among these horizons, as they are critical elements of women's uncertain honor. Even when she appears to be "only" negotiating over school fees, a young Beti woman is also managing the conditions under which she will become a mother. She may be confronted with extraordinary uncertainty that makes strictly means-ends rational choice—and indeed most planning—tenuous at best, but the educated Beti woman nonetheless tries to draw together conditions favorable to the outcomes she desires.

Epilogue

Because there is no substitute for vigorous and exact
description, I would like to say how
your eyes, at twilight, reflect, at the same
time, the beauty of the world, and its crimes.
— Mary Oliver, *The Leaf and the Cloud*

In the summer of 2001, I returned to Cameroon for the first time since the accident that sent me home in 1998. In between, I had written my dissertation, gotten married, and found a job. I was not working in the fields, as some in Mbeya had feared, but nor did I have a baby, as many had wished for me. By the standards of Beti womanhood, I had achieved an uncertain honor. I was eager to visit with people in Mbeya and Yaoundé, to give copies of the dissertation to Père Amerin and the others, to learn how Claudette, Nathalie, and Marie were faring. I also needed to show myself that I could return: that the nerves crushed by the crash were only physical ones.

The flight to Yaoundé was canceled and I was rerouted on a much-delayed flight into Douala. Arriving after midnight, I found a cheap hotel and recalled my first visit to Cameroon, in 1996. Then I had also arrived in Douala—the connection to Yaoundé had been grounded, reportedly because President Biya was traveling—and I had spent a similarly sleepless night owing to the bikutsi music, jetlag, and excitement. Then, Douala had seemed vast and dangerous and lurid, the moist heat of the port city blending in my memory with the perfume of the red-lipsticked women in the hotel lobby. This time, the city felt subdued, pale, and quiet, like a western bar on a weekday morning.

The next day I made my way to the bus station. As I rode on to Yaoundé, I considered the changing landscape—changing both as we rose from sea level toward Yaoundé's twenty-five-hundred feet, and changing with time. It seemed to me that the crisis was easing somewhat: new buildings had appeared alongside the road and the mood on the bus seemed less troubled. The newspapers were still full of stories of *la crise,* but now these tales were published alongside announcements for job openings. Stopping briefly in Edea, Michel's natal town, reminded me of him, and then of Nathalie. The bus sighed and leapt forward again, back onto the glossy blacktop. I wondered whether her family had ever accepted the bridewealth.

Yaoundé is about four degrees north of the equator, so even at the solstices, days and nights are almost equal in length. By the time the bus pulled into Yaoundé, the six o'clock twilight was settling over the seven hills of the city. I slid into the city with the darkness, enjoying the anonymity of the capital and the night.

At first it seemed that everything had changed. Yaoundé itself had undergone a dramatic transformation for the France-Africa Summit in January 2001. Père Amerin was no longer at Mbeya. My other favorite priest had gone to Europe to continue his studies. As la Trinité was closed for the summer, the Foyer de la Grande Famille was empty. But then I began to find my bearings. Nathalie and Michel had moved, but their old neighbors knew where they had gone. Marie's parents still lived in the same house, and her brother took me to her room near the university. And Marie helped me to find Claudette. All three were in Yaoundé, as indeed were many other former students of la Trinité. I never managed to see Père Amerin, but left him a copy of my dissertation.

Marie had done well on the *baccalauréat* and was at the University of Yaoundé studying medicine. We talked first in her room, one of a block of student rooms opening onto a narrow walk, and then at my insistence at the open-air *café-resto* at the corner of the paved road edging the student quarter. I know that respectable women don't go to open-air cafés, especially unaccompanied, but I like them, and like the sweet Nescafé au lait that they serve. Although Marie said that she regretted not being able to do research science—she had hoped for a career in marine biology—she liked medicine. She explained that her father had wanted her to stay in Cameroon, rather than going to study in France, and that she could not have done marine biology in Cameroon. Besides, she added, the people her father knew were in the medicine faculty. If she was going to get a place, like everyone else she would need "someone up front" to give her a hand: the hands to which she had access were in medicine. Marie's educational success showed the wisdom of practicing judicious opportunism, of learning to capitalize on the possible, perhaps particularly in Cameroon.

Yes, she had a boyfriend, and yes, she was coy about it. Was he serious? Would it lead to anything? I don't know. Although they had been together for more than a year, Marie had not introduced him to her parents. "I am still observing him," she explained, as if speaking from a script for honorable Beti sexual relationships. As for her son and the Manguissa family that she almost joined, Marie never saw them. She would have children one day, but she was focused on her studies for now. As she pointed out, I of all people should understand that! Marie teased me about being so old and not yet having any children, and then said that she, too, was going to wait until she got a first-rate job and husband before she had children.

A few days later, I was taken to Claudette's house by her sister, who worked in a *téléboutique* in the university quarter, and whom Marie knew. Yaoundé has a population of over one million, and yet it sometimes feels like a small town: everything functions on relationships, and people are much more sophisticated about knowing who knows whom than in Chicago or Oakland. Former schoolmates are resources to be cultivated, as are relatives and occasional visitors from America. Claudette had failed her exams and transferred to another school in Yaoundé, returning to her parents' home. Living with her parents had been horrible, she explained, because they were always checking on her; she had missed the relative freedom of the *foyer* and la Trinité. Between the lack of uniforms, the independent room, and the group of friends she had there, Mbeya had become a kind of magic time in her memory. Over cokes and roasted peanuts, Claudette recounted how her return to Yaoundé clarified for her that she was not a "girl of the school bench." Tired of the round of schools, her parents, and—perhaps especially—the hideous school uniforms, Claudette decided she would try one more year but no more. Soon after arriving at the new school, she met a man who was "serious" and "kind": two of the most important descriptors of potentially marriageable men. When, at the end of the next school year (1998–99), Claudette again failed the *probatoire,* she told her parents that she would not return to school. "I brought Jean-Pierre to them," she recounted, "and he explained everything, everything, everything." She moved into his house soon thereafter, and they began planning for the bridewealth ceremony, which had been completed in February of 2001. In between, she had a baby—a beautiful little girl with the same long, thin proportions as her mother.

Claudette's house was small and tidy, with a clean cement floor. In the front room hung not only the usual framed images of President Biya and the pope, but also of a blonde child holding an armful of kittens, and of a Swiss chalet surrounded by flowers. I have seen the same posters in Kenya, and I think that they are produced in China; they index a specific aesthetic sense, like doilies and porcelain figurines, and with it a tentative claim to middle-class privilege. It was a nice little house, and she seemed well. Claudette was not working, but hoped to start soon, perhaps in an office or store, or even in a *téléboutique* as her sister did. It had to be somewhere clean, she explained, as Jean-Pierre refused to have his wife smell like the "dried fish or beignets" often sold in outdoor markets or alongside the road. Knowing Claudette even a little bit, I suspected that her husband's pride suited her well: it was almost impossible to imagine the delicate woman, whose constitution prevented her from eating the local staple *kpem,* selling dried fish in a dusty market. She wouldn't go back to night school, I asked, to try to finish the *bac?* Claudette said no, she had had enough of school, and anyway, Jean-Pierre would take care of her. Her willingness to rely on a husband surprised me, but then so did her excitement about her baby. She had dropped out of school to get married—not at all her intention when I had known her three years earlier—and yet Claudette appeared serene, even happy.

I got the directions to Nathalie's new house from her old neighbors. When I first arrived, both she and Michel were away at work. Michel's mother had come from Edea to live with them and take care of her grandson. We had never met, and yet she seemed not at all surprised to see me standing in her yard. As she put down the laundry she was washing and dried her hands, the three-year-old boy stared at me the way some children do. "He's not used to you!" the grandmother exclaimed, half scolding that I had not come sooner. The new house was more comfortable than the old one; they were still renting, but this house had running water and ceiling boards to quiet the sound of rain on the tin roof. Nathalie had done a night course in typing and computers and was working at one of the mushrooming number of cyber-cafés, mostly typing documents and e-mail messages. Her sparkly eyes and quick, sometimes mordant humor were back as she recounted some of the messages that people dictated to her. Mostly sex, she summarized when we were alone, most of what the clients want to write is about sex.

Nathalie had indeed baptized her son in the Catholic Church, and one of her brothers had started to visit at the house. But there was still no talk of a bridewealth marriage, and Michel's mother was driving her crazy. Although Michel himself had largely come to terms with Nathalie's persistence as a Catholic, the older woman was adamant in her Jehovah's Witness beliefs and alternated between trying to convert Nathalie and trying to persuade her son to abandon her for a more religiously suitable wife. "She thinks that we Catholics do no better than worshipping skulls!" Nathalie exclaimed in disgust, referring to the common local representation of pre-Christian Beti religion. In particular, Nathalie said, her work at the cyber-café infuriated her mother-in-law, who believed, perhaps not altogether incorrectly, that the Internet was a dangerous force of secular modernity, streaming sex, commodity consumption, and other wicked things through invisible wires around the world. I suspected that this alone might be enough to ensure that Nathalie never quit this job.

Nathalie had in fact tried a third time to pass the *bac*, studying on her own at night and registering for the exam as a *candidat libre*. But between caring for her son and lacking the structure of regular classes, she had again failed it. It was then that she had attended typing and computer classes at an unlicensed, private school, earning an ornate certificate after three months. Michel was still working as a builder during the day, and he was also working in the evening to produce an herbal health soap, which they sold out of the house. Although not the ideal son-in-law owing to his ethnicity, religion, and low-status work, Michel was serious, hardworking, and devoted to his wife and son. Nathalie's family may have refused to accept bridewealth from him, but they had to admit that she had not done too badly.

All three young women had made significant transitions in the three years between 1998 and 2001. All three were making their way into honorable adulthood, albeit along different paths and with differing degrees of success. Only Marie had finished high school with a degree and continued at university, and only Claudette had been married with bridewealth. Yet in some ways it was Nathalie who best fit the descriptions of what Beti schoolgirls hope for: working in a respectable job, she had her own money and also a serious husband and healthy son. Becoming an honorable educated mother in contemporary southern Cameroon requires compromise and hope. The technique is to wait and see what alternatives come along, and then grasp tightly to the most promising ones. The path that is possible is not always the one you would have wished for, or imagined. Still, sometimes what comes along works out fine.

Looking backward, the vital conjunctures through which these young women came—both the ones recounted in chapter 7 and the ones that occurred between our interviews then and my return in 2001—fade away. The unexplored alternatives that appeared vibrant, so undeniable when they were possible futures, dissolve in retrospect, like a boat's wake in choppy water. What remains is a provisional outcome, a framing of events and actions that applies at least until the next conjuncture. Gell has argued that we should think of events in time as fixed, and uncertainty as the result of our lack of knowledge about some of those events. "Four-dimensional space-time," he claims, "is a stable field, rather than a process of becoming, and we have the idea that events 'happen' only because we 'encounter' them in a particular causal order, not because time itself actually progresses from future to present to past" (1992: 155). Although he acknowledges that social actors may "imagine" other worlds and even act accordingly, Gell rejects the notion of fundamental, foundational, real uncertainty in the world. Regardless of the philosophical merits of his position, social life in southern Cameroon does indeed entail fundamental uncertainty. Time matters: not just as a coordinate system, but as a basic aspect of experience (see Munn 1992).

The gentrification of Yaoundé that the government had undertaken for the 2001 France-Africa Summit transformed the feel of the city. Around the main post office, the street hawkers had disappeared, replaced by stately plantings and fluttery banners. Everywhere roads were paved or widened. My favorite haphazard book market had been disbanded: the booksellers dispersed and moved off out of sight. The loading stop for the minibuses to Mbeya had been cleared out of the center city. Even the city shysters and story peddlers, who before had crowded street corners to lure the unsuspecting into some complicated escapade that only ever ended with money moving in one direction, were gone. Seeing Douala somewhat tamed had surprised but not moved me. But I was stunned by the change in Yaoundé, this horrendous city that had so cowed me with its petty thieves and pretty vices. In 1998, I had come to see Yaoundé as a reflection of the both the "beauty of the world and its crimes" as Mary Oliver writes (2000). Visiting in 2001, that reflection had changed. In a way it was a loss, like losing your strongest opponent, the one who always demanded the most of you. Or finding that they have installed an ATM machine in the village where you did your first fieldwork, back before it even had a paved road, let alone electricity. There is a certain pleasure in the difficulty that defines your first relationship to a place, and the street cheaters had been part of mine.

And yet it was not only because of the summit that the city looked better. Yaoundé, and indeed Cameroon as a whole, was doing better economically. Although people still talked about *la crise*, the economic indicators had already turned around and incomes were rising again. People were still worse off than they had been in 1985, but things were better than they had been in fifteen years; in a country where some 40 percent of the population had not yet been born at the onset of the crisis, that should mean quite a lot. Of course, the social organization and cultural representations of permanent crisis would be slower to change in Cameroon; they may never really disappear. Still, on some level, things were getting better.

I thought intently about the parallels between the changes in the city and the partial resolutions of all four of our stories. It seemed too tidy, too blithe: the happy ending that makes for satisfying fiction but Whig history. But then, the resolutions are partial, temporary, unfinished. And they will never be finished. The transition to honorable female adulthood in contemporary Cameroon is necessarily always a work in progress, because there is no clearly established life stage that can be neatly entered with a single event and then sustained. Just as there is no way to achieve all of the competing, contradictory components of honorable adulthood, such that every life trajectory is necessarily a series of compromises, there is no point of closure. Marie and I raise eyebrows because we do not yet have children. Nathalie has a serious conflict with her mother-in-law and her own family about religion. Claudette will need to find a way to earn her own money, and thereby some limited independence from her husband. It's as if we had each fought our way through devil's club and underbrush to come to a small clearing in the woods: a good place, a respite. But soon enough, we each will foray back into the woods.

After returning to Berkeley, I spent many mornings rereading my field notes. Strong coffee—not Nescafé—and a filtered view of San Francisco marked my distance from the experiences that I had recorded in these little blue notebooks. One experience in particular held my attention, and I returned to it several times. The story concerns a young woman who had been a student at la Trinité, but whom I knew hardly at all. After dark one evening she came to my room in the *presbytère* and asked to come in. We sat in an awkward quiet for a few minutes while I boiled water for tea, talking first about the lessons and then about the unseasonably cold weather—small things we had in common. Then she explained the purpose of her visit. Her family was very poor, and her father's cacao trees were no longer producing well; they were not able to continue paying her school

fees. However, recently a man had offered to pay for her to continue studying. He had not requested anything in return, and his office would normally
prevent him from marrying, but she had heard stories about girls who accepted money from such men, and then later were expected to repay them
in other ways. She wanted my advice, and perhaps also some financial assistance. I was surprised, moved, and unable to think of anything useful to
say. I asked about her alternatives (they were few), and her network of potential protectors (they were somewhat more numerous). We talked about
how to decide when a risk is worth taking, and what is most important.
Although I thought that we did not make much progress—just discussed
the same things several times—when she stood to leave she thanked me.
"You explained that we cannot know the future," I quoted in my field notes
after she left, "we can only make our little actions [*on ne peut que poser
ses petits actes*]." In contemporary southern Cameroon, education, sex, and
childbearing intersect in women's striving for honorable adulthood. Their
honor is ever uncertain. And as for the young woman who came and left in
the night, I never found out whether she accepted the gift or not, or what
happened afterward.

Notes

Chapter One

1. In a different critique of the same kinds of outcome-focused research, Basu (1996) argues that the discourse of small desired family size is so hegemonic in the developing world that stated desires are meaningless; actual numbers of children represent the best proxy for desired numbers of children.

2. In this way (although not in others), the vital conjuncture resembles the stand-offs so expertly analyzed by Wagner-Pacifici (2000).

3. Sahlins cites Braudel and Firth, rather than Bourdieu, in reference to his concept of conjuncture.

Chapter Two

1. This association between kinship and residential communities remains visible even today. In Mbeya, the members of the dominant *mvog* occupy the center of the village. In Yaoundé, several *quartiers* are known by the names of the *mvog* that formally comprised them.

2. For the Beti, see Laburthe-Tolra 1977: 880; Guyer 1984; cf. Berry 1993; Bledsoe 1980; Herskovits 1938; Miers and Kopytoff 1977.

3. For an elegant history of Duala hegemony of the European trade, see Austen and Derrick 1999: 48–92.

4. Zenker came to Africa as part of a scientific expedition to Gabon. At the end of the research, he traveled to Cameroon and sought employment with the colonial government. When relieved of duty in Yaoundé, he continued collecting biological specimens on the coast. One of the few Germans permitted to stay in the French mandate territory, Zenker remained in Cameroon until his death in 1934 (Laburthe-Tolra 1970).

5. However, Kuczynski suggests that the census figures were derived only a third

from enumeration and two-thirds from estimates. He gives the population of the district of Yaoundé as 300,000 for 1909–10 (1939: 22, 25).

6. The war, as well as the duration between the departure of the Germans and the effective establishment of the French, was a time of substantial hardship. Medical centers were closed, the leprosy and sleeping-sickness campaigns were suspended (Kuczynski 1939: 68), and many of the schools were shut.

7. This situation bears a certain resemblance to the contemporary role of international NGOs in fulfilling state functions in many African countries, including Cameroon.

8. Since my mother's father was an Alsatian Catholic, some small hope was also held out for my being able to understand. In casual conversation, southern Cameroonians generally compare Cameroon either to Alsace or to Canada. In both cases, the similarity is first of all linguistic: in the 1910s and 1920s, southern Cameroonians had to attend school in German and then in French as did Alsatians at several points in history; today, the country is officially French-English bilingual, like Canada.

9. The renowned Cameroonian historian Englebert Mveng reiterates the widely held Cameroonian view that Vogt's appointment as the first Cameroonian bishop was an act of providence, as Vogt "was a saint." According to Mveng, the bishop "traveled his immense diocese on foot, despite the uninterrupted suffering imposed on him by his poor health" (1963: 465).

10. The priests I knew in Mbeya usually cited 90 percent, a figure that they said came from the bishop of Mbalmayo. However, according to the Mbalmayo diocese page on the Catholic-Hierarchy Web site published by David M. Cheney (http://www.catholic-hierarchy.org/diocese/dmbal.html), only 44 percent of the population of Yaoundé and some 60 percent of the populations of the dioceses of Mbalmayo and Obala are Catholic.

11. For a discussion of the rise of the UPC and the resistance, see Mbembe 1996.

12. See, for example, the reference document "In the Logic of Democratie Avancée" on the Web site of the Social Democratic Front of Cameroon (http://www .sdfparty.org/english/references/188.php).

13. "Back in 1982, Cameroonians drank as much champagne per head of population as West Germans. On average each Cameroonian earned about $880 that year (each West German $13,400), but this newly oil-rich West African state knocked back 495,000 bottles of bubbly, which made it Africa's biggest importer of the stuff" ("Hung Over," *Economist* 346, no.8057 [February 28, 1998]).

14. Figures for 1998 are reported in "World Study Senses High Corruption," *Chicago Tribune*, September 23, 1998. Figures for 1999 are available at the Web site of Transparency International (http://www.transparency.de).

15. In one of the few quantitative sources from the early twentieth century, Dr. Külz published that the women of the "Etóns" bore an average of six children (cited in Kuczynski 1939: 39).

16. See also Guyer's discussion of the etymology of *mevungu* (1984: 16).

17. However, neither Tsala nor Laburthe-Tolra recognizes the distinction between *ngon* and *ngal*, which could also be a dialectical difference between Eton and Ewondo.

18. These shared taxis have equivalents in many African cities. Standing at the side of the road, you call out your destination to the taxi drivers, who decide whether it can be incorporated into the route they have planned, based on the other passengers.

Chapter Three

1. But not in Camfrançais more generally. As Feldman-Savelsberg pointed out to me, the Beti distinction between *dignité* and *respectabilté* is not held by Bangangté speakers of French (personal communication).

2. I would thus disagree with Weber's representation of Catholic virtue as "the gradual accumulation of individual good works to one's credit." Instead, I would argue that, at least in southern Cameroon, Catholicism, like Protestantism, is experienced as "a systematic self-control . . . at every moment" (Weber 1958: 115).

3. These folk histories may be traceable, in part, to the late-nineteenth-century European travelers who described the Beti as unusually tall, graceful, and substantially less barbarian than their neighbors (cited in Laburthe-Tolra 1977).

4. This may be compared to the Sarakatsani concept of honor: "One aspect of honour, then, is a struggle of self-discipline over cowardice and sensuality, flaws of animal nature that continually threaten to limit the natural nobility of man" (Campbell 1974: 269).

5. A related discussion can be found in Gable 1997.

6. There is also a term, written *nzine* by my research assistants, which can indicate "internal honor." However, the term is used neither by Laburthe-Tolra (1981) nor by Tsala (1957), and appears to be a borrowing from the French *digne*.

7. The calls for a partially independent Cameroonian church seem to me somewhat different from the ordinary Catholic disregard for hierarchy and earthly authority. These latter, however, are as much in play in Cameroon as anywhere. One elderly gentleman in Mbeya who had constructed an elaborate altar to Mary in his living room told me that if you love your neighbor, all the other commandments are "flexible." In a similar vein, and much to my Protestant annoyance, my interpreter in 1996 insisted on referring to papal bulls and Vatican encyclicals jointly as "recommendations." He argued that the church "can only suggest" that people conform to its teachings. In the end, people will do as they like anyway.

8. Laburthe-Tolra's use of *digne* in this quote requires discussion. He employs the term according to contemporary usage in Camfrançais, indicated by his quotation marks. But the context being described is precolonial, and it is unclear to what

degree current understandings of *être digne* would have applied. Yet, his claim that a woman's renown relied in part on her *dignité* is significant, and resonates with the current situation.

Chapter Four

1. Historically, even this form may have been somewhat ambivalent, rather than entirely dangerous and negative. Laburthe-Tolra (1985) notes that only a woman possessed by *evu* could officiate at the *mevungu*, or ceremony of female fecundity.

2. I am thinking of the conversion of educational capital in the sense used by Bourdieu, who writes: "The accumulation of economic capital merges with the accumulation of symbolic capital, that is, with the acquisition of a reputation for competence and an image of respectability and honorability that are easily converted into political position as a local or national *notable*" (1984: 291).

3. The distinction between general education and technical training occurs at much younger ages in the Cameroonian school system than here. By the time students are ready to take the BCE (about fifth grade), the two tracks have diverged.

4. In contrast to metropolitan French, Camfrançais uses the term *lycée* for public high schools and *collège* for private ones, rather than using these terms to distinguish between the upper and lower levels of high school, respectively.

Chapter Five

1. It is unclear whether school-based honorability among the Beti can rightly be called "educational capital," as used by Bourdieu (1984).

2. The principal is a priest. However, the surveillant general and the vice-principal, who together are responsible for most daily management of the school, are both laity. This laitization may be compared to a similar trend in Zambia described by Carmody (1990).

3. Although the numbers are too small to constitute strong evidence, it is intriguing that these data conform to the pattern of unequal selection described by Bourdieu and Passeron (1971).

4. Francanglais is a Cameroonian pidgin, spoken primarily by street vendors in Douala. Recently, however, it has been picked up by young urbanites. Among these *yos* and *yoyettes*, Francanglais consists primarily of English words incorporated into French grammar. *Yoyettes* are trendy young women, who usually reside in the city and perceive themselves as part of an international youth culture. The term is derived from "Yo!" as used in American rap music.

5. Similarly, Simon-Hohm claims that French schools failed in Cameroon be-

cause the curriculum failed to address "African reality," as well as because the process of family socialization produced an individual who "cannot correspond in his being and behavior to the norms and values of a colonial or capitalist society" (1983: 3).

6. This is a necessary part of the "fertility awareness method," which uses the woman's monthly temperature fluctuations and changes in cervical mucus to know on which days she is fecund. In fact, most Beti women using periodic abstinence use the less-effective but easier method of counting days.

7. Feldman-Savelsberg expertly describes how infertility and political impotence are symbolically equated in West Cameroon (1999). In contrast to the case she explores, Mr. Ebene's view is remarkably nationalist.

8. In fact, the Cameroonian population is growing by about 2.5 percent per year, according to data from the World Bank (http://devdata.worldbank.org/dataonline).

Chapter Six

1. Among his citations for this claim is the passage from which the epigraph to this chapter is taken (Tessman 1913, 2:253), although Laburthe-Tolra mistakenly assigns it to volume 1, rather than volume 2.

2. Both Mviena and Tabi are not only Beti scholars, but also priests. Their relationships to the ethics of Beti social practice are therefore doubly fraught.

3. The related changes in age at marriage are discussed in chapter 2.

4. Part of the difference between demographic and popular interpretations of the sex ratio relates to the social availability of sexual or marital partners, as compared to counts of the population per se. On the one hand, in a growing population where women are usually significantly younger than their male partners, there will always be more potentially available women than men, because their birth cohorts were later, and therefore larger. Thus, the popular experience of excess numbers of women is an accurate description of the relative size of cohorts of probable sex partners, although it is not an accurate description of the overall sex ratio. At the same time, it is critical to note that temporary abstinence works in the opposite direction: since most Beti women abstain from sex during their menstrual periods, and some also abstain during the fecund period, the effective number of sexually available women at any given time is significantly lower than the number available over the course of a month.

5. It is, of course, possible that in a small sample of births, a third should be female, just as it is possible to get heads in a third of a small number of coin tosses; as the size of the sample increases, the probability of such an outcome decreases. Although the sex ratio at birth does vary somewhat, in the absence of sex-selective abortion it varies only between about 103 to 108 male births for every 100 female births.

6. The exception is its use as punishment under unusual circumstances (Ombolo 1990: 77).

7. There is some disagreement among young Beti women whether infidelity is a trait of Beti men or of men in general. This debate was particularly pointed among those women hoping to marry a European man, for example, by seeking a marriage partner on Internet.

8. This may be changing somewhat, at least among highly educated and urban youth, who are beginning to view dating publicly as a modern, specifically American, form of romance. None of the women I knew in 1998 were willing to risk this degree of *modernisme,* however.

9. For example, my informants recognized neither *la titulaire,* nor *cacao* (Calvès 1996: 173–74), although they liked both terms.

10. Eton and Ewondo have five tones, but those tones are often redundant in the sense that words distinguished by tone also differ on another feature as well: minimal oppositions based *only* on tone are rare in Eton.

11. Cameroon is, to my knowledge, unique in legally recognizing monogamous and polygamous marriages as distinct forms, or "regimes," which are voluntary, but once signed, legally binding. Although South Africa recognizes "traditional" marriage, which may be polygamous, there is no form of civil polygamous marriage (Chambers, n.d.).

12. Because of the small sample size, age-specific transition rates are calculated over the ten years prior to the study.

13. I count 155. That is, there are 75 ways to complete all four transitions (24 if you do one at a time, plus 42 for the paths that include performing two transitions at once, plus 8 ways if you do three at a time, plus 1 way if you do all four). Then there are 52 paths through only three transitions, 24 paths through two, and 4 paths that end after only one transition.

14. Among women who had attended secondary school, 22 percent were using periodic abstinence, 6 percent condoms, 5 percent the pill, and 9 percent all other methods combined. These data are available on the DHS Web site (http://www .measuredhs.com).

15. As one particularly eloquent American Catholic said of why confession was unnecessary: "You tell your sins to the Man upstairs; the rest are only men."

16. Most Beti women use the simplest "calendar" method of rhythm, meaning that they abstain from about the eighth to the eighteenth day of their menstrual cycle.

17. See Johnson-Hanks 2002c for a more extensive discussion of the perceived modernity of periodic abstinence.

18. There seems to be a significant change in the kinds of talk that are acceptable once a woman is formally engaged or married. At that point, the identity of her sexual partner is publicly known, and she can no longer talk about his talents (or lack thereof) anonymously. Such talk therefore is quickly limited to close intimates.

19. Cameroon is somewhat unusual among sub-Saharan African countries in this regard, owing to the large proportion of schools that are private and the large number of school transfers. Although technically, women who have borne a child are not supposed to enroll in public school, they frequently do, by withdrawing from one school before the pregnancy is too visible and enrolling in another after the birth. In addition, the private schools (including the very popular Catholic schools) have no rules against the attendance of young mothers.

Chapter Seven

1. Thanks to Elizabeth Kuhn-Wilken for the terms "malleable motherhood" and "relinquishing claims to children."

2. The term "unwanted" is systematically ambiguous in the demographic litera-ture. In addition to the definition above, which refers to a woman's retrospectively stated intentions about specific births, it may refer more generally to fertility in excess of some stated desire. Work using this definition compares the number of children that a woman has borne to the number she says she would want if she were to begin all over again, classifying births in excess of her stated desired number as "unwanted" (Bongaarts 1990). This usage differs in practically every way from the one I advocate here, as it negates the importance of social timing inherent in an understanding of vital conjunctures.

3. The semantic conflation of abortions and miscarriages is widespread: both are called *avortement* in Camfrançais, it takes an additional question to distinguish between an *avortement spontanée* (miscarriage) and *avortement provoquée* (abor-tion).

4. The total abortion rate is the number of abortions that a woman would have over the course of her life if she had abortions at the age-specific rates calculated from the data. The crude abortion rate is simply the number of births per 1,000 women aged fifteen to forty-nine.

5. Although interesting to an order of magnitude, these crude rates cannot be directly compared because the age structure of the populations differs, and younger women are more likely than older women to have abortions in any given year.

6. Although foster children may be a burden to the receiving household, their presence does not necessarily require a complete reorganization. Most receiving households already have children, and as we saw in chapter 3, children are given substantial freedom and older children perform much of the direct care of younger ones.

7. The rare cases where a desperate mother leaves an infant alone on the street, or in a trash receptacle, receive substantial attention in the Cameroonian press. But these incidents are strongly distinguished from the form of relinquishment of claims to children that I am describing here.

8. In a few cases, two points are superimposed, as two or three women experienced both events at the same ages (say, first birth at eighteen and first marriage at twenty-one). The number of superimposed points is very small, however.

9. This is not to imply that the age limits in public schools are a major or consistent impediment: there is a thriving and lucrative business in falsified attestations of birth and certifications of passing certain exams—the prices of these false documents are high, but many students are willing to pay them.

10. *Mal aux nerfs* is characterized by terrible headaches brought on by stress and by the heat. People who suffer it are often unable to attend classes or work in the afternoon in the dry season. It is particularly common among young women and recent brides, and essentially unknown among men.

Chapter Eight

1. Although scholars and policymakers have long known that illegal abortion is dangerous, only a few reliable studies of the rates and health consequences of illegal abortion in the developing world have been conducted over the past two decades. A growing number of hospital-based studies have sought to establish the degree of mortality and morbidity related to illegal and clandestine abortion (Makokha 1980; Narkavonnakit and Bennett 1981; Rochat et al. 1981). A second group of studies have sought to estimate the population prevalence of abortion, primarily relying on residual techniques derived from Bongaarts's model (1982) of proximate determinants (Johnston and Hill 1996; Foreit and Nortman 1992), and more recently on a method of third-person report in which each woman in a population sample is asked to report the abortions of her close confidantes (Rossier 2002).

2. Notice how the former novitiate describes how she found herself pregnant after having sex when she "didn't know what took her," using the same phrase as Nathalie. Compare this to Marie's recounting that under peer pressure, she went with the "first boy who came" up to her. In the stories of women who conceived unintentionally in school, especially with a man that they did not later marry, there is often an implied sense of randomness and disorder in the actions that led to the pregnancy. One woman emphasized that she got pregnant on the twenty-third day of her cycle, and that she and her partner had been systematically avoiding sex during the typically fecund period using rhythm method. She said this to demonstrate that the pregnancy was out of her hands—it occurred despite her concerted effort to avert pregnancy through periodic abstinence. Unforeseen births systematically occur in the context of unplanned unions perceived not to have a future. It is noteworthy that throughout all of the surveys, unforeseen pregnancies are always blamed on accidents or fate, and never on the men. In none of the interviews did a woman say that pregnancy resulted when the man forced her to have sex, that

she was tricked, or drunk, or coerced, although women do indeed talk about sexual coercion in nonreproductive contexts.

3. The argument is that in order to baptize a baby, the parents must commit themselves to raise the child in the church. If the mother bore the child outside of marriage but then repented, she can still do so; however, if the parents are together rearing a child without being married, they cannot have truly repented, and thus are not fit Christian parents.

References

Abu-Lughod, Lila. 1986. *Veiled Sentiments: Honor and Poetry in a Bedouin Society*. Berkeley: University of California Press.

Adamchak, Donald, and Peggy Gabo Ntseane. 1992. "Gender, Education and Fertility: A Cross-National Analysis of Sub-Saharan Nations." *Sociological Spectrum* 12:167–82.

Ainsworth, Martha. 1988. *Socioeconomic Determinants of Fertility in Cote d'Ivoire*. New Haven: Economic Growth Center, Yale University.

Ainsworth, Martha, Andrew Nyamete, and Kathleen Beegle. 1995. "The Impact of Female Schooling on Fertility and Contraceptive Use: A Study of 14 Sub-Saharan Countries." Living Standard Measurement Working Papers, no. 110. Washington, D.C.: World Bank.

Alan Guttmacher Institute. 2002. *Facts in Brief: Induced Abortion*. New York: Alan Guttmacher Institute.

Alexandre, Pierre, and Jacques Binet. 1958. *Le groupe dit Pahouin (Fang-Boulou-Beti)*. Paris: Presses Universitaires de France. Translated as Alexandre and Binet 1985.

———. 1985. *The Group Called Pahouin (Bulu-Beti-Fang)*. New Haven, N.J.: Human Relations Area Files.

Al-Khayyat, Sana. 1990. *Honour and Shame: Women in Modern Iraq*. London: Saqi Books.

Alter, George. 1988. *Family and Female Life Course: The Women of Verviers, Belgium, 1849–1880*. Madison: University of Wisconsin Press.

Amanor, Kojo Sebastian. 1994. *The New Frontier: Farmer's Response to Land Degradation*. Geneva: UNRISD.

Anon. 1998. "L'histoire d'un malaise programmé." *Perspectives Hebdo*, no. 167 (July 27–August 1), 6.

Anyon, Jean. 1983. "Intersections of Gender and Class: Accommodation and Resistance by Working-Class and Affluent Females to Contradictory Sex-Role

Ideologies." In *Gender, Class and Education,* edited by Stephen Walker and Len Barton. Sussex: Falmer Press.

Appadurai, Arjun, ed. 1986. *The Social Life of Things: Commodities in Cultural Perspective.* Cambridge: Cambridge University Press.

Argenti, Nicolas. 1998. "Air Youth: Performance, Violence and the State in Cameroon." *Journal of the Royal Anthropological Institute* 4:753–55.

Aronowitz, Stanley, and Henry Giroux. 1991. *Postmodern Education: Politics, Culture and Social Criticism.* Minneapolis: University of Minnesota Press.

Asuagbor, Greg. 1994. "Democratization and Modernization in Africa: The Case of Cameroon." Ph.D. diss., University of Nevada, Reno.

Atangana, J. J. Mebenga. 1998. "Scandale autour du bacc session 98." *La Nouvelle Expression,* no. 398 (15 July), 6.

Atangana-Mebara, Jean Marie, et al. 1982. *Education, emploi et saliare au Cameroun.* Paris: UNESCO.

Austen, Ralph, and Jonathan Derrick. 1999. *Middlemen of the Cameroon Rivers: The Duala and Their Hinterland, c. 1600–c. 1960.* Cambridge: Cambridge University Press.

Axinn, William G., and Arland Thornton. 1992. "The Relationship between Cohabitation and Divorce: Selectivity or Causal Influence?" *Demography* 29:357–74.

Azébazé, Alex G. 1998. "Comment on a dévalué le bacc." *Le Messager,* o. 797 (August 5), 6.

Bankole, Akinrinola, and Charles Westoff. 1998. "The Consistency and Validity of Reproductive Attitudes: Evidence from Morocco." *Journal of Biosocial Science* 30:439–55.

Barnes, Sandra. 1986. *Patrons and Power: Creating a Political Community in Metropolitan Lagos.* Bloomington: Indiana University Press.

Barreto, Thalia, et al. 1992. "Investigating Induced Abortion in Developing Countries: Methods and Problems." *Studies in Family Planning* 23, no. 3: 159–70.

Basu, Alaka Malwade. 1996. "Maternal Education, Fertility and Child Mortality: Disentangling Verbal Relationships." *Health Transition Review* 4:205–15.

Bauer, Annemarie, and Herbert Bergmann. 1984. *Erziehungstraditionen und Schule in Schwartzafrika.* Saarbruwcken: Verlag Breitenbach.

Bayart, Jean-Francois. 1989. *The State in Africa: The Politics of the Belly.* Translated by Mary Harper et al. London: Longman Press.

Becker, Gary. 1991. *A Treatise on the Family.* Cambridge: Harvard University Press.

Belman, Dale, and Jean S. Heywood. 1989. "Government Wage Differentials: A Sample Selection Approach." *Applied Economics* 21:427–38.

Bennett, Neil G., et al. 1988. "Commitment and the Modern Union: Assessing the Link between Premarital Cohabitation and Subsequent Marital Stability." *American Sociological Review* 53:127–38.

Berger, Heinrich. 1978. *Mission und Kolonialpolitik: Die Katolische Mission in*

Kamerun Während der Deutschen Kolonialzeit. Immensee: Neue Zeitschrift für Missionswissenschaft.

Bernstein, Michael Andre. 1994. *Foregone Conclusions: Against Apocalyptic History.* Berkeley and Los Angeles: University of California Press.

Berry, Sara. 1993. *No Condition Is Permanent: The Social Dynamics of Agrarian Change in Sub-Saharan Africa.* Madison: University of Wisconsin Press.

Beti, Mongo. 1958. *Mission to Kala.* Translated by Peter Green. Oxford: Heinemann Press.

Blake, Judith. 1989. *Family Size and Achievement.* Berkeley and Los Angeles: University of California Press.

Blanc, Ann, and Cynthia Lloyd. 1990. "Women's Childrearing Strategies in Relation to Fertility and Employment in Ghana." Working Papers, no. 16. New York: Population Council.

Bledsoe, Caroline. 1980. *Women and Marriage in Kpelle Society.* Stanford: Stanford University Press.

———. 1984. "The Political Use of Sande Ideology and Symbolism." *American Ethnologist* 11, no. 3: 455–72.

———. 1990a. "No Success without Struggle: Social Mobility and Hardship for Foster Children in Sierra Leone." *Man* 25:70–88.

———. 1990b. "School Fees and the Marriage Process for Mende girls in Sierra Leone." In *Beyond the Second Sex: New Directions in the Anthropology of Gender,* edited by P. R. Sanday and R. G. Goodenough. Philadelphia: University of Pennsylvania Press.

———. 1990c. "The Politics of Children: Fosterage and the Social Management of Fertility among the Mende of Sierra Leone." In *Births and Power: Social Change and the Politics of Reproduction,* edited by W. P. Handwerker. Boulder: Westview Press.

———. 1992. "The Cultural Transformation of Western Education in Sierra Leone." *Africa* 62, no. 2: 182–201.

———. 1993. "The Politics of Polygyny in Mende Education and Child Fosterage Transactions." *Sex and Gender Hierarchies,* edited by Barbara Diane Miller. Cambridge: Cambridge University Press.

———. 2002. *Contingent Lives: Fertility, Time and Aging in West Africa.* Chicago: University of Chicago Press.

Bledsoe, Caroline, Fatoumatta Banja, and Allan Hill. 1998. "Reproductive Mishaps and Western Contraception: An African Challenge to Fertility Theory." *Population and Development Review* 24:15–57.

Bledsoe, Caroline, and Uche Isiugo-Abanihe. 1989. Strategies of Child-Fosterage among Mende Grannies in Sierra Leone. In *Reproduction and Social Organization in Sub-Saharan Africa,* edited by Ron Lesthaeghe. Berkeley and Los Angeles: University of California Press.

Bledsoe, Caroline, and Kenneth Robey. 1993. "Arabic Literacy and Secrecy among the Mende of Sierra Leone." *Cross-Cultural Approaches to Literacy,* edited by Brian Street. Cambridge: Cambridge University Press.

Bledsoe, Caroline, et al., eds. 1999. *Critical Perspectives on Schooling and Fertility in the Developing World.* Washington, D.C.: National Academy Press.

Boddy, Janice. 1989. *Wombs and Alien Spirits: Women, Men and the Zar Cult in Northern Sudan.* Madison: University of Wisconsin Press.

Bongaarts, John. 1982. "The Fertility-Inhibiting Effects of the Intermediate Fertility Variables." *Studies in Family Planning* 13:179–89.

———. 1990. "The Measurement of Wanted Fertility." *Population and Development Review* 16:487–506.

———. 1991. "The KAP-Gap and the Unmet need for Contraception." *Population and Development Review* 17, no. 2: 293–313.

Bongaarts, John, and Judith Bruce. 1994. "The Causes of Unmet Need in Contraception and the Social Content of Services." Working Papers, no. 69. New York: Population Council.

Bongaarts, John, and Susan Cotts Watkins. 1996. "Social Interactions and Contemporary Fertility Transitions." *Population and Development Review* 22, no. 4: 639–83.

Bourdieu, Pierre. 1977. *Outline of a Theory of Practice.* Cambridge: Cambridge University Press.

———. 1984. *Distinction: A Social Critique of the Judgement of Taste.* Translated by Richard Nice. Cambridge: Harvard University Press.

———. 1990. *The Logic of Practice.* Stanford: Stanford University Press.

———. 1993. *The Field of Cultural Production.* New York: Columbia University Press.

Bourdieu, Pierre, and Jean-Claude Passeron. 1971. *Reproduction in Education, Society and Culture.* London: Sage Publications.

Brazza, Savorgnan de. 1887–88. "Voyages dans l'Ouest Africain, 1875–1887." *Le Tour de Monde.* Paris and London.

Bruel, Max. 1940. *Kampf im Urwald: Von Urwaldgottern und Schicksalen deutscher Planzer und Soldaten in Kamerun.* Leipzig: Julius Klinthardt.

Cain, Mead T. 1977. "The Economic Activities of Children in Bangladesh." *Population and Development Review* 3, no. 3: 201–27.

Caldwell, John. 1980. "Mass Education as a Determinant of the Timing of Fertility Decline." *Population and Development Review* 6, no. 2: 225–55.

———. 1982. *Theory of Fertility Decline.* London: Academic Press.

———. 1997. "The Global Fertility Transition: The Need for a Unifying Theory." *Population and Development Review* 23, no. 4: 803–12.

Caldwell, John, and Pat Caldwell. 1987. "The Cultural Context of High Fertility in Sub-Saharan Africa." *Population and Development Review* 13, no. 3: 409–37.

Caldwell, John, P. H. Reddy, and Pat Caldwell. 1985. "Educational Transition in Rural South India." *Population and Development Review* 11, no. 1: 29–51.

Calvert, Albert. 1917. *The Cameroons.* London: T. Werner Laurie.

Calvès, Anne-Emmanuèle. 1996. "Youth and Fertility in Cameroon: Changing Patterns of Family Formation." Ph.D. diss., Pennsylvania State University.

Campbell, J. K. 1974. *Honour, Family and Patronage.* Oxford: Oxford University Press.

Carmody, Brendan. 1990. "Denominational Secondary Schooling in Post-Independence Zambia: A Case Study." *African Affairs* 89, no. 355: 247–63.

Carter, Anthony. 1995. "Agency and Fertility: For an Ethnography of Practice." *Situating Fertility: Anthropological and Demographic Inquiry,* edited by Susan Greenhalgh. Cambridge: Cambridge University Press.

————. 1999. "What Is Meant, and Measured, by 'Education'?" *Critical Perspectives on Schooling and Fertility in the Developing World,* edited by Caroline Bledsoe et al. Washington, D.C.: National Academy Press.

Casterline, John, et al. 1997. "Factors Underlying Unmet Need for Family Planning in the Philippines." *Studies in Family Planning* 28, no. 3: 173–91.

Castiglioni, Maria, Gianpiero Dalla Zuanna, and Marzia Loghi. 2001. "Planned and Unplanned Births and Conceptions in Italy, 1970–1995." *European Journal of Population* 17, no. 3: 207–33.

Castro Martin, Teresa. 1995. "Women's Education and Fertility: Results from 26 Demographic and Health Surveys." *Studies in Family Planning* 26, no. 4: 187–202.

Chambers, David. N.d. "Civilizing the Natives: Marriage in Post-Apartheid South Africa." Manuscript.

Chambon, Adrienne. 1995. "Life History as Dialogical Activity: 'If You Ask Me the Right Questions, I Could Tell You.'" *Current Sociology* 43, no. 2/3: 125–35.

Clark, Gracia. 1994. *Onions Are My Husband: Survival and Accumulation by West African Market Women.* Chicago: University of Chicago Press.

Cleland, John, and Georgia Kaufman. 1998. "Education, Fertility and Child Survival: Unraveling the Links." *The Methods and Uses of Anthropological Demography,* edited by Alaka Basu and Peter Aaby. Oxford: Clarendon Press.

Cleland, John, and German Rodriguez. 1988. "The Effect of Parental Education on Marital Fertility in Developing Countries." *Population Studies* 42:419–42.

Coale, Ansley. 1973. "The Demographic Transition." In *International Population Conference,* vol. 1. Liege: IUSSP.

Coale, Ansley, and James Trussell. 1974. "Model Fertility Schedules: Variations in the Age Structure of Childbearing in Human Populations." *Population Index* 40:185–258.

Cochrane, Susan H. 1979. *Fertility and Education: What Do We Really Know?* Baltimore: Johns Hopkins University Press.

Coeytaux, Francine. 1988. "Induced Abortion in Sub-Saharan Africa: What We Do and Do Not Know." *Studies in Family Planning* 19, no. 3: 186–90.

Cohen, Barney, and William House. 1994. "Education, Experience, and Earnings in the Labor Market of a Developing Economy." *World Development* 22, no. 10: 1529–65.

Collier, David. 1995. "Translating Quantitative Methods for Qualitative Researchers: The Case of Selection Bias." *American Political Science Review* 89, no. 2: 461–66.

Collier, Jane Fishburne and Sylvia Junko Yanagisako. 1987. *Gender and Kinship: Essays Toward a Unified Analysis.* Stanford: Stanford University Press.

Comaroff, Jean L. 1985. *Body of Power, Spirit of Resistance: The Culture and History of a South African People.* Chicago: University of Chicago Press.

Comaroff, Jean, and John Comaroff. 1991. *On Revelation and Revolution.* Vol. 1, *Christianity, Colonialism and Consciousness in South Africa.* Chicago: University of Chicago Press.

Comaroff, John. 1980. *The Meaning of Marriage Payments.* London: Academic Press.

Comaroff, John, and Jean Comaroff, eds. 1993. *Modernity and Its Malcontents: Ritual and Power in Postcolonial Africa.* Chicago: University of Chicago Press.

Commissariat de la Republique Française au Cameroun. 1923. *Guide de la colonisation au Cameroun.* Paris: Emile Larose.

Coquery-Vidrovitch, Catherine. 1993. "La ville coloniale 'lieu de colonisation' et metissage culturel." Special issue *Afrique Contemporaire,* no. 4.

Courgeau, Daniel, and Eva Lelièvre. 1992. *Event History Analysis in Demography.* Oxford: Clarendon Press.

Cunningham , F. Gary, et al. 2001. *Williams Obstetrics,* 21st ed. New York: McGraw-Hill Medical Publishing Division.

Delaney, Carol. 1991. *The Seed and the Soil.* Berkeley and Los Angeles: University of California Press.

Delaunay, Valérie. 1994. *L'entrée en vie féconde: Expression démographique des mutations socio-économique d'un milieu rural sénégalais.* Paris: Centre Français sur la Population et le Développement.

Deloria, Philip. 1999. *Playing Indian.* New Haven: Yale University Press.

Denzer, LaRay. 1992. "Domestic Science Training in Colonial Yorubaland, Nigeria." *African Encounters with Domesticity,* edited by Karen Hansen. New Brunswick: Rutgers University Press.

Desgrées du Lou, A., et al. 1999. "Le recours à l'avortement provoquée à Abidjan: Une cause de la baisse de la fécondité?" *Population* 54, no. 3: 427–46.

Devische, Renaat. 1993. *Weaving the Threads of Life: The Khita Gyn-Eco-Logical Healing Cult among the Yaka.* Chicago: University of Chicago Press.

Dillinger, Edmund. 1991. *Kirche in Kamerun—Kirche der Hoffnung: Zur Hundertjahrfeier der Gründung der katolischen Kirche in Kamerun.* Friedrichsthal: Verlag der CV- Afrika-Hilfe eV.

Easterlin, Richard. 1980. *Birth and Fortune: The Impact of Numbers on Personal Welfare.* New York: Basic Books.

Easterlin, Richard A., and Eileen M. Crimmins. 1985. *The Fertility Revolution.* Chicago: University of Chicago Press.

Ebenson, Christel. 1998. "Fighting Feminine Delinquency." *L'Effort Camerounais,* no. 102 (March 12–18).

Eisenhart, Margaret. 1995. "The Fax, the Jazz Player and the Self-Story Teller: How Do People Organize Culture?" *Anthropology and Education Quarterly* 26, no. 1: 3–26.

Ellison, Peter. 2001. *On Fertile Ground: A Natural History of Human Reproduction.* Cambridge: Harvard University Press.

Eloundou-Enyegue, Parfait. 1997. "Demographic Responses to Economic Crisis in Cameroon: Fertility, Child Schooling and Quantity/Quality Trade-Off." Ph.D. diss., Pennsylvania State University.

Eloundou-Enyegue, Parfait, et al. 2000. "Are There Crisis-Led Fertility Declines? Evidence from Central Cameroon." *Population Research and Policy Review* 19, no. 1: 47–72.

Emecheta, Buchi. 1979. *The Joys of Motherhood.* New York: George Braziller.

Escherich, Georg. 1938. *Kamerun.* Berlin: Hans Reigler.

Evans-Pritchard, E. E. 1951. *Kinship and Marriage among the Nuer.* Oxford: Oxford University Press.

———. 1969. *The Nuer.* New York: Oxford University Press.

Eyoh, Dickson. 1998. "Through the Prism of a Local Tragedy: Political Liberalisation, Regionalism and Elite Struggles for Power in Cameroon." *Africa* 41, no. 2: 338–60.

Fardon, Richard. 1996. "The Person, Ethnicity and the Problem of Identity in West Africa." In *African Crossroads,* edited by Ian Fowler and David Zeitlyn. Oxford: Berghan Books.

Fehring, Richard, and Andrea Matovina Schmidt. 2001. "Trends in Contraceptive Use among Catholics in the United States, 1988–1995." *Linacre Quarterly,* May, 170–185.

Feldman-Savelsberg, Pamela. 1994. "Plundered Kitchens and Empty Wombs: Fear of Infertility in the Cameroonian Grassfields." *Social Science and Medicine* 39, no. 4: 463–74.

———. 1995. "Cooking Inside: Kinship and Gender in Bangangte Idioms of Marriage and Procreation." *American Ethnologist* 22, no. 3: 483–502.

———. 1999. *Plundered Kitchens, Empty Wombs: Threatened Reproduction and Identity in the Cameroon Grassfields.* Ann Arbor: University of Michigan Press.

Ferguson, James. 1999. *Expectations of Modernity: Myths and Meanings of Urban Life on the Zambian Copperbelt.* Berkeley and Los Angeles: University of California Press.

Fernandez, James. 1982. *Bwiti: An Ethnography of the Religious Imagination in Africa.* Princeton: Princeton University Press.

Fisiy, Cyprian, and Mitzi Goheen. 1998. "Power and the Quest for Recognition:

Neotraditional Titles among the New Elite in Nsó, Cameroon." *Africa* 41, no. 2: 383–401.

Foreit, Karen, and Dorothy Nortman. 1992. "A Method for Calculating Rates of Induced-Abortion." *Demography* 29, no. 1: 127–37.

Fortes, Meyer. 1969. *The Dynamics of Clanship among the Tallensi.* London: Oxford University Press.

Fotso, Medard, et al. 1999. *Enquête démographique et de santé, Cameroun 1998.* Calverton, Md.: Macro International.

Foucault, Michel. 1979. *Discipline and Punish: The Birth of the Prison.* Translated by Alan Sheridan. New York: Vintage Books.

———. 1990. *The History of Sexuality.* Vol. 1. New York: Vintage Books.

Franqueville, André. 1984. *Yaoundé: Construire une capital.* Collections Memoires, no 104. Paris: ORSTOM.

———. 1987. *Une Afrique entre le village et la ville: Les migrations dans le sud du Cameroun.* Paris: ORSTOM.

Frehill, Lisa M. 1999. "Education and Occupational Sex Segregation: The Decision to Major in Engineering." *Sociological Quarterly* 38, no. 2: 225–49.

Froelich, Jean-Claude. 1956. *Cameroun—Togo: Territoires sous tutelle.* Paris: Berger-Levrault.

Fuller, Bruce, and Xiaoyan Liang. 1999. "Which Girls Stay in School? The Influence of Family Economy, Social Demands, and Ethnicity in South Africa." In *Critical Perspectives on Schooling and Fertility in the Developing World,* edited by Caroline Bledsoe et al. Washington, D.C.: National Academy Press.

Fuller, Bruce, et al. 1995. "Why Do Daughters Leave School in Southern Africa? Family Economy and Mothers' Commitments." *Social Forces* 74:657–82.

Gable, Eric. 1996. "Women, Ancestors and Alterity among the Manjoco of Guinea-Bissau." *Journal of Religion in Africa* 26, no. 2S: 104–21.

———. 1997. "A Secret Shared: Fieldwork and the Sinister in a West African Village." *Cultural Anthropology* 12, no. 2: 213–33.

Gaillard, Phillippe. 1989. *Le Cameroun.* Paris: Editions L'Harmattan.

Gell, Alfred. 1992. *The Anthropology of Time: Cultural Constructions of Temporal Maps and Images.* Oxford: Berg Publishers.

Geschiere, Peter. 1997. *The Modernity of Witchcraft: Politics and the Occult in Post-colonial Africa.* Charlottesville: University Press of Virginia.

Gilmore, David. 1982. "Anthropology of the Mediterranean." *Annual Review of Anthropology* 11:175–205.

Ginsburg, Faye, and Rayna Rapp. 1991. "The Politics of Reproduction." *Annual Review of Anthropology* 20:311–43.

———, eds. 1995. *Conceiving the New World Order: The Global Politics of Reproduction.* Berkeley and Los Angeles: University of California Press.

Gintis, Herbert, and Bowles, Samuel. 1976. *Schooling in Capitalist America: Ed-*

ucational Reform and the Contradictions of Economic Life. New York: Basic Books.

Glick, Peter, and David Sahn. 2000. "Schooling of Girls and Boys in a West African Country: The Effects of Parental Education, Income, and Household Structure." *Economics of Education Review* 19:63–87.

Godong, Serge Alain. 1998. "300 diplômes suspendus à une signature." *Mutations,* no. 138 (August 3).

Goffman, Erving. 1967. *Interaction Ritual: Essays on Face-to-Face Behavior.* New York: Pantheon Books.

Goody, Jack. 1968. *Literacy in Traditional Societies.* Cambridge: Cambridge University Press.

Goody, Jack, and Ian Watt. 1963. "The Consequences of Literacy." *Comparative Studies in Society and History* 5:304–45.

Greenhalgh, Susan, ed. 1995. *Situating Fertility: Anthropology and Demographic Inquiry.* Cambridge: Cambridge University Press.

Greenhalgh, Susan, and Jaili Li. 1995. "Engendering Reproductive Policy and Practice in Peasant China: For a Feminist Demography of Reproduction." *Signs* 20, no. 3: 601–42.

Gronau, Reuben. 1974. "Wage Comparisons—a Selectivity Bias." *Journal of Political Economy,* November/December 1974.

Guyer, Jane. 1984. *Family and Farm in Southern Cameroon.* Boston: Boston University African Studies Center.

———. 1985. "The Economic Position of Beti Widows, Past and Present." In *Femmes du Cameroun: Mères pacifique, femmes rebelles,* edited by J.-C. Barbier. Paris: ORSTOM.

———. 1987. "Feeding Yaoundé." In *Feeding African Cities: Studies in Regional African History,* edited by Jane Guyer. Bloomington: Indiana University Press.

———. 1993. "Wealth in People and Self-Realization in Equatorial Africa." *Man* 28:243–65.

———. 1996. "Traditions of Invention in Equatorial Africa." *African Studies Review* 39, no. 3: 1–28.

Hammel, Eugene A. 1990. "A Theory of Culture for Demography." *Population and Development Review* 16:455–485.

Hanks, William. 1996. *Language and Communicative Practice.* Boulder: Westview Press.

———. 2000. "Converting Words." Paper presented in the Department of Anthropology, University of California at Berkeley, January 27.

Hansen, Judith Friedman. 1979. *Sociocultural Perspectives on Human Learning.* Prospect Heights, Ill.: Waveland Press.

Hardiman, David. 1995. "Community, Patriarchy, Honour: Raghu Bhanagre's Revolt." *Journal of Peasant Studies* 23, no. 1: 88–130.

Hari, M. 1991. "Modernization, Status of Women and Fertility." *Journal of Family Welfare* 37, no. 2: 62–67.

Hatch, Elvin. 1989. "Theories of Social Honor." *American Anthropologist* 91, no. 2: 341–53.

————. 1992. *Respectable Lives: Social Standing in Rural New Zealand.* Berkeley: University of California Press.

Hawhee, Debra. 2004. *Bodily Arts: Rhetoric and Athletics in Ancient Greece.* Austin: University of Texas Press.

Hayden, Corinne P. 2003. *When Nature Goes Public: The Making and Unmaking of Bioprospecting in Mexico.* Princeton: Princeton University Press.

Heath, Shirley Brice. 1983. *Ways with Words.* Cambridge: Cambridge University Press.

Heckman, James. 1976. "The Common Structure of Statistical Models of Truncation, Sample Selection and Limited Dependent Variables and a Simple Estimator for Such Models." *Annals of Economic and Social Measurement* 5, no. 4: 475–92.

Henry, Louis. 1961. "Some Data on Natural Fertility." *Eugenics Quarterly* 8:81–91.

Henshaw, Stanley, et al. 1999. "The Incidence of Abortion Worldwide." *International Family Planning Perspectives* 25:S30–38.

Herskovits, Melville. 1938. *Dahomey: An Ancient West African Kingdom.* 2 vols. New York: J. J. Augustine.

Herzfeld, Michael. 1980. "Honour and Shame: Problems in the Comparative Analysis of Moral Systems." *Man*, n.s., 15, no. 2: 339–51.

Hirschman, Charles. 1994. "Why Fertility Changes." *Annual Review of Sociology* 20:203–33.

Hobsbawm, Eric, and Terence Ranger. 1982. *The Invention of Tradition.* Cambridge: Cambridge University Press.

Hochschild, Arlie Russell. 2003. *The Commercialization of Intimate Life.* Berkeley and Los Angeles: University of California Press.

Hoerning, Erika, and Peter Alheit. 1995. "Biographical Socialization." *Current Sociology* 43, no. 2/3: 101–14.

Holland, Dorothy, and Margaret Eisenhart. 1990. *Educated in Romance: Women, Achievement, and College Culture.* Chicago: University of Chicago Press.

Hunt, Nancy Rose. 1990. "Domesticity and Colonialism in Belgian Africa: Usumbra's 'Foyer Social,' 1946–1960." *Signs* 15, no. 3: 447–72.

Inhorn, Marcia. 1994. *Quest for Conception: Gender, Infertility, and Egyptian Medical Traditions.* Philadelphia: University of Pennsylvania Press.

IUSSP (International Union for the Scientific Study of Population). 1982. *Multilingual Demographic Dictionary, English Section.* Liege: Ordina Editions.

Jacobs, John Arthur. 1996. "Gender Inequality and Higher Education." *Annual Review of Sociology* 22:153–85.

Jejeebhoy, Shireen J. 1995. *Women's Education, Autonomy, and Reproductive Behavior: Experience from Developing Countries.* Oxford: Clarendon Press.

Johnson, Brooke R., et al. 1993. "Contraception and Abortion in Romania." *Lancet* 341, no. 8849: 875–78.

Johnson, Noris Brock. 1985. *West Haven: Classroom Culture in a Rural Elementary School.* Chapel Hill: University of North Carolina Press.

Johnson-Hanks, Jennifer. 2002a. "On the Limits of the Life Cycle in Ethnography: Toward a Theory of Vital Conjunctures." *American Anthropologist* 104, no. 3: 865–80.

———. 2002b. "The Lesser Shame: Adolescent Abortion in Cameroon." *Social Science and Medicine* 55, no. 8: 1337–49.

———. 2002c. "The Modernity of Traditional Contraception." *Population and Development Review* 28, no. 2: 229–49.

———. 2003. "Ethnicity, Education and Reproductive Practice in Contemporary Cameroon." *Population* 58, no. 2: 171–200.

———. 2004. "Uncertainty and the Second Space: Modern Birth Timing and the Dilemma of Education." *European Journal of Population* 20, no. 4: 351–73.

———. 2005. "When the Future Decides: Uncertainty and Intentional Action in Contemporary Cameroon." *Current Anthropology* 46, no. 3: 363–385.

Johnston, Heidi Bart, and Kenneth Hill. 1996. "Induced Abortion in the Developing World: Indirect Estimates." *International Family Planning Perspectives* 22:108–14.

Joyce, Theodore, and Robert Kaestner. 2001. "The Impact of Mandatory Waiting Periods and Parental Consent Laws on the Timing of Abortion and the State of Occurrence among Adolescents in Mississippi and South Carolina." *Journal of Policy Analysis and Management* 20, no. 2: 263–82.

Kapchan, Deborah. 1995. "Performance." *Journal of American Folklore* 108, no. 430: 479–508.

Keane, Webb. 1997. "From Fetishism to Sincerity: On Agency, the Speaking Subject, and Their Historicity in the Context of Religious Conversion." *Comparative Studies in Society and History* 39, no. 4: 674–93.

Kemner, Wilhelm. 1937. *Kamerun: Dargestellt in Kolonialpoliticher, Historischer, Verkehrtechnischer, Rassenkundlicher and Rohstoffwirtschaftlicher Hinsicht.* Berlin: Freiheits-Verlag.

Kertzer, David. 1993. *Sacrificed for Honor: Italian Infant Abandonment and the Politics of Reproductive Control.* Boston: Beacon Press.

Ketchoua, Thomas. 1989. *De l'apparition de la Vierge Marie à Nsimalen.* Yaoundé: SOPECAM.

Kimball, Solon. 1974. *Culture and the Educative Process: An Anthropological Perspective.* New York: Teachers College Press.

Klerman, Lorraine. 2000. "The Intendedness of Pregnancy: A Concept in Transition." *Maternal and Child Health Journal* 4:155–62.

Knodel, John. 1987. "Starting, Stopping, and Spacing during the Early Stages of Fertility Transition: The Experience of German Village Populations in the 18th and 19th Centuries." *Demography* 24:143–62.

Koenig, Delores. 1981. "Education and Fertility among Cameroonian Working Women." *Women, Education, and Modernization of the Family in West Africa,* edited by Helen Ware. Canberra: Department of Demography, Australian National University.

Kressel, Gideon. 1992. "Shame and Gender." *Anthropological Quarterly* 65:34–46.

Kuczynski, Robert. 1939. *The Cameroons and Togoland: A Demographic Study.* London: Oxford University Press.

Laburthe-Tolra, Phillipe. 1970. *Yaoundé d'apres Zenker (1895).* Yaoundé: Université Federale du Cameroun.

———. 1977. *Minlaaba.* 3 vols. Paris: Honoré Champion.

———. 1981. *Les seigneurs de la foret: Essai sur le passé historique, l'orginisation sociale et les normes éthiques des anciens Beti du Cameroun.* Paris: Publications de la Sorbonne.

———. 1985. "Le mevungu et les rituels féminins à Minlaaba." In *Femmes du Cameroun: Mères pacifique, femmes rebelles,* edited by J.-C. Barbier. Paris: ORSTROM.

Largeau, Victor. 1901. *Encyclopédie pahouine.* Paris: Ernst Laroux.

Lave, Jean. 1988. *Cognition in Practice.* Cambridge: Cambridge University Press.

Lave, Jean, and Etienne Wenger. 1991. *Situated Learning: Legitimate Peripheral Participation.* Cambridge: Cambridge University Press.

Lazaridis, Gabriella. 1995. "Sexuality and Its Cultural Construction in Rural Greece." *Journal of Gender Studies* 4, no. 3: 281–95.

Lee, Valerie, and David Burkam. 1992. "Transferring High-Schools: An Alternative to Dropping Out." *American Journal of Education* 100, no. 4: 420–53.

Leete, Richard, ed. 1999. *Dynamics of Values in Fertility Change.* New York: Oxford University Press.

Lembezat, Bertrand. 1954. *Le Cameroun.* Paris: Editions Maritimes et Coloniales.

Lesthaeghe, Ron. 1989. "Production and Reproduction in Sub-Saharan Africa: An Overview of Organizing Principles." In *Reproduction and Social Organization in Sub-Saharan Africa,* edited by Ron Lesthaeghe. Berkeley: University of California Press.

LeVine, Robert, and Beatrice LeVine. 1966. *Nyansongo: A Gusii Community in Kenya.* New York: Wiley Press.

LeVine, Robert, and Merry White. 1986. *Human Conditions: The Cultural Basis of Educational Developments.* New York: Kegan Paul.

LeVine, Robert, et al. 1991. "Women's Schooling and Child Care in the Demographic Transition: A Mexican Case Study." *Population and Development Review* 17:186–91.

Lloyd, Cynthia, and Anastasia Gage-Brandon. 1992. "Does Sibsize Matter? The

Implications of Family Size for Children's Education in Ghana." Working Papers, no. 45. New York: Population Council.

MacCormack, Carol, ed. 1994. *Ethnography of Fertility and Birth.* 2nd ed. Prospect Heights, Ill.: Waveland Press.

Mahmood, Saba. 2001a. "Feminist Theory, Embodiment and the Docile Agent: Some Reflections on the Egyptian Islamic Revival." *Cultural Anthropology* 16:202–36.

———. 2001b. "Rehearsed Spontaneity and the Conventionality of Ritual." *American Ethnologist* 28:827–53.

Makokha, A. E. 1980. "Maternal Mortality in Kenyatta National Hospital, 1972–1977." *East African Medical Journal* 57, no. 7: 451–60.

Malinowski, Bronislaw. 1984. *Argonauts of the Western Pacific.* Prospect Heights, Ill.: Waveland Press.

Malkal, Hervé Charles. 1998. "Le directeur de l'Office Avoue." *Mutations,* no. 134 (July 20), 5.

Malthus, Thomas. 1970. *An Essay on the Principle of Population.* New York: Penguin Classics.

Mana, Haman. 1998. "L'école à l'assemblée." *Mutations,* no. 96, 3.

Mann, Kristin. 1985. *Marrying Well: Marriage, Status, and Social Change among the Educated Elite in Colonial Lagos.* Cambridge: Cambridge University Press.

Marshall, D. Bruce. 1973. *The French Colonial Myth and Constitution-making in the Fourth Republic.* New Haven: Yale University Press.

Martin, Emily. 1989. *The Woman in the Body.* New York: Milton Keynes.

Martin, Gustave. 1921. *L'existence au Cameroun: Etudes sociales, études medicales, études d'hygiene et de prophylaxie.* Paris: Emile Larose.

Mason, Karen Oppenheim. 1997. "Explaining Fertility Transitions." *Demography* 34:443–55.

Maurer, William. 1997. *Recharting the Caribbean: Land, Law, and Citizenship in the British Virgin Islands.* Ann Arbor: University of Michigan Press.

Mbala Owono, Rigobert. 1982. "L'education Beti." In *La quête du savoir: Essais pour une anthropologie de l'education camerounaise,* edited by Renaud Santèrre and Celine Mercier-Tremblay. Montreal: Les Presses de l'Université de Montréal.

Mbembe, Achille. 1996. *La naissance du maquis dans le Sud-Cameroun, 1920–1960.* Paris: Karthala.

Mbembe, Achille, and Janet Roitman. 1995. "Figures of the Subject in Times of Crisis." *Public Culture* 7:323–52.

McLaren, Peter. 1993. *Schooling as Ritual Performance.* 2nd ed. London: Routledge.

McRobbie, Angela. 1978. "Working Class Girls and the Culture of Femininity." In *Women Take Issue: Aspects of Women's Subordination,* edited by the University of Birmingham Women's Studies Group. London: Hutchinson Press.

Meekers, Dominique. 1992. "The Process of Marriage in African Societies." *Population and Development Review* 18, no. 1: 61–78.

Miers, Suzanne, and Igor Kopytoff, eds. 1977. *Slavery in Africa: Historical and Anthropological Perspectives*. Madison: University of Wisconsin Press.

Miescher, Stephan. 1997. "Becoming a Man in Kwawu: Gender, Law, Personhood, and the Construction of Masculinities in Colonial Ghana, 1875–1957." Ph.D. diss., Northwestern University.

Mikell, Gwendolyn. 1989. *Cocoa and Chaos in Ghana.* New York: Paragon House.

Miyazaki, Hiro. 2004. *The Method of Hope.* Stanford: Stanford University Press.

Mombio, Michel. 1998. "Les raisons d'un ajustement décrié." *Le Messager,* no. 791 (July 22), 7.

Monga, Célistin. 1998. "Notre société encourage la facilité." *L'Effort Camerounais,* no. 122 (July 30–August 5).

Montgomery, Mark, and Cynthia Lloyd. 1999. "Excess Fertility, Unintended Births, and Children's Schooling." In *Critical Perspectives on Schooling and Fertility in the Developing World,* edited by Caroline Bledsoe. Washington, D.C.: National Academy Press.

Moore, Henrietta. 1986. *Space, Text, and Gender: An Anthropological Study of the Marakwett of Kenya.* Cambridge: Cambridge University Press.

Moore, Henrietta, and Todd Sanders. 2001. *Magical Interpretations, Material Realities: Modernity, Witchcraft and the Occult in Postcolonial Africa.* New York: Routledge.

Moran, Mary. 1990. *Civilized Women: Gender and Prestige in Southeastern Liberia.* Ithaca: Cornell University Press.

Morgen, Curt von. 1893. *Durch Kamerun von Süd nach Nord.* Leipzig: Brockhaus.

Morson, Gary Saul. 1994. *Narrative and Freedom: The Shadows of Time.* New Haven: Yale University Press.

Munn, Nancy. 1992. "The Cultural Anthropology of Time: A Critical Essay." *Annual Review of Anthropology* 21:93–123.

Murphy, William. 1980. "Secret Knowledge as Property and Power in Kpelle Society: Elders versus Youth." *Africa* 50, no. 2: 193–207.

Mveng, Englebert. 1963. *Histoire du Cameroun.* Paris: Presence Africaine.

Mviena, Paul. 1970. *Univers culturel et religieux du peuple Beti.* Yaoundé: L'Imprimerie Saint Paul.

Narkavonnakit, Tongplaew, and Tony Bennett. 1981. "Health Consequences of Induced Abortion in Rural Northeast Thailand." *Studies in Family Planning* 12, no. 2: 58–66.

National Geography Division of Cameroon. 1989. *Atlas regional du Sud-Cameroun.* Yaoundé: National Geography Division of Cameroon.

Ndongko, Wilfred, and Franklin Vivekananda. 1989. *Economic Development in Cameroon.* Stockholm: Bethany Books.

Ngoa, Henri. 1968. *Le mariage chez les Ewondo.* Paris: Université du Paris.

Ngoh, Victor Julius. 1987. *Cameroon, 1884–1985: A Hundred Years of History.* Yaoundé: Navi-Group Publishers.

Ngongo, Louis. 1987. *Histoire des institutions et des faits sociaux du Cameroun.* 2 vols. Paris: Berger-Levrault.

Ngumu, Pie Claude. 1977. *Ein Beitrag zur Religion der Ewondo-Sprechenden Beti (Kamerun) auf Grunde Schriftlicher und Mündlicher Quellen.* Vienna: Verlag Ferdinand Berger und Söhne.

Nkoe, Benjamin. 1991. *De la procuration à la conviction: Cent ans d'evangélisation du Cameroun.* Yaoundé: SOPECAM.

Nouwou, David. 1998. "La peur d'une mise en examen." *La Nouvelle Expression,* no. 392 (July 22), 8.

Ntonga, Sylvestre Ndoumou. 1998. "Fête de jeunesse message d'espoir: Faut-l-y croire?" *L'Effort Camerounais,* no. 98 (February 12–18), 2.

Nwatsok, Sanam. 1998. Santé reproductive: Une politique nationale s'impose. *Mutations,* March 1998, 4.

Ochs, Elinor. 1993. "Indexing Gender." In *Sex and Gender Hierarchies,* edited by Barbara D. Miller. Cambridge: Cambridge University Press.

Ochs, Eilinor, and Lisa Capps. 1996. "Narrating the Self." *Annual Review of Anthropology* 25:19–43.

Ogbu, John. 1974. *The Next Generation.* New York: Academic Press.

Oliver, Mary. 2000. *The Leaf and the Cloud: A Poem.* Da Capo Press.

Ombolo, Jean-Pierre. 1990. *Sexe et societé en Afrique noir.* Paris: Karthala.

Ong, Walter. 1982. *Orality and Literacy: The Technologization of the Word.* London: Methuen Press.

Oppong, Christine, et al., eds. 1976. *Marriage, Fertility, and Parenthood in West Africa.* Canberra: Australian National University Press.

Orwell, George. 1977. *1984: A Novel.* New York: Signet Classic.

Page, Hillary. 1989. "Childrearing versus Childbearing: Coresidence of Child and Mother in Sub-Saharan Africa." In *Reproduction and Social Organization in Sub-Saharan Africa,* edited by Ron Lesthaeghe. Berkeley and Los Angeles: University of California Press.

Peel, John David. 1983. *Ijeshas and Nigerians.* Cambridge: Cambridge University Press.

Pelissier, Catherine. 1991. "The Anthropology of Teaching and Learning." *Annual Review of Anthropology* 20:75–95.

Péristiany, John G, ed. 1966. *Honour and Shame: The Values of Mediterranean Society.* London: Weidenfeld and Nicolson.

Péristiany, John, and Julian Pitt-Rivers, eds. 1991. *Honor and Grace in Anthropology.* New York: Cambridge University Press.

Pitt, Mark. 1995. "Women's Schooling, the Selectivity of Fertility, and Child Mortality in Sub-Saharan Africa." Living Standard Measurement Working Papers, no. 119. Washington, D.C.: World Bank.

Pitt-Rivers, Julian A. 1977. *The Fate of Shechem; or, The Politics of Sex: Essays in the Anthropology of the Mediterranean.* Cambridge: Cambridge University Press.

Porter, Theodore. 1986. *The Rise of Statistical Thinking 1820–1900.* Princeton: Princeton University Press.

Pritchett, Lant. 1994. "Desired Fertility and the Impact of Population Policies." *Population and Development Review* 20, no. 1: 1–55.

Quinn, Frederick. 1987. "The Impact of the First World War and Its Aftermath on the Beti of Cameroun." In *Africa and the First World War,* edited by Melvin Page. New York: St. Martin's Press.

Rabinow, Paul. 1996. *Making PCR: A Story of Biotechnology.* Chicago: University of Chicago Press.

————. 1999. *French DNA: Trouble in Purgatory.* Chicago: University of Chicago Press.

Radcliffe-Brown, A. R., and Daryll Forde, eds. 1967. *African Systems of Kinship and Marriage.* London: Oxford University Press.

Rana, Ashma, Neelam Pradhan, Geeta Gurung, and Meeta Singh. 2004. "Induced Septic Abortion: A Major Factor in Maternal Mortality and Morbidity. *Journal of Obstetrics and Gynaecology Research* 30, no. 1:3.

Raum, Otto. 1940. *Chaga Childhood: A Description of Indigenous Education in an East African Tribe.* Oxford: Oxford University Press.

Reisman, Paul. 1992. *First Find Your Child a Good Mother.* New Brunswick: Rutgers University Press.

Riles, Annelise. 2000. *The Network Inside Out.* Ann Arbor: University of Michigan Press.

Rioux, Jean-Pierre. 1987. *The Fourth Republic, 1944–1958.* New York: Cambridge University Press.

Robert, Paul. 1972. *Dictionnaire alphabétique et analogique de la langue française.* Paris: Societé du Nouveau Littré.

Robertson, A. F. 1991. *Beyond the Family: The Social Organization of Human Reproduction.* Berkeley and Los Angeles: University of California Press.

Rochat, Roger, et al. 1981. "Maternal and Abortion Related Deaths in Bangladesh, 1978–1979." *International Journal of Gynecology and Obstetrics* 19:155–64.

Rossier, Clementine. 2002. "Measure and Meaning of Induced Abortion in Rural Burkina Faso." Ph.D. diss., University of California, Berkeley.

Rowlands, Michael. 1994. "The Material Culture of Success: Ideals and Life Cycles in Cameroon." In *Consumption and Identity,* edited by Jonathan Friedman. Geneva: Harwood Academic Publishers.

Rowlands, Michael, and Jean-Pierre Warnier. 1988. "Sorcery, Power, and the Modern State in Cameroon." *Man,* n.s., 23, no. 1: 118–32.

Ruppel, Dr. 1912. *Die Landesgesetzgebung für das Schutzgebiet Kamerun.* Berlin: E. Siegfried Mittler und Sohn.

Rutenberg, Naomi, and Susan Cotts Watkins. 1997. "The Buzz outside the Clinics: Conversations and Contraception in Nyanza Province, Kenya." *Studies in Family Planning* 8, no. 4: 290–307.

Sahlins, Marshall. 1985. *Islands of History*. Chicago: University of Chicago Press.

Sargent, Carolyn. 1989. *Maternity, Medicine and Power: Reproductive Decision in Urban Benin*. Berkeley and Los Angeles: University of California Press.

Schieffelin, Bambi. 1990. *The Give and Take of Everyday Life: Language Socialization of Kaluli Children*. Cambridge: Cambridge University Press.

Schieffelin, Bambi, and Elinor Ochs. 1986. "Language Socialization." *Annual Review of Anthropology* 15:163–91.

Schneider, Jane. 1971. "Of Vigilance and Virgins: Honor, Shame and Access to Resources in Mediterranean Societies." *Ethnology* 10:1–24.

Schneider, Jane, and Peter T. Schneider. 1996. *Festival of the Poor: Fertility Decline and the Ideology of Class in Sicily, 1860–1980*. Tucson: University of Arizona Press.

Schultz, T. Paul. 1993. "Investments in the Schooling and Health of Women and Men: Quantities and Returns." *Journal of Human Resources* 28, no. 4: 684–725.

Schutz, Alfred. 1967. *The Phenomenology of the Social World*. Evanston: Northwestern University Press.

Schwartzman, Helen B. 1978. *Transformations: The Anthropology of Children's Play*. New York: Plenum Press.

Serpell, Robert. 1993. *The Significance of Schooling: Life-Journeys in an African Society*. Cambridge: Cambridge University Press.

Setel, Philip. 1999. *A Plague of Paradoxes: AIDS, Culture and Demography in Northern Tanzania*. Chicago: University of Chicago Press.

Shapiro, David, and B. Oleko Tambashe. 1997. "Education, Employment, and Fertility in Kinshasa and Prospects for Changes in Reproductive Behavior." *Population Research and Policy Review* 16, no. 3: 259–87.

Simon-Hohm, Hildegard 1983. *Afrikanische Kindheit und Koloniales Schulwesen: Erfahrungen aus Kamerun*. Cologne: Boehlau Verlag.

Southall, Aidan William. 1966. "The Concept of Elites and Their Formation in Uganda." In *The New Elites of Tropical Africa*, edited by P. C. Lloyd. Oxford: Oxford University Press.

SPECC (Secretariat Permanent de l'Enseignement Catholique au Cameroun). 1992. *L'Enseignement Catholique au Cameroun, 1890–1990*. Yaoundé: Publication de Centenaire.

Spindler, George, ed. 1963. *Education and Culture: Anthropological Approaches*. New York: Holt, Rinehart and Winston.

———. 1974. *Education and Cultural Process: Toward an Anthropology of Education*. New York: Holt, Rinehart and Winston.

Stambach, Amy. 2000. *Lessons from Mount Kilimanjaro: Schooling, Community, and Gender in East Africa*. New York: Routledge.

Starrett, Gregory. 1995. "The Hexis of Interpretation: Islam and the Body in the Egyptian Popular School." *American Ethnologist* 22, no. 4: 953–69.

Stewart, Frank Henderson. 1994. *Honor.* Chicago: University of Chicago Press.

Stoller, Paul. 1984. "Horrific Comedy: Cultural Resistance and the Hauka Movement in Niger." *Ethos* 12, no. 2: 165–88.

Stoyanova, Vassela, and Jan H. Richardus 1999. "Induced abortions in Bulgaria: Trends during the periods 1986–1996." *European Journal of Public Health.*" 9(3): 223–228.

Strathern, Marilyn. 1988. *The Gender of the Gift.* Berkeley and Los Angeles: University of California Press.

———. 1992a. *After Nature: English Kinship in the Late Twentieth Century.* Cambridge: Cambridge University Press.

———, ed. 1992b. *Reproducing the Future: Anthropology, Kinship and the New Reproductive Technologies.* New York: Routledge.

———. 1995. "Future Kinship and the Study of Culture." *Futures* 27, no. 4: 423–35.

Street, Brian, ed. 1993. *Cross-Cultural Approaches to Literacy.* Cambridge: Cambridge University Press.

Sugar, Melissa. 1991. "Adolescent Pregnancy in the USA: Problems and Prospects." Part 1, "The Problems." *Adolescent and Pediatric Gynecology* 4, no. 4: 171–82.

Tabi, Isadore. N.d. *La Théologie des rites Beti: Essai d'explication religieuse des rites Beti et ses implications socio-culturelles.* Yaoundé: AMA-CENC.

Tagne, David. 1998. "Ce bacc s'annule de lui même." *Le Messager,* no. 797 (August 5), 7.

Tchankam, Marc. 1998. "Rentrée scolaire: Le dernier virage." *Le Quotidien,* no. 349 (April 3–5), 11.

Tchasse, Jean Claude. 1998. "Lettre ouverte au ministre d'état chargé de l'education nationale." *Le Messager,* no. 785 (July 8), 3.

Tessman, Günther. 1913. *Die Pangwe: Völkerkundliche Monographie eines westafrikanischen Negerstammes.* 2 vols. Berlin: Ernst Wasmuth.

Thé, M. P. de. 1965. *Influence des femmes sur l'évolution des structures sociales chez les Beti du Sud-Cameroun.* Paris: Mémoire, E.P.H.E.

Thomas, Lynn. 1998. "Imperial Concerns and 'Women's Affairs': State Efforts to Regulate Clitoridectomy and Eradicate Abortion in Meru, Kenya, 1910–1950." *Journal of African History* 39, no. 2: 121–45.

Thorne, Barrie. 1993. *Gender Play: Girls and Boys in School.* New Brunswick: Rutgers University Press.

Tonye, Victor. 1986. *Catéchése pour jeunes et adults.* Yaoundé: SOPECAM.

Townsend, Nicholas. 1997. "Reproduction in Anthropology and Demography." In *Anthropological Demography: Toward a New Synthesis,* edited by David I. Kertzer and Tom Fricke. Chicago: University of Chicago Press.

Trilles, Rene-Pierre. 1912. *Le totemisme chez les Fan.* Muenster: Bibliotheque Anthropos.

Tsala, Theodore. 1957. *Dictionnaire Ewondo-Français*. Lyon, Emm. VITTE.

———. 1985. *Mille et un proverbes Beti*. Paris: SELAF.

Turner S. E., and William G. Bowen. 1999. "Choice of Major: The Changing (Unchanging) Gender Gap." *Industrial and Labor Relations Review* 52, no. 2: 289–313.

United Nations. 1994. "Programme of Action of the International Conference on Population and Development." A/CONF.171/13. Report presented at the United Nations International Conference on Population and Development (ICPD), September 5–13, Cairo, Egypt. http://www.iisd.ca/Cairo/program/p00000.html.

———. 1995. "Women's Education and Fertility Behavior: Recent Evidence from the Demographic and Health Surveys." New York: United Nations Department for Economic and Social Information and Policy Analysis.

United States Catholic Conference. 1994. "Catechism of the Catholic Church." In *Libreria Editrice Vaticana*. Mahwah, N.J.: Paulist Press.

Van de Walle, Etienne. 1992. "Fertility Transition, Conscious Choice, and Numeracy." *Demography* 29, no. 4: 487–502.

Veblen, Thornstein. 1899. *The Theory of the Leisure Class: An Economic Study in the Evolution of Institutions*. New York: Macmillan.

Vernon-Jackson, Hugh Owen Hardinge. 1968. "Schools and School Systems in Cameroon: 1844–1961." Ed.D. thesis, Columbia University.

Vincent, Jeanne-Francoise. 1976. *Traditions et transistion: Entretiens avec des femmes Beti du Sud-Cameroun, l'homme d'outre mer*. Paris: ORSTROM.

Wagner-Pacifici, Robin. 2000. *Theorizing the Standoff: Contingency in Action*. Cambridge: Cambridge University Press.

Warren-Sohlberg, Luann, et al. 1998. "Implementing and Evaluating Preventive Programs for High-Risk Transfer Students." *Journal of Educational and Psychological Consultation* 9, no. 4: 309–24.

Weber, Max. 1958. *The Protestant Ethic and the Spirit of Capitalism*. New York: Charles Scribner's Sons.

———. 1978. *Economy and Society: An Outline of Interpretive Sociology*. Berkeley and Los Angeles: University of California Press.

Weis, Lois. 1988. "High School Girls in a De-Industrializing Economy." In *Class, Race and Gender in American Education,* edited by Lois Weis. Albany: State University of New York Press.

Whyte, Susan Reynolds. 1997. *Questioning Misfortune: The Pragmatics of Uncertainty in Eastern Uganda*. Cambridge: Cambridge University Press.

Willis, Paul. 1977. *Learning to Labour: How Working Class Kids Get Working Class Jobs*. New York: Columbia University Press.

Wilson, Monica. 1951. *Good Company: A Study of Nyakyusa Age Villages*. London: Oxford University Press.

Wolcott, Harry. 1967. *A Kwakiutl Village and School.* New York: Holt, Rinehart and Winston.

Woll, Nikolaus. 1933. *Als Urwalddoktor in Kamerun.* Gotha: P. Ott Press.

Wright, Gwendolyn. 1991. *The Politics of Design in French Colonial Urbanism.* Chicago: University of Chicago Press.

Ze, Bishop Raphael-Marie. 1998. "L'education, notre mission." *L'Effort Camerounais,* no. 92 (December 24–January 7), 2.

Zelizer, Viviana. 1994. *Pricing the Priceless Child: The Changing Social Value of Children.* Princeton: Princeton University Press.

Zenker, Georg. 1895. "Yaunde." *Mitheilungen von Forshungsreisended und Gelehrten aus den deutschen Schutzgebeiten* (Berlin) 8:35–70.

Index